Capitalism vs. Socialism

Comparing Economic Systems

Edward F. Stuart, Ph.D.

THE
GREAT
COURSES

PUBLISHED BY:

THE GREAT COURSES

Corporate Headquarters
4840 Westfields Boulevard, Suite 500
Chantilly, Virginia 20151-2299
Phone: 1-800-832-2412
Fax: 703-378-3819
www.thegreatcourses.com

Edward F. Stuart, Ph.D.

Professor Emeritus of Economics
Northeastern Illinois University

Edward F. Stuart is a Professor Emeritus of Economics at Northeastern Illinois University, where he has been a member of the faculty since 1986. He earned his Ph.D. in Economics at the University of Oklahoma, specializing in International Economics and Russian and Eastern European Studies.

Professor Stuart teaches courses in international economics, the economics of the European Union, comparative economic systems, European economic history, and macroeconomic theory. He is also the chair of the Faculty Advisory Committee on International Programs and has led study tours to France, Germany, Austria, Italy, and Spain.

Professor Stuart has been a visiting guest professor at the University of Salzburg in Austria, the Burgundy School of Business in France, the Ural State Pedagogical University in Russia, and the Warsaw School of Economics and the University of Warsaw in Poland. In January 2014, he served as a guest professor at the China University of Petroleum-Beijing's Academy of Chinese Energy Strategy, where he lectured in macroeconomic theory and forecasting. Professor

Stuart has also served as an adjunct faculty at Loyola University Chicago's Quinlan School of Business, where he has taught classes in microeconomics, macroeconomics, and international business economics for students in the MBA program.

For the past 15 years, Professor Stuart has worked as a consultant to several international relocation firms and has made presentations on the histories, economic and political systems, geographies, and current events in a wide range of countries. These presentations have the objective of preparing the participants to be effective and successful professionals in the foreign countries to which they have been transferred.

Professor Stuart has published widely in the field of economics. His most recent publication is "Building Regional Competitive Advantage: Lessons from U.S. Experiences for Poland and Other New EU Member States." Professor Stuart is completing a textbook introducing the economics of the European Union to American college students and interested scholars. The book is being coauthored by his colleague at the Burgundy School of Business, Professor Jean-Guillaume Ditter.

Professor Stuart has been an economic analyst on radio and television programs, including NPR, Chicago's *WGN Morning News*, FOX 32 Chicago's evening news, WTTW's *Chicago Tonight*, and News Talk 980 CKNW in Vancouver, Canada. He has also given interviews to print and online media, including MSNBC.com, the Associated Press, *Bloomberg Businessweek*, and the French business daily *Les Echos*. ◆

Table of Contents

Introduction

Guides

Supplementary Material

Capitalism vs. Socialism
Comparing Economic Systems

This course covers the important economic systems in the world today. It also addresses the historical background and big ideas that created the different economic systems.

The course explains the key insights of Adam Smith, the first great economist and intellectual godfather of free market capitalism. Then, the course analyzes the ideas of Karl Marx, the chief critic of the capitalist system and the first major proponent of a socialist system. In the modern era, the contrasting ideas of John Maynard Keynes and Milton Friedman help explain the conflict between the arguments for and against active government intervention in a market economy.

The actual development of British and American capitalism highlights the advances and problems created by industrial capitalism. The reaction to the excesses of early industrial capitalism created the first socialist movements that attempted to reform and improve the capitalist system. Early "utopian" socialists, who often had a religious and moral zeal to improve the lives of ordinary workers, created the first socialist political parties, trade unions, and worker cooperatives. Some of the most interesting reform attempts were the New Lanark mills in Scotland, the Amana Colonies in Iowa, and the Mondragon cooperative society in the Basque region of Spain.

The first country to create a brand-new economic system was the Soviet Union. The course examines the history of the Russian Empire and the forces and events that led to the Bolshevik Revolution and the creation of the Union of Soviet Socialist Republics. How did the Bolsheviks under Vladimir Lenin and Leon Trotsky organize an economy with little or no private property? The answer is this: with little or no market institutions and no price and profit information. After Lenin died and Joseph Stalin established himself as the supreme and unquestioned leader of the Soviet Union, the Soviet economy created the first command planning system. The course analyzes the key institutions in this system and the incentives and behaviors of the economic planners, enterprise managers, and ordinary Soviet workers and farmers.

After World War II, the Soviet economic and political system was imposed on the countries of eastern Europe by the victorious Red Army. How were the economies of Poland, Hungary, Czechoslovakia, and East Germany transformed from market economies to government-owned and planned economies? The contrasting economies of East and West Germany provide an almost laboratory experiment in comparative economic systems. These two countries have the same history, the same language and culture, and the same people. The only difference between them is their economic systems. What were the key institutions of the West German economy and its social market economic system? How did the centrally planned economy of East Germany function? What eventually led to the collapse of the socialist economies of eastern Europe? And what forces unleashed by the reforming efforts of Mikhail Gorbachev led to the collapse of the Soviet Union?

The course examines some economies that attempt to capture the best aspects of capitalism with some reforms and government regulation advocated by the early utopian socialists and social democrats. In contrast to the private enterprise economy of the United States, the economies of Great Britain, France, and Sweden have a significant governmental involvement in the areas of health care, education, housing, transportation, and public utilities. These countries also do a considerable amount of income redistribution through progressive income taxes and a comprehensive social welfare system.

The course examines the economy of the People's Republic of China and its fascinating attempt to combine Communist Party control with private enterprise in agriculture and manufacturing. The course then analyzes the so-called Asian Tiger economies of South Korea, Taiwan, and Singapore. They all have used a strong central government to develop a modern, capitalist economy that competes successfully in world markets. Finally, the course examines the economy of Slovenia and its attempt to transform itself from a communist-type, planned economy into a mixed economy with significant private enterprise but retaining much of the social welfare policies that create an egalitarian society.

The course ends with the question of whether the world's economic systems are converging—becoming more similar—or whether there are still significant differences in national cultures and values that cause different societies to choose different economic systems. ◆

Lecture 1

Gorbachev's Hello and the Soviet Goodbye

THERE ARE DIFFERENT WAYS OF LOOKING AT THE world, and differences in values manifest themselves in different social policies. Comparative economics is a fascinating subject that attempts to analyze, and answer, many important social questions. Comparative economics is the study of different systems of economic organization—notably capitalism, socialism, communism, and mixed economies. ◆

Debates about Comparative Economics

◀ Virtually all countries and societies around the world debate the role of governments and market institutions. Some of the questions that debates about comparative economics raise and seek to answer are as follows:

⬥ What are the goals of a good society?
⬥ How should societies be organized?
⬥ What is the best way to make sure that people have a decent standard of living?
⬥ Are people best motivated by self-interest and individual success, or do we have a basic moral sense of solidarity? Are we motivated by altruism and regard for others?

Health Care

◀ In the United States, the perennial health-care debate is, in an important sense, a debate about comparative economic systems. Should health care be provided by the government? Should health care be a purely individual responsibility and left to a free market, consumer-driven system?

◀ There are many different forms of health care in between the extremes of a completely government, or public, system and a completely free enterprise system of individual choice and payment. Governments could subsidize health care but let individuals decide what kind of health care they should purchase. Governments could mandate that individuals must have private health insurance.

Different countries have vastly different health-care systems.

◀ In the United Kingdom, the government—through the National Health Service—is the sole provider of health care, and all of its citizens are treated in public hospitals and clinics, paying no out-of-pocket costs. Taxes on all residents are the source of revenue to pay for this government-provided health care.

◀ In France, all residents get a health-care card for services that may be purchased from a variety of sources at the patient's discretion. Again, the funding comes from a fairly significant level of taxation. Japan has a similar system to France's.

◀ In the former Soviet Union, all citizens typically were assigned to a particular clinic and hospital, where they would receive their medical care. Often, the clinic and hospital were attached to the enterprise where the Soviet citizen worked, and his or her family had little or no choice as to who would be their doctor or surgeon.

Education

◀ Another important social question—which again can be viewed through the lens of comparative systems—is that of education.

◀ Should education be funded by the government and be free to all residents? Should individual families have choices about where their children go to school?

◀ Is a mixed system of public and private education better, because it offers more choices? Or does a system of mixed public and private education inevitably lead to a situation where the poor and working-class families send their children to underfunded public schools and upper-income, rich families send their children to private schools that have more resources and better-paid, more-talented teachers? If so, would this undermine a commitment to democracy and equal opportunity?

◀ Maybe there can be private schools and individual choice, but the government could provide subsidies and vouchers to poorer families to help them choose better schools for their children.

Mass Transportation

◀ In many crowded cities, maybe not everyone should be driving their own cars to work, or school, or shopping. Should mass transportation be an alternative to private automobiles?

◀ You can certainly make the case that a car is a source of freedom and individual choice. But if everybody is driving, what about the congestion this causes? What about the pollution? What about traffic accidents and the lives of pedestrians? Are you free only to be stuck in someone else's traffic?

◀ If a society is to provide mass transportation as an alternative to private automobiles, who should pay for the trains, buses, subways, trams, and ferries we'd need? Should riders pay the whole cost of the bus trip?

◀ If more people ride the bus and you keep driving your car, aren't you—as an automobile driver—much better off because all the people on the bus are not driving? If so, then your freeway trip is much less congested and you can get to work in much less time. But, then again, shouldn't you pay for some portion of that bus travel, because you are getting some of the benefits?

◀ The nature of transportation is taking on ever-greater social and global importance. Does your driving a gas-powered car contribute to the problems of climate change? If so, should governments tax gasoline more heavily?

◀ The United States has relatively cheap gasoline in comparison to the social welfare states of the European economy, where gasoline is much more expensive. And the reason for this has to do with choices. The high price of gasoline in Europe relative to that in the United States reflects radically higher taxes—and political decisions about how transportation of all forms should be financed and produced.

◀ Another important question—in addition to the questions of how mass transportation is to be paid for—is how mass transportation should be produced.

The late British Prime Minister Margaret Thatcher thought that mass transportation was a type of socialism. And—as a self-described supporter of free enterprise and individual rights—she believed that citizens should be free to drive cars whenever and wherever they liked.

◀ Should mass transportation be provided by private enterprises that make a profit? If they can't make a profit, should they be subsidized by the government? Or should mass transportation be produced by public enterprises that are owned by a government and financed, at least partially, by all taxpayers?

◀ Should there be a difference between local mass transportation (such as city buses) and intercity transportation (such as airlines and long-distance trains)?

◀ Many different transportation systems exist throughout the world. In France, for example, the intercity trains—including the famous TGVs—are a government-owned enterprise.

◀ Japan has partially privatized some of its intercity trains, and some of Japan's famous bullet trains are the property of private railroad companies.

◀ Some governments own a national airline, such as Singapore Airlines, which is owned by the government of Singapore. The United States has purely private commercial airlines, although sometimes they have been bailed out by the U.S. government.

◀ Here's a similar question: Should large industrial enterprises sometimes be owned by governments—or be partially owned by governments—to promote the public good?

◀ The German automobile company Volkswagen is partially owned by the state government of Lower Saxony, where Volkswagen has its headquarters and main factory. The government of Lower Saxony also places some representatives on Volkswagen's board of directors. And, at least in theory, these representatives represent the citizens of the surrounding region, who are affected by anything such a large enterprise does. Large private enterprises in Germany must also include workers' representatives on their boards of directors.

◀ This German system is called *Mitbestimmung*, or codetermination. It's a variation of private property and its control. And it's different than in the United States, where only private shareholders typically get a place on a company's board of directors.

Housing

◀ One more example of comparative systems in economics is seen in the provision of housing.

◀ Most housing in the United States is owner-occupied, or rental housing owned by a private landlord. There are some examples of public housing, usually in urban areas. But many countries have much more extensive government-owned, or cooperatively owned, housing than commonly is found in the United States.

◀ If you consider basic housing a human right, then it might make sense for public bodies to build and own housing units and let poor or disadvantaged residents live in them for free or minimal costs. Or you might make the argument that private construction and private ownership is the most efficient way to produce housing.

◀ In this case, if you want to provide the poor and underprivileged with housing they could not afford on their own income, then government subsidies might be a better way of providing everyone with an adequate level of basic housing.

◀ So, even in a private market economy, such as that of the United States, many issues and problems have, at their base, a comparative-systems argument. Is the public sector and government the best provider of some products and services, or should human needs be left mostly to the private sector, albeit with some modest amount of government regulation or subsidy?

REID, *The Healing of America.*
STIGLITZ, *Whither Socialism?*

Questions

1   How would your different political, moral, and
    religious values cause you to prefer a particular kind of
    economic system?

2   Do you think that most people are motivated by
    self-interest or by concerns for their fellow human
    beings? What does this have to do with capitalism
    versus socialism?

Lecture 1 Transcript

Gorbachev's Hello and the Soviet Goodbye

O n May 21, 1985, I happened to be in the bar at the Hotel Europe on Nevsky Prospekt in Leningrad. I was an economics professor from Chicago—leading a student tour of the Soviet Union—six years before the Soviet Union's collapse. By chance, Mikhail Gorbachev—the newly chosen leader of the Soviet Communist Party—was in Leningrad that day to give his first major speech to a group of leading Communist Party officials. And the speech was televised. Two months earlier, the communist party's Central Committee had named Gorbachev as its new general secretary. That made him the political and governmental leader of the entire country. In his memoirs, Gorbachev said later that he knew at the time that profound changes had to be made. And now, the moment had arrived. He was in Leningrad, the Soviet Union's second-biggest city, to describe the types of reforms he had in mind.

Accompanying me on this tour was a man named Don Davis, a professor of Russian history at Illinois State University, where we both taught. Don was extremely knowledgeable about Soviet and Russian history, and fluent in Russian. So, as we sat at the bar drinking Cognac, and watching Gorbachev on TV, Don interpreted what the new Soviet leader was saying to the Leningrad party bigwigs. Even without the translation, I could tell by looking at the faces of the party bosses on that small TV screen that they were not terribly happy about what they were hearing.

One of the reasons Gorbachev had chosen Leningrad for his initial pronouncements on the need for change was that the city was one of the most corrupt and inefficient centers of the Soviet economy. Being from Chicago, Don and I knew something about that. But here, Gorbachev was explaining the need for a major restructuring, "perestroika" in the Russian language, along with economic reforms throughout the entire Soviet economy.

To demonstrate one consequence of this proposed restructuring, Gorbachev reached in his pocket, and rattled some change to illustrate his determination that policies would reduce the amount of graft and corruption that ended up in the pockets of the party leaders. Needless to say—however well-received this message might have been by the Soviet public at large—his immediate audience among the party oligarchs was not overjoyed by the presentation, or its implications. Even from the hotel bar, I can tell you that the faces in the crowd were disapproving, and you didn't need to understand Russian to understand why.

After Gorbachev's appointment to dual leadership posts in the Communist Party and the Soviet Union government, many of us found that the United States' longtime Cold War competitor had, at last, become a very interesting and important subject to study and teach once again. Put simply, courses on comparative economic systems and capitalism versus socialism suddenly became quite popular in university economics and history departments. Comparative economics is the study of different systems of economic organization, notably capitalism, socialism, communism, and mixed economies. And all of a sudden, debates about the nature of socialism and communism—and whether either could be reformed to function better in the interests of the general population—were common once more.

When I was a young boy growing up in Texas, I wouldn't have known what comparative economic systems meant. But even as a boy, I was surrounded by heated arguments about the nature of governments, free enterprise, markets, and private property. My mom and dad were rather different in their political leanings. My dad was a native Texan and quite conservative. He worked for an independent oil company in Houston that went bankrupt in the late 1950's.

Through him, I got my first experience with the volatile nature of capitalism.

Centuries earlier, even before the first European contact with North America, native Indians had found oil seeping from Texas soil, and believed it held medicinal value. In January 1901, the famous gusher erupted at Spindletop, Texas, near Beaumont. Oil spouted more than 100 feet into the air for nine days, until it was capped. Even today, the oil business centered in Houston is still a very up-and-down kind of business, and a great example of the highs and lows of a market economy.

My dad was always preaching about how the government should get out of the business of regulating the economy, and how taxes were a bad idea. My mom, on the other hand, was a liberal Catholic in the tradition of a New York-born woman named Dorothy Day, who led a progressive initiative called the Catholic Worker Movement. Some people would describe Dorothy Day as a saint—not necessarily my dad. She launched the Catholic Worker Movement in May 1933—during the Great Depression—with a penny newspaper by that name that addressed itself to its readers with these words:

> For those who are sitting on the park benches in the warm spring sunlight. For those who are huddling in shelters trying to escape the rain. For those who are walking the street in the all but futile search to find work. For those who think that there is no hope for the future, no recognition of their plight, this little paper is addressed. It is printed to call their attention to the fact that ... there are men of God who are working not only for their spiritual, but for their material welfare.

The Catholic Worker Movement was dedicated to a liberal view of social justice and favored strong trade unions, expanded social welfare benefits, and significant regulation of private business.

In those days, Texas itself was often bitterly divided between different factions of the Democratic Party. There was no meaningful Republican Party influence up through the '40s and '50s. One wing of the Texas Democratic Party in the '30s and '40s came to be led by a young congressman named Lyndon Johnson, and like-minded followers of president Franklin Roosevelt's New Deal. The other wing of the Democratic Party was quite conservative, and in favor of unregulated markets and free-enterprise capitalism. The conservative wing was led by the crusty, sharp-tongued John Nance Garner, who likened serving FDR in the office of vice president to "a bucket of warm spit." After getting off the presidential ticket, he became a critic of FDR's, and his conservative faction eventually turned into the modern Texas Republican Party.

Growing up Catholic, I was influenced by my teachers in church schools, especially the Jesuits who taught me during high school. They were a pretty radical bunch, and always referring to the part of Saint Matthew's gospel about how hard it was for a rich man to get into heaven. The Jesuits also spent a lot of time quoting the Sermon on the Mount, especially about the poor in spirit and the meek inheriting the earth.

My mom was in favor of Texas having an income tax, and a progressive one at that. My dad's boss, who owned the oil company where dad was the accountant, lived in a big mansion in River Oaks, the ritziest neighborhood in Houston, Texas. Mom thought he should pay taxes on his income to the state of Texas so that poor kids—white, black, and brown—would have better schools. She said this one night at the dinner table, and my dad blew up. "That's nothing but communism" he thundered. "Do you want some politician to steal your hard-earned money and give it away? That's what those commies do in Russia!" To this day, Texas doesn't have a state income tax.

The nature of my mom's Catholicism—and my later interest in the Soviet economy—unexpectedly came together a few years ago when my mom joined me on the Trans-Siberian Express across Russia. Riding the Trans-Siberian Railway is one of the world's great adventures. It links Moscow to Beijing through Siberia and Mongolia. We traveled more than 5,000 miles of the route—from Khabarovsk (near China, in the southeast) to Moscow—over the course of 11 days. And we stopped in a couple of places. One of these was the city of Irkutsk in Siberia, on the shores of Lake Baikal, which is the deepest fresh-water lake in the world.

While in Irkutsk, we visited an old Russian Orthodox monastery. Our guide was a very charming woman who related to us her education when she was a little girl in early Soviet communist Russia. She explained how her teachers had emphasized the brotherhood of man, and the responsibility to help the poor; the necessity of solidarity with all people; and the dangers of focusing on material possessions. My mom exclaimed, "She sounds just like the Sisters of the Sacred Heart who taught me at Saint Aloysius grade school in Spokane, Washington." And it's true. They were both products of a time in history, not just a place.

By comparison, my experience of growing up Catholic in Baptist-dominated Texas was an early education in contrasting philosophies and cultures. It was an early introduction to the idea that there were different ways of looking at the world, and differences in values that manifested themselves in different social policies. By the time I got to college, the Vietnam War was dominating the headlines, and sparking heated arguments about war and peace; capitalism and communism; and the nature of a just society. The Cold War between the United States and Russia—and between Western Europe and Eastern Europe—dominated the political atmosphere of the time. It was widely assumed that this was a life-and-death struggle between two incompatible systems.

A student's years as an undergraduate should be a time for questioning and exploring differing ideas. And it certainly was for me, as a young man, and for my fellow students. I took classes in comparative economic systems, Soviet economics, and government regulation of market economies. Comparative economics, as I indicated a moment ago, is a fascinating subject that attempts to analyze, and answer, many important social questions.

For instance, virtually all countries and societies around the world debate the role of governments and market institutions. Here are some of the questions that debates about comparative economics raise and seek to answer: What are the goals of a good society? How should societies be organized? What is the best way to make sure that people have a decent standard of living? Are people best motivated by self-interest and individual success, or do we have a basic moral sense of solidarity? And are we motivated by altruism, and regard for others?

In the United States, the perennial health-care debate is, in an important sense, a debate about comparative economic systems. Should health care be provided by the government? Should health care be a purely individual responsibility, and left to a free market, consumer-driven system? There are many different forms of health care in between the extremes of a completely government or public system, and a completely free enterprise system of individual choice and payment. Governments could subsidize health care, but let individuals decide what kind of health care they should purchase. Governments could mandate that individuals must have private health insurance.

Different countries have vastly different systems. In the United Kingdom, the government—through the National Health Service—is the sole provider of health care, and all of its citizens are treated in public hospitals and clinics, paying no out-of-pocket costs. Taxes on all residents are the source of revenue to pay for this government-provided health care. In France, all residents get a health-care card for services that may be purchased from a variety of sources at the patient's discretion. Again, the funding comes from a fairly significant level of taxation. Japan has a similar system to France's. In the former Soviet Union, all citizens typically were assigned to a particular clinic and hospital where they would receive their medical care. Often, the clinic and hospital were attached to the enterprise where the Soviet citizen worked. And his or her family had little or no choice as to who would be their doctor or surgeon.

Another important social question—which we can again view through the lens of comparative systems—is that of education. Should education be funded by the government, and free to all residents? Should individual families have choices about where their children go to school? Is a mixed system of public and private education better, because it offers more choices? Or does a system of mixed public and private education inevitably lead to a situation where the poor and working class families send their children to underfunded public school, and upper-income, rich families send their children to private schools that have more resources, and better paid and talented teachers? If so, would this undermine a commitment to democracy, and equal opportunity? Maybe there can be private schools and individual choice, but the government could provide subsidies and vouchers to poorer families to help them choose better schools for their children.

And how about mass transportation? In many crowded cities, maybe not everyone should be driving their own cars to work, or school, or shopping. Should mass transportation be an alternative to private automobiles? The late British prime minister, Margaret Thatcher thought that mass transportation was a type of socialism. And—as a self-described supporter of free enterprise, and individual rights—she believed that citizens should be free to drive cars whenever, and wherever they liked. You can certainly make the case—and understand the nature of your own car—as a source of freedom, and individual choice. But if everybody is driving, what about the congestion this causes? What about the pollution? What about traffic accidents and the lives of pedestrians? Are you free only to be stuck in my traffic?

If a society is to provide mass transportation as an alternative to private automobiles, who should pay for the trains, buses, subways, trams, and ferries we'd need? Should riders pay the whole cost of the bus trip? If more people ride the bus, and I keep driving my car, aren't I—as an automobile driver—made much better off because all the people on the bus are not driving? If so, then my freeway trip is much less congested, and I can get to work faster, and with much less time. But then again, shouldn't I pay for some portion of that bus travel, because I am getting some of the benefits?

The nature of transportation is taking on ever-greater social and global importance. Does my driving a gas-powered car contribute to the problems of climate change? If so, should governments tax gasoline more heavily? In the United States, we have relatively cheap gasoline. But I can reach a few years back to demonstrate how comparatively expensive gasoline is in the social-welfare states of the European economy. And the reason for this has to do with choices.

Back in 2003, I flew from the United States to Sweden to pick up a new Saab automobile that I would ship home myself, on the gray market. "Gray market" means it was a legal transaction, or purchased through authorized, or semi-authorized channels. Sometimes there are opportunities to save a little money buying a car this way. Besides, for me, it meant a trip to Europe. So, I collected my car at the Saab factory in Trollhattan, Sweden, and drove to Norway to see the capital, Oslo. On the way back to Gothenburg, Sweden—to drop off my vehicle at the port to be loaded onto a freighter for the United States—I stopped at a Shell station to fill up.

My tank was only about half-empty but I didn't want to take any chances of running out of gas in the middle of the Swedish countryside. So, I filled up, and went to the cashier to pay. Once I did the calculations of changing liters into gallons—and Norwegian kroner into dollars—I realized that the roughly nine gallons I'd put into my tank had cost about $90. And remember, that was several years ago. Real pocketbook effects are a powerful kind of knowledge.

The high price of gasoline in Europe relative to that in the United States reflects radically higher taxes—and political decisions about how transportation of all forms should be financed and produced. It's an example of government regulation, or partial control of a market transaction, such that filling up at the pump in Norway—a leading European producer of crude oil and natural gas—is not an exercise in free-market economics.

Another important question—in addition to the questions of how mass transportation is to be paid for—is how mass transportation should be produced. Should mass transportation be provided by private enterprises that make a profit? If they can't make a profit, should they be subsidized by the government? Or should mass transportation be produced by public enterprises that are owned by a government and financed, at least partially, by all taxpayers?

Should there be a difference between local mass transportation (like city buses) and intercity transportation (like airlines and long distance trains)?

Many different transportation systems exist throughout the world. In France, for example, the intercity trains—including the famous TGVs—are a government-owned enterprise. Japan has partially privatized some of its intercity trains, and some of Japan's famous "bullet trains" are the property of private railroad companies. Some governments own a national airline, like Singapore Airlines, which is owned by the government of Singapore. In the United States, we have purely private commercial airlines, although sometimes they have been bailed out by the U.S. government.

Here's a similar question: should large industrial enterprises sometimes be owned by governments—or be partially owned by governments—in order to promote the public good? The German automobile company, Volkswagen, is partially owned by the state government of Lower Saxony, where Volkswagen has its headquarters and main factory. The government of Lower Saxony also places some representatives on Volkswagens' board of directors. And, at least in theory, these representatives represent the citizens of the surrounding region, who are affected by anything such a large enterprise does. Large private enterprises in Germany must also include workers' representatives on their boards of directors. This German system is called *Mitbestimmung*, or "co-determination." It's a variation of private property, and its control. And it's different than in the United States, where only private shareholders typically get a place on a company's board of directors.

One more example of comparative systems in economics is seen in the provision of housing. Most housing in the United States is owner-occupied, or rental housing owned by a private landlord. We do have some examples of public housing, usually in urban areas. But many countries have much more extensive government—or cooperatively—owned housing than commonly is found in the United States.

Now, if you consider basic housing a human right, then it might make sense for public bodies to build and own housing units, and let poor or disadvantaged residents live in them for free or minimal costs. Or you might make the argument that private construction and private ownership is the most efficient way to produce housing. In this case, if you want to provide the poor and underprivileged with housing they could not afford on their own income, then government subsidies might be a better way of providing everyone with an adequate level of basic housing.

So even in a private market economy like that of the United States, many issues and problems have, at their base, a comparative-systems argument. Is the public sector and government the best provider of some products and services? Or should human needs be left mostly to the private sector, albeit with some modest amount of government regulation or subsidy?

This course on comparative economic systems will take us around the world. We'll begin with the world of ideas, and look at the major thinkers and ideas that propelled the development of different economic systems. These include Adam Smith, the Scottish social philosopher who is considered the father of economics as a distinct social science. We'll also examine the ideas of Germany's Karl Marx, the most famous and important critic of capitalism, and the first important proponent of communism.

A more contemporary figure is John Maynard Keynes, the 20th-century English economist who revolutionized the role of government in a free-market economy, and provided the theoretical basis for managed capitalism and the modern social welfare state. Something of an antidote to Britain's Lord Keynes is the American Nobel laureate Milton Friedman, and his critique of Keynesian welfare economics. Friedman was a lively proponent of free-market capitalism, and the intellectual godfather of the Margaret Thatcher/Ronald Reagan revolution that rolled back the role of the state in the U.K. and U.S. economies of the 1980s. Friedman also influenced the free-market advocates that appeared after the fall of communism in Eastern Europe.

Our tour of the world's economies will encompass Europe, both East and West—and the related antagonisms between market economies and socialist economies, since they differed during the Cold War—and also Asia and the rise of the Peoples' Republic of China. China presents a unique model of a communist state, with dominant public ownership that, at the same time, permits capitalist-style private businesses, and entrepreneurs who have turned into some of the world's wealthiest individuals. Along with China, we will also cover the "Tiger" economies of Asia, including South Korea, Singapore, and Taiwan. These economies present another unique mix of public and private economic institutions, which seems to be a successful way to build economic progress.

Throughout this course, I will address some of the ways that economists and other researchers in the field of comparative economic systems try to measure the success—or failure—of an economic system. I tell my university students that just like when you go to your physician for an annual checkup, and leave with pages of numbers that say something about how healthy you are, economists use pages of data and statistics to assess how well an economy is doing.

In addition to all of this, we will spend a good deal of time examining the foundations and the functioning of the former Soviet Union's economy in the 20th century. It was the first attempt to put Karl Marx's ideas into practice, and served as a template for all other communist systems that followed: from East Germany to the Peoples Republic of China. Problems in the Soviet economy eventually led to its collapse, and the collapse of all communist economies in Eastern Europe.

In turn, we'll also describe key features of the U.S. economy: the most privately owned, and market-oriented economy in the group of advanced industrial high-income economies. Between the U.S. economy and the former Soviet-type economies of Russia and Eastern Europe, the mixed economies of Western Europe present an array of economic models that differ in crucial ways from both the U.S. economy and the former Soviet type economies. And so we will examine these models, as well—the

United Kingdom, France, Germany, and Sweden—to see how such issues as health care, education, transportation, and housing policy are handled in different (and possibly instructive) ways.

Finally, I'll pose and discuss some of the big questions in comparative economic systems: Are economies converging and so becoming more similar? If they are becoming more similar, what are the key similarities?

And what will the dominant economic system of the future look like? Or are peoples, cultures, different value systems destined to always create very different societies and economic systems? And if so, does this provide a basis for argument and disagreement about what is the best way to organize an economy?

Lecture 2

Adam Smith, Karl Marx, Keynes, and Friedman

E VERY ECONOMIC SYSTEM IS BASED ON THE IDEAS of one or more big thinkers. While there are many important economic thinkers, four men—Adam Smith, Karl Marx, John Maynard Keynes, and Milton Friedman—represent virtually all of the major ideas in practice about how an economy should be organized and how it should work. This includes ideas about private property versus state ownership, government regulation versus free market decisions, and high taxes versus low taxes on consumption spending. ◆

Adam Smith

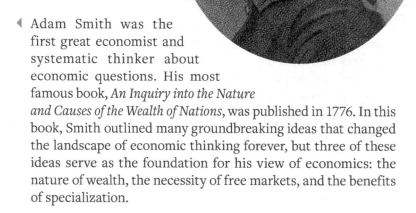

"Humans have a natural propensity to truck, barter, and exchange."

— SMITH

◀ Adam Smith was the first great economist and systematic thinker about economic questions. His most famous book, *An Inquiry into the Nature and Causes of the Wealth of Nations*, was published in 1776. In this book, Smith outlined many groundbreaking ideas that changed the landscape of economic thinking forever, but three of these ideas serve as the foundation for his view of economics: the nature of wealth, the necessity of free markets, and the benefits of specialization.

◀ During Smith's time, most people thought that national wealth meant lots of gold in the king's treasury, or a big army, or impressive government buildings. But he disagreed. He said that the most important kind of wealth was a nation's production of goods and services that made the lives of ordinary people better.

◀ In the same way, in assessing or examining the health of a nation's economy today, typically we focus on gross domestic product—that is, the total production of goods and services in an economy.

◀ Smith's thinking about how to increase the wealth of nations rests on his ideas about human nature and human motivation. He believed that most people were concerned about other people and could be motivated by sympathy for their fellow human. But he thought that a stronger human motivation was self-love and concern for immediate family and close friends.

◀ Taking into account humans' self-interest—along with the human desire to interact—Smith recognized that people, by their very nature, love to trade and shop. He thought that bargaining and exchange activities were unique to human beings.

◀ What emerges from this view is Smith's belief that a commercial society—based on market institutions—is the best economic system humans could create and sustain. He didn't use the label "capitalism" for this ideal system, because that word didn't exist yet; it would be invented by another great thinker, Karl Marx, in the 1840s.

◀ Smith put all of his ideas together in the thesis that a rational human economy would be based on exchange, motivated by self-interest. He believed that by appealing to the self-interest of individual producers and businesses, they would produce what society wanted, and the general good of the society would be promoted.

◀ This is also where Smith's most famous idea, known as the invisible hand, comes in: In an economy based on self-motivated exchange, the economy is guided by an invisible hand—a hand that benefits all parties participating in the exchange.

The word "economics" comes from the Greek word for management of household expenses, and it first appears in the writings of Aristotle in the 4th century B.C.

The word "economist" was invented late in the 18th century by a group of professors at the University of Paris known as the physiocrats, who believed that all wealth derived from land. They adapted the Greek term *okionomia* to label their own nascent profession *economiste.*

◀ Smith was a great believer in freedom. At the time he was writing, an individual's job and social position were mainly determined by what kind of family you came from. But he thought that people should be free to choose their own occupations and professions.

◀ Smith believed that there should a lot of freedom when it comes to who could sell in a market. No one person, or small group, should have a monopoly in the sale of a good or service.

◀ Although Smith was very much in favor of markets, he was also very suspicious of businessmen. He assumed that when people in the same business got together, they were usually cooking up some scheme to rig the market and cheat the consumer. So, he was a firm believer in the necessity of the state to keep a close eye on the markets and watch out for anticompetitive behavior.

◀ Smith also recognized that the successes of some would lead to inequality in incomes. In other words, some people would get rich and some people would be poor. The reasons could be differences in skill, luck, effort, and the training needed to succeed in some occupations. Therefore, it would be necessary for the state to provide some basic standard of living.

◀ Smith saw inequality in incomes as a necessary evil of a market society. The best way to prevent too much inequality was to promote as much competition as possible and make the market as big and wide as could be. Competition from other regions and other countries would limit the power of local businessmen to control the market for their benefit.

◀ Smith was a big believer in free trade, which is the basis for specialization. He saw specialization as a second main source of increased wealth, in addition to self-interested, market-based exchanges. If people could specialize and trade, each person could focus on what they were good at—and trade for everything else they'd need.

◀ Specialization was also a source of innovation and progress. If people specialize, they learn—or figure out—ways to do the job better and faster.

Karl Marx

◀ Karl Marx authored many books, pamphlets, and articles—the most famous of which was *Das Kapital*. Like Adam Smith, Marx set forth several key ideas that would change the face of economics, four of which are class society; the development of capitalist industry; the rise of the working class, or proletariat; and the inevitability of socialism.

" The philosophers have only interpreted the world, in various ways. The point, however, is to change it. "

— MARX

◀ Unlike Smith—who saw markets as a way to bring people together—Marx insisted that different groups in society have conflicting interests. Marx assumed that as market societies develop, some men would become rich and own more and more of the productive machinery and factories. Everyone else would have to sell their own labor to earn enough to live.

- The rich capitalists would come from landlords, successful merchants, and traders. The working class consisted of former peasants, poorer landowners, and unsuccessful artisans who were bankrupted by industrial capitalists who mass-produced cheaper products.

- Marx lamented the decline of artisan work and handicraft production, which gave the maker some direct control over the product and satisfaction at seeing the finished good produced. But he stipulated that industrialization offered benefits to society and set the stage for a higher standard of living. Here, we find a surprising area where Marx and Smith agreed.

- In Marx's view, the great cities of capitalist countries would be the places of giant factories and large populations. These factories would turn out countless numbers of products cheaply and efficiently. And that would, indeed, improve the lives of those entering from rural societies.

- The major problem Marx found with this form of development was that most profits from this production went to the owners of the factories, and not to the workers.

- Marx also argued that as growing numbers of workers came to work in the factories, their bargaining power would diminish. He envisioned more and more workers competing against each other for the same or fewer jobs, having the effect of driving down wages.

- The capitalists would become more and more monopolistic. And, therefore, fewer and fewer would dominate the market, as well as politics and society.

◀ The declining power of workers and the growing power of the capitalists would force wages to subsistence levels—just enough income to keep the workers and their families alive.

◀ Marx believed that the workers' only hope was to band together in trade unions and in support of political parties formed around these trade unions. The labor parties, social democratic parties, and socialist parties of Europe all derive some of their ideas from Marx.

◀ Marx envisioned that the labor parties and workers' organizations would be powerful enough to overthrow capitalism and establish social control of industry. This control would be used to benefit workers and to divide the total revenues and profits of industry among the entire population. This would be the way in which inequality would be eliminated and democratic control of industry would be established.

◀ Marx thought that a successful workers' revolution would begin in an advanced economy, such as that of Great Britain or Germany. A society ripe for revolution would be highly developed, where workers were skilled at industrial labor and manufacturing processes. But the first workers' revolution actually occurred in poor and underdeveloped Russia. And it didn't turn out so well.

◀ Social equality—and the idea of everybody being paid the same—sounds humane and democratic. But they can have some unintended consequences.

John Maynard Keynes and Milton Friedman

"Capitalism is the astounding belief that the most wickedest of men will do the most wickedest of things for the greatest good of everyone."

—KEYNES

◀ Two 20th-century thinkers loom large over most modern economies: John Maynard Keynes and Milton Friedman.

◀ Modern macroeconomics—which is the scientific analysis of the overall economic performance of national economies—owes its existence to Keynes and his followers. Most governments around the world today practice some macroeconomic policies to stabilize their economies and to promote growth. We see the influence of Keynes as governments manipulate taxes and government spending levels to influence overall economic performance.

◀ Milton Friedman was a free market advocate who created an entire school of modern economics at the University of Chicago. He believed that Keynes was wrong and that activist governments created more problems in the economy than they solved.

◀ Friedman derived his ideas from Adam Smith's belief that free markets—if left to themselves—would produce beneficial results for all of society and that too much government interference, in contrast, would damage the workings of demand and supply and the profit motive. Such damage created economic inefficiency and reduced economic growth.

◀ Most conservative political parties and thinkers owe a great deal to Friedman's ideas and arguments. Margaret Thatcher in the United Kingdom and Ronald Reagan in the United States are just two of the most prominent political leaders to put his ideas into practice.

"*There's no such thing as a free lunch.*"

— FRIEDMAN

BUCHAN, *Capital of the Mind.*
FRIEDMAN AND FRIEDMAN, *Free to Choose.*
MARX AND ENGELS, *Selected Works in One Volume.*
SKIDELSKY, *Keynes.*

1   What did Adam Smith think about the basic nature of
    human beings? How did this influence his advocacy of a
    market system?

2   Where did Karl Marx get his initial ideas about class
    conflict? How did Marx think class conflict could
    be eliminated?

Adam Smith, Karl Marx, Keynes, and Friedman

Adam Smith. Karl Marx. John Maynard Keynes. And Milton Friedman. Every economic system is based upon the ideas of one or more big thinkers. And most arguments today about what an economy is supposed to be—and what it's supposed to do—find their origins in the ideas of these four men. This includes arguments about: private property versus state ownership, government regulation versus free-market decisions, high taxes versus low taxes on consumption spending, and other questions. So, while it's true that there are many other important economic thinkers, these four men represent virtually all the major ideas in practice about how an economy should be organized, and how it should work.

Let's start with Adam Smith, the first great economist and systematic thinker about economic questions. Adam Smith was born in Glasgow, Scotland, in 1723. This was during the period known as the Scottish Enlightenment—a period of great debate about social policy, ethics, and the nature of humanity. Smith studied "moral philosophy" at the University of Edinburgh, in Scotland's capital. The subject of moral philosophy eventually turned into economics, political science, and sociology.

During Adam Smith's time, Edinburgh was a fast-growing city of merchants, manufacturers, bankers, lawyers, politicians, and professors. Precisely the kind of people who'd be interested in debating ideas about economic policy; a just society; and a rational political order. Smith also studied for at time at Oxford University, then—as now—one of the most important universities in the world. Smith didn't like Oxford very much. He thought it was too conservative, and filled with stuffy old professors.

He was once caught reading a book by the famous Scottish philosopher David Hume. Oxford had banned the book because of its critical views about religion. And the professor who caught him reprimanded Smith. As a believer in free and independent thinking, Adam Smith was not happy to have his intellectual life ruled by some sanctimonious old academic. Students to the present-day rebel against being told what to do, and what to think. Some things never change.

After Oxford, Smith got a teaching position at the University of Edinburgh as the main professor in the department of moral philosophy. Most biographies say he was an outstanding lecturer, and his students were happy to enroll in his lively classes. He seemed to take teaching seriously, and spent a lot of time thinking about his presentations. But Smith was also a great example of the absent-minded professor. Often, he could be seen walking around Edinburgh talking to himself, and rehearsing his classroom disputations. Once, he walked 30 miles before he realized how far—and for how long—he'd been wandering. So, you see the old cliché about absent-minded professors has a long and famous history—and some basis in fact.

Adam Smith's title at the university was not professor of economics. But that's what he really taught. The word "economist" didn't come into existence until some years later—late in the 18th century—when it was invented by a group of professors known as the physiocrats, at the University of Paris. The word "economics" actually comes from the Greek word for management of household expenses, and we first see it in the writings of Aristotle in the 4th century BC. The physiocrats believed that all wealth derived from land. And they adapted the Greek term *oikonomia* to label their own nascent profession *economiste*.

Some time later, in the 19th century, a new subject—"political economy"— was added to university studies and public debate. But well before then, you could say Adam Smith was already a "big thinker" in economics. Smith wasn't concerned with some narrow topic like the price of bread or the annual production of wood. Instead, he concerned himself with questions of national wealth, economic growth, social policy, and justice. We can get a sense of Adam Smith's main ideas by thinking about the title of his most famous book, *An Inquiry into the Nature and Causes of the Wealth of Nations*.

Most people refer to the book as *The Wealth of Nations*, but by taking note of the complete title, we gain a more nuanced understanding of what Smith was all about. His big book—and it is a big book; about 1,000 pages long—was published in 1776. That's an easy date to remember, as other big things happened that year as well. And there is a connection between the ideas of Adam Smith and the American Revolution that will become clear as we continue. Now, Smith outlined many groundbreaking ideas, in a classic book that changed the landscape of economic thinking forever. But for now, I want to focus on three that serve as the foundation for Smith's view of economics. These are: the nature of wealth; the necessity of free markets; and the benefits of specialization.

Let's first examine Smith's view of what exactly was the nature of the wealth of a nation. During Smith's time, most people thought national wealth meant lots of gold in the king's treasury; or a big army; or impressive government buildings. But Smith disagreed. He said the most important kind of wealth was a nation's production of goods and services that made the lives of ordinary people better. It wasn't how much gold and silver the king or the emperor had. Instead, the food, clothing, shelter, and health of the general population made a nation wealthy. Smith was concerned about ordinary folks who make up a country's population. How well did they live? To Smith, the activities of bakers, tailors, shoemakers, carpenters, and butchers were more important than the comings and goings of kings and queens. In the same way, in assessing or examining the health of a nation's economy today, typically we focus on gross domestic product, or GDP: that is the total production of goods and services in an economy.

The next part of Smith's book title—the *Causes of the Wealth of Nations*—is still the most important question for the majority of the world's population. How do we make a country wealthier, in the Adam Smith sense? How do we make people's lives better? These are big questions in Africa, Asia, and South America, as well as in Europe and the United States. Think about any national debate, from healthcare to taxes to national defense. Adam Smith's thinking about how to increase the wealth of nations rests on his ideas about human nature and human motivation.

Smith believed that most people were concerned about other people, and could be motivated by sympathy for their fellow-man. But he thought that a stronger human motivation was self-love, and concern for immediate family and close friends. Smith thought it would be foolish to view human society with the belief that people's main objective is to improve the lives of all humanity. We all know people who truly are generous, and thoughtful, and concerned about the fate of the entire world. But Smith believed most of us have to spend our time and energy worrying about ourselves—and our nearest and dearest.

Smith also believed that most people are social creatures who like to participate in society, interacting with fellow human beings. So, the trick is to recognize that while people want to engage with one another, they still mostly look out for themselves. Taking into account humans' self-interest—along with our desire to interact—Adam Smith recognized that people, by their very nature, love to trade and shop. One of Adam Smith's most-quoted phrases is that "humans have a natural propensity to truck, barter, and exchange." Smith thought that bargaining and exchange activities were unique to human beings. He would always ask his students if they had ever seen two dogs making a bargain about exchanging bones. What emerges from this view is Smith's belief that a commercial society—based on market institutions—is the best economic system humans could create and sustain.

Smith didn't use the label "capitalism" for this ideal system. That word didn't exist yet. It would be invented by another great thinker, Karl Marx, in the 1840s. But Smith put all of his ideas together in the thesis that a rational human economy would be based on exchange, motivated by self-interest. He said we should appeal to the self-interest of the baker for our daily bread. Sure, there might be very charitable and friendly bakers who give us bread out of the goodness of their hearts, but it would be risky to depend on their generosity on a daily basis. Much better, instead, to give the baker something he or she values—and that will improve the baker's life, and his or her family's well-being—in exchange for the bread provided to us.

When I go into my local coffee shop each morning, I know the barista likes me because I'm a rather pleasant fellow for an economics professor, or maybe it's because I'm buying coffee there every day. And you know, that can get pretty expensive! Now, maybe the barista is so pleased to see me that she'll give me my *grande misto* for free.

And believe or not, this happens on occasion. But I know enough to not depend on this. I always bring money with me, since coffee is one of the most necessary parts of my daily life!

So here we see that Smith believed that by appealing to the self-interest of individual producers and businesses, they would produce what society wanted—and the general good of the society would be promoted. This is also where Smith's most famous idea comes in: the "invisible hand." The idea of the invisible hand basically goes like this: in an economy based on self-motivated exchange, the economy is guided by an invisible hand—a hand that benefits all parties participating in the exchange.

Smith was a great believer in freedom. At the time he was writing, an individual's job (or occupation), and social position were mainly determined by what kind of family you came from. If you were born into nobility, you'd be a nobleman. If you were born into a family of bakers, you'd be a baker. But Smith thought people should be free to choose their own occupations and professions. He thought that what made a great baker was someone with a passion to be really good at baking bread. And if they were really good at baking bread—and consumers were free to buy their bread from whomever they wanted—the person satisfying their customers' desires for bread would make a lot of dough! Sorry about that. Couldn't resist.

Anyway, Smith believed there should a lot of freedom, as to who could sell in a market. No one person, or small group, should have a monopoly in the sale of a good or service. But though Smith was very much in favor of markets, he was also very suspicious of businessmen. He assumed that when people in the same business got together, they were usually cooking up some scheme to rig the market, and cheat the consumer. So, Smith was a firm believer in the necessity of the state to be keep a close eye on the markets, and watch out for anti-competitive behavior.

Smith also recognized that the successes of some would lead to inequality in incomes. In other words, some people would get rich and some people would be poor. The reasons could be differences in skill, luck, effort, and the training needed to succeed in some occupations. Therefore, it would be necessary for the state to provide some basic standard of living. Smith saw inequality in incomes as a necessary evil of a market society. The best way to prevent too much inequality was to promote as much competition as possible, and make the market as big and wide as could be. Competition from other regions and other countries would limit the power of local businessmen to control the market for their benefit. So, as you can imagine, Smith was a big believer in free trade. And free trade is the basis for the final idea of Smith's that I'll talk about today: specialization.

Smith saw specialization as a second main source of increased wealth, in addition to self-interested, market-based exchanges. If people could specialize and trade, each person could focus on what they were good at—and trade for everything else they'd need. Specialization was also a source of innovation and progress. The thinking goes that if people specialize, they learn—or figure out—ways to do the job better, and faster.

For instance, I used to be on the newsletter-mailing committee of Chicago's Lincoln Park running club. The usual practice was to give everybody on the committee a stack of pages, and let them put them all together—fold, staple, peel off the mailing label, stick the mailing label on—and then add the postage stamp. Offering my best impression of Adam Smith, I said, "We can make this process much more efficient and quicker if we divide the tasks and specialize." So, one person was assigned the task of organizing the sheets of paper. The next person was the folder. The next person was the stapler. And so on. As we progressed, each person figured out ways to make the process quicker and more precise. There was now more time for drinking beer, and telling running stories—and that was the real reason people volunteered for the committee!

Karl Marx, a very different person from Adam Smith, was born in 1818, in the city of Trier—on the Moselle River—in what is now Germany. Trier was part of the Prussian Rhineland. At the time of Marx's birth, Prussia was a very conservative and undemocratic state. And this was to play a part in Marx's career prospects. Marx studied law, history, and philosophy—first at the University of Bonn, and then in Berlin. Because of his radical and progressive views, he was forbidden the luxury of having an academic career, which is what he originally wanted for himself. Maybe if he'd been allowed to be just another stuffy German professor, history would have been quite different.

Instead, he got a job writing for a radical newspaper in Cologne—another lovely city along the Rhine River. Because of his radical views on politics and economics, that job got Marx into trouble with the Prussian authorities.

One issue that was especially troublesome, at the time, was the Moselle peasantry taking wood from a landlord's forest. The peasants needed the wood for heat in the winter. But they were prosecuted in the local courts, and sentenced to prison. Marx took the peasants' side, and aroused the authorities' displeasure. Eventually, he would move to Great Britain, which was more democratic and tolerant. But the experience of the Moselle peasantry convinced Marx that he needed to learn a lot more about economics.

Now, when we think of Karl Marx, many of us picture a radical political figure with bushy beard and moustache—and a real mover and shaker in the economic world. Technically that's accurate. But you might be surprised to learn Marx's life wasn't very exciting at all. In London, he spent a great deal of time studying in the library of the British Museum. He earned a little bit of money writing articles for newspapers like the *New York Herald Tribune.*

But mostly, he was supported by his friend, Frederick Engels, the son of a rich industrialist.

Marx was a prolific writer, and authored many books, pamphlets, and articles. His most famous was *Das Kapital.* And it was Marx who gave us the label "Capitalism" for the economic system centered on private property, markets, and profits. Like Adam Smith, Marx set forth several key ideas that would change the face of economics. Today, we'll concentrate on four of them: class society; the development of capitalist industry; the rise of the working class, or proletariat; and the inevitability of socialism. Let's look at each of these ideas, and then contrast the ideas of Adam Smith and Karl Marx.

Marx begins the first section of one of his most famous essays, *The Communist Manifesto*, with this statement: "The history of all hitherto existing society is the history of class struggles. Freeman and slave, patrician and plebian, lord and serf, guild-master and journeyman, in a word, oppressor and oppressed." Here, we can see the effects of Marx's early exposure to the conflict between the Moselle landlords and the peasants who were trying to get some wood for their heating and cooking.

Unlike Adam Smith—who saw markets as a way to bring people together—Marx insisted that different groups in society have conflicting interests. Marx assumed that as market societies develop, some men would become rich—and own more and more of the productive machinery and factories. Everyone else would have to sell their own labor to earn enough to live. The rich capitalists would come from landlords, successful merchants, and traders. The working class consisted of former peasants, poorer landowners, and unsuccessful artisans who were bankrupted by industrial capitalists who mass produced cheaper products.

Marx lamented the decline of artisan work, and handicraft production, which gave the maker some direct control over the product—and satisfaction at seeing the finished good produced. But he stipulated that industrialization offered benefits to society, and set the stage for a higher standard of living. Here we find a surprising area where Marx and Adam Smith agreed.

Marx even had words of praise for the contributions of the rich capitalists, or bourgeoisie. Here again we can quote from *The Communist Manifesto*: "The bourgeoisie has subjected the country to the rule of the towns. It has created enormous cities, has greatly increased the urban population as compared with the rural, and thus rescued a considerable part of the population from the idiocy of rural life." Right after World War I, there was a popular song in the United States about the changed thinking of American soldiers coming home after serving in Britain and France. The refrain went: "How you gonna keep 'em down on the farm after they've seen Paree" I won't sing it for you because it would be obvious why I decided not to be a singer. But in Marx's view, the great cities of capitalist countries would be the places of giant factories and large populations. These factories would turn out countless numbers of products cheaply and efficiently. And that would, indeed, improve the lives of those entering from rural societies.

The major problem Marx found with this form of development was that most profits from this production went to the owners of the factories, and not to the workers. What's more, Marx argued that as growing numbers of workers came to work in the factories, their bargaining power would diminish. He envisioned more and more workers competing against each other for the same or fewer jobs, having the effect of driving down wages. The capitalists would become more and more monopolistic. And, therefore, fewer and fewer would dominate the market, as well as politics and society.

The declining power of workers, and the growing power of the capitalists, would force wages to subsistence levels—just enough income to keep the worker and his family alive. Marx believed the workers' only hope was to band together in trade unions, and in support of political parties formed around these trade unions. The labor parties, social democratic parties, and socialist parties of Europe all derive some of their ideas from Marx. We can see one result of this in the modern British Labour Party, originally funded by the British Trades Union Congress.

Finally, Marx envisioned that the labor parties and workers' organizations would be powerful enough to overthrow capitalism, and establish social control of industry. This control would be used to benefit workers, and to divide the total revenues and profits of industry among the entire population. This would be the way in which inequality would be eliminated, and democratic control of industry would be established. Marx thought that a successful workers' revolution would begin in an advanced economy like Great Britain or Germany. A society ripe for revolution would be highly developed, where workers were skilled at industrial labor and manufacturing processes. As we know, the first workers' revolution actually occurred in poor—and underdeveloped—Russia. As we also know, it didn't turn out so well.

Social equality—and the idea of everybody being paid the same—sound humane and democratic. But they can have some unintended, if easily understood, consequences. For example, on my first trip to the former Soviet Union in 1985, I ran into the strange phenomenon of restaurants closing for lunch and dinner so the workers wouldn't have their meals interrupted by customers. They were being paid a fixed income, tipping was illegal—considered a remnant of exploitive capitalism—and they had guaranteed jobs.

In this example, the Soviet system of socialism didn't fully account for the role that material incentives play in human behavior. The result was a lot of hungry consumers who had to wait until late afternoon to have their Borscht. Borscht, by the way, is a piping hot beet and cabbage soup that's a favorite of diners during the hard, cold winters in Russia. It helped keep me alive during the semester I spent teaching in the Urals region near Siberia.

Now, capitalists would say that the failure to realize the self-interested nature of human behavior was one of the leading causes for the failures of the Soviet economy, and its eventual breakdown. It might also explain why the current government of the Peoples' Republic of China—although they refer to themselves as Marxist communists—nevertheless decided to let farmers own their own land, and sell their products in free markets. In its own way, this shows that economic systems are always evolving. And in reality, there is no purely market—or socialistic—economy.

Two 20th-century thinkers loom large over most modern economies. They are John Maynard Keynes and Milton Friedman. Keynes was an upper crust Englishman who studied math—and later politics and economics, at Cambridge University. His flamboyant personality and vivid intellect made him a centerpiece of the society of artists and writers known as the Bloomsbury Group. Keynes rose to prominence in the British treasury during World War I, and in post-war settlement talks at Versailles—which he harshly criticized in his book, *The Economic Consequences of the Peace*. But his most lasting contributions to economic theory emerged from his thinking and proposals arising out of the Great Depression of the 1930s.

Modern macroeconomics—which is the scientific analysis of the overall economic performance of national economies—owes its existence to Keynes and his followers. Most governments around the world today practice some macroeconomic policies to stabilize their economies—and to promote growth. We see the influence of Keynes as governments manipulate taxes and government spending levels to influence overall economic performance.

In turn, Milton Friedman—born nearly 30 years after Keynes, and whose life would encompass most of the 20th and part of the 21st century—was a free-market advocate, who created an entire school of modern economics at the University of Chicago. Friedman believed that Keynes was wrong, and that activist governments created more problems in the economy than they solved.

Friedman derived his ideas from Adam Smith's belief that free markets—if left to themselves—would produce beneficial results for all of society; and that too much government interference, in contrast, would damage the workings of demand and supply, and the profit motive. Such damage created economic inefficiency, and reduced economic growth. Most conservative political parties and thinkers owe a great deal to Milton Friedman's ideas and arguments. Margaret Thatcher in the United Kingdom, and Ronald Reagan in the United States, are just two of the most prominent political leaders to put Friedman's ideas into practice.

Today—all over the world—political leaders, academics, journalists, bloggers, and activists echo the ideas of Smith, Marx, Keynes, and Friedman. They argue strongly about how an economy should be organized; about what are the goals of a good society; how production and distribution should be organized; whether we should tolerate differences in income and wealth; and other questions about the future.

One reason I try to always be prepared to buy my cup of morning coffee, and not rely on the barista, is influenced by Milton Friedman's statement, "There's no such thing as a free lunch." But Friedman also said, "If you put the federal government in charge of the Sahara Desert, in five years there'd be a shortage of sand." What would Adam Smith say to that? What about Karl Marx? And what about John Maynard Keynes?

Keynes had great wit. And one thing he said is this: "Capitalism is the astounding belief that the most wickedest of men will do the most wickedest of things for the greatest good of everyone." He might have been parodying Adam Smith—while not disagreeing with him. In turn, Marx said: "The philosophers have only interpreted the world, in various ways. The point, however, is to change it." So, as you can see, the argument goes on.

Lecture 3

How to Argue GDP, Inflation, and Other Data

THIS LECTURE WILL EXPLORE DIFFERENT WAYS IN which economies can be compared and evaluated. Many of these differences reflect national values, ideologies, and opinions. This lecture will examine some of the most commonly used measures of comparative economic performance and learn how they help us judge which economies are doing better than others. ◆

Gross Domestic Product

◀ The most commonly used measure of economic performance is gross domestic product (GDP). This statistical concept attempts to capture the value of all goods and services that an economy produces in a given time period, usually one calendar year.

◀ Most countries calculate and publish their economy's annual GDP. And this number is becoming more and more standard. The Organization for Economic Cooperation and Development (OECD) in Paris is one of the main international organizations to advise countries on how to calculate their GDP so that it is comparable with other countries' GDPs. The OECD provides advice, studies, and statistical consulting to high-income countries around the globe, including to the United States, Canada, and Japan.

◀ The GDP statistic was invented by a Russian American immigrant economist in the United States named Simon Kuznets, who was tasked by the administration of President Franklin D. Roosevelt to come up with a measure of the economic potential of the entire U.S. economy. Kuznets was awarded the Nobel Prize in Economics for his development of the GDP statistic.

◀ GDP is an aggregate number. It is a summing up of all the sectors of an economy and all the products and services that an economy produces.

◀ In the United States, the calculation of GDP is performed by the Bureau of Economic Analysis, which is part of the Department of Commerce.

◀ Exports are part of U.S. GDP because they are goods and services produced in the United States and sold to foreigners. Imports are subtracted from U.S. GDP because they are part of some other country's production. However, most of what we buy in the United States is produced in the United States. The biggest household expenditure category is housing, and most housing is produced in the United States.

◀ Business investment spending on buildings, equipment, and capital goods is also included in GDP. Finally, governments buy goods and services, too. Military goods, police protection, fire protection, education services, government buildings, and medical care are all mostly produced in the United States.

◀ The United States has the world's largest GDP. But that doesn't mean that it has the richest citizens. The United States distributes its GDP among approximately 320 million residents. You can't judge living standards by GDP alone; you must adjust for population. GDP per capita, or GDP per person, is calculated by dividing a country's GDP by its population.

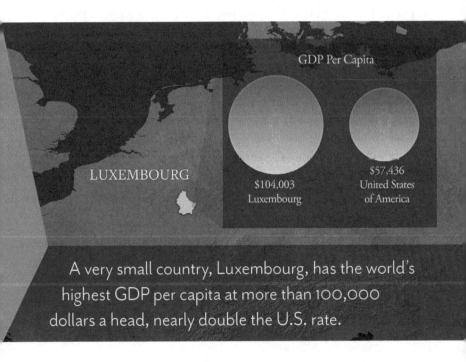

GDP Per Capita

LUXEMBOURG

$104,003
Luxembourg

$57,436
United States
of America

A very small country, Luxembourg, has the world's highest GDP per capita at more than 100,000 dollars a head, nearly double the U.S. rate.

◀ Many countries with a growing GDP might have falling living standards because their populations are growing faster than their GDP. China introduced the one-child policy decades ago for this reason. Since then, Chinese GDP per capita has risen very quickly. Ironically, the Chinese abandoned the one-child policy because it was too successful. Today, China's population is aging, threatening to slow the growth of the Chinese economy.

◀ Another important adjustment that frequently needs to be made to the GDP statistic is to account for the problem of inflation. GDP is calculated by adding up all the monetary values of current production.

◀ The people who calculate GDP actually produce two versions: current-dollar GDP, which measures GDP using current prices; and constant-dollar GDP, which uses some base year—or constant price standard—to calculate what is also called real GDP. When economists use the adjective "real" before some monetary statistic, this means that the statistic has been adjusted for inflation.

◀ Real per capita GDP is the main comparative statistic with which to compare societies. It's the best measure available to us for comparing most countries in the world.

Income Distribution

◀ Another important question is how income is distributed. Are most residents of a country similar in incomes, or is there a big gap between the rich and the poor? Just dividing GDP by population doesn't tell you anything about how evenly, or unevenly, total income is distributed. Averages—what real GDP per capita is—can be quite misleading.

◀ To illustrate this, consider what happens when Bill Gates walks into a room. Let's say that the room holds 20 people and that the occupants have an average income of $50,000. Then, Bill Gates, one of the world's wealthiest men, walks into the room. Now, the average income in the room shoots up into the billions of dollars. Of course, that doesn't give an accurate picture of the living standards of those 21 people.

◀ A more descriptive statistic might be median income, based on the income of the person in the exact middle of the group. If the original 20 people all had very similar incomes, the median income might not change, even after Bill walked in.

◀ Other common measures also give us a picture of the distribution of income in a country, including income inequality. These measures include calculating the share of total income received by the top 1 percent or top 10 percent of the population.

◀ Other, more complicated measures are the ratio of incomes of the top 10 percent to the bottom 10 percent and the ratio of the top 20 percent to the bottom 20 percent. These are called decile and quintile ratios, respectively, and they get larger as income gets more unevenly distributed.

◀ This topic has become more important as income in the United States flattened out relative to some other high-income countries.

◀ A last and most complicated measure of income inequality is called the Gini coefficient, named after Italian economist and statistician Corrado Gini. The Gini coefficient can vary between 0 and 1. The closer the Gini coefficient is to 1, the more uneven income distribution is in a country.

◀ Many societies place a high value on social solidarity and seek to minimize the extremes of rich and poor. These countries usually have high progressive tax systems—that is, the higher the income, the bigger the tax rate—and significant social welfare programs.

◀ Progressive taxes are usually personal income taxes rather than sales or excise taxes, which typically are a fixed percentage of the price of some good or service.

◀ There's no objectively correct level of income distribution or inequality. Some societies value individual freedom and self-sufficiency, while others place a higher value on social equality and avoiding extreme income differences. These conflicting values are one of the most important and interesting differences among competing economic systems.

◀ One goal of socialism was to eliminate, or at least drastically reduce, income and class inequality. Socialists criticized capitalism for creating these differences. In some ways, socialist or communist countries did reduce inequality, though not completely.

◀ In capitalist economies, big debates are under way today about how much inequality is supportive of economic growth and whether it is possible to have too much inequality.

> As George Orwell noted about communist economies: "All were equal, but some were more equal than others."

◀ Most economists argue that some inequality is necessary to encourage innovation and business performance.

◀ But some minimum level of income needs to be available for everyone in an economy so that all citizens can lead healthy and productive lives. There should be adequate levels of food, shelter, health care, and education for an economy to produce at its maximum potential. A society of malnourished and uneducated people won't be able to provide efficient workers for capitalist entrepreneurs, nor consumers for retail businesspeople.

◀ One key reason for the rapid economic growth of the American economy in the 19th century was the country's development of a public education system—first at the primary- and secondary-school levels and later at the college level. Land-grant public universities, which charged little or no tuition, gave many Americans a higher education that was available in Europe only to the very upper classes and nobility.

Quality of Life and Health

◀ A new field of comparative economic achievement has focused directly on the quality of life and health of a country's population. These new measures and statistics have a variety of names, such as the Human Development Index.

◀ Life expectancy and infant mortality rates are correlated with real GDP per capita. Higher-income countries almost always have better food, medical care, and education and more access to important information.

◀ A new field of comparative economic performance that focuses on human health and development is called anthropometry, developed by American economists John Komlos and Richard Steckel. Their unique contribution was to focus on differences in average height among different populations.

◀ It turns out that height is a pretty good measure of all kinds of social conditions, such as nutrition, health care, prenatal and neonatal conditions, economic status, income distribution, and education. Today, many studies compare the height of different countries' populations.

◀ This is also a simple and direct way of comparing standards of living. Countries that have high standards of living will have taller populations. In countries with improving economies, populations will be growing taller.

◀ Height differences tell a much larger story about health, education, and economic opportunity. Countries with improving economies will observe significant gains in average height over time.

◀ For all of these reasons, it's disconcerting that average height in the United States has not been increasing in the last few decades. Economists and public health specialists have some possible explanations, including worsening nutrition and diet, uneven access to health care, and increasing economic inequality and opportunity.

As of 2017, the tallest populations are in the Netherlands and Latvia. Dutch men are the tallest in the world, and Latvians are the tallest women. The shortest men are in East Timor, and the shortest women are in Guatemala.

Employment and Unemployment

◀ Two more pieces of data are commonly used to measure the ability of an economy to provide jobs for its residents and a dependable money supply.

◀ Employment and unemployment statistics provide a measure of how well people who want to work can find jobs. Low unemployment rates mean jobs for new graduates, new opportunities for workers looking to change careers or location, and optimism for individuals and families about their futures. High unemployment rates contribute to anxiety and a stagnant economy.

◀ Employment and unemployment statistics are collected somewhat differently in each country but are becoming more comparable thanks to the OECD and the International Labour Organization (ILO), which is an office of the United Nations devoted to promoting policies to better the lives and working conditions of labor around the world. The ILO also advises countries on proper ways to collect and publish employment and unemployment data so that comparative analysis is possible—and realistic.

Inflation

◀ Another measure of comparative economic performance is inflation, which is defined as a general rise in the cost of living. It doesn't refer to the price of one product or another getting more expensive, but rather an economy-wide rise in prices. Inflation hurts almost everyone, especially the poor and the old.

◀ In the United States, inflation is measured by the Bureau of Labor Statistics, which is part of the Department of Labor.

◀ Hyperinflation is usually defined by economists as inflation of more than 50 percent a year. Under hyperinflation, nobody wants to exchange goods and services for money, and barter becomes much more common. But barter is very inefficient and time consuming. And very often, hyperinflation is a precursor of political and social upheaval.

Readings

BUREAU OF ECONOMIC ANALYSIS, "Survey of Current Business."
BUREAU OF LABOR STATISTICS, "Beyond the Numbers."
ORGANIZATION FOR ECONOMIC COOPERATION AND
　　DEVELOPMENT, *OECD Factbook 2015–2016.*

Questions

1 What do you think are the most important measurements of how well an economy is doing?

2 Why won't people ever agree on what is the most important measure of economic success and performance?

How to Argue GDP, Inflation, and Other Data

If you like baseball, and get into a conversation about who has the best Major League Baseball team, you can always get some argument. But there are pretty easy ways to end that argument. The answer comes down to numbers: like winning percentages, and World Series victories. When assessing who has the world's best economy, there are a lot more numbers—and not much agreement—about the most important measures. This question can start a lot of arguments. And they're difficult to end. Scholars like me, who study comparative economic systems, spend a lot of time—and thought—trying to come up with answers to the question.

In this lecture, we'll explore different ways in which economies can be compared and evaluated. Many of these differences reflect national values, ideologies, and opinions. The Harvard economist Greg Mankiw—who was the White House's chief economic advisor under President George W. Bush—once compared economic performance to medical statistics. When you ask how is an economy doing, an economist can spout off hundreds of different statistics.

In the same way, I often tell my students that the ways in which economists judge the health and performance of an economy is somewhat similar to what happens following your annual medical checkup. After the examination, you might ask the doctor, "How am I doing?" You don't get a simple answer. What you're most likely to get, instead, are several pages of data: blood pressure, heart rate, weight, height, blood counts, cholesterol, temperature, etc. In fact, these days you don't just get cholesterol, you get total cholesterol, high-density lipoprotein, low-density lipoprotein, very low-density lipoprotein, and a cholesterol ratio. (One of the few things my parents had in common was high cholesterol.) So, you won't get an answer like, "You're fine" or "You're sick." Instead, you'll get a long discussion with all of the good things about the results, and all of the not-so-good things about the results. Often, I leave these discussions confused about how healthy I am.

Comparative economic measurement and evaluation is a lot like that. We look at lots of numbers and data, and come to some conclusions. But we don't expect to come to clear-cut, definitive judgments that let us say, "This economy is great," or "This economy is terrible." We might be able to conclude that some economies are doing better, in a wide range of performance measures; and some economies are doing worse, on some commonly accepted measures of performance. But definite and conclusive judgements are hard to come by. So, let's examine some of the most commonly used measures of comparative economic performance, and see how they help us judge which economies are doing better than others.

The most commonly used measure of economic performance is gross domestic product, or GDP. This statistical concept attempts to capture the value of all goods and services that an economy produces in a given time period, usually one calendar year. Most countries calculate and publish their economy's annual GDP. And this number is becoming more and more standard. The Organization for Economic Co-operation and Development, or OECD, in Paris, is one of the main international organizations to advise countries on how to calculate their GDP, so that it is comparable with other countries' GDPs.

The OECD has its roots in the United States' "European Recovery Program," which most of us know as the Marshall Plan—named after former Secretary of State George Marshall. Originally it was named the Organization for European Economic Cooperation, or OEEC. After World War II, Secretary Marshall laid out the U.S. plan for helping Europe recover from the devastation of war, in a speech at Harvard University in 1947.

One of the brilliant components of the plan was that all the European countries—winners and losers alike—had to cooperate in determining how U.S. financial aid was to be used. This began the momentum for economic cooperation, and peaceful relations, between the former belligerent countries of Europe. Even the newly communist countries of eastern Europe and the Soviet Union were invited to join. But Joseph Stalin—fearing American influence—forbade the eastern European countries under his control from participating. This was a tough decision for Stalin, because the Soviet Union was devastated at the end of the war.

And initially, he thought about accepting the U.S. money. But Stalin's ideology—and his desire for control—was larger than his need for economic assistance.

More broadly, the Organization for European Economic Cooperation, founded in April 1948, needed ways to tell how well the American aid was being used—and how well member economies were recovering from the war. So, it began using the GDP approach, which had been invented a few years before by a Russian-American immigrant economist in the United States named Simon Kuznets. The administration of Franklin Delano Roosevelt had asked Kuznets to come up with some measure of the economic potential of the entire U.S. economy. This had been crucial information for a country going to war. How much war materiel could be produced and still have enough goods and services left over for civilians who would be producing the war goods? Kuznets was awarded the Nobel Prize in economics for his development of the GDP statistic.

In many ways, the Organization for European Economic Cooperation led the way towards the creation of the European Economic Community, or EEC, in 1957—known more commonly as the Common Market. The Common Market evolved over the years into the European Union. So, in some fundamental ways, the European Union is also an American creation. Once the countries of western European recovered, the OEEC changed its focus and name. In September 1961, it became the Organization for Economic Co-operation and Development, or OECD, a worldwide body rather than a strictly European one. And today, the OECD provides advice, studies, and statistical consulting to high-income countries around the globe, including to the United States, Canada, and Japan.

Gross domestic product is an aggregate number. It is a summing up of all the sectors of an economy; and all the products and services that an economy produces. Some years ago, I asked a class of mine, "What does the word 'aggregate' mean?" A young lady in the back answered, "It's a rock." I said, "No, you're wrong." Some years later I learned she was correct. Unfortunately, I never had a course in geology. So, I was totally ignorant of the fact that an aggregate is, indeed, a form of rock, like gravel, sand, or crushed stone. But it is somewhat similar in concept to GDP, in that an aggregate rock is a combination of different elements forced together.

In the United States, the calculation of GDP is performed by the Bureau of Economic Analysis, which is part of the Commerce Department. I have a soft spot in my heart for the BEA. I wrote my Ph.D. dissertation on the foreign trade patterns of the United States. And for a key part of my research, I needed some foreign trade statistics that weren't widely available. I made a trip to BEA headquarters in Suitland, Maryland, and was advised and helped by some very capable and friendly government staff. The data helped me with my statistical work. After writing my dissertation—and successfully defending it—I sent a dozen roses to the woman who was the most helpful, and I mentioned her in the dissertation's acknowledgement section.

Foreign trade has since become an increasingly important contributor to the U.S. economy. At the end of World War II, the U.S. had almost no imports or exports. No matter what your opinion is of globalization, it's a fact the foreign trade today is a growing part of the U.S. economy. Exports are part of U.S. GDP because they are goods and services produced in the United States, and sold to foreigners. Imports are subtracted from U.S. GDP because they are part of some other country's production.

However, most of what we buy in the United States is produced in the United States. The biggest household expenditure category is housing. And most housing is produced in the United States. Business investment spending on buildings, equipment, and capital goods is also included in GDP. And finally, governments buy goods and services, too. Military goods, police protection, fire protection, education services, government buildings, and medical care are all mostly produced in the United States.

The United States has the world's largest GDP. But that doesn't mean we have the richest citizens. The United States distributes its GDP among approximately 320 million residents. This brings us to another measure called GDP per capita, or GDP per person. It's calculated by dividing a country's GDP by its population. A very small country, Luxembourg, has the world's highest GDP per capita at more than $100,000 a head, nearly double the U.S. rate. So, you can't judge living standards by GDP alone. You must adjust for population.

Many countries with a growing GDP might have falling living standards because their populations are growing faster than their GDP. China introduced the one-child policy decades ago for this reason. Since then, Chinese GDP per capita has risen very quickly. Ironically, the Chinese abandoned the one-child policy because it was too successful. Today, China's population is aging, threatening to slow the growth of the Chinese economy. Economics is never simple!

One other important adjustment frequently needs to be made to the GDP statistics. That's to account for the problem of inflation. GDP is calculated by adding up all the monetary values of current production. So, if there are 1 million bushels of wheat produced and a bushel sells for $4.00, then $4 million is added to this year's GDP. Suppose that next year 1 million bushels are produced again, but the price goes up to $6.00 a bushel. We now have $6 million of wheat. But do we really have more? No. In this example, the increase in monetary value of wheat production is solely the result of inflation—rising prices.

So, the people who calculate GDP actually produce two versions. One is called "current dollar GDP," which measures GDP using current prices. The other is called "constant dollar GDP," and uses some base year—or constant price standard—to calculate what is also called "Real GDP." When economists use the adjective "real" before some monetary statistic, this means the statistic has been adjusted for inflation. For example, if this year you get a raise in your salary of 2 percent but all the goods and services that you buy have gone up in price by 3 percent, you have a gain in current income but a decrease in real income of 1 percent.

A dramatic example of the difference in "current" versus "constant"—or real—GDP is the country of Venezuela. In recent years, the current dollar GDP of Venezuela rose about 50 percent. But after adjusting for its high rate of inflation, Venezuelan constant dollar, or real, GDP actually fell. The living standards of the average Venezuelan citizen also decreased. This led to much dissatisfaction, and disgust, with the government and its economic policies.

Demonstrations and political conflict is often a manifestation of falling living standards.

We now have the main comparative statistic with which to compare societies: real per capita GDP. It's the best measure available to us for comparing most countries in the world. Let's take the examples of China and Taiwan. In one recent year, China had GDP of $11.4 trillion and Taiwan $529 billion, according to *The Economist* magazine.

But China had a population of 1.4 billion people compared to just 24 million in Taiwan. So, China's per capita GDP was just $15,424—compared to Taiwan's per capita GDP of $47,790.

Another important question is how income is distributed. Are most residents of a country similar in incomes? Or is there a big gap between the rich and the poor? Just dividing GDP by population doesn't tell you anything about how evenly, or unevenly, total income is distributed. Averages—that's what real GDP per capita is—can be quite misleading. To illustrate, let me tell you the story about what happens when Bill Gates walks into the room.

Let's say the room holds 20 people, and the occupants have an average income of $50,000. Then Bill Gates, one of the world's wealthiest men, walks into the room. Now, the average income in the room shoots up into the millions of dollars. Of course, that doesn't give an accurate picture of the living standards of those 21 people. A more descriptive statistic might be "median" income, based on the income of the person in the exact middle of the group.

That wouldn't change much even after Bill Gates walked into the room. If the original 20 people all had very similar incomes, the median income might not change at all, even after Bill walked in.

Other common measures also give us a picture of the distribution of income in a country, including income inequality. These measures include calculating the share of total income received by the top 1 percent or top 10 percent of the population. Other, more complicated, measures are the ratio of incomes of the top 10 percent to the bottom 10 percent; or the ratio of the top 20 percent to the bottom 20 percent. These are called decile and quintile ratios, and get larger as income gets more unevenly distributed. This topic has become more important as income in the United States has become more unequal relative to some other high-income countries.

A last and most complicated measure of income inequality is called the Gini coefficient, named after the Italian economist and statistician Corrado Gini. The Gini coefficient can vary between 0 and 100. So, it will be some numerical value. The closer the Gini coefficient is to 100, the more uneven income distribution is in a country.

Many societies place a high value on social solidarity, and seek to minimize the extremes of rich and poor. These countries usually have high progressive tax systems—that is, the higher the income, the bigger the tax rate—and significant social welfare programs. Progressive taxes are usually personal income taxes rather than sales or excise taxes, which typically are a fixed percentage of the price of some good or service.

There's no objectively correct level of income distribution or inequality. Some societies value individual freedom and self-sufficiency, while others place a higher value on social equality and avoiding extreme income differences.

These conflicting values are one of the most important, and interesting, differences among competing economic systems.

One goal of socialism was to eliminate, or at least drastically reduce, income and class inequality. Socialists criticized capitalism for creating these differences. In some ways, socialist or communist countries did reduce inequality, though not completely. As George Orwell noted about communist economies: "All were equal, but some were more equal than others."

In capitalist economies, big debates are under way today about how much inequality is supportive of economic growth; and is it possible to have too much inequality? Most economists argue that some inequality is necessary to encourage innovation and business performance. But some minimum level of income needs to be available for everyone in an economy so that all citizens can lead healthy and productive lives. There should be adequate levels of food, shelter, health care, and education for an economy to produce at its maximum potential. A society of malnourished, uneducated people won't be able to provide efficient workers for capitalist entrepreneurs, nor consumers for retail businesspeople.

One key reason for the rapid economic growth of the new American economy in the 19th century was the country's development of a public education system—first at the primary and secondary school levels, and later at the college level. Land-grant public universities, which charged little or no tuition, gave many Americans a higher education that was available in Europe only to the very upper classes and nobility.

After my father got out of the Army Air Corps—a predecessor of the Air Force—following World War II, he attended the University of Texas on the G.I. Bill. Most economists who specialize in the study of economic growth and productivity name the G.I. Bill as one of the most important economic and social policies of the United States. It created a mass of well-educated professionals, scientists, and engineers who fueled future increases in U.S. real GDP.

A new field of comparative economic achievement has focused directly on the quality of life and health of a country's population. These new measures and statistics have a variety of names: such as the Human Development Index, created by the World Bank. Incidentally, the World Bank provides a wealth of high-quality statistics on comparative economic performance around the world. It provides tables of data on everything from GDP to GDP per capita, educational attainment, health statistics, income distribution statistics, access to technology, access to clean water, percentages of the population attending school or university, and hundreds of other descriptive and interesting numbers.

When *The Economist* magazine compared China to Taiwan, it noted that life expectancy in China was 76 years while in Taiwan it was 80. When I was a young undergraduate, the difference between a life expectancy of 76 versus 80 was trivial to me. Now that I am a bit older, those extra four years seem a lot more important. In China, the infant mortality rate was 9.2 deaths per 1,000 live births while in Taiwan the rate was 4.4. Life expectancy and infant-mortality rates are correlated with real GDP per capita. The correlation isn't perfect, but it's a dependable relationship. Higher-income countries almost always have better food, medical care, education, and more access to important information.

A new field of comparative economic performance that focuses on human health and development is called anthropometrics, from the Greek words for human and measurement. It was developed by two American economists, John Komlos and Richard Steckel. Their unique contribution was to focus on differences in average height among different populations. Professor Komlos assembled data on armies as far back as Napoleon. Most countries didn't have censuses until the 20th century, and there are no comprehensive statistics on heights in the entire population. But armies quite often measured a soldier's height, if for no other reason than to make sure uniforms and armor were appropriately sized. It turns out the height is a pretty good measure of all kinds of social conditions, like nutrition, health care, prenatal and neonatal conditions, economic status, income distribution, and education.

Today, many studies—including some sponsored by the World Health Organization—compare the height of different countries' populations. This is also a simple and direct way of comparing standards of living. Countries that have high standards of living will have taller populations. In countries with improving economies, populations will be growing taller. Currently, the tallest populations are in the Netherlands and Latvia. Dutch men are the tallest in the world, and Latvians are the tallest women. At the other end of the spectrum, the shortest men are in East Timor, and the shortest women in Guatemala.

Height differences tell a much larger story about health, education, and economic opportunity. Countries with improving economies will observe significant gains in average height, over time. Of late, the largest gains in height have occurred for South Korean women and Iranian men. For all of these reasons, it's disconcerting that average height in the United States has not been increasing in the last few decades. Economists and public health specialists have some possible explanations. These include: worsening nutrition and diet, uneven access to health care, and increasing economic inequality.

Two more pieces of data are commonly used to measure the ability of an economy to provide jobs for its residents, and a dependable money supply. Employment and unemployment statistics provide a measure of how well people who want to work can find jobs. Low unemployment rates mean jobs for new graduates, new opportunities for workers looking to change careers or location, and optimism for individuals and families about their futures. High unemployment rates contribute to anxiety and a stagnant economy.

Employment and unemployment statistics are collected somewhat differently in each country, but are becoming more comparable thanks to the OECD and the International Labor Organization. The International Labor Organization, or ILO, is an office of the United Nations devoted to promoting policies to better the lives and working conditions of labor around the world. The ILO also advises countries on proper ways to collect and publish employment and unemployment data, so that comparative analysis is possible—and realistic.

A final measure of comparative economic performance to examine today is inflation. Inflation is defined as a general rise in the cost of living. It doesn't refer to the price of one product, or another product getting more expensive, but rather an economy-wide rise in prices. Inflation hurts almost everyone, especially the poor and the old.

In the United States, inflation is measured by the Bureau of Labor Statistics, which is part of the Labor Department. During World War I, the Labor Department created the United States' chief measure of inflation— the consumer price index, or CPI—to help settle a labor dispute in the New England shipyards. Shipyard workers were arguing for higher wages, to keep up with rising prices. The shipyard owners disputed that prices were rising. Without an objective measure, there was no way to settle the dispute. So, the shipyard owners and labor leaders asked the Department of Labor to create a statistic that would measure the changes in the cost of living for the average worker.

When I was teaching in Russia during the mid-1990s, the inflation rate there was about 100 percent a month. That means prices for most goods and services were doubling every month. Because the availability—and quality—of food in the city I was living in was pretty bad, I ended up eating a lot of Snickers candy bars. They were imported, and a good source of quick calories. When I arrived in Russia one September, a Snickers bar cost about 100 rubles. By the time I left a few months later, the same Snickers cost more than 1,000 rubles.

For the average Russian worker, schoolteacher, or student living on a fixed income, inflation was disastrous, and a major source of stress in their lives. No-one wants to save money when very soon it will be worth much less. And if nobody is saving, there'll be no funds in financial institutions available to lend to businesses who want to buy new equipment to modernize or improve productivity. There'll be no money to lend to new businesspersons and entrepreneurs.

Hyperinflation is usually defined by economists as inflation of more than 50 percent a year. Under hyperinflation, no-one wants to exchange goods and services for money, and barter becomes much more common. But barter is very inefficient and time consuming. And very often, hyperinflation is a precursor of political and social upheaval.

So, we've seen that there are many different measures of how well or badly an economy is doing. People can argue forever using whatever statistics prove their point. And people have different values so they can argue about what is the most important measure of an economy. Is it best to have low inflation? Low unemployment? Rapid economic growth? Economic equality? There are no right answers, and no definite conclusions.

Lecture 4

British Revolution: Industry and Labor

G REAT BRITAIN LAUNCHED MODERN INDUSTRIAL capitalism in the late 18th century by combining a series of essential but previously uncoordinated economic and political institutions. In the political sphere, these institutional innovations included the basic liberties outlined in the Magna Carta and safeguarded by parliamentary democracy. In the economic sphere—on which this lecture will concentrate—they included trade finance, shipping insurance, and a corporate form of ownership facilitated by stock markets and public investors. Together, these developments helped propel Britain to become the first country in the world to create large factories and export its products to foreign markets. ◆

Financial Innovations

◀ Financing foreign trade depends on the existence of insurance contracts, which were developed during the Middle Ages by the first Venetian merchants, who shipped their goods all over the Adriatic Sea and eastern Mediterranean.

◀ At first, this insurance was created by several wealthy merchants, who would pool their funds to insure each individual voyage. When a ship was lost to storms or pirates or foreign navies, each individual investor would lose a small share of the cost of the insurance. But successful voyages typically more than covered the costs of such losses, thereby generating profits to finance other voyages—and to pay for the insurance.

◀ The ad hoc collections of merchants called on to insure individual voyages was gradually replaced by companies set up to be permanent insurers of shipping and other types of commerce. And individual businessmen skilled at determining the risks of various business enterprises became insurance brokers.

◀ Another financial innovation was the rise of corporate ownership and investment. The Dutch perfected the joint-stock company form of corporate ownership and the first fully functioning stock exchange in Amsterdam. This innovation enabled large numbers of investors to pool rather small individual sums of money to underwrite a new enterprise.

◀ The key aspect of a joint-stock company is that each investor can lose only the amount of money the individual puts into the company. The collective resources of individual investors combined with limited personal liability makes it possible to gather large sums of money to build, for example, large factories with complicated machinery and equipment.

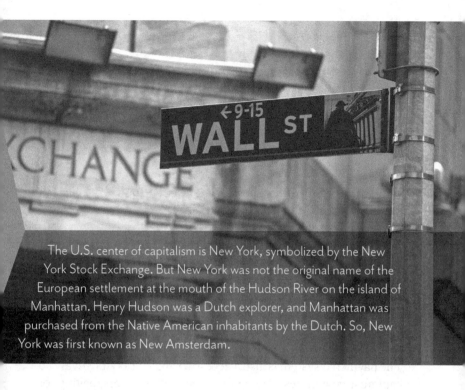

The U.S. center of capitalism is New York, symbolized by the New York Stock Exchange. But New York was not the original name of the European settlement at the mouth of the Hudson River on the island of Manhattan. Henry Hudson was a Dutch explorer, and Manhattan was purchased from the Native American inhabitants by the Dutch. So, New York was first known as New Amsterdam.

◀ In early market economics, most production was small-scale and accomplished with a few simple tools. The individual baker or shoemaker produced one item—or a few at a time—and did not need large amounts of money to start or maintain the business.

◀ What made large-scale British industrial capitalism different was massive factories producing thousands of items a day. Because no individual could raise all the funds necessary for these large-scale enterprises, the joint-stock company was vital to raise the necessary funds.

◀ An individual investor with a few shares of stock typically could sell these shares fairly easily and get out of any enterprise the investor deemed too risky or possibly unprofitable. This was made possible by a functioning stock market, where buyers and sellers of stocks could trade shares of companies on a regular and regulated basis. And it further reduced the risks of ownership.

◀ But the honesty of stock market participants—and the true value of the companies they own—is a continuing problem in the functioning of most stock markets.

◀ The Dutch began the process of regulating the companies that could sell their shares on the Amsterdam Stock Exchange. But even today, this regulatory process has not been perfected—and never will be. So, stock market crises have continued to disrupt capitalist economies and create economic instability. It's one of the chief problems of every capitalist economy.

◀ The payments system is also a necessary institution for advanced capitalist economies. Paying for goods and services, paying for raw materials and labor, and borrowing and lending money all historically depend on a banking system that is both sound and dependable.

◀ The northern Italians of the late Middle Ages invented modern banking and perfected it as merchant capitalism began to grow. But even with central banking systems and government deposit insurance systems—two innovations of later centuries—banking crises persist even today.

Building Industrial Capitalism

◀ One of Britain's main advantages in building industrial capitalism was that by the beginning of the 18ᵗʰ century, it was the largest single market in Europe. Britain's single market had a much larger customer base than elsewhere in Europe. So, British manufacturers could enjoy the benefits of mass production—which was the key to lower unit costs of production and lower prices for individual goods. This gave British capitalists a great competitive advantage compared to other European economies.

◀ Another key advantage for British capitalists was the Royal Navy. By the beginning of the 19ᵗʰ century, Britain had the largest and most modern navy in the world. Its sailors and fleets could protect British ships carrying the goods of British manufacturers around the world.

◀ One of the important institutions that Britain created was parliamentary democracy and the rule of law regarding property rights. The English first began to limit the power of the central government with the Magna Carta of 1215: the concession by King John to his nobles that subjected the sovereign to the rule of law and identified certain liberties as rights belonging to all free men. A further limitation on capricious governmental power was the Glorious Revolution of 1688 and 1689 and the execution of England's Charles I.

◀ Property rights are crucial to a market economy. Manufacturers, merchants, bankers, investors, and property owners must feel secure that their property, assets, money, and resources won't be taken away at the whim of the government, but rather only after an independent judicial process concludes that some law or regulation has been violated.

British Political Economy

- The most important British contribution to the development of industrial capitalism was British political economy.

- The Scottish philosopher, historian, and economist David Hume and the economist Adam Smith were both intellectual leaders of the Scottish Enlightenment. This period of revolutionary thought about economics, politics, and the just order of a commercial society lasted from roughly 1748 to 1789.

- Smith and Hume laid out the basic preconditions for a just and efficient commercial society based on private property and market exchanges. Their ideas were antiroyalist, antitraditional, and inherently democratic. They believed that people should be free to choose their own occupations and govern their own purchases and sales.

- If many people could choose to be shoemakers, for example, they would compete robustly for customers, and good shoes would be produced at fair and competitive prices. Furthermore, this competition would drive the search for better and more efficient ways of producing current goods and lead to the development of new goods and services finding a profitable market.

- The English political economist David Ricardo provided an intellectual argument for free trade and international competition. In his groundbreaking book, *On the Principles of Political Economy and Taxation*, published in 1817, he introduced the concept of comparative advantage, which remains one of the most important principles of economic theory.

◀ Ricardo explained that countries should specialize in the products they produce with the lowest opportunity cost. In other words, whatever choice an economic actor makes about production, he or she will necessarily sacrifice other opportunities as a result of the investment and ingenuity required to make the product of choice. Ideally, in the interests of efficiency, your choice should come with the lowest cost.

◀ While there are some exceptions to this principle, such as national defense, it's still an approximation of why certain countries specialize and export certain products while importing the products that are very costly for them to produce.

The Labour Party

◀ By the 1800s, Britain was the world's foremost industrial power and its richest country. The cities of Manchester, Birmingham, Sheffield, and London were all growing rapidly and pulling in rural citizens to work in factories near urban areas. The port cities of Bristol and Plymouth—and shipyards in the north—also grew commensurately.

◀ With a growing urban working class, the problems of unequal incomes, poverty, industrial accidents and death, and urban crime quickly followed. Popular agitation and campaigns for improvement in the lives of factory workers began around 1845, when Karl Marx's collaborator and fellow revolutionary Friedrich Engels wrote *The Condition of the Working Class in England*, which provided graphic details about the long and dangerous work of factory laborers and the slum conditions in which they lived.

◀ The first British organized labor movement, the Trades Union Congress, was formed in 1868. Eventually, this gave rise to a political party based on the British labor movement: the British Labour Party, one of two principal political parties in the country today.

◀ The Labour Party's original program called for the abolition of capitalism and its replacement by a socialist economy, though it advocated peaceful change through victories in democratic elections rather than revolution and violent overthrow of the existing government.

◀ In 1924, for the first time, the Labour Party won the most votes in a national election—but not a majority—and led a governing coalition for less than a year, partially as a result of the disaster of World War I. But the Labour Party swiftly lost again, in the next election, to the Conservative Party.

◀ The Labour Party returned to power with the onset of the Great Depression, ruling from 1929 to 1931. The Depression was an economic blow to capitalist economies and its workers and also a challenge to the idea that capitalism was the most efficient and dynamic economic system.

◀ With millions of workers unemployed, businesses bankrupt, financial institutions failing—and farmers thrown off their land—political movements and parties that advocated an alternative to capitalism found newfound acceptance and support.

◀ In the 1930s, the Labour Party began to implement Keynesian macroeconomic policies of fiscal stimulus and a greater social safety net. These measures included government funding of public works, extended social welfare benefits, and taking Britain off the gold standard to allow for a more flexible monetary policy.

- After World War II, the British Labour Party won a huge electoral victory and mandated for much more comprehensive social welfare programs. With this, Britain began the National Health Service, unemployment compensation, public housing construction, labor union rights, mandatory holidays for workers, and nationalization of some industries.

- Although the Labour Party never instituted a Soviet-style state takeover of all private property and businesses, it did nationalize several key enterprises, including British Telephone, British Petroleum, and the expansion of the British Broadcasting Corporation (BBC) into television and radio.

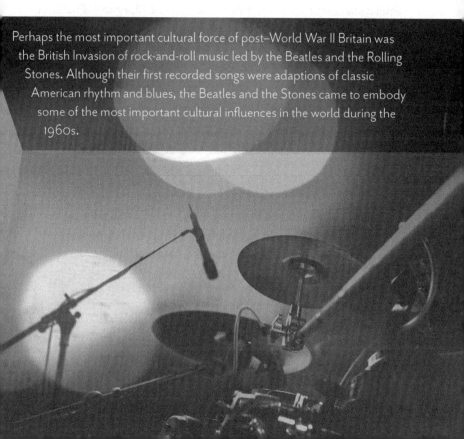

Perhaps the most important cultural force of post–World War II Britain was the British Invasion of rock-and-roll music led by the Beatles and the Rolling Stones. Although their first recorded songs were adaptions of classic American rhythm and blues, the Beatles and the Stones came to embody some of the most important cultural influences in the world during the 1960s.

◀ In other words, Britain evolved one of the world's oldest, most orthodox free market economies into a much-modified capitalist system with some government ownership and control. This was a far cry from the economy advocated by Adam Smith and the thinkers of free market capitalism.

◀ It had some positive benefits. British incomes and living standards became much less unequal. The health and housing conditions of the average British worker improved markedly. The cultural life of the British citizen arguably grew richer, through the programs of BBC television, radio, and the British film industry.

◀ After less than half of a century, the short-lived era of Labour Party socialism ended with the election of Margaret Thatcher and the Conservative Party in 1979.

Readings

DICKENS, *Hard Times.*
ENGELS, *The Condition of the Working Class in England.*

Questions

1 The British created industrial capitalism, but did they create all the necessary institutions for its development?

2 David Ricardo thought that free trade would be good for British workers and capitalists. Who did he think it would harm?

British Revolution: Industry and Labor

G reat Britain launched modern industrial capitalism in the late 18th century by combining a series of essential but previously uncoordinated economic and political institutions. In the political sphere, these institutional innovations included the basic liberties outlined in the Magna Carta, and safeguarded by parliamentary democracy. In the economic sphere—which I'll concentrate on here—they included trade finance, shipping insurance, and a corporate form of ownership facilitated by stock markets and public investors. Together, these developments helped propel Britain to become the first country in the world to create large factories, and export its products to foreign markets.

Financing foreign trade depends upon the existence of insurance contracts. Insurance contracts were developed during the middle ages by the first Venetian merchants who shipped their goods all over the Adriatic Sea and eastern Mediterranean. At first, this insurance was created for each individual voyage. Several wealthy merchants would pool their funds to insure a particular voyage. When a ship was lost to storms or pirates or foreign navies, each individual investor would lose a small share of the cost of the insurance. But successful voyages typically more than covered the costs of such losses, thereby generating profits to finance other voyages—and to pay for the insurance.

My grandmother used to have an expression for when anyone offered to buy her dinner or a present. She would say, "When your ship comes in, you can buy that for me." Not until I started studying the history of capitalism did I understand the origins of that phrase.

The ad hoc collections of merchants called upon to insure individual voyages was gradually replaced by companies set up to be permanent insurers of shipping and other types of commerce. A seamen's coffee house in London established by Edward Lloyd around the mid-17th century grew into one such institution: Lloyd's of London. And individual businessmen skilled at determining the risks of various business enterprises became insurance brokers.

Big capitalist projects are risky. Insurance helps spread the risk.

Another financial innovation was the rise of corporate ownership and investment. The Dutch perfected the joint-stock company form of corporate ownership, and the first fully functioning stock exchange in Amsterdam. This innovation enabled large numbers of investors to pool rather small individual sums of money to underwrite a new enterprise. The key aspect of a joint-stock company is that each investor can lose only the amount of money the individual puts into the company, and nothing more. The collective resources of individual investors, combined with limited personal liability, makes possible gathering large sums of money to build, for example, large factories with complicated machinery and equipment.

The U.S. center of capitalism is New York, symbolized by the New York Stock Exchange. But New York was not the original name of the European settlement at the mouth of the Hudson River, on the island of Manhattan. Henry Hudson was a Dutch explorer. And Manhattan was purchased from the Native inhabitants by the Dutch. So, New York was first known as New Amsterdam.

A few years ago, I took a group of students to the original Amsterdam— and also to Haarlem, by which I mean not the Harlem on the north side of Manhattan but rather the capital of North Holland province. For centuries, it was a Dutch trading city for merchants traveling the world.

In early market economies, most production was small-scale, and accomplished with a few simple tools. The individual baker, brewer, tailor, and shoemaker produced one item—or a few items at a time—and did not need large amounts of money to start or maintain his business. What made large-scale British industrial capitalism different was massive factories producing thousands of items a day. Because no individual could raise all the funds necessary for these large-scale enterprises, the joint-stock company was vital to raise the necessary funds.

An individual investor with a few shares of stock typically could sell these shares fairly easily, and get out of any enterprise he deemed too risky or possibly unprofitable. This was made possible by a functioning stock market, where buyers and sellers of stocks could trade shares of companies on a regular and regulated basis. And it further reduced the risks of ownership. But the honesty of stock market participants—and the true value of the companies they own—is a continuing problem in the functioning of most stock markets.

The Dutch began the process of regulating the companies that could sell their shares on the Amsterdam Stock Exchange. But even today, this regulatory process has not been perfected—and probably never will be. So, stock-market crises have continued to disrupt capitalist economies, and create economic instability. It's one of the chief problems of every capitalist economy.

The payments system is also a necessary institution for advanced capitalist economies. Paying for goods and services, paying for raw materials and labor, and borrowing and lending money all historically depend upon a banking system that is both sound and dependable. The northern Italians of the late Middle Ages invented modern banking, and the double-entry system of bookkeeping. Double-entry bookkeeping essentially refers to the two sides of a financial statement, or bookkeeping ledger: one accounting for assets, the other liabilities. Stated otherwise, it's a way to record income and expenses; debts and monies payable.

It might not have been the Medicis themselves—in Renaissance Florence—who invented banking. But banking was perfected by the northern Italians, as merchant capitalism began to grow. And the House of Medici flourished in Florence and Tuscany from 1434 to 1737. The first Italian bankers were goldsmiths. And the first circulating money was usually pieces of gold and silver. When a merchant sold a lot of his product, he ended up with a lot of gold. Needing a secure place to keep this gold, he naturally looked for the persons who had the best safes. This was usually the local goldsmith, who needed to hold quantities of gold leaf and gold bars to produce jewelry, or plates and goblets, and other luxury objects. So, merchants and other wealthy individuals began keeping their gold with the local goldsmith.

When a merchant made a sale, he would bring the gold to this craftsman. And when he needed to pay a supplier, he would return to withdraw the necessary payment. Often the supplier would also have an account with the same goldsmith. Eventually, goldsmiths began to issue receipts for the gold deposits, and these receipts were used for payment, thus eliminating the need to keep going back and forth to the goldsmiths. Over time, goldsmiths noticed that the amount of gold held in their safes stayed fairly constant. On any given day, the amount deposited was about equal to the amount withdrawn. This phenomenon is known at the "goldsmith's principle," and is the basis for current fractional-reserve banking. (Fractional-reserve banking is the practice of accepting deposits, and making loans or other investments, while holding only the fraction of the cash necessary to cover day-to-day liquidity requirements.) The intent is to keep funds circulating in the marketplace.

Most modern banks never have enough cash on hand to settle all of their depositors' balances. But most depositors don't come into their bank every day, and withdraw all of their deposits. So, clever goldsmiths began to "create" a paper form of money by issuing deposit receipts—with balances in excess of the amount of gold they actually held in their safes. Naturally, they charged interest for providing this service. And many of them earned enough of a profit as financial intermediaries to give up the goldsmith business, and become full-time service providers: taking deposits, making loans, and earning interest income. The very first places for such business were on benches in main town squares. It won't surprise you to know the Italian word for bench is *banca*. The German word for bench is "bank."

Paper and paper money had actually been invented by the Chinese centuries earlier. But Florentine, Venetian, Milanese—and other Italian— "bankers" developed the use of paper receipts backed by gold deposits as the basis for modern banking. You might ask yourself, "What's to stop unscrupulous bankers from creating as much paper money as they want, and flooding the market with worthless paper?" The answer is nothing. Reputation did serve as something of a brake on unscrupulous behavior. The regulation of town businesses by the local council of merchant guilds was another check on economically damaging behavior. But even with central banking systems, and government deposit insurance systems— two innovations of later centuries—banking crises persist even today.

One of Britain's main advantages in building industrial capitalism was that by the beginning of the 18th century it was the largest single market in Europe. By comparison, the Austrian, Russian, and Ottoman empires were collections of different nationalities, customs, laws, religions, and levels of economic development. Italy was not a unified country until the 1860s. Germany was united in 1871.

Britain's single market had a much larger customer base than elsewhere in Europe. So, British manufacturers could enjoy the benefits of mass production. And mass production was the key to lower unit costs of production, and lower prices for individual goods. This gave British capitalists a great competitive advantage compared to other European economies. Another key advantage for British capitalists was the Royal Navy. By the beginning of the 19th century, Britain had the largest—and most modern—navy in the world. Its sailors and fleets could protect British ships carrying the goods of British manufacturers around the world.

The Dutch developed much of the technology for ocean-going sailing ships, and Dutch merchants were active in the world market as well. But the Netherlands was a much smaller country, and couldn't afford to build both merchant ships and warships to protect them. For that reason, the Dutch had to rely more heavily than the British, French and Spanish did on international agreements and treaties to protect their shipping. Sometimes this wasn't enough. After all, the British succeeded in driving the Dutch out of New Amsterdam, in the New World.

Many historians point out that one real advantages the British had was their receptivity to foreign ideas. Some of the world's most skilled engineers and mechanics also came to Britain as refugees. Prominent among them were the Huguenots—French protestants fleeing religious persecution in Catholic France. The Huguenots were bankers, businessmen, and skilled engineers and craftsmen. By the way, many Huguenots also fled across the French border into Switzerland, and created the Swiss watchmaking industry.

The British did create some important institutions of their own. One of these, as I mentioned at the outset, was parliamentary democracy, and the rule of law regarding property rights. The English first began to limit the power of the central government with the Magna Carta of 1215: That is the concession by King John to his nobles that subjected the sovereign to the rule of law, and identified certain liberties as rights belonging to all free men. Of course, this "innovation" was granted only under the threat of civil war. A further limitation on capricious governmental power was the so-called Glorious Revolution of 1688 and 1689, and the execution of my forebear, England's Charles I—the rather imperious Stuart king.

I often ask my students in classes on European history and comparative economic systems to compare the execution of kings in various European societies, and the development of functioning democracies. The English executed their king in 1648, and established a parliamentary democracy by the 19th century. The French executed their king in 1793, and didn't have a functioning democracy until the 20th century. The Russians executed their emperor in 1918, and, I think it's fair to say, we're still waiting on Russian democracy.

Property rights are crucial in a market economy. Manufacturers, merchants, bankers, investors, and property owners must feel secure that their property, assets, money, and resources won't be taken away at the whim of the government, but rather only after an independent judicial process concludes that some law or regulation has been violated. The most important British contribution to the development of industrial capitalism was British political economy. That's "British," as opposed to "English," because many of the most important thinkers on political economy were Scottish.

Scotland became part of Britain in 1707. David Hume, the Scottish philosopher, historian, and economist, was born a few years after that, in 1711, followed by the economist Adam Smith in 1723. Smith and Hume were intellectual leaders of the "Scottish Enlightenment" during the second half of the 18th century: a period of revolutionary thinking about economics, politics, and the just order of a commercial society lasting from roughly 1748 to 1789. This period began with the defeat of the Stuart dynasty, and ended with the outbreak of the French Revolution.

Smith and Hume laid out the basic preconditions for a just and efficient commercial society based upon private property and market exchanges. Their ideas were anti-royalist, anti-traditional, and inherently democratic. They believed that people should be free to choose their own occupations, and govern their own purchases and sales. If many people could choose to be shoemakers, for example, they would compete robustly for customers, and good shoes would be produced at fair and competitive prices.

Furthermore, this competition would drive the search for better and more efficient ways of producing current goods, and lead to the development of new goods and services finding a profitable market.

The English political economist David Ricardo provided an intellectual argument for free trade and international competition. Ricardo started out as a stock market speculator who made a fortune at a young age. He grew bored with making money, and decided to go into politics, securing a seat in Parliament as Britain's battles with Napoleon were concluding. During the Napoleonic Wars from 1803 to 1815, the British government prohibited the import of grains from France, in the hope that this would reduce the income of French farmers, and limit their ability to fund Napoleon's military campaigns. When the wars ended, British farmers wanted the embargo on French grain to continue. It's a universal truth that all businesspeople are in favor of free trade in general, just not in their particular commodity.

The British policy of restricting imports of foreign grain was formally known as the "Corn Laws." A word to the wise: While Americans label a specific plant, maize, as corn, much of the rest of the world uses the term "corn" to refer to all grains. My American students are often confused about the British restricting "corn" from France, since maize per se doesn't grow in France.

David Ricardo was an adamant opponent of the Corn Laws because he saw their true purpose as being to raise the income of British farmers and landlord, at the expense of British workers and capitalists. In fact, the Corn Laws were reducing the profits of emerging British capitalists because higher grain prices meant capitalists had to pay higher wages to their workers so that the labor force could afford its daily bread. And higher workers' wages meant lower profits for the capitalists.

As an economist, Ricardo wasn't concerned that the capitalists would see their own living standards decline. He was worried that British capitalists would have fewer funds with which to make new investments, and create a dynamic British capitalist economy. Ricardo explained this in a ground-breaking book, *The Principles of Political Economy and Taxation*, published in 1817. In it, he introduced the concept of "comparative advantage," which remains one of the most important principles of economic theory.

Ricardo explained that countries should specialize in the products they produce with the lowest opportunity cost. What is an opportunity cost? The answer is that whatever choice an economic actor makes about production, he or she will necessarily sacrifice other opportunities as a result of the investment and ingenuity required to make the product of choice. Ideally, in the interests of efficiency, your choice should come with the lowest cost.

In Ricardo's book, his example was trade and exchange between Britain and Portugal. Owing to differences in soil, climate, labor, and other factors, Britain could produce wool with a smaller cost in foregone wine, whereas Portugal could produce wine with a smaller foregone cost of wool. Therefore, Britain should produce wool and trade some of it to Portugal for wine. After specialization—and trade—Britain and Portugal each would end up with both more wool, and more wine. Viewed this way, trade was not a zero-sum game but a win-win situation for both trading partners. While there are some exceptions to this principle, such as national defense, it's still an approximation of why certain countries specialize and export certain products while importing the products that are very costly for them to produce. To this day, Britain exports fashionable Harris Tweed jackets from Scotland, and imports Harvey's Bristol Cream Sherry from Portugal.

A classic example of the rising capitalist during the early stages of the British industrial revolution was Josiah Wedgewood, who lived from 1730 to 1795. Wedgewood was an apprentice potter. But he developed a disease that crippled his legs so that he couldn't operate the peddles on pottery wheel. So, he looked for other sources of power to replace human power. He established his first factory in Manchester, England, near a river. Manchester would become the most important city in the development of British industrial capitalism, in part because as it was situated near to that river, whose current provided the power to turn mechanical water wheels.

Another innovator of the age was James Watt, an energetic Scottish engineer. In 1769, he patented an improvement to an early model of the Newcomen steam engine. Watt's engine was first installed in a factory in 1785. And Manchester was on its way to becoming the center of the British textile industry, and numerous other British industries.

Among the beneficiaries were Joseph Wedgewood's beloved porcelain industry. Wedgewood was more than a potter. He was a true commercial entrepreneur. He pioneered the use of direct mail to market and deliver his products all over Britain, and, eventually, all over the world. He did so to take advantage of British colonial expansion and British shipping. Wedgewood also pioneered the consumer-financing concept of extended payments, and the money-back guarantee. He marketed his porcelain first to the nobility and upper classes, and then used the publicity this earned to market the products as luxury goods to the middle classes. He sold them all over Europe, China, India, Canada, South Africa—and even in the new United States of America.

Like many rising new British capitalists, Wedgewood was a devout Protestant. His faith drove him to be a fervent abolitionist, and to campaign against slavery and the British involvement in the slave trade. Britain didn't abolish slavery until after Wedgewood's death, but his energy and fortune were important forces in the campaign to end this barbaric practice. Wedgewood is an early example of the rich capitalist using his good fortune and success for noble social and cultural causes, a tradition that is still in practice today—though not always.

By the 1800s, Britain was the world's foremost industrial power, and its richest country. The cities of Manchester, Birmingham, Sheffield and London were all growing rapidly, and pulling in rural citizens to work in factories near urban areas. The ports cities of Bristol and Plymouth—and shipyards in the north—also grew commensurately. With a growing urban working class, the problems of unequal incomes, poverty, industrial accidents and death, and urban crime, quickly followed. A picture of these miserable conditions is found in the novels of Charles Dickens, especially *Hard Times*.

In 1845, Karl Marx's collaborator and fellow revolutionary, Friedrich Engels, wrote *The Condition of the Working Class in England*. In it, he penned one graphic detail after another about the long and dangerous work of factory laborers, and the slum conditions in which they lived. Not surprisingly, popular agitation—and campaigns for improvement in the lives of factory workers—began at about the same time.

The first British organized labor movement, the Trades Union Congress, was formed in 1868. Eventually, this gave rise to a political party based on the British labor movement: the British Labour Party (one of two principal political parties in the country today). The Labour Party's original program called for the abolition of capitalism, and its replacement by a socialist economy, though it advocated peaceful change through victories in democratic elections rather than revolution and violent overthrow of the existing government. In 1924, for the first time, the Labour Party won the most votes in a national election but not a majority, and led a governing coalition until 1924, partially as a result of the disaster of World War I. But Labour swiftly lost again, in the next election, to the Conservative Party.

As often happens when political parties, or movements, win elections and take power, the difficulties of governing, changes tend to modify and limit the actual changes that take place. Once the Labour Party realized the complicated nature of achieving economic and political change, it began to modify its goals and political platform. The Labour Party returned to power with the onset of the Great Depression, ruling from 1929 to 1931.

The Depression was an economic blow to capitalist economies, and its workers, and also a challenge to the idea that capitalism was the most efficient and dynamic economic system. With millions of workers unemployed, businesses bankrupt, financial institutions failing—and farmers thrown off their land—political movements and parties that advocated an alternative to capitalism found newfound acceptance and support.

In the 1930s, the Labour Party began to implement Keynesian macroeconomic policies of fiscal stimulus and a greater social safety net. These measures included government funding of public works, extended social welfare benefits, and taking Britain off the gold standard to allow for a more flexible monetary policy.

After World War II, the British Labor Party won a huge electoral victory and mandate for much more comprehensive social welfare programs. With this, Britain began the National Health Service, unemployment compensation, public housing construction, labor union rights, mandatory holidays for workers, and nationalization of some industries. Although the Labour Party never instituted a Soviet-style state takeover of all private property and businesses, it did nationalize several key enterprises. These included British Telephone, British Petroleum, and British Overseas Airlines—and the expansion of the British Broadcasting Corporation into television as well as radio. In other words, Britain evolved one of the world's oldest, most orthodox free-market economies into a much-modified capitalist system with some government ownership and control. This was a far cry from the economy advocated by Adam Smith, and the thinkers of free market capitalism.

It had some positive benefits. British incomes and living standards became much less unequal. The health and housing conditions of the average British worker improved markedly. The cultural life of the British citizen arguably grew richer, through the programs of BBC television and radio. Even the British film industry had a revival with productions like *The Third Man, The Loneliness of the Long-Distance Runner, Darling,* and my personal favorite, *Alfie*—that's the Michael Caine version, not the Jude Law version.

Maybe the most important cultural force of post-World War II Britain was the "British Invasion" of rock and roll led by the Beatles and the Rolling Stones. Although their first recorded songs were adaptions of classic American rhythm and blues, the Beatles and the Stones came to embody some of the most important cultural influences in the world during the 1960s.

In modern, post-industrial economies, cultural exports are large earners. Movies, television shows, and music are often major sources of income for culturally ascendant economies. After less than a half-century, the short-lived era of "Labour Party Socialism" ended with the election of Margaret Thatcher and the Conservative Party in 1979.

Not all institutions created by the British Labour Party have disappeared since. By no means. But as demonstrated by the nation's decision to withdraw from the community of social welfare states—bound up in the European Union—Britain has returned to a somewhat more orthodox vision of itself: as an island apart; on its own.

Lecture 5

American Capitalism: Hamilton and Jefferson

ALTHOUGH THE SPANISH WERE THE FIRST EUROPEANS to settle and explore the Americas, the Dutch and the British gave the future United States of America the institutional structures that were so beneficial for its own brand of capitalism. The early Dutch brought with them the key institutions of banking, stock markets, and insurance. While the Dutch created modern finance, the British established private-property rights—on which modern capitalism is based—and the common law legal system of contracts, which is also necessary in a capitalist society. ◆

Economy of the American Revolutionary War

◀ The author Kevin Phillips draws a clear historical line between the mid-17th-century English Civil War and the subsequent economic and political history of the British colonies in America; and the nascent United States of America.

◀ The American Revolutionary War emerged from a continuing sense of restriction felt by the New England settlers against their colonial rulers. The British monarchy, and British capitalists, wanted the new Americans to fulfill the usual function of a lesser-developed colony—that is, the American colonies should provide raw materials for the industries of the British capitalists and the American colonists should buy the finished manufactured goods of the British industrialists.

◀ This is the classic recipe for keeping colonial land underdeveloped and dependent and for concentrating higher profits earned from producing finished manufactured goods in the home country.

◀ Furthermore, British colonial policy dictated that American raw materials and other exports should be shipped only on British vessels. This created a monopoly for British shipping. It's a basic law of economics that monopolies charge higher prices, and provide poorer service, than businesses who face serious competition.

◀ In addition, the British Crown was imposing taxes on the Americans' own business activities. The taxes were not particularly onerous, but they did make American goods more expensive and gave British goods an added advantage.

◀ Maybe the most serious British restriction was the passage of the Quebec Acts, which extended the border of the Quebec territory into the Ohio territory and Mississippi Valley, reinforcing the Proclamation of 1763 that forbade American colonists from settling lands west of the Allegheny Mountains.

◀ The Virginian surveyor, soldier, and aspiring colonial officer George Washington had plans to expand his farm farther west and profitably exploit the potential of this property.

◀ Fortunately for the rebellious American colonists, the French monarchy at the time hated the British more than they hated uprisings against monarchs. The French gave the American revolutionaries support and superior forces when combined against the British.

◀ After the success of the American Revolution, the expansionary nature of American capitalism was unshackled to push westward, farther and faster. To make sure that American manufacturing would flourish, Alexander Hamilton, the first U.S. Secretary of the Treasury, established policies to nourish American industries.

◀ Language known as the Commerce Clause was inserted in the Constitution to help support as large a market as possible for the output of American businesses. Larger and larger production runs—and an increasing scale of production—are hallmarks of successful capitalist enterprises, and the clause prevented individual states from hindering or blocking the sale of goods from one to another.

◀ Additionally, to protect American industry from competition by the leading British and other European capitalist powers, Hamilton advocated a system of high tariffs on imported goods, thus protecting American producers. As a consequence, the United States had one of the highest tariff rates from the nation's beginning until after World War II.

◄ Hamilton also insisted on the federal government assuming the debts of the individual states and issuing federal debt certificates. Although it's fashionable today to oppose any kind of federal debt, there are some good reasons for it. Mainly, it creates low-risk assets for savers and investors and supports the formation of a bond market—a necessary financial component of a modern capitalist economy.

◄ Hamilton also wanted a central bank that would be an issuer of money and a lender of last resort. He lost that battle to the Anti-Federalists. The United States did not get a true central bank until 1913—after the Panic of 1907—with the creation of the Federal Reserve System.

In modern international economics, one argument for tariffs in developing countries is the "infant industry" argument to protect new industries. Alexander Hamilton invented this phrase.

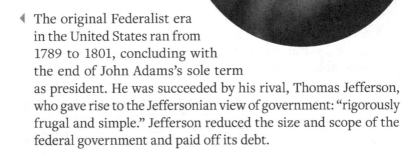

> *" I am for a government rigorously frugal and simple, applying all the possible savings of the public revenue to the discharge of the national debt. "*
>
> — JEFFERSON

◀ The original Federalist era in the United States ran from 1789 to 1801, concluding with the end of John Adams's sole term as president. He was succeeded by his rival, Thomas Jefferson, who gave rise to the Jeffersonian view of government: "rigorously frugal and simple." Jefferson reduced the size and scope of the federal government and paid off its debt.

◀ But then, the Napoleonic Wars of 1803 to 1815—against France's European rivals—gave Jefferson the opportunity to purchase the French-held Louisiana Territory, an 828,000-square-mile landmass that doubled America's footprint and set in motion the creation of 15 new states.

◀ At the time of the Louisiana Purchase in 1803, Napoleon was fighting nearly every other European power, and he needed money to fund his war efforts. So, he sold French lands reaching all the way to the Rocky Mountains and from the Gulf of Mexico to Canada. This greatly increased the potential scope of American industry and agriculture.

Economy of the American Civil War

◀ But the new lands also planted the seeds for conflicts that culminated in the Civil War. Were the new states created from the Louisiana Purchase to be free states or slave-holding ones?

◀ If the new states were to extend slavery, then the new senators and representatives of these states would invariably vote to maintain slaves as property, and slave-based agriculture likely would dominate the American economy. But if the new states were free states, then their senators and representatives would almost certainly vote to abolish slavery.

Private property is almost always the most efficient agricultural system for the production of food and raw materials. Farmers seem to produce best when they own their own land and reap the economic rewards of their efforts.

The United States was the first country in the world to create a system of mass, publicly funded, essentially free higher education.

◀ During the Civil War that followed—with Congress in the hands of radical Republicans and no Southern conservatives sitting in the Senate or House of Representatives—Congress passed two of the most important pieces of legislation in the development of American capitalism: the Homestead Act and the Morrill Act, both passed in 1862.

◇ The Homestead Act provided for the free distribution of new lands west of the Allegheny Mountains. By limiting the size of the property and distributing it for free, millions of new property-owning farmers were created. This was an enormous extension of private property and solidified the American economy as a system of widely held private property with significant political support.

◇ The Morrill Act established a system of land-grant colleges in the newly created western states. Each state university was given an allotment of land that was to be the main source of revenue for the college. Tuition rates would be low or nothing. Many economists who specialize in economic development believe that the high level of human capital possessed by American workers was the most important factor in the rise of the U.S. economy to become the world's richest in subsequent decades.

◀ After the Civil War, the American capitalist economy resumed its westward expansion.

◀ One of the first significant postwar actions of the U.S. government and the federal army was the removal of the Native Americans from their traditional lands to make room for private-property agriculture and also for the coming of the railroads, which were a great stimulus to American capitalist development.

◀ With the development of the railroads, new industries were created and existing industries were expanded. Customers all over the United States could order all manner of goods from a catalog and send their orders through the mail, which was carried in railway cars.

◀ The development of large American capitalist industries also created some serious problems. These problems were related to the industries' powerful size and uncompetitive behavior.

◀ Soon, big oil companies, large steel companies, and expansive food companies combined into trusts that monopolized markets. This led to increases in prices and poor-quality goods and services.

Much of the early investments in American railroads came from foreign investors in England, the Netherlands, and Germany. Another source of capital came from the profits of businessmen who had made fortunes supplying the Union Army in the Civil War—including John D. Rockefeller, J. P. Morgan, and Andrew Carnegie.

A Growing Economy

◀ To counter the excessive developments of capitalist society and its Gilded Age, the Progressive movement was started and had some significant successes in curbing the abuses of the dominant market power of the trusts.

◀ The Interstate Commerce Commission was created in 1887 to regulate the railroads and ensure fair pricing for transportation services. President Theodore Roosevelt pushed through legislation that created the Food and Drug Administration in 1906 to regulate the production and distribution of food products. The Federal Trade Commission was created in 1914 to police the competitive situation in the American economy and to prevent the buildup of monopoly power by large corporations.

◀ In the long run, these policies helped make the American economy more competitive and more beneficial to consumers and small businesses. But none of these reforms fully addressed another recurrent problem of capitalist economies: the persistent cycle of boom and bust.

◀ Before depressions and recessions were known by those terms, they were called panics. Panics are a macroeconomic problem: They cause a general decline in the entire economy, not in just one sector. With capitalism and some of its excesses accelerating at full throttle through the second half of the 19th century, there were panics in 1873, 1893, and 1907.

◀ The Panic of 1907 culminated in a financial crash that led to the creation of the Federal Reserve System and of a central bank to monitor the money supply and interest rates. But the problems of system-wide collapses of capitalist economies was not fully addressed until the time of the Great Depression of 1930 and later again after World War II.

◀ Following World War II, the United States took up greater leadership at home and around the world, most clearly among its European allies. It sought to develop more concentrated and sophisticated efforts to prevent, or at least lessen, the damaging effects of depressions, recessions, and other economic dislocations. The belief, then as now, was that capitalism has a much better chance of flourishing—and even surviving—in a growing and stable economy.

Readings

CHERNOW, *Alexander Hamilton*.
COHEN AND DELONG, *Concrete Economics*.
LINDERT AND WILLIAMSON, *Unequal Gains*.

Questions

1 What key capitalist institutions did American capitalism get from the Dutch? Where were these located in the new American economy?

2 Why didn't Alexander Hamilton believe in free trade? What trade policies did he advocate for the new American government?

American Capitalism: Hamilton and Jefferson

E arly American capitalism started off with many advantages. Some were gifts of Mother Nature. Others were human creations. The North American continent is rich in natural resources. Native Americans lived in a land of abundance until they were pushed off their traditional lands, and decimated by the diseases brought to the continent by European colonizers. And although the Spanish were the first Europeans to arrive on the Americas, it was the Dutch and the British who gave the future United States of America the institutional structures that were so beneficial for its own brand of capitalism.

The first permanent British settlements in North American were at Jamestown, Virginia where they established plantations to grow tobacco and indigo. Tobacco was considered a wonder drug. It was a pleasurably addictive plant that found a large and expanding market in Europe. Indigo was an expensive dye used to turn raw wool and linen into darkly colored fabric. It was the hallmark of luxury clothing. European nobility and rich merchants clothed themselves in dark fabrics to show the world their high status and income.

In turn, the British landowners of the Jamestown estates were known as Cavaliers, after their allegiance to the Stuart cause in the English Civil Wars of the mid-17th century. They brought Irish, Scottish, and Welsh peasants to work in the tobacco and indigo fields. These fair-skinned European peasants—used to northerly climates—were poorly suited to the heat, humidity, and pests of the mid-Atlantic and southern-Atlantic coasts. Many of these poor men and women died from the unfamiliar climate, or decided to go back to the British Isles.

Eventually the planters of Virginia, Carolina, and Georgia had to import African slaves to work in their fields.

At first, the establishment of slave-based agriculture in the American South was to prove economically profitable for the American colonies. But eventually, it was a source of political and economic conflict that would result in the American Civil War.

While the slave economy produced indigo and tobacco, it was a third crop—cotton—that made wealthy the slave-owning upper class of the South. Cotton was also the primary raw material of the early Industrial Revolution. It fed the young textile industry developing in New England. Exports of cotton from the American colonies, and later from the southern states, provided funds to finance the import of capital goods and technology to unleash American capitalism.

The most important early immigrant groups—at the beginning of American capitalism—were, as I've indicated, the Dutch settlers of New Amsterdam (later New York); and the English Puritans who arrived and settled throughout New England. The early Dutch brought with them the key institutions of banking, stock markets, and insurance. It's no coincidence that the most important financial center in the United States today is New York. That's thanks to the Dutch, who'd developed early financial institutions at home in Amsterdam, and throughout the Netherlands, starting in the late 16th century.

A modern capitalist economy depends upon a well-functioning system of finance that channels savings into investment. Without funds from a developed financial system, new capitalist enterprises cannot be created, and existing capitalist enterprises cannot borrow the resources they need to operate and expand.

Capitalism's need for borrowing arises from the basic fact that production comes before sales. Goods must be produced before they are sold; and to produce goods, capitalists need machinery, raw materials, and workers. These resources must be paid well before the capitalist owner sees any revenue from the sales of the products. The same is also true of farmers who need to buy seed before they can sell their crops. The source of these funds is usually the banking system, especially for new enterprises. Established enterprises might also have the ability to sell stock to investors, if the enterprise is well-known or has a positive reputation.

The Dutch perfected modern banking after it was invented by the Italians. The Dutch also created the first stock market, based upon the concept of limited liability for shareholders. This principle of limited liability opened the floodgate to raising large sums of money that are necessary for mass production and large corporate enterprises.

Now, while the Dutch created modern finance, the British established private property rights, and the common law legal system of contracts.

Modern capitalism is based upon private property rights. Adam Smith understood the entire system of a commercial economy in terms of the self-interest of private owners of businesses. The reward of private gain is what motivates a business owner to produce desired products as efficiently as possible. And without a secure system of property rights, a modern capitalist economy has a very limited foundation, and will not function well.

Paradoxically, this means that a free-market, private enterprise economy needs a strong government to protect the property rights of its citizens and businesses. Adam Smith was emphatic about the need for key governmental institutions such defense, public education, and protection of private property, to ensure the proper functioning of a private enterprise economy.

A system of enforceable contract rights is also necessary in capitalist society. That's because capitalist economic exchange is based upon voluntary exchanges. Goods and resources are sold for money. Quite often, the transfer of goods, resources, and money occur at different points in time. So, the provider of goods—who is promised payment by the buyer—must be certain that the agreed-upon amount will be paid at the agreed-upon time. If there is a dispute, it should be settled by an impartial judge in an accepted legal system.

When I was teaching in post-Soviet Russia in 1994, I was often asked by my American friends and colleagues what the Russians needed. My friends had visions of poor Russians longing for scarce American blue jeans and cigarettes. But by 1994, any Russian with enough money could buy all the blue jeans and cigarettes he or she wanted. What the Russians really needed couldn't be shipped over on a plane or in a truck. What the

Russians needed was a functioning financial system—and an unbiased legal system with guaranteed private property rights. There is some question as to whether the Russians ever got them.

The English Puritans turned out to be the most important of all the European immigrant groups who came to America. Important to the development of American capitalism that is. After leaving Plymouth, England, these Puritans who landed at Plymouth Rock could not advertise creativity and originality as a strong suit. They were a rather peculiar bunch. Firm believers in the Protestant Reformation—and in the theologies of Luther and Calvin—the English Puritans believed, however, that ordinary men and women should read the Bible, and make up their own minds as to the road to salvation. This required that they be literate—something that was relatively rare in the 17th century. And literacy meant that these early American settlers could learn theology from books but also mechanics, and mathematics, and other practical knowledge.

Puritan theology, therefore, was individualistic. It created a drive in each person to better himself and herself, not just for life after death but also during our time on earth. John Calvin's view of predestination stated that God had chosen those for heaven at their birth. And how could you get some idea of whether or not you'd been chosen? One way was to be successful in your vocation, and use the talents you had been given. So, Puritan theology placed earthly economic success in the realm of spiritual success.

The English Puritans came mainly from East Anglia, England—that's places like Norfolk, and Suffolk, and Cambridgeshire, and Essex. And they were mostly artisans, craftsmen, printers, and other entrepreneurs. The American writer and commentator Kevin Phillips, in his masterful history *The Cousins' Wars: Religion, Politics, & The Triumph Of Anglo-America*, explores how this particular group succeeded in becoming the richest, and most successful, group of European colonists in the New World.

They'd go on to lead the forces of revolution in 1776, and successfully prosecute the American Civil War in 1865.

Those were two of the so-called "cousins' wars." The third cousins' war was the first: It was the mid-17th-century English Civil War between the Royalist Stuarts and the Protestant Parliamentarians, led by Oliver Cromwell. The parliamentarians won. They executed King Charles I, and ruled England from 1648 to 1660. Then, Cromwell died, and the English grew tired of puritanical restrictions on wine, women, and song. So, they brought back the Stuarts (some of my ancestors), and put Charles II back on the throne. This restoration of monarchy and nobility led to many more puritans leaving for New England to practice their own anti-royal and anti-hierarchical religion.

We Stuarts, by the way, have always been in favor of wine, woman, and song. My father, Edward Francis Stuart II, was married four times, and he loved his martinis. Late in life one of his ex-mothers-in-law took to asking about Dad as, "How's Henry the VII?"

The author Kevin Phillips draws a clear historical line between the mid-17th-century English Civil War—fought between cousins, as it were—and the subsequent economic and political history of the British colonies in America, and the nascent United States of America. The American Revolutionary War itself emerged from a continuing sense of restriction felt by the New England settlers against their colonial rulers.

The British monarchy—and British capitalists—wanted the new Americans to fulfill the usual function of a lesser developed colony. That is, the American colonies should provide raw materials for the industries of the British capitalists. And the American colonists should buy the finished manufactured goods of the British industrialists.

This is the classic recipe for keeping colonial land underdeveloped and dependent, and for concentrating higher profits earned from producing finished manufactured goods in the home country.

Furthermore, British colonial policy dictated that American raw materials and other exports should be shipped only on British vessels. This created a monopoly for British shipping. It is a basic law of economics that monopolies charge higher prices, and provide poorer service, than businesses who face serious competition.

In addition, the British crown was imposing taxes on the Americans' own business activities. The taxes were not particularly onerous, but they did make American goods more expensive and gave British goods an added advantage. Maybe the most serious British restriction was the passage of the Quebec Acts, which extended the border of the Quebec Territory into the Ohio Territory and the Mississippi Valley reinforcing the proclamation of 1763 that forbad American colonists from settling lands west of the Allegheny Mountains.

The Virginian surveyor, soldier, and aspiring colonial officer George Washington had plans himself to expand his farm farther west, and profitably exploit the potential of this property. Fortunately, for the rebellious American colonists, the French monarchy, at the time, hated the British more than they hated uprisings against monarchs. The French gave the American revolutionaries support and superior forces when combined against the British.

After the success of the American Revolution, the expansionary nature of American capitalism was unshackled to push westward, further and faster. To make sure American manufacturing would flourish, the Constitution and Treasury Secretary Alexander Hamilton, established policies to protect and nourish American industries. Language known as the Interstate Commerce Clause was inserted in the Constitution to help support as large a market as possible for the output of American businesses.

Larger and larger production runs—and an increasing scale of production—are hallmarks of successful capitalist enterprises. And the Interstate Commerce Clause prevented individual states from hindering, or blocking, the sale of goods from one to the other. This idea is also the basis for the Single Market Act in today's European Union.

Additionally, to protect American industry from competition by the leading British and other European capitalist powers, Hamilton advocated a system of high tariffs on imported goods, thus protecting American producers.

In modern international economics, one argument for tariffs in developing countries is the "infant industry" argument to protect new industries. Hamilton invented this phrase.

As a consequence, the United States had one of the highest tariff rates from the nation's beginning until after World War II, when American industries were anything but infant. Hamilton also insisted on the federal government assuming the debts of the individual states, and issuing federal debt certificates.

Although it's fashionable today to oppose any kind of federal debt, there are some good reasons for it. Mainly, it creates low-risk assets for savers and investors, and supports the formation of a bond market—a necessary financial component of a modern capitalist economy. Hamilton also wanted a central bank that would be an issuer of money and a lender of last resort. He lost that battle to the anti-Federalists. The United States did not get a true central bank until 1913—after the Panic of 1907—with the creation of the Federal Reserve System.

The original Federalist era in the United States ran from 1789 to 1801, concluding with the end of John Adams' sole term as president. He was succeeded by his rival Thomas Jefferson, who gave rise to the Jeffersonian view of government: "rigorously frugal as simple." Jefferson reduced the size and scope of the federal government, and paid off its debt. But then, the Napoleonic Wars of 1803-1815—against France's European rivals— gave Jefferson the opportunity to purchase the French-held Louisiana Territory. This was an 828,000-square mile land mass that doubled America's footprint, and set in motion the creation of 15 new states.

At the time of the Louisiana Purchase in 1803, Napoleon was fighting nearly every other European power, and he needed money to fund his war efforts. So, he sold French lands reaching all the way to the Rocky Mountains, and from the Gulf of Mexico to Canada. This greatly increased the potential scope of American industry and agriculture.

But the new lands also planted the seeds for conflicts that culminated in the Civil War. Were the new states created from the Louisiana Purchase to be free states or slave-holding?

The American Revolution had been all about independence and freedom— but that wasn't about freedom for the African slaves of the southern states. If the new states were to extend slavery, then the new senators and representatives of these states would invariably vote to maintain slaves as property, and slave-based agriculture likely would dominate the American economy. On the other hand, if the new states were free states, then their senators and representatives would almost certainly vote to abolish slavery.

During the Civil War that followed—with Congress in the hands of radical Republicans, and no southern conservatives sitting in the House or the Senate—Congress passed two of the most important pieces of legislation in the development of American capitalism. Lincoln's Emancipation Proclamation of 1863—and later amendments to the Constitution—transformed human and political rights. But these two other acts had enormous influence on the creation of a successful American capitalist economy. They were the Homestead Act and the Morrill Act, both passed in 1862.

The Homestead Act provided for the free distribution of new lands west of the Allegheny Mountains. Each settler was given perpetual title to 160 acres of land, if you could build a home and a farm on your new land. Free distribution was different from auctioning the land to the highest bidder. The auction system would have created large tracts of land owned by rich landlords, like the nobility in Europe and the *latifundia* in Mexico. But by limiting the size of the property, and distributing it for free, millions of new property-owning farmers were created.

One thing you learn from studying comparative economics is that private property is almost always the most efficient agricultural system for the production of food and raw materials. All other agricultural systems—including state-owned farms, collectively owned farms, and communal farms—have been tried, and almost uniformly failed. Farmers seem to produce best when they own their own land, and reap the economic rewards of their efforts.

A system of millions of small farmers who owned their land—and thus enjoyed economic freedom and political freedom—was a Jeffersonian ideal. It provided the basis not only for large increases in agricultural productivity but was also a foundation of American democracy. The farmers' land was theirs in perpetuity, and could be disposed of, sold, or bequeathed as they saw fit. The government guaranteed a citizen's rights, but had no further control over their ownership. This was an enormous expansion of private property, and solidified the American economy as a system of widely held private property with significant political support.

The other piece of groundbreaking legislation in 1862 was the Morrill Act, which established a system of land-grant colleges in the newly created western states. Each state university was given an allotment of land that was to be the main source of revenue for the college. Tuition rates would be low or nothing. The United States was the first country in the world to create a system of mass, publicly funded, essentially free higher education. A modern, technologically advanced economy needs highly educated and trained workers, scientists, agronomists, business leaders, and teachers.

Many economists who specialize in economic development believe the high level of human capital possessed by American workers was the most important factor in the rise of the U.S. economy to become the world's richest in subsequent decades. So, these two acts—the Homestead Act and the Morrill Act—are classic examples of government policy fostering the development of private agriculture and private industry.

After the Civil War, the American capitalist economy resumed its westward expansion. One of the first significant post-war actions of the U.S. government and the federal army was the removal of the Native Americans from their traditional lands to make room for private property agriculture, and also for the coming of the railroads. General George Custer might have lost at Little Big Horn, but in the long run Native Americans were no match for federal troops.

Before railroads, canals and rivers were the primary means of transportation for commercial goods produced by American businesses. The Erie Canal, the most famous of these projects, connected the Great Lakes economy with the port of New York and Atlantic trade routes. But the railroads were an even greater stimulus to American capitalist development. Railroads were the single-most important industry immediately after the Civil War. They increased demand for steel, wood, engines, and coal.

Still, the construction of new tracks and lines west of Chicago and St. Louis required the actions of the U.S. Army, as well as the U.S. Geological Survey—and subsidies provided by the federal government to the railroads themselves. These subsidies were mainly free land along rights of way. This land would be extremely valuable once the railroads were built. It was a powerful incentive to the railroads to build out the new lines, and was a valuable asset they could use to raise funds and purchase equipment.

Much of the early investments in American railroads came from foreign investors in England, the Netherlands, and Germany. Another source of capital came from the profits of businessmen who had made fortunes supplying the Union Army in the Civil War. Indeed, many American capitalists got started by supplying oil, armaments, metals, and textiles to Union forces. Names such as Rockefeller, Morgan, and Carnegie all recorded their first fortunes from what historians have referred to as the "Great Barbecue" of federal money flowing out of Washington, D.C. between 1861 and 1865.

With the development of the railroads, new industries were created, and existing industries were expanded. Steelmakers benefited from the transportation of pig iron and coal from the mines to the factories. The meat industry could now ship cattle from the western plains to the slaughterhouses and meatpacking plants of Chicago. Wheat farmers could get their grain to Chicago, and then on ships through the Great Lakes to the Atlantic; or on barges down the Mississippi River to the port of New Orleans. And the oil industry could get crude oil from Texas and Oklahoma to refineries on the East Coast.

As a resident of Chicago, I'm steeped in the history of Sears, Roebuck and Co., and Montgomery Ward. These two retail giants owed their early dominance to the building of the railroads. Customers all over the United States could order all manner of goods from a catalog, and send their orders through the mail, which was carried in railway cars.

The U.S. Postal Service built the world's largest post office directly over the tracks just south of Union Station, at the edge of the Chicago Loop. Customers' orders from all over the young expanding country would be received there and filled from the vast warehouses in the city. (Many of these warehouse buildings still exist but now are mostly converted condos, lofts, and art galleries.) The goods would be shipped out by rail from the gargantuan post office to the waiting customer in Cut Bank, Montana, let's say; on the route of the Great Northern Railway.

The development of large American capitalist industries also created some serious problems. These problems were related to the industries' powerful size and uncompetitive behavior. Soon, big oil companies, large steel companies, and expansive food companies combined into trusts that monopolized markets. This led to increases in prices and poor-quality goods and services.

Railroad trusts raised the rates that farmers had to pay. Oil trusts raised the prices that consumers paid. Food trusts raised prices and produced dangerous products that threatened the health of consumers. The American writer Upton Sinclair exposed the dangers of the meatpacking industry in his classic book expose, *The Jungle*. The famous muckraking journalist Ida Tarbell described the damaging behavior of John D. Rockefeller and Standard Oil.

To counter the excessive developments of capitalist society and its Gilded Age, the Progressive movement was started, and had some significant successes in curbing the abuses of the dominant market power of the trusts. The Interstate Commerce Commission was created in 1887 to regulate the railroads and insure fair pricing for transportation services. In turn, the Standard Oil trust was broken up in 1911, and several independent oil firms were created in the hopes of fostering more competition.

President Theodore Roosevelt—an upper-crust product of the Gilded Age who became a Progressive lion—pushed through legislation that created the Food and Drug Administration in 1906 to regulate the production and distribution of food products. The Federal Trade Commission was created in 1914 to police the competitive situation in the American economy, and to prevent the buildup of monopoly power by large corporations. In the long run, these policies helped to make the American economy more competitive, and more beneficial to consumers and small businesses. But none of these reforms fully addressed another recurrent problem of capitalist economies: the persistent cycle of boom and bust.

Before depressions and recessions were known by those terms, they were called "panics." Panics are a macroeconomic problem. They cause a general decline in the entire economy; not in just one sector. With capitalism, and some of its excesses, accelerating at full throttle through the second half of the 19th century, there were panics in 1873, 1893, and 1907. The Panic of 1907 culminated in a financial crash that led to the creation of the Federal Reserve System, and the creation of a central bank to monitor the money supply and interest rates. This was in the hopes of reducing the devastating effects of widespread economic catastrophes. Even so, the problems of system-wide collapses of capitalist economies was not fully addressed until the time of the Great Depression of the 1930s, and later again after the end of World War II.

Following World War II, the United States took up greater leadership at home and around the world, most clearly among its European allies, it sought to develop more concentrated, and more sophisticated efforts to prevent (or at least lessen) the damaging effects of depressions, recessions, and other economic dislocations. The belief, then as now, was that capitalism has a much better chance of flourishing—and even surviving—in a growing and stable economy.

Lecture 6

Utopian Socialism to Amana Microwave Ovens

W HILE INDUSTRIAL CAPITALISM BROUGHT IMPORTANT benefits to society in terms of new wealth and opportunity, it also created great problems. The conditions of working-class life in America's big cities during the late 19th and early 20th centuries were miserable. The unsatisfactory—and often exploitative—conditions inspired many different social and political movements. Some were predominantly religious in nature, seeking spiritual inspiration and solution. Others, such as the trade unions, had economic orientations. Many approaches were a mixture, combining political, social, economic, and religious answers to alleviate the miserable conditions of the increasing numbers of the poor, urban working class. The more religious or philosophical movements got the label of "utopian socialist." ◆

Utopian Socialism

◀ The term "utopian socialist" was probably first used by Friedrich Engels, the intellectual collaborator of Karl Marx. Engels used the term as a pejorative to make a distinction with the more revolutionary and political movement that he and Marx favored.

◀ In 1892, Engels wrote *Socialism: Utopian and Scientific*, in which he promoted the Marxist version of socialism and criticized views and programs that Engels characterized as utopian socialist. The Marxist view of socialism is of an economy with a high level of state ownership, achieved through violent revolution.

◀ The term "utopian" signifies a model, or perfect, stage. It does a good job of describing the aims of many people who were attempting to improve humanity's lot in the face of the evils of industrial capitalism.

◀ Many utopian socialists had a strong moral or religious basis for their beliefs. Their religious and moral philosophies were based either on extreme views of the Protestant Reformation or the social gospel tradition of the Catholic Church.

◀ The 16th-century Protestant Reformation—led by such men as Martin Luther and John Calvin—challenged papal authority and the Bible as mankind's principal spiritual guides. The gospel tradition refers to the teachings of Jesus through his eyewitness followers and chroniclers.

◀ The rise of capitalism was made possible, in part, by the Protestant Reformation and its insistence on the primacy of the individual and the necessity of work and earthly success.

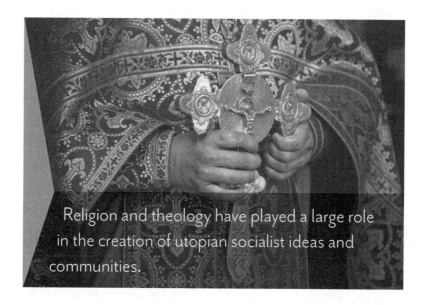

Religion and theology have played a large role in the creation of utopian socialist ideas and communities.

◀ The German sociologist Max Weber—in his most famous work—described this connection with a phrase that became the book's title, *The Protestant Ethic and the Spirit of Capitalism*. Weber said that encouraging people to work as individuals for worldly success was one of the key foundations of the rise of capitalism in preindustrial Europe.

◀ The teachings of Luther and Calvin criticized the other-worldly focus of the Catholic religion: the Catholics' focus on the afterlife and the excessive time spent in church and on holidays and feast days.

◀ After the Protestant Reformation, with its emphasis on literacy and practical vocations, the northern part of Europe became rich, while the southern part of Europe (the Catholic part of Europe) remained quite poor. And it would take the aftermath of World

War II to make the southern part of Germany the richest part of the country. This transformation was the work of the U.S. Army, the Marshall Plan, and Soviet-style socialism.

◀ Catholic theology was always more social and communal. It was also much less interested in worldly success for its believers. The role of the Catholic peasant or craftsman was to worship and obey. This philosophy is not the driver of individualistic acquisitiveness in the pursuit of worldly profits.

Socialist Reformers

◀ Although Engels was critical of the utopian socialists, he was not completely dismissive. Instead, he had sincere praise for the efforts of a few early socialist reformers.

◀ The first of these early reformers was the French philosopher Charles Fourier, who rejected the entire system of industrial capitalism—factories, cities, and large groups of exploited workers. Instead, he favored voluntary groups of people choosing to live communally in nature and dividing necessary tasks based on their individual passions and desires.

◀ Fourier saw industrial capitalism as a system that alienated humans from nature and their own community. Fourier's concept of alienation was later to be taken up by Marx, as one of his first criticisms of capitalism.

◀ A much more practical utopian socialist was the Welsh industrialist Robert Owen. Owen was a philanthropist and social reformer who came into possession of a cotton mill located in the village of New Lanark near Glasgow, Scotland. Water mills were the chief source of power for early British industry, before the advent of coal-fired steam power. At its peak, the mill employed about 2,500 workers.

◀ When Owen took over, he was appalled at the poor conditions that the mill workers and their families lived in. He raised wages and established schools for the workers' children. He made sure that the work and home environments of his workers were clean, aesthetically pleasing, and safe. He was a pioneer of urban planning for ordinary workers and citizens.

◀ It came as a shock to Owen's fellow industrialists that such efforts could be profitable. His New Lanark enterprise was an example of what contemporary economists call the efficiency theory of wages: Sometimes it is more profitable and efficient for employers to pay workers more than they are required to by labor market conditions. Workers who are paid above the norm may work more efficiently and more industriously and have less absenteeism. And if they are well fed, it's more likely that these workers will be healthier and stronger.

◀ The mills at New Lanark continued working until 1968, when they were no longer competitive with textiles and fabrics from newly industrializing countries in the Third World. Low-wage workers from India, Pakistan, Korea, and Taiwan shifted the comparative advantage to their own countries, outstripping the relative worker efficiency of comparatively wealthy Britain.

◀ This is one of the Achilles' heels of utopian socialist projects: They remain subject to the ups and downs of the predominantly capitalist world market and the forces of globalization.

◀ Today, New Lanark is a tourist destination and a UNESCO World Heritage site.

The Amana Colonies

◀ By far the most famous of the utopian communities established in the United States were the Amana Colonies, which owe their inspiration to German Protestant theology.

◀ The Amana movement grew out of opposition to the official Lutheran Church and its increasingly dogmatic theology, which was viewed as becoming increasingly like the Catholic Church: hierarchical, centralized, and dogmatic. The founders of the faith believed that God gave to individuals the inspiration to discover truth; therefore, followers were called Inspirationalists. And they were persecuted by the official Lutheran Church.

One of most impressive modern utopian social organizations is the Mondragon Corporation in Spain, which employs more than 70,000 workers and generates about $12 billion in sales a year. It has been cited as a model for cooperative enterprises all over the world. Catholic social theology, emphasizing humanist values and a spirit of social solidarity, was the philosophy behind Mondragon.

◀ Eventually, in the face of ever-increasing persecution, they decided to leave Germany in 1842 and move to America. At first, they bought land from the Seneca Nation near Buffalo, New York, but after being unable to afford the land they needed to expand their operation and receive more immigrants from Germany, the community moved in 1855 to the newly constituted state of Iowa.

◀ The basic form of property ownership in the original colonies was communal. There was no private property. Under Iowa state law, the community had to incorporate as a business. But although the community was incorporated, it had a communistic property system—common ownership, no private property— and a democratic government.

◀ The colony was divided into villages that were self-contained communities. Each village had a church, bakery, school, dairy, wine cellar, post office, sawmill, and general store. All workers in community enterprises were compensated in roughly the same amounts. Members were expected to shop at the village stores and budget their spending wisely. Members who became indebted, or ran out of money due to mismanagement, could be expelled.

◀ Cooking and eating were communal experiences. There was gender specialization: Women could choose among eight occupations that were traditional female jobs, such as cooking, gardening, and laundry, while men had their choice of more than 30 jobs. Children stayed with their mothers until the age of two, and then they were sent to school.

◀ The Great Depression intervened and crushed the economic viability of the Amana Colonies in 1931. Just as millions of American businesses and farms were bankrupted by the Depression, so Amana had to reorganize to survive.

Two different institutions emerged. One was given the task of tending to the spiritual needs of the community. This was the Amana Church Society. The other entity was created as a joint-stock company to manage the colonies' land, industry, and community services. This was the for-profit Amana Society, which exists to present day, producing bread, meats, furniture, clocks, and woolens.

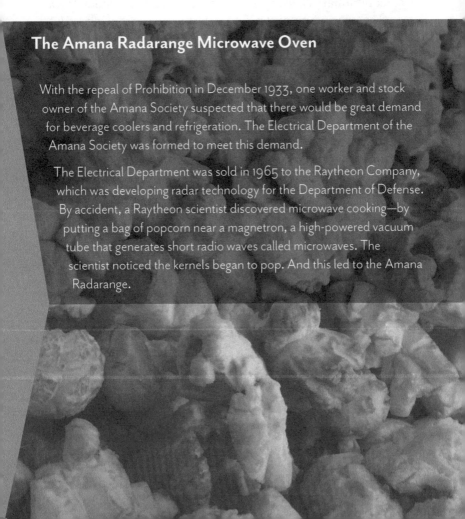

The Amana Radarange Microwave Oven

With the repeal of Prohibition in December 1933, one worker and stock owner of the Amana Society suspected that there would be great demand for beverage coolers and refrigeration. The Electrical Department of the Amana Society was formed to meet this demand.

The Electrical Department was sold in 1965 to the Raytheon Company, which was developing radar technology for the Department of Defense. By accident, a Raytheon scientist discovered microwave cooking—by putting a bag of popcorn near a magnetron, a high-powered vacuum tube that generates short radio waves called microwaves. The scientist noticed the kernels began to pop. And this led to the Amana Radarange.

Readings

ENGELS, *Socialism.*
TAYLOR, *Political Ideas of Utopian Socialists.*
WHITE AND WHITE, *Making Mondragon.*

Questions

1 What ideas and policies of the reformer Robert Owen might be beneficial for capitalist managers?

2 What do you think are the main pros and cons of the Mondragon Corporation? How does Mondragon benefit its worker/members?

Utopian Socialism to Amana Microwave Ovens

You can read the novels of Theodore Dreiser and Upton Sinclair to grasp some of the stark conditions of working-class life in America's big cities during the late 19th and early 20th centuries. *Sister Carrie, Jennie Gerhardt, The Financier,* and *The Titan*—all by Dreiser—relate the ruthlessness and amorality of the age's bankers and its industrial barons; as well as certain tales of sexual submission by female workers coming to terms with the machine age. *The Jungle,* about Chicago's meatpacking plants, and *King Coal,* and *Oil!*—by Sinclair—ripped the oozing lid off corporate and political corruption.

So, as you can see, while industrial capitalism brought important benefits to society in terms of new wealth and opportunity, it created great problems, as well. Factory workers in the early Progressive era often worked 12-hour days, seven days a week. Sometimes, they rotated day and night shifts every other week, so that when the pattern changed, the worker would have to work 24 hours straight at the beginning of the new rotation. Children as young as seven and eight went to work in textile mills because their small hands and fingers were so well-suited to close work with threads and fabrics. Industrial labor was hired and fired at management's will—with little to no control over their working lives.

Some of the new factory workers had previously been independent craftsmen and artisans who exercised much greater control of their work. They might also have taken pride in the products of those labors. But the factory system put most artists and craftsmen out of business. The development of the factory system beginning in the mid-19th century is a classic example of the economic benefits and costs of such dramatic social change.

Take the example of the small-scale shoemaker. He has his own little workshop, with maybe an assistant or apprentice. He makes, perhaps, one pair of shoes a day. They are well made, and the shoemaker stands by the quality of his work. The problem, of course, is that his shoes are rather expensive, and can be afforded only by the upper classes.

In contrast, a factory that mass produces hundreds or thousands of shoes a day can turn out shoes much more cheaply, making them affordable to a much larger part of the population. The widespread availability of this essential product—shoes—raises the living standards of many people. But it also puts some craftsmen and artisans out of business, with little choice other than to become factory workers, relinquishing control over their working lives and the products they make. Many critics of industrial capitalism focus on this separation of work from the products of the individual worker, calling the phenomenon "alienation." Even today, it remains an important issue of negotiation and dispute between labor and management.

Some factory workers in early industrial Great Britain and America were former farm workers who'd migrated from the countryside to the city. Others were immigrants, whether starving Irish in the textile mills of Manchester, or displaced Europeans—including many Catholics and Jews—in the garment shops, sawmills and steel factories of the United States. Early on, some of them had been pushed off the land in Britain by the enclosure movement between 1795 and 1815. The enclosure movement was the conversion of grain fields into pasture land, mainly for sheep.

With the rise of textile factories, there was a big increase in the demand for wool as a raw material for fabric. So, for landowners, it became much more profitable to raise wool-bearing sheep than to grow wheat or barley or oats. Sheep production was less labor intensive than grain growing. And displaced farm workers frequently had to move to urban areas to make a living.

One real disadvantage of moving from the countryside to the city is that unhealthy conditions often were prevalent in rapidly expanding urban centers. During the 19th century, the overcrowding and the proximity of poor people close to one another made the spread of disease quite common. Drinking water was polluted by industrial waste and sewage, and the air was fouled by the smoke from coal-fired factories. Life expectancy in the city was much less than in the country. But most working-class people had little choice other than to live in these miserable conditions.

The unsatisfactory—and often exploitative—conditions inspired many different social and political movements. Some were predominantly religious in nature, seeking spiritual inspiration and solution. Others, like the trade unions, had economic orientations. Many approaches were a mixture—combining political, social, economic and religious answers—to alleviate the miserable conditions of the increasing numbers of the poor, urban working class.

The more religious or philosophical movements got the label of "utopian socialist." And the more political and revolutionary movements referred to themselves as "scientific socialism." The term utopian socialist probably first was used by Frederick Engels, the intellectual collaborator of Karl Marx. Engels used the term utopian socialist as a pejorative to make a distinction with the more revolutionary and political movement that he and Marx favored.

You could say the Engels wrote the book on utopian socialism because he did, indeed, write the book *Socialism: Utopian And Scientific* in 1892. In it, Engels promoted the Marxist version of socialism, and criticized views and programs that Engels characterized as utopian socialist. The Marxist view of socialism is of an economy with a high level of state ownership, achieved through violent revolution.

The term "utopian" itself signifies a model, or perfect, stage. It does a pretty good job of describing the aims of a lot of people who were attempting to improve humanity's lot, in the face of the evils of industrial capitalism. Many utopian socialists had a strong moral or religious basis for their beliefs. Their religious and moral philosophies were based either on extreme views of the Protestant Reformation, or the social gospel tradition of the Catholic Church.

The 16th-century Protestant Reformation—led by such men as Martin Luther and John Calvin—challenged papal authority, and the Bible as mankind's principal spiritual guide. The gospel tradition refers to the teachings of Jesus through the eyewitness followers and chroniclers.

One key theme I will continue to emphasize is the role of religion and theology in the creation of utopian socialist ideas and communities. The rise of capitalism was made possible, in part, by the Protestant Reformation, and its insistence on the primacy of the individual, and the necessity of work and earthly success. The German sociologist Max Weber—in his most famous work—described this connection with a phrase that became the book's title, *The Protestant Ethic and the Spirit of Capitalism*. Weber said that encouraging people to work as individuals for worldly success was one of the key foundations of the rise of capitalism in preindustrial Europe. The teachings of Luther and Calvin criticized the other-worldly focus of the Catholic religion: the Catholics' focus on the after-life, and the excessive time spent in church, and on holidays and feast days.

Luther's most serious criticism was the role of the Catholic hierarchy in siphoning off so much of the resources of preindustrial Europe to support the luxurious lifestyles of popes, cardinals, and bishops. He felt these resources should have been put to more practical and profitable uses. One of the things I was not taught in my Catholic grade school in Bellaire, Texas—or even by the Jesuits in my high school—was the role of religion in dividing Europe into rich and poor areas.

After the Protestant Reformation, with its emphasis on literacy and practical vocations, the northern part of Europe became rich indeed. The southern part of Europe (the Catholic part of Europe), remained quite poor. And it would take the aftermath of World War II to make the southern part of Germany—around Stuttgart and Munich—the richest in Germany.

This transformation—making Munich and the south rich compared to Berlin, Leipzig and Dresden—was the work of the U.S. Army, the Marshall Plan—and Soviet-style socialism. The U.S. Army occupied Baden-Wurttemberg, in southwest Germany—bordering on France and Switzerland. And Bavaria, with Munich at its center, poured in resources. The Marshall Plan gave them more resources. The Soviets, meanwhile, took everything in eastern Germany that was (and wasn't nailed) down back to Russia, and saddled the new state of East Germany with its own inefficient communist economic system.

Catholic theology was always more social and communal. It was also much less interested in worldly success for its believers. The role of the Catholic peasant or craftsman was to worship and obey—and to pray to be taken into heaven when Saint Peter called. This philosophy is not the driver of individualistic acquisitiveness in the pursuit of worldly profits. As an altar boy, I remember vividly hearing many sermons about the avoidance of earthly riches, and the duty to give to the poor. In the Basque region of Spain, a workers' cooperative named for the town of Mondragon is based on the principles of Catholic social teaching. And Jewish theology underpins the kibbutz movement of collective agriculture in Israel. So, you see, the spirit of the utopian socialists is alive, and not merely an historical artefact.

Although Frederick Engels was critical of the utopian socialists, he was not completely dismissive. Instead, he had sincere praise for the efforts of a few early socialist reformers. The first of these early reformers was the French philosopher Charles Fourier. Fourier rejected the entire system of industrial capitalism—factories, cities, and large groups of exploited workers. Instead, he favored voluntary groups of people choosing to live communally in nature, and dividing necessary tasks based on their individual passions and desires. Fourier saw industrial capitalism as a system that alienated man from nature and his own community. Fourier's concept of alienation was later to be taken up by Marx, as one of his first criticisms of capitalism.

A much more practical utopian socialist was the Welsh industrialist Robert Owen. Owen was a philanthropist and social reformer who came into possession of a cotton mill near Glasgow, Scotland, through his father-in-law. The mill was located in the village of New Lanark on the River Clyde. Water mills were the chief source of power for early British industry, before the advent of coal-fired steam power. At its peak, the mill employed about 2,500 workers. And when Owen took over, he was appalled at the poor conditions that the mill workers and their families lived in. Owen raised wages, and established schools for the worker's children. He made sure that the work and home environments of his workers were clean, aesthetically pleasing, and safe. Owen was a pioneer of urban planning for ordinary workers and citizens.

It came as something of a shock to Owen's fellow industrialists that such efforts could be profitable. His New Lanark enterprise was an example of what contemporary economists now call the "efficiency theory of wages."

Put simply, it's the understanding that sometimes it is more profitable and efficient for employers to pay workers more than they are required to by labor market conditions. That's because workers who are paid above the norm may work more efficiently, work more industriously, have less absenteeism. And if they are well fed, it's all the more likely that these workers will be healthier and stronger. The mills at New Lanark continued working until 1968, when they were no longer competitive with textiles and fabrics from newly industrializing countries in the Third World.

Low-wage workers from India, Pakistan, Korea, and Taiwan shifted the comparative advantage to their own countries, outstripping the relative worker efficiency of comparatively wealthy Britain. Here, we see one of the Achilles heels of utopian socialist projects. They remain subject to the ups and downs of the predominantly capitalist world market, and the forces of globalization. New Lanark is, today, a tourist destination and a UNESCO World Heritage Site. There is a New Lanark Mill Hotel—managed by the New Lanark Conservation Trust.

Scotland's Robert Owen eventually sold his New Lanark mill, and moved to the United States to create a second utopian community in New Harmony, Indiana. It was a failure two years after it began. New Harmony's troubles included some of the managers running off with most of the enterprise's operating funds. The community itself continued to exist, and made some important social and economic contributions to the U.S. economy. Chief among these was its role as a center of science and technology education. It was also the home of the U.S. Geological Survey.

By far the most famous of the utopian communities established in the United States were the Amana Colonies. These settlements owe their inspiration to German Protestant theology. The Amana movement grew out of opposition to the official Lutheran Church and its increasingly dogmatic theology, which they thought was becoming increasingly like the Catholic Church hierarchy: centralized and dogmatic.

The founders of the faith believed that all individuals could be instruments of God's word, and that they did not need the professional Lutheran clergy to instruct them in their faith. They believed that God gave to individuals the inspiration to discover truth, and so were called "Inspirationalists." And they were persecuted by the official Lutheran Church.

The Inspirationalists refused military service, and refused to send their children to the Lutheran public schools.

Eventually, in the face of ever-increasing persecution, they decided to leave Germany in 1842, and move to America. At first, they bought land from the Seneca Nation near Buffalo, New York. But Buffalo was growing due to the stimulus provided by the building of the Erie Canal. The Inspirationalists were unable to afford the land they needed to expand their operations, and to receive more immigrants from Germany. So, they sent a group of men westward to find suitable acreage for a new settlement. Their representatives were drawn to the possibilities of new federal land grants in the west, and purchased tracts of land near the Iowa River.

In 1855, the community moved from New York to the newly constituted state of Iowa. The original name of this colony was Bleibetreu, a word derived from the German term *bleiben* for remain, and *treu* for faithful or true. But Bleibetreu was difficult for non-German speakers to pronounce. Something about the diphthong "eu" still gives Americans trouble. It's the reason we refer to the German settlers of Pennsylvania as "Pennsylvania Dutch." They're not Dutch. They're Deutsch. But Deutsch is too hard to pronounce. So, instead of the German word for remaining faithful, they chose a Biblical name—Amana—which means nearly the same thing.

The basic form of property ownership in the original colonies was communal. There was no private property. Under Iowa state law, the community had to incorporate as a business. But though the community was incorporated, it had a communistic property system—that's common ownership, no private property—and a democratic government.

The popular vote elected the community's Great Council of the Brethren, which decided most important matters.

The colony was divided into villages, and each one was governed by a group of elders known as the *Bruderrath*. This nice German word is derived from the word for brother (Bruder) and council (Rath). The Bruderrath was selected from among the most pious and hard-working villagers. In turn, these villages were self-contained communities. Each village had a church, bakery, school, dairy, wine-cellar, post office, sawmill and general store. All workers in community enterprises were compensated in roughly the same amounts. And members were expected to shop at the village stores and to budget their spending wisely. Members who became indebted, or ran out of money due to mismanagement, could be expelled.

Cooking and eating were communal experiences. There was gender specialization, and women usually worked in the communal kitchens under the direction of the *Kuchebaas*—another great German word that's isn't hard to translate. Women could choose among eight occupations that were traditional female jobs, such as cooking, gardening, and laundry. Men had their choice of more than 30 jobs. Children stayed with their mothers until the age of two, and then they were sent to a *Kinderschule*. At the age of seven, they would attend combined grade school and high school, until the age of 15. The children learned reading, writing, and arithmetic as well as how to shell seed corn and pick fruit.

The Great Depression intervened, and crushed the economic viability of the Amana colonies in 1931. Just as millions of American businesses and farms were bankrupted by the Depression, so Amana had to reorganize to survive. Two different institutions emerged. One was given the task of tending to the spiritual needs of the community. This was the Amana Church Society. The other entity was created as a joint-stock company to manage the colonies' land, industry, and community services. This was the for-profit Amana Society. It exists to present day, producing bread, meats, furniture and clocks, woolens, a toy store and a general store founded in 1858.

The path to the Amana Radarange microwave oven has something of a spirited origin. With the repeal of Prohibition in December 1933, one worker and stock owner of the Amana Society suspected there would be great demand for beverage coolers and refrigeration. The electrical department of the Amana Society was formed to meet this demand. It also profited from Defense Department contracts during World War II.

The electrical department was sold to the Raytheon Corporation in 1965. In turn, Raytheon was developing radar technology for the Defense Department, and—rather by accident—discovered microwave cooking.

According to legend, a Raytheon scientist put a bag of popcorn near a magnetron. A magnetron is a high-powered vacuum tube that generates short radio waves called microwaves. The scientist noticed the kernels begin to pop. And this led to the Amana Radarange. Today, the radar range division is part of the Whirlpool Corporation.

One of most impressive, modern utopian social organizations is the Mondragon cooperative in Spain, which employs more than 70,000 workers and generates about $12 billion in sales a year. It has been cited as a model for cooperative enterprises all over the world. And here we see the influence of Catholic teaching as a basis for organizing economic enterprise on communal and egalitarian ideals. The founder of the Mondragon cooperative was a Catholic priest, Father Jose Maria Arizmendiarrieta. After the Spanish Civil War from 1936 to 1939, this Catholic priest set out to help the Basque region in northern Spain recover from the war's devastation.

The war had pitted a leftist political group known as the Republicans against a conservative and authoritarian movement known as the Nationalists. The Nationalists were led by certain military officers, including Generalissimo Francisco Franco. The war was extremely destructive, leaving Spain poorer and more underdeveloped. The Nationalists under Franco won, and formed a very conservative government. Nevertheless, a rather utopian communal organization thrived in the government's shadow.

In 1943, Father Arizmendiarrieta founded a technical school to train engineers, managers, and skilled labor.

At the time, Spain was a predominantly agricultural economy, with low levels of literacy and technical knowledge. Human capital had to be developed. The Mondragon Cooperative Corporation was founded in 1955. Its first manufactured products were paraffin heaters—a rather primitive product but well-suited to the underdeveloped nature of the

Spanish power system of the day. Catholic social theology, emphasizing humanist values and a spirit of social solidarity, was the philosophy behind Mondragon.

Solidarity is one of the key words, or concepts, frequently used in European discussions of economic and social policy. Its usage is not as common in the United States, where the emphasis tends to be on economic growth, and success measured in monetary terms. This difference in cultural or theological values is a key factor in the development of different economic systems. It also makes it impossible to declare one economic system superior to another. That's because different economic systems pursue different goals and objectives. Students of comparative economic systems—and experts, too—must always consider the cultural, ethical, and social values of the people who live in a particular economic system.

The Mondragon organization established many different cooperatives over the years—a network of some 100 of them exists today. But each follows the same core values. These principles include a sense of social responsibility that emphasizes equitable, or relatively equal, distribution of wealth and income. There are established ratios of incomes between the cooperatives' managers and workers, usually not exceeding a level of nine to one.

Contrast this to a CEO pay ratio in the United States. One widely cited report puts the average CEO-to-worker pay ratio at 70-to-1—rising to more than 300-to-1, and even more than 400-to-1! Should these corporate executives be paid such orders of magnitude more than their workers? Should they be paid orders of magnitude more than the managers of the Mondragon cooperatives? These are interesting questions in comparative economic systems.

Another Mondragon value was democratic decision making by all workers and managers in the cooperative. Industrial democracy is a key value in many economic organizations, not just cooperatives. One recurring problem of socialist-type organizations and economies is stagnation, and lack of growth. One benefit of a profit-seeking enterprise in a market economy is the constant pressure to innovate; to improve production processes, and create new products and services.

In a cooperative enterprise where members are less pressured by the threat of bankruptcy or job loss, the pressure to innovate may also be less forceful. Yet the non-profit cooperative Mondragon University—which is part of the Mondragon Corporation—specializes in engineering, business management, entrepreneurship, and the media, and even gastronomic sciences. It's designed, in its own words, "to quickly adapt to technological and socio-economic changes."

And the Mondragon cooperatives themselves produce a range of sophisticated products for the automotive and construction materials industries, as well as industrial design and logistics. The U.S. Steel Corporation is one of its many partners. Although Mondragon has been a successful economic institution that embodies many of the ideals of the early utopian socialist thinkers, it also has been the subject of intense criticism.

The American radical thinker Noam Chomsky, for instance, argues that Mondragon can hardly fail to commit some of the same excesses of other participants in a capitalist system: the pollution of some of its industrial factories, for example. Chomsky also maintains that Mondragon exploits some workers by paying the prevailing low wages in some developing countries where its cooperatives operate subsidiaries.

Another critic has pointed out that not all Mondragon employees are owners, and, therefore, the organization maintains two tiers of employees, and discriminates against the non-owner employees. When one Mondragon enterprise had to lay off workers, it reportedly fired non-owner employees in much greater numbers.

This gets to another, more frequent criticism of the cooperative movement. Mondragon does not protect worker-members from all vagaries and vicissitudes of the capitalist system. You might be part of an organization that practices solidarity and worker democracy, but you're still at risk of unemployment and insecurity because you operate in a capitalist market economy.

A more conservative critique of the cooperative movement holds that only private, for-profit companies create the dynamism and economic growth sufficient to improve the lives of broader society. In this view, too much equality creates complacency and stagnation. Of course, this gets us back to a happy oxymoron: Some are more equal than others.

Lecture 7

The Bolsheviks: Lenin, Trotsky, and Stalin

O N JULY 16, 1918, SEVERAL MEMBERS OF THE RUSSIAN royal family were murdered by Bolshevik revolutionaries. The royal family patriarch, Tsar Nicholas II, had been deposed months before his murder, ending 300 years of Romanov family rule. Revolution was under way across all segments of society—the military, radical leftists, and elites—with many of them fleeing. What would follow is the creation of a vast new state known as the Soviet Union, at a time when World War I had exhausted the Russian people and led to the deaths of millions of Russian peasants conscripted into the tsarist army. ◆

Vladimir Lenin

◀ Two revolutions occurred in Russia in 1917. The first was the February Revolution that deposed Tsar Nicholas II while maintaining the Romanov dynasty and Russian participation in the war. The second was the October Revolution led by the Bolsheviks under Vladimir Lenin, which founded the Union of Soviet Socialist Republics as a communist state under the control of one party.

◀ The Bolsheviks seized power in St. Petersburg and Moscow but were attacked by opposing forces known as the White Army in a civil war that lasted from 1917 to 1922.

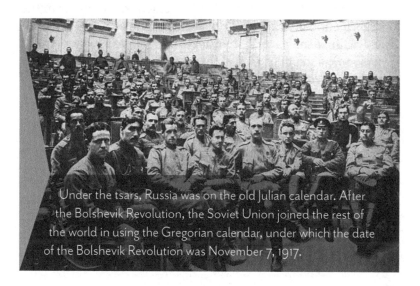

Under the tsars, Russia was on the old Julian calendar. After the Bolshevik Revolution, the Soviet Union joined the rest of the world in using the Gregorian calendar, under which the date of the Bolshevik Revolution was November 7, 1917.

◀ Karl Marx left no detailed description of what a real, functioning communist economy would look like. Consequently, Vladimir Lenin and his fellow Russian Bolshevik communists had to make up their new economic system when they seized power.

◀ The Bolsheviks—who constituted the majority faction of the Russian Social Democratic Party that had seized power— decided on a system of direct control over the economy. This was eventually called War Communism, and for many revolutionaries, it was what their ideal economy would look like even in peacetime. War Communism lasted from 1917 to 1921 and was a system of complete state ownership and control of all important economic sectors.

◀ Because the Bolsheviks had taken over a society with very few factories and industrial resources, their labor force consisted of illiterate peasants who had to be recruited from the countryside.

◀ Furthermore, the Bolshevik wing of the Russian Social-Democratic Workers' Party that had emerged victorious in the larger political struggle against the old Romanov monarchy— and against the party's Menshevik wing—was led by political personnel and philosophical thinkers such as Lenin. They were not experienced or skilled at economics and business. The Bolsheviks also tended to be city boys who knew very little about farming and agriculture.

◀ Meanwhile, many of society's elite—scientists, managers, and industrialists—had already fled during the civil war. In this, we begin to understand the cause of some of the continuing difficulties of Soviet agriculture throughout the entire history of the Soviet Union.

◀ The Bolsheviks' economic and political philosophy positioned them as enemies of private property and as hostile to factory owners and land owners. And this antagonism was one of the reasons the Bolsheviks decided that they had to take direct control over the country's means of production.

◀ Many observers and scholars who study the Soviet system believe that dictatorship is inherent in socialism and communism. Others contend that the Soviet dictatorship arose out of the unique conditions of Russian and Soviet society.

◀ The argument that dictatorship grew out of the Soviet Union's unique circumstances is based on several particular forces in prerevolutionary Russia and in the newly created society.

◀ Tsarist Russia was nobody's idea of a modern democracy. The tsar was considered a divine ruler, and no protest or criticisms of the policies of the divine ruler were tolerated. Secret police spying on citizens, exile to Siberia, and banishment were not creations of the new Bolshevik rulers of Soviet Russia but instead were instruments of dictatorial rule employed by the Russian aristocracy.

◀ Any political opposition or independent thinking in prerevolutionary Russia had to be done in secret and underground. There was no history of open, public, democratic debate. Anyone outside your group could be spies, enemies, or police agents. Tight control over any group by its leaders was necessary to preserve the group from outside harm.

◀ Not only did the Bolsheviks have to fight against domestic enemies in the White Army, but for a brief period of time, British and America forces—although exhausted by the horrors of World War I—also fought in Russia against the Bolshevik Red Army.

◀ After the Red Army and the Bolshevik leadership emerged victorious in the political and military battles unfolding across the new Soviet Union, they still faced the almost impossible task of providing food and the basic necessities to a desperate population exhausted by war.

◀ Furthermore, Lenin and the other Bolshevik leaders also realized that they did not have sufficient personnel or trusted comrades to oversee the economy. Many Bolshevik leaders and partisans had been killed in the civil war. And Russia is such a vast country that it stretched across 11 time zones.

◀ The Bolsheviks had no alternative but to relax their initial attempt to command the new Soviet economy, because they had limited ability to manage it. This relaxation of control meant that individual landowners initially could make their own decisions as to what to grow, how to grow it, when and where to market their produce, and what to charge for it in agricultural markets that were now permitted.

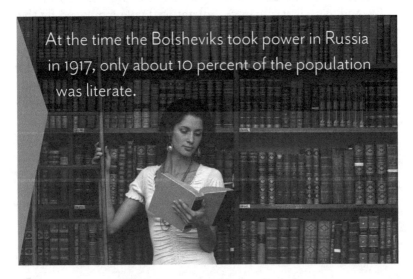

At the time the Bolsheviks took power in Russia in 1917, only about 10 percent of the population was literate.

◀ The allowance of private farming was a significant ideological retreat for the new Soviet Russian communist leadership. As a result, a leadership that had promised to eliminate the inequalities of private property now had to allow some private property.

◀ Along with private agriculture, the new Soviet leadership also had to allow small private retail and manufacturing enterprises to exist, such as bakeries and furniture shops. This new system of relaxed control over the economy was given the label of the New Economic Policy (NEP), and it was in force from 1921 to 1928.

◀ Along with a somewhat relaxed approach to economic control, this was a time of open debate and artistic experimentation. Sergei Eisenstein revolutionized the making of modern film, Kazimir Malevich broke new ground in art and theory with a series of sculptures called the *arkhitektons*, and Vladimir Mayakovsky and Anna Akhmatova wrote modern poetry.

◀ Lenin died in early 1924. Prior to his death, an unsuccessful assassination attempt had left him weak and unable to vigorously exert his command over Bolshevik personnel. This set the stage for one of the most important and prolonged conflicts in the Soviet leadership: the Great Industrialization Debate.

◀ The Great Industrialization Debate concerned how long private ownership should be allowed to continue and how much economic freedom would be given to private Russian landowners and farmers. There were also debates about democracy, and, most importantly, there was the struggle to replace Lenin.

◀ One faction, known as the Right Opposition, favored a long run for the NEP and a slower road to true communism. A leader of this faction was Nikolai Bukharin, the Bolshevik leader most knowledgeable about economics and economic development.

Leon Trotsky

◀ At the opposite extreme from the Right Opposition were the leftists. The left wing of the party was led by Bolshevik intellectual Leon Trotsky, the most famous Bolshevik after Lenin. Trotsky had written several books on politics and revolution, as well as a famous three-volume history of the Russian Revolution.

◀ Like Lenin, Trotsky spent several years outside of Russia after being banished by the tsarist government for revolutionary activity. While Lenin went to Zurich, Trotsky spent most of his prerevolutionary exile in the salons of Vienna.

Born as Lev Bronstein, Trotsky used his family name while hiding in Vienna.

◀ Trotsky opposed the continuation of the NEP and advocated a much swifter transition to complete communism. One of the developments leading to this conclusion was the so-called scissors crisis, which was the result of an increase in farm prices and the resulting enrichment of some successful farmers.

◀ The leftist opposition assumed that these rich farmers—whom the Bolsheviks labeled kulaks—would keep getting richer and richer. If, as the leftists envisioned, agricultural prices increased, this would lead farmers to plant more crops, eventually increasing the supply of farm products and bringing prices back down. This is an example of the new Soviet leadership's fundamental misunderstanding of how markets work.

◄ According to the Left Opposition, personified by Trotsky, the kulaks might eventually become rich and powerful enough to oppose the Soviets politically, leading to a counterrevolution and the establishment of a capitalist society.

◄ The left advocated taxing the kulaks to secure the funds necessary to finance rapid investment in heavy industry and manufacturing. The left also said that the state should directly manage and procure key agricultural outputs, either by direct requisition or establishment of state-owned agricultural enterprises.

◄ The Left Opposition feared continuous counterrevolution and attack by hostile foreign powers, and it believed that the Soviet Union needed to acquire its own base of heavy industry to produce the matériel for modern industrial warfare.

◄ The left was deeply concerned that the Soviet Union did not have the luxury of time to wait while Russian agriculture slowly and gradually produced the extra output required to generate sufficient economic development.

Joseph Stalin

◄ The Great Industrialization Debate was about the timing and the nature of Soviet economic development. How long could the new Soviet economy remain as a primarily agricultural and mixed economy? The economy was mixed between central control of key parts of the economy but with significant private property and production in the hands of rich kulaks and petty capitalists.

- In the middle of these two viewpoints was Joseph Stalin, who was appointed by Lenin as general secretary of the Communist Party, a somewhat secondary position in the intraparty bureaucracy. Stalin was not a leading Bolshevik theoretician or intellectual, but he was a master of bureaucratic infighting and manipulation.

- Another factor in Stalin's favor was that his enemies tended to underestimate his skill and ambition. Because Stalin was not among the leaders of the political, economic, and theoretical debates, Trotsky, Bukharin, and others did not consider him to be a leading contender for the leadership role left vacant after Lenin's death.

- But they were mistaken. Stalin began his drive for power by allying himself with the Right Opposition and its battle with Trotsky. Stalin had decided that Trotsky was his most formidable rival, due to Trotsky's reputation both inside the new Soviet Union and internationally among communists in other countries.

- By isolating Trotsky and eventually driving him into exile, Stalin thereby eliminated his chief rival. Ultimately, Trotsky was assassinated by a member of the NKVD, the Soviet secret police.

- After disposing of Trotsky and his followers in the Left Opposition, Stalin turned on Bukharin and the Right Opposition. First, the Right Opposition leadership was expelled from the Soviet Communist Party. Then, they were charged with various political offenses. And then they were jailed and put on trial. Finally, Bukharin and most of the rest of the opposition were executed following a series of purges and the show trials.

◀ While the physical elimination of Stalin's opponents was accomplished by the mid-1930s, he had crushed meaningful political opposition to his economic and political plans much earlier. By 1928, Stalin was in complete control of the direction of the Soviet Union. And he oversaw the rapid industrialization of Soviet society that achieved dramatic results at great human costs and that became the template for nearly all new communist governments in eastern Europe, Asia, and Cuba for decades to follow.

Readings

MASSIE, *The Romanovs.*
NOVE, *An Economic History of the USSR.*
RIASANOVSKY, *A History of Russia.*

Questions

1   What specific historical circumstances led to the Bolshevik Revolution in 1917?

2   How did the new Soviet economy "solve" the problems facing Russian society at the beginning of the 20th century? At what cost?

The Bolsheviks: Lenin, Trotsky, and Stalin

O n July 16, 1918, several members of the Russian royal family—including a father, his wife, their five children, and servants—were murdered by Bolshevik revolutionaries, and dumped into unmarked graves. The royal family patriarch, Tsar Nicholas II, had actually been deposed months before his murder, ending 300 years of Romanov family rule. And now, revolution was under way across all segments of society: the military, radical leftists, and the elites, many of them fleeing.

What would follow is the creation of a vast new state known as the Soviet Union—this was a major experiment that would test the communist theories of Karl Marx—as well as endless subsets of this experiment with such names as the Great Industrialization Debate, NEP, and their nadir, the star trials of the 1930s, in which brute force prevailed over collective aims or ideals. So, the origins of the Soviet Union go back to a time when World War I had exhausted the Russian people, and led to the deaths of millions of Russian peasants conscripted into the Tsarist army.

Actually, two revolutions occurred in Russia in 1917. The first was the February Revolution that deposed Tsar Nicholas II while maintaining the Romanov dynasty and Russian participation in the war. The second was the October Revolution led by the Bolsheviks under Vladimir Lenin, which founded the Union of Soviet Socialist Republics as a communist state under the control of one party. There's confusion as to the dates and name of the Revolution that brought the Bolsheviks to power. Under the Tsars, Russia was on the old Julian calendar. After the Bolshevik revolution, the Soviet Union joined the rest of the world in using the Gregorian calendar. So, under the Gregorian calendar, the date of the Bolshevik revolution was November 7, 1917.

The Bolsheviks seized power in St. Petersburg and Moscow but were attacked by opposing forces known as the White Army in a civil war that lasted from 1917 to 1922. Russia's Civil War was extremely brutal and bloody. One of the most gruesome events was the murder of Tsar Nicholas II and his family. The Tsar's family and servants had been sent to Ekaterinburg in the Ural Mountains in 1918 to prevent them for giving direct support and inspiration to the White Army. After Lenin gave the order to have them killed, the entire family—along with their servants—was massacred in the basement of the Ipatiev House in the center of Ekaterinburg. Much later, the late-20th-century communist leader Boris Yeltsin ordered the house to be demolished to eliminate it as a place of potential honor and remembrance. The site is now home to a Russian Orthodox church.

Karl Marx left no detailed description of what a real, functioning communist economy would look like. But he assumed that communism would first triumph in a modern developed capitalist economy, with sophisticated managers and literate, skilled workers. He certainly didn't envision communism starting in such a poor, backward, agricultural, and largely illiterate society as early-20th-century Russia. Consequently, Vladimir Lenin and his fellow Russian Bolshevik communists had to more or less make up their new economic system on their own when they seized power. The Bolsheviks—who constituted the majority faction of the Russian Social Democratic Party that had seized power—decided on a system of direct control over the economy. This was eventually called "War Communism." And for many revolutionaries, it was what their ideal economy would look like even in peacetime. War Communism lasted from 1917 to 1921, and was a system of complete state ownership and control of all important economic sectors.

Because the Bolsheviks had taken over a society with very few factories and industrial resources, their labor force consisted of illiterate peasants who had been recruited from the countryside. Furthermore, the Bolshevik wing of the Russian Social-Democratic Workers Party that had emerged victorious in the larger political struggle against the old Romanov monarchy—and against the party's Menshevik wing—was led by political personnel and philosophical thinkers such as Lenin. They were not experienced or skilled at economics and business. The Bolsheviks also tended to be city boys who knew very little about farming and agriculture.

Meanwhile, many of society's elite—scientists, managers, and industrialists—had already fled during the civil war. In this we begin to understand the cause of some of the continuing difficulties of Soviet agriculture throughout the entire history of the Soviet Union.

Big picture: the Bolsheviks' economic and political philosophy positioned them as enemies of private property, and as hostile to factory owners and land owners. And this antagonism was one of the reasons the Bolsheviks decided they had to take direct control over the country's means of production. Many observers and scholars who study the Soviet system believe that dictatorship is inherent in socialism and communism. Others contend that the Soviet dictatorship arose out of the unique conditions of Russian and Soviet society. The argument that dictatorship grew out of the Soviet Union's unique circumstances is based upon several particular forces in prerevolutionary Russia, and in the newly created society.

Tsarist Russia was nobody's idea of a modern democracy. The tsar was considered a divine ruler, chosen by God to rule over his obedient subjects. No protest or criticisms of the policies of the divine ruler were tolerated. Secret police spying on citizens, exile to Siberia, and banishment were not creations of the new Bolshevik rulers of Soviet Russia but instead were instruments of dictatorial rule employed by the Russian aristocracy. Any political opposition or independent thinking in prerevolutionary Russia had to be done in secret and underground—figuratively, if not literally. There was no history of open, public, democratic debate. Anyone outside your group could be spies, enemies, or police agents. Tight control over any group by its leaders was necessary to preserve the group from outside harm.

I've often asked my students if Russia or the Soviet Union ever invaded the United States. The correct answer is no, unless you count some examples in movies like the comedy, *The Russians are Coming, the Russians are Coming.*

I also ask my students if the United States ever invaded Russia, and the answer is yes. That's because not only did the Bolsheviks have to fight against domestic enemies in the White Army but for a brief period of time, British and America forces—although exhausted by the horrors of World War I—also fought in Russia against the Bolshevik Red army.

Some 10,000 American soldiers were engaged in this conflict. They landed in Soviet Russia at the port of Murmansk, above the Arctic Circle. But they didn't stay long. Imagine you're a young American soldier who's spent months fighting in the muddy trenches of World War I, in France and

Belgium and Germany. And now you're told that you're going to land in fight in the Russian Civil War, which you probably have a hard time understanding. American officers and soldiers had little desire to fight in such a cold and strange and confusing place.

Thomas Jefferson believed that democracy depended on an educated population. One of the glories of 19th- and 20th-century America was its system of mass, public education, available to all American citizens. Russia had no such system, or institutional belief in educating its citizens, most of whom were peasants tied to their landlords' fields. Political parties were forbidden. Literacy was for only the urban aristocracy, and bureaucrats serving the tsar. Even much of the lower nobility and clergy were illiterate. Finally, the Russian economy the Bolsheviks took over was barely capable of feeding its population. Prerevolutionary Russia was constantly afflicted with periods of starvation and epidemic diseases. When society has to be preoccupied with questions of survival, then political discussion and debate is a luxury not available to the mass of the population.

Many scholars of the American Revolution point to the fact that prerevolutionary America, by comparison, was already a land of literate, prosperous, and politically aware people. In other words, economic and social conditions in America in 1776 were completely different from the economic and social conditions of 1917 Russia. Many American revolutionary leaders—and the ordinary American soldiers in the Continental army—were quite well prepared to take over self-government in the new country.

In contrast, the Bolshevik leadership took over a country that was poor, illiterate, weak from war and hunger, and unfamiliar with even many basics of government and public life. Specifically, at the time the Bolsheviks took power in Russia in 1917, only about 10 percent of the population was literate. After the Red Army and the Bolshevik leadership emerged victorious in the political and military battles unfolding across the new Soviet Union, they still faced the almost impossible task of providing food and the bare necessities to a desperate population exhausted by war.

Furthermore, Lenin and the other Bolshevik leaders also realized they did not have sufficient personnel, or trusted comrades, to oversee the economy. Many Bolshevik leaders and partisans had been killed in the civil war. And Russia is such a vast country that it stretched across 11 time zones. So, the Bolsheviks had no alternative but to relax their initial attempt to command the new Soviet economy, because they had limited ability to manage it.

This relaxation of control meant that individual landowners initially could make their own decisions as to what to grow, how to grow it, when and where to market their produce, and what to charge for it in agricultural markets that were now permitted. The allowance of private farming was a significant ideological retreat for the new Soviet Russian communist leadership. As a result, a leadership that had promised to eliminate the inequalities of private property now had to allow some private property. The Russian land that had been spontaneously expropriated by peasants during the Russian revolutions—as their landlords were killed or left— was of uneven quality. Some land was very fertile and productive. Some land was barren and rocky.

So, private ownership of farmland would inevitably lead to differences in economic success. If you got your hands on good land, you had an advantage. And, of course, some peasants were better farmers than others. Even the weather, always a formidable and unpredictable force, would play a part in making some farmers prosperous and successful and some farmers unlucky and poor.

Along with private agriculture, the new Soviet leadership also had to allow small private retail and manufacturing enterprises to exist. We're not talking about big, modern industrial enterprises but little bakeries, furniture makers, weavers and tailors, leather workers, and retail shopkeepers. This new system of relaxed control over the economy was given the label of the New Economic Policy, or NEP. Along with small private farmers and small business owners, a class of intermediaries, or retail agents—or wheelers and dealers—now appeared. These "Nepmen," as they were called, provided a key function of linking the country producers and consumers with the city producers and consumers.

Farmers who produced wheat needed to get their crops to millers and bakers in the city. Bakers needed to get their bread to shops in the city and stores in the rural areas where grains were not produced. And naturally, the Nepmen made a little profit on every transaction. But profits were anathema to true believers in communism. And these Nepmen—along with the more prosperous farmers and businessmen—became objects of scorn and derision rather than gratitude by the Bolshevik leadership.

The New Economic Policy was in force between 1921 and 1928. Along with a somewhat relaxed approach to economic control, this was a time of open debate and artistic experimentation. I'm just a simple economics professor but I do know that some great Russian cultural contributions came at this time: Sergei Eisenstein was revolutionizing the making of modern film; Kazimir Malevich was breaking ground in architecture; Vladimir Mayakovsky and Anna Akhmatova were writing modern poetry. It was a time of new thinking, and experimentation, and vigorous debates.

There were limits to these debates, and to this new thinking. But soon, the limits were to get much narrower, as the struggle for ultimate leadership in the Soviet Union intensified. Lenin died in early 1924. Previously, there had been an unsuccessful assassination attempt that left him weak, and unable to vigorously exert his command over Bolshevik personnel. And this set the stage for one of the most important and prolonged conflicts in the Soviet leadership. This argument about the future economic development of the Soviet Union is known as the Great Industrialization Debate. And it divided the Bolshevik Party from 1924 to 1928.

The conflict concerned how long such private ownership should be allowed to continue, and how much economic freedom would be given to private Russian landowners and farmers. After his death, a power struggle began in earnest. This was really several struggles rolled into one. There were debates about democracy across the country, and within the ruling Bolshevik Party. There were debates about how long the New Economic Policy would be allowed to persist, and how long private, capitalist enterprises would continue in Soviet Russia. And, most importantly, there was the struggle to replace Lenin as the leader of the Soviet Communist Party, and of the new Soviet Union.

At first, several factions and personalities vied for the job. One faction, known as the Right Opposition, favored a long run for the New Economic Policy, or NEP, and a slower road to true communism, which would call for the abolition of private property and market activity. One leader of the party's right was Nikolai Bukharin, who proclaimed that Russia would shuffle towards communism on the back of a mule. He meant that private agriculture would be a dominant feature of the Soviet economy for decades to come. Bukharin was probably the Bolshevik leader most knowledgeable about economics, and economic development.

At the opposite extreme were the leftists led by the Bolshevik intellectual Leon Trotsky, the most famous Bolshevik after Lenin. Trotsky had written several books on politics and revolution, as well as a famous three-volume history of the Russian Revolution. Like Lenin, he had spent several years outside of Russia, having been banished by the Tsarist government for revolutionary activity. And indeed, all the leading Bolsheviks adopted pseudonyms to help conceal their identities from the Tsarist secret police. Lenin's family name was actually Ulyanov, and Stalin's was Djugashvili.

While Lenin had spent some time in Zurich, writing and communicating with the underground Bolshevik leadership back home in Russia, Trotsky spent most of his prerevolutionary exile in salons of Vienna. Born as Leon Bronstein, Trotsky used his family name while hiding in Vienna, and spent a good bit of time at the Café Central, on Herrengasse, while thinking and writing about revolution. This marvelous café still exists, and is a lovely place for apple strudel and coffee. When I'm in Vienna, I always make a pilgrimage to the Café Central to see if I can detect the spirit of Trotsky there.

When the Russian revolution broke out, a Viennese who heard the news dismissed it with the unwitting observation, "What Russian can lead a revolution? Herr Bronstein from the Café Central?" But of course, it was being led by Lenin and Trotsky—Herr Bronstein.

Trotsky opposed the continuation of the New Economic Policy, and advocated a much swifter transition to complete communism. One of the developments leading to this conclusion was the so-called "Scissors Crisis." When I was a graduate student at the University of Oklahoma, and first came upon the phrase while studying Soviet economic history, I imagined some shortage of cutting tools for Russian tailors. No, the term "scissors" refers to two different lines on a graph.

When prices of Soviet farm products and industrial goods were plotted on a time line, the line for farm products was going upwards and the line representing the prices of industrial goods was headed downwards. The two lines looked like the two blades of a pair of scissors opening up. This "Scissors Crisis" was the result of farm prices increasing, and some successful farmers getting rich. The leftist opposition assumed that these rich farmers—whom the Bolsheviks labeled "Kulaks"—would keep getting richer and richer. The Russian term kulak comes from the word for fist—a fist that holds tight to money and property. It has connotations of greed and power.

According to the Left Opposition, personified by Trotsky, the Kulaks might eventually become rich enough and powerful enough to oppose the Soviets politically, leading to a counter-revolution and the establishment of a capitalist society. This fundamental misunderstanding of how markets works is a good illustration of the lack of basic economic knowledge by a good part of the new Soviet leadership.

If, as the leftists envisioned, agricultural prices increased, this would lead farmers to plant more crops, and put more land into production, eventually increasing the supply of farm products. And that would bring prices back down. Not up. Similarly, the relatively low prices of industrial and manufactured goods would lead some businessmen to stop or decrease production, eventually bringing up the prices of those goods. The blades of the scissors would eventually close.

But just as Marx had not given anyone a plan for a communist economy, most of the new Bolshevik leadership was relatively unfamiliar with economic theory. They were especially unfamiliar with the new theories of market behavior being created in England—by economists like Alfred Marshall, the inventor of the demand and supply curve. Marshall also proved to be a tormentor of generations of freshmen economics students. He demonstrated that surpluses and shortages often cure themselves through changes in demand, as well as changes in supply, and changes in market prices.

The early revolutionary leaders' ignorance of market forces and market behavior was to remain characteristic right up through the Soviet Union's very last leader, Mikhail Gorbachev. The Left Opposition proposed a much more radical and rapid transformation of the Soviet Union into an industrial planned economy than did the Bukharin wing. The left advocated taxing the Kulaks to secure the funds necessary to finance rapid investment in heavy industry and manufacturing. Additionally, the state should directly manage and procure some key agricultural outputs, either by direct requisition or by the establishment of state-owned agricultural enterprises.

As I mentioned a moment ago, almost all Soviet leadership consisted of "city boys" who believed that farms could be organized and run like factories. Farmers would behave just like workers, and could be corralled into large production teams like large industrial enterprises. But agricultural organization and production is a recurring problem in communist economies. It's almost a fact of nature that farmers want their own land, and to manage their own crops. And so, in communist economy after communist economy—from China across southeast Asia to eastern Europe and Cuba—agricultural inefficiencies have remained an Achilles heel.

The Left Opposition feared continuous counter-revolution and attack by hostile foreign powers, and it believed that the Soviet Union needed to acquire its own base of heavy industry to produce the materiel for modern industrial warfare. The left was deeply concerned that the Soviet Union did not have the luxury of time to wait while Russian agriculture slowly, and gradually, produced the extra output required to generate sufficient economic development.

The Great Industrialization debate was about the timing and the nature of Soviet economic development. How long could the new Soviet economy remain as a primarily agricultural and mixed economy? Mixed between central control of key parts of the economy but with significant private property and production in the hands of rich Kulaks and petty capitalists.

In the middle of these two viewpoints was Joseph Stalin. Lenin had appointed Stalin as general secretary of the Communist Party. This somewhat secondary position in the intra-party bureaucracy was not considered all that important by leading party theoreticians and intellectual combatants. But Stalin used the position to place his allies in key jobs, and in offices throughout the Soviet system. The positions usually had privileged access to food and housing, still in very short supply in post-revolutionary Russia. This created a relationship of patronage and personal loyalty to Stalin, who made his appointees beholden to him. The precedent of political placement determining a person's standard of living was also to become a hallmark of nearly all communist societies all over the world.

Stalin was not a leading Bolshevik theoretician or intellectual, but he was a master of bureaucratic infighting and manipulation. Another factor in Stalin's favor was that his enemies tended to underestimate his skill and his ambition. Because Stalin was not among the leaders of the political, economic, and theoretical debates, Trotsky, Bukharin, and others did not consider him to be a leading contender for the leadership role left vacant after Lenin's death.

They were mistaken. Stalin began his drive for power by allying himself with the Right Opposition, and its battle with Trotsky. Stalin had decided that Trotsky was his most formidable rival, due to Trotsky's reputation both inside the new Soviet Union and internationally among communists in other countries. By isolating Trotsky and eventually driving him into exile—first in Alma-Ata (present-day Almaty in Kazakhstan), then Turkey, and finally to Mexico—Stalin thereby eliminated his chief rival. Ultimately, Trotsky was assassinated in Mexico by a member of the NKVD, the Soviet secret police.

After disposing of Trotsky and his followers in the Left Opposition, Stalin turned on Bukharin and the Right Opposition. Nikolai Bukharin had been born to two primary school teachers in Moscow on October 9, 1888. Like other radicals, he faced the threat of constant arrest during the movement's early years. He felt into exile in 1910, and moved between Vienna, Zurich, London, Stockholm, Copenhagen, and Krakow. In 1916, he moved to New York where he met Leon Trotsky. Having worked at one time for the newspaper *Pravda*, he and economist Evgenii Preobrazhensky wrote one of the more important books on the beginnings of the Soviet economy, *The ABC of Communism*.

But he and Lenin had frequently clashed over theoretical and practical matters, including even Russia's withdrawal from World War I. Bukharin saw it as an opportunity to provoke a pan-European communist revolution. And now, Stalin proceeded in stages to eliminate any challenges from the leaders of the Right Opposition, as well as he had from the left.

First, the Right Opposition leadership was expelled from the Soviet Communist Party. Then they were charged with various political offenses. And then they were jailed, and put on trial. Finally, Bukharin and most of the rest of the opposition were executed following a series of purges and the show trials. While the physical elimination of Stalin's opponents was accomplished by the mid-1930s, he had crushed meaningful political opposition to his economic and political plans much earlier.

By 1928, Stalin was in complete control of the direction of the Soviet Union. And he oversaw the rapid industrialization of Soviet society that achieved dramatic results at great human costs, and which also became the template for nearly all new communist governments in eastern Europe, Asia, and Cuba, for decades to follow.

Soviet Planning and 1,000 Left-Foot Shoes

JOSEPH STALIN GAINED COMPLETE CONTROL OF THE Soviet Union and its Communist Party in the four years between Vladimir Lenin's death in 1924 and the initiation of forced collectivization in 1928. In the years to come, the chief instrument that Stalin would use to exercise his all-encompassing control was the five-year plan, which attempted to organize all productive activity in the entire Soviet economy. The plan required hundreds of state personnel to calculate all the input and output requirements of the entire economy. ◆

The Five-Year Plan

◀ The problem of coordinating millions of factories, stores, farms, transport vehicles, and water and power providers was overwhelming. Many observers of the Soviet planning system have remarked that the amazing thing about the Soviet economy was that it worked at all. A separate government agency—known as Gosplan, headquartered in the center of Moscow—was set up to produce the planning documents.

◀ The Soviets' five-year plans were broken up into one-year and monthly plans to help make more comprehensible the enormous task of carrying out the nation's planning objectives. Every factory manager, farm director, school principal, hospital administrator, and store manager in the country was given a target goal for each monthly planning period.

If you were a manager of a shoe factory, your monthly plan goal—or "output target"—might be expressed in terms of producing a set number of shoes. A single production run of a single object is the easiest type of production process.

One of numerous jokes about the Soviet economic system is about the shoe factory manager who was given a monthly target of 1,000 shoes. He produced 1,000 size-10 black shoes—for the left foot.

◀ A continuing problem of centrally planned production is the difficulty of anticipating and satisfying the need for many different styles and forms of products, especially consumer products that will end up meeting the requirements of real people.

◀ The most important person in the production process was the factory or farm manager, usually called the enterprise director, who was subject to a rather complicated system of controls. The layout of this system of control and planning was to be a template for nearly all communist economic and political systems throughout the world.

◀ At the top was the Communist Party. Its leader was the general secretary of the Central Committee of the Communist Party. In the Soviet Union, this position of power was created by Stalin, and it remained a station of power in the USSR through the rule of Mikhail Gorbachev, the last general secretary.

◀ The general secretary presided over the regular meetings of the politburo—a small group of party leaders who decided the most important questions for the economy and society at large. The politburo and the general secretary were elected by the Central Committee, which in turn was elected at a party congress that convened every few years. Members of the Communist Party were the only citizens who were allowed to vote in these all-important elections.

◀ In local towns, factories, farms, schools, and stores, party members were the eyes and ears of the party to make sure that the plans and decisions of the top leadership were carried out. Each enterprise director was closely watched and checked on by the party member, or members assigned to his particular enterprise. Depending on the importance of the enterprise, the director himself might also be required to be a member of the party.

◀ This system of party leadership was the main mechanism of political control over the economy. However, there was also a nominally independent government system. The government of the Soviet Union was led by a premier, or prime minister, who was elected by the Supreme Soviet—ostensibly, the governing legislature of the country.

◀ In the early days of the Soviet Union and the Russian Bolshevik Party—that is, the Russian Social-Democratic Party—the new economic and political system was supposed to be governed by elected councils of workers and peasants. This idealized democratic system was run by elected representatives of ordinary workers and farmers.

◀ To pay tribute to this ideal, the Supreme Soviet was established to give the appearance of a democratically elected government. In reality, the Supreme Soviet had no independent power, and the elected representatives had to be approved by the Communist Party.

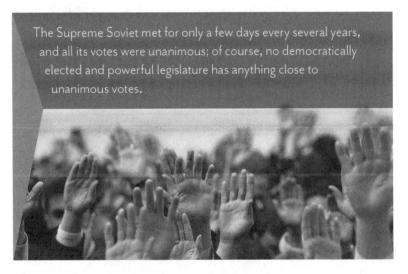

The Supreme Soviet met for only a few days every several years, and all its votes were unanimous; of course, no democratically elected and powerful legislature has anything close to unanimous votes.

◀ Below the Supreme Soviet was the council of ministers, the personnel charged with running the individual components of the Soviet planned economy. Each minister was in charge of a particular branch of the economy. Each enterprise was a component of a particular ministry, and each enterprise director would answer to his or her boss at the appropriate ministry.

◀ The minister of state planning was given the task of developing each component of the five-year plans. An enterprise director was given the part of the plan that related to his or her ministry. The minister of state would then decide how the objectives of the plan would be allocated among the various enterprises within the ministry.

◀ To demonstrate the superiority of the Soviet economy—and, by implication, the superiority of Stalin—gigantic enterprises were created. This would lead to all kinds of problems, such as communication and coordination of enterprise functions.

◀ Capitalist enterprises suffer from this problem as well, but eventually, the higher costs of production will force a capitalist firm to scale back and cut costs. There was no such cost pressure at work in the Soviet economy to limit the size of an enterprise.

◀ That's because most Soviet enterprises were organizationally linked to worker apartment complexes, schools, grocery and clothing stores, medical clinics, sports, and cultural centers. Each of these providers of goods and services supported enterprise workers and their families.

◀ So, in the Soviet system, where you worked determined almost everything about your daily life. Access to apartments, schools, retail goods and services, sports, and culture was all under the control of the enterprise director and served as a tool to organize and motivate workers.

◀ Soviet workers were also organized into trade unions. But unlike labor unions in capitalist countries—which often are the antagonists of corporate bosses and managers—Soviet trade unions were yet another means for the Communist Party to exercise control. Trade unions usually had control over issues such as workers' pensions and vacations.

State Farms and Collectives

◀ Soviet agriculture was organized into state farms or collectives. Collective farms were theoretically run by all members of the collective, but in reality, the key decisions were made by the farm manager and his Communist Party colleague.

Farm machinery drivers were elite workers in Soviet agriculture, so tractor and combine drivers were among the highest-paid farm workers.

Before Mikhail Gorbachev went off to Moscow to study law at Moscow State University, he worked as a combine driver in Stavropol, in southern Russia, where he grew up.

◄ Collective farm members were paid according to revenues raised, including sales to the state. Member incomes would vary according to hours worked and the skill level of their particular occupation.

◄ State farms were managed directly by an appointee of the ministry of agriculture and were supposed to be run on an industrial basis, just like a city factory. State farm workers received hourly pay, just like an urban factory worker.

◄ State and collective farms also provided housing, education, medical care, and basic consumer goods and services—just like industrial employers in the cities.

◄ At the beginning of the Soviets' five-year plans in the early 20th century, agriculture was crucial to the country's industrial development.

◄ Stalin had decided that the Soviet Union must industrialize rapidly if it were to survive as the lone communist society surrounded by capitalist enemies. In the Great Industrialization Debate, there were two camps: the Right Opposition, led by Bukharkin, who advocated a gradual approach to development; and the Left Opposition, led by Leon Trotsky, who advocated much more rapid industrialization, concentrating first on heavy industry.

◄ Essentially, Stalin adopted the ideas of the Left Opposition and implemented these ideas and proposals ruthlessly. In the beginning, Soviet agricultural had to perform four critical functions: provide food for a growing urban and industrial labor force, supply some of its workers for the growing industrial force, provide raw materials for Soviet industrial production, and deliver exports that would earn foreign exchange.

The United States—and, for that matter, every advanced industrial economy—saw the majority of its workers move from farms to factories amid urbanization and industrialization. But the process in the United States took almost a century. The Soviet Union made this transition in less than 10 years.

◀ One tiny pocket of private agriculture existed on most Soviet collective and state farms. These were the private plots allocated to almost every member or worker. On these very tiny plots of land—only a few yards square—Soviet farm workers would grow a few potatoes, and maybe some cabbage, and raise a few chickens. This meager output was a primary food source for many Soviet agricultural workers.

◀ Even up to modern times, Soviet industrial workers in the cities were also given access to their own private plots. This concession to private property, and individual initiative, was necessary to avoid mass starvation, as nearly all of the output of state and collective farms was delivered to state agencies so that state planners could achieve their larger objectives.

◀ Many private landowners resisted Soviet efforts to force them into collective or state farms. Some were shot or imprisoned, their machinery and their livestock seized by the state. The rash and irrational organization of Soviet agriculture was to plague the Soviet Union with serious food and crop problems throughout the country's history.

Education

◀ To develop the more skilled workers required to industrialize, the Soviet Union had to build primary and secondary schools to teach the basics of reading, science, and arithmetic.

◀ The Soviet Union provided primary (and, later, secondary) education to nearly all of its citizens, but university education was rather rare and very specialized. The most important areas of study in Soviet universities involved production questions. Therefore, engineering, math, and science were the critical departments, and the most prestigious.

◀ The university system was fundamental to Soviet class structure. Where you graduated from determined where you would end up in Soviet society and in the Soviet hierarchy, including your job, apartment, medical care, vacations, and status.

◀ Property or financial wealth could not be passed on, or inherited, in the Soviet Union for the simple reason that there were no financial assets or private property. What could be bequeathed to your children—if you were a high-ranking Soviet official—was preferred access to a good university.

◀ In the Soviet Union, a degree in engineering or the hard sciences was a necessity for appointment to enterprise management and a start up the ladder in an important ministry in Moscow. The only other important university department taught Marxist political theory. If your ambition was to be a top Communist Party official, such academic training was necessary to understand the terminology and beliefs underlying the Soviet political system.

Soviet Russia pioneered one original method of increasing the industrial labor force: bringing women into factory work in large numbers. In fact, the majority of the adult female population was so employed—a first in history. The United States didn't achieve such levels until sometime after 1970.

The Soviet Economy

◀ The Soviet economy was a planned economy, but it did use the basic elements of a monetary system to add another mechanism of calculation and control. That said, banking in the Soviet Union was not part of an independent financial system as you would find in a market economy. The possession of money didn't provide much in the way of purchasing power, or direct command over products or resources, in the Soviet economy unless provided for in the plan itself.

◀ The relative unimportance of money, and the critical importance of political position and bureaucratic connection, is the main explanation why Soviet leaders never retired. Retirement meant losing access to the best cars, apartments, clinics, and stores associated with political power and position.

◀ For all its inherent contradictions and faults, the early Soviet economy did achieve impressive rates of economic growth. By the time of World War II, the Soviets had achieved an industrial base capable of eventually defeating the bulk of Adolph Hitler's army.

◀ Yet the costs in human suffering and death were often hidden, or ignored, by Soviet leadership. Such problems eventually came to the surface.

◀ With the fall of the Berlin Wall in 1989 and the collapse of the Soviet Union in 1991, many senior academics found that the knowledge they possessed was worthless in the new postcommunist societies that were developing market institutions and democratic political systems.

Readings

MALIA, *Russia under Western Eyes.*
SPUFFORD, *Red Plenty.*

Questions

1 How did the organization of the Soviet economy create big problems?

2 Why did the one-party state structure of the Soviet Union create strong incentives for Soviet bureaucrats and leaders to never retire?

Lecture 8 Transcript

Soviet Planning and 1,000 Left-Foot Shoes

Joseph Stalin gained complete control of the Soviet Union and its Communist Party in the four years between Vladimir Lenin's death in 1924, and the initiation of forced collectivization in 1928. Collectivization concentrated individual landholdings into state and collective farms. Stalin used the collectivization cudgel to also rid himself of his rival, Nikolay Bukharin—whom he denounced for opposing the program. In the years in-between, Stalin thoroughly undermine all his other rivals, too: Leon Trotsky, Grigory Zinovyev, and Lev Kamenez.

So now he was in complete control of the Soviet economy. There'd be no system of checks and balances. No countervailing powers were allowed to exist. No competing political parties with opposing ideas or political programs. No independent newspapers, radio, or cultural institutions.

In the years to come, the chief instrument Stalin would use to exercise this all-encompassing control was the Five-Year Plan. This process attempted to organize all productive activity in the entire Soviet economy. The Five-Year Plan required hundreds of state personnel to calculate all the input and output requirements of the entire economy.

So, a separate government agency was set up to produce the planning documents. It was known as "Gosplan" from the Russian abbreviation for the words "state" (*gosudarstva*) and "planning" (*plannirov*). It was headquartered in the center of Moscow, just outside the Kremlin walls.

The problem of coordinating millions of factories, stores, farms, transport vehicles, water and power providers was rather overwhelming. Many observers of the Soviet planning system have remarked that the amazing thing about the Soviet economy was that it worked at all. Like the bumble bee, it doesn't seem designed to work but somehow it does! With no computers and very little in the way of any type of office equipment, the first Soviet planners worked with principally paper and pencils.

The Soviets' five-year plans were broken up into one-year and monthly plans to help make more comprehensible the enormous task of carrying out the nation's planning objectives. Every factory manager, farm director, school principal, hospital administrator, and store manager in the country was given a target goal for each monthly planning period. As you might imagine, these planning goals were rather simple at the beginning. If you were a manager of a shoe factory, your monthly plan goal—or "output target"—might be expressed in terms of producing a set number of shoes.

And there are numerous jokes about the Soviet economic system—many of them underground jokes in the Soviet Union itself. One is about the shoe factory manager who was given a monthly target of 1,000 shoes. He produced 1,000 size 10 black shoes—for the left foot. And there is the manager of a nail factory, who was given a target of 1,000 pounds of nails. So, he produced one nail weighing 1,000 pounds. These stories are apocryphal, perhaps. But they do contain large elements of truth.

A continuing problem of centrally planned production is the difficulty of anticipating and satisfying the need for many different styles and forms of products, especially consumer products that will end up meeting the requirements of real people. The most important person in the production process was the factory or farm manager, usually called the enterprise director. He—and almost always it was a "he"—was subject to a rather complicated system of controls.

I'll describe the layout of this system of control and planning, which was to be a template for nearly all communist economic and political systems throughout the world. At the very top was the Communist Party. Its leader was the general secretary of the central committee of the Communist Party—a rather large title for a business card. In the Soviet Union, this position of power was created by Stalin. And it remained a station of power in the USSR all the way to the rule of Mikhail Gorbachev, as the last general secretary. The general secretary presided over the regular meetings of the politburo—a group of about seven or eight party leaders who decided the most important questions for the economy, and society, at large.

These were big questions, like the overall direction of the economy, and the economic sectors that were to be given priority. Those sectors that would be relatively unimportant were also decided by the politburo, under the direction of the general secretary. The politburo and the general secretary were elected by the central committee, which, in turn, was elected at a party congress that convened every few years. Members of the Communist Party were the only citizens allowed to vote in these all-important elections.

In local towns, factories, farms, schools, and stores, party members were the eyes and ears of the party to make sure the plans and decisions of the top leadership were carried out. Each enterprise director was closely watched, and checked on, by the party member, or members assigned to his particular enterprise. Depending on the importance of the enterprise, the director himself might also be required to be a member of the party. This system of party leadership was the main mechanism of political control over the economy. However, there was also a nominally independent government system, as well.

The government of the Soviet Union was led by a premier or prime minister who was elected by the Supreme Soviet, ostensibly, the governing legislature of the country. "Soviet" is a Russian word that means council. In the early days of the Soviet Union and the Russian Bolshevik party— that is, the Russian Social Democratic Party—the new economic and political system was supposed to be governed by elected councils of workers and peasants.

This idealized democratic system would be run by elected representatives of ordinary workers and farmers. To pay tribute to this ideal, the supreme soviet was established to give the appearance of a democratically elected government. In reality, the supreme soviet had no independent power, and the elected representatives had to be approved by the Communist Party.

The supreme soviet met for only a few days every several years, and all its votes were unanimous. Of course, no democratically elected and powerful legislature has anything close to unanimous votes—except for unusual circumstances such as patriotically declared wars. And even then, there might be some dissenters who cast minority votes.

Below the supreme soviet was the council of ministers, the personnel charged with running the individual components of the Soviet planned economy. Each minister would be in charge of a particular branch of the economy. The minister of transportation would be in charge of the railroads, for example. This minister's job would be to keep everything on track. (Sorry!)

Each enterprise would be a component of a particular ministry, and each enterprise director would answer to his or her boss at the appropriate ministry. One of the most important ministries was Gosplan. The minister of state planning was given the task of developing each component of the five-year plans. An enterprise director was given the part of the plan that related to his or her ministry. The minister of state would then decide how the objectives of would be allocated among the various enterprises within the ministry.

On the surface, this is not very different from a corporate vice president deciding which particular factories get what part of the corporate plan to fulfill. The difference is that an enterprise director in the Soviet system presided over a geographically specific location of production. So, while the Soviet enterprise director managed a single plant or firm, the executive of a capitalist corporation might be responsible for factories spread over many different countries.

At the same time, the Soviet enterprise director would have a much, much wider range of responsibilities than most corporate executives. And Soviet enterprises tended to be much larger than their counterparts in capitalist economies. One Russian critic of the Soviet system, Roy Medvedev, referred to this tendency as Soviet "gigantism" and said that it arose from Stalin's megalomania. Bigger was better. And to demonstrate the superiority of the Soviet economy, and by implication, the superiority of Stalin, gigantic enterprises were created. This gigantism would lead to all kinds of problems like communication and coordination of enterprise functions. The larger an enterprise, the more difficulty it is to communicate with all the component sections.

Capitalist enterprises suffer from this problem as well but, eventually, the higher costs of production will force a capitalist firm to scale back and cut costs. There was no such cost pressure at work in the Soviet economy to limit the size of an enterprise. That's because most Soviet enterprises were organizationally linked to worker apartment complexes, schools, grocery and clothing stores, medical clinics, sports, and cultural centers. Each of these providers of goods and services supported enterprise workers and their families.

So, in the Soviet system where you worked determined almost everything about your daily life. Access to apartments, schools, retail goods and services, sports and culture was all under the control of the enterprise director, and served as a tool to organize and motivate workers. Good work might mean access to a better and bigger apartment. Housing was in chronically short supply in the Soviet Union. So, access to housing was a strong motivational tool.

Soviet workers were also organized into trade unions. But, unlike labor unions in capitalist countries—which often are the antagonists of corporate bosses and managers—Soviet trade unions were yet another means for the Communist Party to exercise control. Trade unions served as cheerleaders for greater production, and the fulfillment of the current five-year plan. Soviet trade unions usually had control over issues like workers' pensions and worker holidays and vacations.

When I visited the Soviet Union in 1985, late in its existence, one of the places my students and I toured was a vacation center for the coal miner's union in Yalta, on the Black Sea. Coal miners who had worked well, and fulfilled the production targets at their mine—usually expressed in tons of coal—could look forward to enjoying a couple of weeks of vacation in a dormitory-style building with a cafeteria and access to the beach.

This same approach also applied to farming. Soviet agriculture was organized into state farms or collectives. Collective farms were theoretically run by all members of the collective. But in reality, the key decisions were made by the collective farm manager, and his Communist Party colleague. Collective farm members were paid according to revenues raised, including sales to the state. Member incomes would vary according to hours worked, and the skill level of their particular occupation. For instance, farm machinery drivers were elite workers in Soviet agriculture. So, tractor and combine drivers were among the highest-paid farm workers. Before Mikhail Gorbachev went off to Moscow to study law at Moscow State University, he'd worked for a while as a combine driver in Stavropol, in southern Russia, where he grew up.

State farms were managed directly by an appointee of the ministry of agriculture. And these state farms were supposed to be run on an industrial basis, just like a city factory. State farm workers received hourly pay, just like an urban factory worker. State and collective farms also provided housing, education, medical care, and basic consumer goods and services—just like industrial employers in the cities.

At the beginning of the Soviets' five-year plans in the early 20th century, agriculture was crucial to the country's industrial development. Stalin had decided that the Soviet Union must industrialize rapidly if it were to survive as the lone communist society surrounded by capitalist enemies. In the Soviet industrialization debate, there were two camps: the Right Opposition, led by Bukharkin, who advocated a gradual approach to development; and the Left Opposition, led by Leon Trotsky, who advocated much more rapid industrialization, concentrating first on heavy industry. Essentially, Stalin adopted the ideas of the Left Opposition and implemented these ideas and proposals ruthlessly.

In the beginning, Soviet agricultural had to perform four critical functions. The first was to provide food for a growing urban, industrial labor force. Factory workers needed a regular food supply to provide the energy for long and taxing factory work—much of it still done by hand, and requiring muscular strength. The second critical function of agriculture was to supply some of its workers for the growing industrial force. In practical terms, this meant that farms had to produce more, with fewer hands, so that some workers could migrate to the city to become part of the urban work force.

The United States—and, for that matter, every advanced industrial economy—saw the majority of its workers move from farms to factories amid urbanization and industrialization. But the process in the U.S. took many decades—almost a century, in fact. The Soviet Union made this transition in less than 10 years.

The third crucial function of Soviet agriculture was to provide raw materials for Soviet industrial production. Bales of wool were needed by textile and clothing enterprises. Wood from forestry was needed for furniture factories. A fourth function of Soviet agriculture was to deliver exports that would earn foreign exchange. The Soviet Union needed foreign exchange to pay for industrial goods and technology. At the time of the revolution, the Soviet Union had almost no industrial or manufactured goods that any foreign buyer would want. In more modern terminology, the Soviet Union was a Third World country with only basic food and raw materials to market to foreign buyers.

One tiny pocket of private agriculture existed on most Soviet collective and state farms. These were the private plots allocated to almost every member or worker. On these very tiny plots of land—literally a few yards square—Soviet farm workers would grow a few potatoes, and maybe some cabbage, and raise a couple of chickens. This meager output was a primary food source for many Soviet agricultural workers.

Even up to modern times, Soviet industrial workers in the cities were given access to their own private plots, as well. This concession to private property, and individual initiative, was necessary to avoid mass starvation, as nearly all of the output of state and collective farms was delivered to state agencies so that state planners could achieve their larger objectives.

Many private landowners resisted Soviet efforts to force them into collective or state farms. Many of these people were shot or imprisoned, their machinery and their livestock seized by the state. The Welsh journalist Gareth Jones, whose writing inspired George Orwell's novel *Animal Farm*, offers this grim real-life account of a Soviet collective farm, first published in October 1931:

> In the Stalin kolkhoz, upon which I stayed, a sharp-eyed, dark-haired peasant approached me in the Village Soviet hut in the presence of the Communist president. He spoke to me of the successes of the kolkhoz, of the enthusiasm of the country for the collective farm movement, amid the affection of the peasants for their young Bolshevist leader. This last statement was accompanied by a friendly clap on the back of the president of the Village Soviet. Next morning, however,

when far away from any of the Communist members of the kolkhoz, the same peasant, who to all appearance was an enthusiastic supporter of the Soviet power, approached me and whispered: 'It is terrible here in the kolkhoz. We cannot speak or we shall be sent away to Siberia as they sent the others. We are afraid. I had three cows. They took them away and now I only get a crust of bread. It is a thousand times worse now than before the Revolution; 1926 and 1927 were fine years, but now we dare not oppose the Communists or we shall be exiled. We have to keep quiet.'

The early days of collectivization were times of famine and bloodshed in the countryside. The rash and irrational organization of Soviet agriculture was to plague the Soviet Union with serious food and crop problems all throughout the country's history.

Soviet Russia did pioneer one original method of increasing the industrial labor force, and that was to bring women into factory work in large numbers. Long before Rosie the Riveter went to work in the United States, producing industrial goods during World War II, Soviet women entered the labor force in such large numbers that the majority of the adult female population was so employed—a first in history. The United States didn't achieve such levels until sometime after 1970.

Female labor did not mean, however, that Soviet women were freed from housework. Soviet men were legendary in their reluctance to work at home. Most cooking, cleaning, washing, child care, and shopping was still done by women. One Soviet joke revolves around the celebration of International Women's Day, on March the 8th of each year. Soviet women would say, "One day for Soviet women, and 364 days for Soviet men!"

To develop the more skilled workers required to industrialize, the Soviet Union had to build primary and secondary schools to teach the basics of reading, science, and arithmetic. Peasant farmers with no perspective of progress did not need—nor want—any change in their centuries-old tasks and responsibilities. To work on their landlord's property, and to have long seasons of idleness—when the Russian weather forbid outside work—was maybe not a rich and satisfying life. But it was the life the peasant knew and accepted.

In contrast, a collective farm laborer or factory worker had to be able to tell time, read numerical plans, and understand basic technical processes. A worker in a shoe factory had to be able to recognize the difference between plans for black shoes of a certain size, and brown shoes of a different size. Right foot and left foot both. Farmers had to understand rudimentary accounting to calculate collective farm revenue and expenses.

The Soviet economy was a planned economy, but it did use the basic elements of a monetary system to add another mechanism of calculation and control. That said, banking in the Soviet Union was not part of an independent financial system as you would find in a market economy. The possession of money didn't provide much in the way of purchasing power, or direct command over products or resources, in the Soviet economy unless provided for in the plan itself.

Even if an enterprise director had stacks of money, he couldn't go out and hire more workers unless he'd been given authorization to do so by the planning authorities. If a worker had stacks of money, he couldn't rent a bigger apartment unless he had authorization to do so by his enterprise director, and if the plan provided for such a move.

Unlike in a capitalist market economy—where, in the words of Cindi Lauper "Money changes everything"—in the Soviet Union, only the plan changed everything.

This relative unimportance of money, and the critical importance of political position and bureaucratic connection, is the main explanation why Soviet leaders never retired. Retirement meant losing access to the best cars, the best apartments, best clinics, and best stores associated with political power and position. Soviet citizens, even leaders, never earned large salaries. So, nobody retired with a portfolio of stocks, bonds, and real estate. There were no stocks, no bonds or privately owned real estate.

When I visited the Soviet Union, and toured its factories and farms, I would almost always meet someone whose title was chief economist. But economists in the Soviet system were essentially accountants who tallied the revenues and receipts of Soviet enterprise. So, whereas economists in market economies talk about macroeconomic issues like gross domestic product and unemployment rates—or microeconomic issues like changes in the price of real estate or shares—Soviet economists worked on adding up totals of income and expenses for their enterprise. And they hoped that those totals added up to the same number.

The Soviet Union provided primary (and, later, secondary) education to nearly all of its citizens, but university education was rather rare and very specialized. The most important areas of study in Soviet universities involved production questions. Therefore, engineering, math and sciences were the critical departments, and the most prestigious. I'll add that most students and faculty in these departments were men.

This male-chauvinist approach to higher education was not unique to the Soviet Union. It was just a little more blatant and pronounced. When I went to teach for a semester in post-communist Russia in 1994, the city I taught in had four universities. The most important one—which that had sent Boris Yeltsin to Moscow, as a key member of Soviet leadership under Gorbachev—was the Polytechnic University. I taught at a different school, the Urals Pedagogic Institute—or UPI, in local speak. It was at the end of the main street of Ekaterinburg, Lenin Prospect, and had a very impressive campus. This was the teacher's college. It had trained primary and secondary school teachers but had now been given the task of creating a new department of business and economics. The Urals State Pedagogical Institute consisted almost entirely of female faculty and students. I had a not totally unpleasant semester teaching there!

In the bigger picture, the university system was fundamental to the Soviet class structure. Where you graduated determined where you would end up in Soviet society, and in the Soviet hierarchy, including job, apartment, medical care, vacations, status—everything. Property or financial wealth could not be passed on, or inherited, in the Soviet Union for the simple reason that there were no financial assets or private property. What could be bequeathed to your children—if you were a high-ranking Soviet official—was preferred access to a good university.

This is similar to the "legacy system" of the Ivy League universities in the United States in the old days, where the children of wealthy alumni could be admitted to excellent universities. In the Soviet Union, a degree in engineering or the hard sciences was a necessity for appointment to enterprise management, and a start up the ladder in an important ministry in Moscow. The only other important university department was that which taught Marxist political theory. If your ambition was to be a top Communist Party official, such academic training was necessary to understand the terminology and beliefs that underlay the Soviet political system.

For all its inherent contradictions and faults, the early Soviet economy did achieve impressive rates of economic growth. By the time of World War II, the Soviets had achieved an industrial base capable of eventually defeating the bulk of Adolph Hitler's army. Yet the costs in human suffering and death were often hidden, or ignored, by Soviet leadership. Such problems eventually came to the surface in profound ways.

With the fall of the Berlin Wall in 1989, and the collapse of the Soviet Union in 1991, many senior academics found the knowledge they possessed was worthless in the new post-communist societies that were developing market institutions and democratic political systems. So, when you hear, or read, of nostalgia for the old communist system, often you're hearing the voices of respected Soviet teachers and professors who no longer taught a valued subject.

Lecture 9

Economic Consequences of European Peace

BEFORE WORLD WAR I, THE GLOBAL CAPITALIST system was extremely open. Most travelers did not need passports, visas, or customs forms, and trade was relatively free. This capitalist world predominantly benefited the rich countries, especially those in western Europe and North America. But it was a world of generally rising standards of living and economic growth. It was also somewhat artificial. ◆

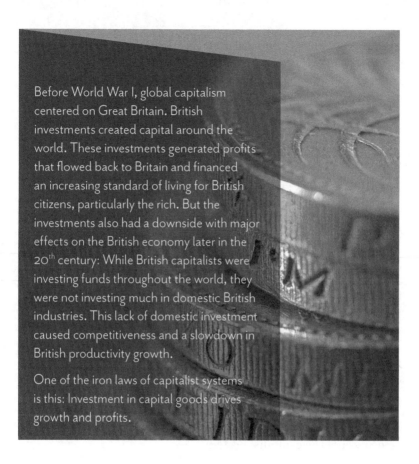

Before World War I, global capitalism centered on Great Britain. British investments created capital around the world. These investments generated profits that flowed back to Britain and financed an increasing standard of living for British citizens, particularly the rich. But the investments also had a downside with major effects on the British economy later in the 20th century: While British capitalists were investing funds throughout the world, they were not investing much in domestic British industries. This lack of domestic investment caused competitiveness and a slowdown in British productivity growth.

One of the iron laws of capitalist systems is this: Investment in capital goods drives growth and profits.

Keynes's Analysis

◀ John Maynard Keynes wrote his famous work *The Economic Consequences of the Peace* in 1919 to protest the British and French government positions in negotiations over the futures of the defeated powers of World War I, Germany and Austria.

◀ Many people wrongly assume that Keynes was some kind of radical, left-wing socialist with a strong anti-capitalist theory. In fact, Keynes found many things commendable about a capitalist society, and he was generally very positive about the benefits of a relatively free market version of capitalism. Keynes, above all, believed that the benefits of a capitalist society should be shared as widely as possible.

◀ Before World War I, commerce, investment, and travel were freer than they'd ever been—and freer than they are today. This was true globalization. At the same time, Keynes realized that this system was based on unequal distribution of incomes. He emphasized that this system would never have been as dynamic if income and wealth were equally distributed.

◀ Keynes pointed out that the system was somewhat artificial, based on what he called a double bluff. On one hand, the working classes had to accept that they would get a small share of the wealth and income that they had helped produce. On the other, the rich would receive a disproportionate share of wealth and income—but they would not spend much of it. The rich saved and invested the lion's share of their incomes and thus contributed to the formation of new capital and industries that fueled the growth of the capitalist system.

◀ Keynes understood the costs and benefits of this arrangement. The cost was the lower standard of living of the working classes. The benefit was the growth of the productive capacity of the capitalist system, which would eventually benefit everyone with greater production and a higher standard of living.

◀ This is an iron law of economics: Economic growth depends on saving. Saving, in economic theory, means not using all of society's resources for current consumer goods and services, but rather also using some resources to produce machinery and factories that will in the future produce more consumer goods and services.

◀ All economic systems that experience economic growth and development must find some way to create savings and channel those savings into productive investment in capital goods.

◀ In the decades before World War I, the bulk of saving was done by the upper classes, who limited their current consumption—to invest in domestic and foreign capital accumulation. This capital accumulation before World War I solved the dire predictions of late-18th-century and early-19th-century British economist Thomas Malthus, who had forecast that population would generally grow faster than food production and that mankind was thus doomed to continual threats of famine.

◀ But investment in agriculture and the cultivation of more land increased the world food supply before 1914 so that more and more people had adequate supplies of food. And the ease of international trade meant that a country's products could be exported all over the world.

◀ The American economist Paul Krugman, a winner of the Nobel Prize in Economics for his work in international trade, points out that by 1900, the telegraph was capable of transmitting price information (including prices of stocks, bonds, and agricultural commodities) around the world in a matter of seconds. This speed of economic information was the basis of Keynes's description of easy flows of capital and spending around the world.

◀ But a peaceful world of growing capitalism and international trade and travel was halted by the outbreak of the Great War. Although it was mostly a European war, it nevertheless affected the entire world due to the interconnected nature of all economies before the war. International trade and investment ground to a halt, and incomes throughout the world were depressed.

◀ This illustrates another facet of modern capitalism: Upheavals in one part of the world have repercussions all around it.

◀ At the end of World War I, the victorious Allied powers—Great Britain, France, and the United States—assembled in Paris to conduct negotiations to formally end the conflict. Yet the terms of this peace agreement—known to history as the Treaty of Versailles—set in motion the chain of events that would lead to the Great Depression and World War II.

◀ David Lloyd George of Great Britain, Georges Clemenceau of France, and Woodrow Wilson of the United States quarreled over the terms of Germany's surrender. In Keynes's view, their demands promised economic hardship for the defeated Germans that would have negative consequences for the victors as well as the vanquished.

Balance of Payments

◀ Countries need to both import and export to provide for their industrial development and the well-being of their citizens. A country's exports pay for its imports. If there is a difference between a country's exports and imports—and provided that the difference is not too large—the difference can be financed with international borrowing.

◀ The record of a country's foreign transactions is its balance of payments. This is a fundamental accounting that sums up the total outflows and inflows of a country's international transactions.

◀ Under the terms of the Treaty of Versailles, Germany was required to make extremely large reparation payments to Great Britain and France for many years. Germany was also required to transfer ownership of all of its railroad stock and merchant shipping. It was required to give France and Britain large amounts of coal and foodstuffs. These very punitive measures were designed to cripple the German economy and make life extremely difficult for the German people.

◀ The United States had a different agenda after World War I. The United States had loaned considerable sums of money to Britain and France to help them pay for war materials. At the end of the war, the United States wanted to be paid back for the loans. This would require Britain and France to run large balance-of-payments surpluses in the postwar years. Their exports would have to exceed imports so that they could accumulate the financial assets necessary to repay the United States.

◀ The difficulty with this situation is that not every country can run a balance-of-payments surplus at the same time. Total world exports must equal total world imports.

◀ If the Germans were going to accumulate the necessary financial assets to meet their obligations, they would have to run large balance-of-payments surpluses for many years. And necessarily, the British and the French would have to run balance-of-payments deficits—at least with Germany.

Many people think that economics is mainly about money, but that's not true. Money is just a means to an end—and a way to measure differing goods, services, and assets.

What economics is really about is people and their lives. In his 1776 book *An Inquiry into the Nature and Causes of the Wealth of Nations*, Adam Smith explained that the real wealth of nations is the goods and services that a nation produces or obtains for its people.

◀ For the German people after World War I to have an obligation to maintain large balance-of-payments surpluses meant that German workers had to produce goods and services that would be sent to other countries to earn money for Germany.

◀ But after World War I, Germany was a damaged country that had suffered human losses—just as the British, French, Belgians, Americans, and others had incurred great losses. Workers of the age received rather low pay and scraped out a meager existence. To reduce this further would have created greater poverty, hunger, disease, and political upheaval.

Tariffs

◀ After the war, Germany attempted to create a democratic government. Kaiser Wilhelm II had abdicated, and the imperial monarchy was replaced with a parliamentary government. But the German government—known as the Weimar Republic, after the city that served as a temporary German capital—could survive only if it provided for its people.

◀ To make matters worse, the British and French governments erected tariff barriers and limits on imports from Germany. This made it impossible for the Germans to fulfill their financial obligations.

◀ When Germany was prevented from earning enough money through exports to pay the reparations, it resorted to the usual tactic of weak governments: It began to print money. The result of this process is inflation. In Germany, it was hyperinflation.

◀ At the same time, the Germans were also unable to import significant amounts of goods and services from France and Great Britain. So, the French and British economies suffered unemployment and business failures as a result.

◀ To make the British economy even worse, the British Treasury decided to go back on the gold standard and set the value of the British pound at four pounds to the U.S. dollar. This was an unrealistically high exchange rate, based on the historical value of the pound in the days before World War I, when the British economy led the world.

◀ It sounds good to have a highly valued, strong currency, but there are some real costs. Those costs are borne by the export industries of an economy. An expensive currency means that your goods and services are expensive to foreigners. And if this is so, then foreigners will buy less from you. Your sales, profits, and employment in export industries will all decline.

◀ The British economy was heavily dependent on exports, so diminished export demand had a significant effect on its entire economy. The British Treasury's decision to set the value of the pound unrealistically high was compounded by the tendency of all countries in the international capitalist system to begin raising tariffs on imported goods.

◀ Tariffs are essentially sales taxes on foreign goods. The idea is to make foreign goods more expensive for domestic consumers and to switch demand from foreign goods to domestic goods. This is thought to aid domestic businesses, increasing the demand for domestic products and thus the capacity to increase employment in those protected industries.

◀ But once one country raises tariffs on foreign goods, other countries retaliate by imposing tariffs of their own. Thus begins a downward spiral of international trade and macroeconomic activity.

Economic Trouble in Europe

◀ During the 1930s, tariffs were at their highest levels in history, and international trade was at its lowest. That is one of the key reasons for a growing recession in Europe at the time.

◀ Britain began to suffer a downturn in economic activity by the mid-1920s. And British employers started demanding wage cuts from their workers to protect sales and profits. In response to these demands, Britain suffered a general strike of all major trade unions in 1926.

◀ Other important economies in Europe, and around the world, began a process of competitive devaluations. A country might gain a trade advantage if its currency becomes cheaper on foreign exchange markets. But this works only if no other countries pursue the same policy. As in the case of tariff policy, once one country attempts to gain a competitive advantage by depreciating its currency, other countries match it, and the world's foreign exchange system breaks down.

◀ Later, during World War II, the United States and several allies created a new multilateral organization—the International Monetary Fund—for the express purpose of providing stability to the world's foreign exchange rate system. Later, the European Union created a single currency, the euro, to accomplish some of the same objectives.

◀ Because Germany was required to run large balance-of-payments surpluses, the Germans began to drive down the value of their currency, the mark, by printing more and more money. This was also Germany's last, and futile, attempt to pay its reparation obligations.

◀ German hyperinflation during the 1920s haunted the national conscious for generations to come and accounts for a near-paranoid fear of inflation among many present-day German bankers, voters, and politicians. The cure for hyperinflation is cancelling the currency and a severe depression to drive down prices and wages.

◀ The depression in Germany at the end of the 1920s and early 1930s fostered the economic and political conditions for the rise of the Nazi Party. The financial turmoil in Germany was also the proximate cause of the start of the European depression in May 1931.

◀ The U.S. stock market had already crashed, but there was not yet a financial breakdown in Europe. That happened when a major bank in Vienna, Creditanstalt, collapsed due to its inability to handle depositors' withdrawals. Creditanstalt declared insolvency and thus set off a chain of events that is common in capitalist systems undergoing financial panic: If there's no lender of last resort—usually a national central bank, with the power to lend—commercial banks all fail in a chain reaction because typically they've lent money and deposited it with each other.

International trade and globalization have many benefits for a capitalist system. Globalization provides wider opportunities for investment and profits and delivers a variety of products and resources at cheaper prices. But globalization also increases the probability that crisis in one economy will be transmitted to all other economies.

Readings

KEYNES, *The Economic Consequences of the Peace.*
SKIDELSKY, *John Maynard Keynes.*

Questions

1 According to the Treaty of Versailles, how would the Germans get the money to pay the British and the French the war reparations they owed?

2 Why were the high tariffs adopted by the British and the French in the 1920s ultimately to prove disastrous for the British, French, and German economies?

Economic Consequences of European Peace

Before World War I, global capitalism centered on Great Britain. London was the financial center of the world. And English was becoming the world language. The breadth of British capitalism stretched from India to China, South America, south and east Africa and the Middle East. The British pound was the principal currency of world trade. And British investments created capital around the world.

In the United States, British financial investments funded the building of railroads, the steel industry, and shipbuilding. These investments generated profits that flowed back to Britain, and financed an increasing standard of living for British citizens, particularly the rich. But the investments also had a down side with major effects on the British economy later in the 20th century. That is, while British capitalists were investing funds throughout the world, they were not investing much in domestic British industries.

This lack of domestic investment was to cause a slowdown in British productivity growth, and competitiveness. It's one of the key reasons the American capitalist system surpassed the British economy later in the 20th century. One of the iron Law of capitalist systems: investment in capital goods drives growth and profits.

Before World War I, the global capitalist system was extremely open. Most travelers did not need passports, visas, customs forms and trade was relatively free. There is no question that this capitalist world predominantly benefited the rich countries, especially those in Western Europe and North America. But it was a world of generally rising standards of living and economic growth. It was also somewhat artificial.

John Maynard Keynes wrote his famous work *The Economic Consequences of the Peace* in 1919, after he resigned from the British delegation to the post-World War I peace talks. Keynes authored the book to protest the British and French government positions in negotiations over the futures of the defeated powers Germany and Austria. Before explaining the reasons for his protest, Keynes provided a clear description of the world capitalist system that existed in the last half of the 19th century and the first decade of the 20th century. Keynes wrote:

> The greater part of the population, it is true, worked hard and lived at a low standard of comfort, yet were, to all appearances, reasonably contented with this lot. But escape was possible, for any man of capacity or character at all exceeding the average, into the middle and upper classes, for whom life offered, at a low cost and with the least trouble, conveniences, comforts and amenities beyond the compass of the richest and most powerful monarchs of other ages. The inhabitant of London could order by telephone, sipping his morning tea in bed, the various products of the whole earth, in such quantity as he might see fit, and reasonably expect their early delivery upon his doorstep; he could at the same moment and by the same means adventure his wealth in the natural resources and new enterprises of any quarter of the world, and share, without exertion or even trouble, in their prospective fruits and advantages; or he could decide to couple the security of his fortunes with the good faith of the townspeople of any substantial municipality in any continent that fancy or information might recommend. He could secure forthwith, if he wished it, cheap and comfortable means of transit to any country or climate without passport or other formality, could dispatch his servant to the neighboring office of a bank for such supply of the precious metals as might seem convenient, and could then proceed abroad to foreign quarters, without knowledge of their religion, language, or customs, bearing coined wealth upon his person, and would consider himself greatly aggrieved and much surprised at the least interference.

Man, that's great writing! It's one of the most famous passages of economic writing describing the world before August 1914. As a graduate student, I discovered Keynes could be read for pleasure as well as insight, and I've never stopped reading his work. I have several things to say about that passage.

First, many people wrongly assume that Keynes was some kind of radical, left-wing socialist with a strong anti-capitalist theory. I think you can see by this passage that Keynes found many things commendable about a capitalist society. And he was generally very positive about the benefits of a relatively free-market version of capitalism. What Keynes wanted, above all, is that the benefits of a capitalist society should be shared as widely as possible.

Keynes wrote this passage in 1919. And some the institutions of the age might seem a bit outdated. Not everyone had a servant, obviously. He used the masculine pronoun. He looked at the world from a Eurocentric or Anglo centric viewpoint. But the key point is still completely relevant.

Before World War I, commerce, investment, and travel were freer than they'd ever been, and freer than they are today. This was true globalization. Even more so than today. At the same time, Keynes realized that this system was based upon unequal distribution of incomes. He emphasizes that this system would never have been as dynamic if income and wealth were equally distributed. Keynes pointed out that the system was somewhat artificial, based on what he called a "double bluff." On the one hand, the working classes had to accept that they would get a small share of the wealth and income that they had helped produce. On the other, the rich would receive a disproportionate share of wealth and income—but they would not spend much of it (even though they could if they wanted).

The rich saved and invested the lion's share of their incomes, and thus contributed to the formation of new capital and industries that fueled the growth of the capitalist system. Keynes understood the costs and benefits of this arrangement. The cost was the lower standard of living of the working classes. The benefit was the growth of the productive capacity of the capitalist system, which would eventually benefit everyone with greater production, and a higher standard of living.

This is another iron Law of economics: economic growth depends on saving. Saving, in economic theory, means not using all of society's resources for current consumer goods and services, but rather also using some resources to produce machinery and factories that will in the future produce more consumer goods and services. All economic systems that experience economic growth and development must find some way to create savings, and channel those savings into productive investment in capital goods.

In the decades before World War I, the bulk of saving was done by the upper classes who limited their current consumption—to invest in domestic and foreign capital accumulation. This capital accumulation before World War I solved the dire predictions of late-18th-century and early-19th-century British economist Thomas Malthus. Malthus had forecast that population would generally grow faster than food production, and mankind was thus doomed to continual threats of famine. It is Malthus whom we can thank for giving economics the label of "the dismal science."

But investment in agriculture, and the cultivation of more land, increased the world food supply before 1914 so that more and more people had adequate supplies of food. And the ease of international trade meant that the grain harvests of the Ukraine, for example, could be exported all over the world.

The American economist Paul Krugman, a winner of the Nobel Prize in Economics for his work in international trade, points out that by 1900 the telegraph was capable of transmitting price information (including prices of stocks, bonds, and agricultural commodities) around the world in a matter of seconds. News of grain harvest changes in the Ukraine could affect wheat prices in Chicago almost instantly. This speed of economic information was the basis of Keynes' description of easy flows of capital and spending around the world.

But a peaceful world of growing capitalism and international trade and travel was halted by the outbreak of the Great War. Although it was mostly a European war, it nevertheless affected the entire world due to the interconnected nature of all economies before the war. International trade and investment ground to a halt, and incomes throughout the world were depressed. This illustrates another facet of modern capitalism: upheavals in one part of the world have repercussions all around it. The real estate and financial crash of 2007 in the United States caused recessions around the world. And this is just one example of that phenomenon.

At the end of World War I, the victorious Allied powers—Great Britain, France, and the United States—assembled in Paris to conduct negotiations to formally end the conflict. Yet the terms of this peace agreement—known to history as the Treaty of Versailles—set in motion the chain of events that would lead to the Great Depression, and World War II. David Lloyd George of Great Britain, Georges Clemenceau of France, and Woodrow Wilson of the United States quarreled over the terms of Germany surrender. Keynes felt that France's Clemenceau was the leading figure of the negotiations, and that he had but one thought: to humble Germany, and make it pay dearly for its war crimes. Clemenceau was not interested in the greater good of the capitalist system, or the health of the world economy.

Britain's Lloyd George, in contrast, was interested in winning the next election, and so did not want to seem soft or conciliatory before a domestic audience to the defeated Germans. Keynes portrayed the American president, Wilson, as a naïve American out of his depth. He portrayed a Wilson who meant well but did not understand the complexity of European politics; and who eventually acquiesced to France's Clemenceau and Britain's Lloyd George. In turn, their demands, Keynes concluded, promised economic hardship for the defeated Germans that would have negative consequences for the victors as well as the vanquished.

Keynes' explanation of the terms of the Treaty of Versailles—and their likely results—provides an excellent analysis of the basics of the modern capitalist system, and its complicated interrelationships. By comparison, this explanation also illustrates that what is generous and thoughtful will often turn out to be most beneficial to the workings of the capitalist system.

To sum up the main conditions of the Versailles Treaty, it's necessary to understand the basics of the British, French, and especially the German economies early in the 20th century. The coal and steel industries were the backbone of their economies. The other important commodities were foodstuffs and other agricultural products.

Countries need to both import and export to provide for their industrial development and the wellbeing of their citizens. A country's exports pay for its imports. If there is a difference between a country's exports and imports—and provided the difference is not too large—the difference can be financed with international borrowing.

The record of a country's foreign transactions is its balance of payments. This is a fundamental accounting that sums up the total outflows and inflows of a country's international transactions. I often explain the basic concepts of the balance of payments to my students by asking them to assume that each student is a separate country. The goods and services they buy are their imports. Whatever work they do for wages and salaries are their exports.

When I was an undergraduate, I worked at a movie theatre as an usher and a ticket taker. I "exported" my services to the General Cinema Corporation. I imported, so to speak, gasoline for my car, textbooks for my college courses, concert tickets for dates, and lots of pizza. If my exports to General Cinema Corporation were greater than my imports, or total spending, then I accumulated financial assets. In my case, this meant my savings account at Southwestern Savings and Loan got a little bigger. If, on the other hand, my imports exceeded my exports, I had to borrow money, or decrease my savings balance at Southwestern Savings.

A country's balance of payments is more complicated than this. It involves millions of transactions, and all types of financial assets. But the basic processes are very similar. To take this personal analogy a bit farther, imagine what would happen if I couldn't work as an usher, and lost my income. Soon I'd have to quit buying gasoline for my car, concert tickets for me and my girlfriend, Lois Anne, and I'd have to stop buying pizzas.

Under the terms of the Versailles Treaty, Germany was required to make extremely large reparation payments to Great Britain and France for many years. Germany was also required to transfer ownership of all of its railroad stock and merchant shipping. It was required to give France and Britain large amounts of coal and foodstuffs. Alsace-Lorraine—and the Saar coal mines—were turned over to France. These were very punitive measures, designed to cripple the German economy, and make life extremely hard for the German people. It's easy to understand the motives for revenge. It's a bit more difficult to understand, and foresee, the negative consequences of such measures.

The United States had a different agenda after World War I. The United States had loaned considerable sums of money to Britain and France to help them pay for war materials. Don't forget that World War I began in August 1914, but the United States didn't enter as a combatant until 1917. At the end of the war, the United States wanted to be paid back for the loans. This would require Britain and France to run large balance-of-payments surpluses in the post-war years. Their exports would have to exceed imports so that they could accumulate the financial assets necessary to repay the United States. The difficulty with this situation is rather obvious.

Not every country can run a balance-of-payments surplus at the same time. Total world exports must equal total world imports. If some country is running a balance-of-payments surplus, then at least one other country must run a balance-of-payments deficit—meaning that its imports must exceed its exports. If the Germans were going to accumulate the necessary financial assets to meet their obligations, they would have to run large balance-of-payments surpluses for many years. And necessarily, the British and the French would have to run balance-of-payments deficits—at least with Germany.

Many people think economics is mainly about money, but that's not true. Money is just a means to an end—and a way to measure differing goods, services, and assets; what economics is really about is people and their lives. Adam Smith explained this in his book, *An Inquiry into the Nature and Causes of the Wealth of Nations* in 1776. Smith explained that the real wealth of nations is the goods and services that a nation produces, or obtains for its people.

So, think about what it meant for the German people after World War I to have an obligation to maintain large balance-of-payments surpluses. It meant that German workers had to produce goods and services that would be sent to other countries to earn money for Germany. But after World War I, Germany was a damaged country that had suffered human losses—just as the British, and French, and Belgians, and Americans, and others had incurred great losses. Workers of the age received rather low pay, and scraped out a meager existence. To reduce this further would have created greater poverty, hunger, disease, and political upheaval.

After the war, Germany attempted to create a democratic government. Kaiser Wilhelm II had abdicated, and the imperial monarchy was replaced with a parliamentary government. But democracy depends on the consent of the governed—to borrow a phrase from Thomas Jefferson. The German government—known as the Weimar Republic, after the city that served as a temporary German capital—could survive only if it provided for its people.

To make matters worse, the British and French governments erected tariff barriers and limits on imports from Germany. This made it impossible for the Germans to fulfill their financial obligations. When Germany was prevented from earning enough money through exports to pay the reparations, it resorted to the usual tactic of weak governments: it began to print money. The result of this process is inflation. In Germany, it was hyperinflation.

At the same time, the Germans were also unable to import significant amounts of goods and service from France and Britain. So, the French and British economies suffered unemployment and business failures, as a result. French farm prices fell. And because agriculture was still a large part of the French economy, the incomes of its people fell. British industry and coal miners also suffered from a lack of German and French demand.

To make the British economy even worse, the British Treasury decided to go back on the gold standard, and set the value of the British pound at four pounds to the U.S. dollar. This was an unrealistically high exchange rate, based on the historical value of the pound in the days before World War I, when the British economy led the world.

It sounds good to have a highly valued, strong currency, but there are some real costs. Those costs are borne by the export industries of an economy. An expensive currency means that your goods and services are expensive to foreigners. If your goods and services are expensive to foreigners, then foreigners will buy less from you. Your sales, profits, and employment in export industries will decline.

The British economy was heavily dependent on exports. So, diminished export demand had a significant effect on its entire economy. The British Treasury's decision to set the value of the pound unrealistically high—and therefore make British goods more expensive to foreign buyers—was compounded by the tendency of all countries in the international capitalist system to begin raising tariffs on imported goods.

Tariffs are essentially sales taxes on foreign goods. The idea is to make foreign goods more expensive for domestic consumers, and to switch demand from foreign goods to domestic goods. This is thought to aid domestic businesses, increasing the demand for domestic products and thus the capacity to increase employment in those protected industries. But like everything else in economics, it's not that simple.

Once one country raises tariffs on foreign goods, other countries retaliate by imposing tariffs of their own. Thus, begins a downward spiral of international trade and macroeconomic activity. During the 1930s, tariffs were at their highest levels in history, and international trade was at its lowest. That is one of the key reasons for the growing recession in Europe, at the time.

Britain began to suffer a downturn in economic activity by the mid-1920s. And British employers started demanding wage cuts from their workers to protect sales and profits. In response to these demands, Britain suffered a general strike of all major trade unions in 1926. Clearly, here were signs of worse things to come.

Other important economies in Europe, and around the world, began a process of competitive devaluations. A country might gain a trade advantage if its currency becomes cheaper on foreign exchange markets. But this works only if no other countries pursue the same policy. As in the case of tariff policy, once one country attempts to gain a competitive advantage by depreciating its currency, other countries match it, and the world's foreign exchange system breaks down.

Later, during World War II, the United States and several allies created a new multilateral organization—the International Monetary Fund—for the express purpose of providing stability to the world's foreign exchange rate system. Later, the European Union created a single currency, the euro, to accomplish some of the same objectives.

Because Germany was required to run a large balance-of-payments surplus—by increasing its exports and its decreasing its imports—the Germans began to drive down the value of their currency, the mark, by printing more and more money. This was also Germany's last, and futile, attempt to pay its reparation obligations. Unable to earn enough British pounds and French francs, it created more of its own currency. German hyperinflation during the 1920s haunted the national conscious for generations to come, and accounts for a near-paranoid fear of inflation among many present-day German bankers, voters, and politicians.

The cure for hyperinflation is cancelling the currency, and a severe depression to drive down prices and wages. The depression in Germany at the end of the 1920s and early 1930s fostered the economic and political conditions for the rise of the Nazi party. The financial turmoil in Germany was also the proximate cause of the start of the European depression in May 1931.

The U.S. stock market had already crashed, but there was not yet a financial breakdown in Europe. That happened when a major bank in Vienna, Creditanstalt Bank, collapsed due to its inability to handle depositors' withdrawals.

Creditanstalt declared insolvency, and thus set off a chain of events that is common in capitalist systems undergoing financial panic. If there's no lender of last resort—usually a national central bank, with the power to lend—commercial banks all fail in a chain reaction because typically they've lent money and deposited it with each other.

Creditanstalt failed for many reasons. It held deposits from German businesses and banks that had been wiped out by hyperinflation and the depression. It held deposits and loans from eastern European businesses and banks that had been customers and suppliers of the German economy.

Now it's true that international trade and globalization have many benefits for a capitalist system. Globalization provides wider opportunities for investment and profits, and delivers a variety of products and resources at cheaper prices. But globalization also increases the probability that crisis in one economy will be transmitted to all other economies.

The process is somewhat like the flu. If there is much contact and travel among the world's citizens, then diseases spread much faster than if they are isolated and kept apart. The Great Depression of the 1930s created new hardships in Europe, and paved the way for the outbreak of World War II— just as John Maynard Keynes had predicted in his book *The Economic Consequences of the Peace.*

Lecture 10

How FDR and Keynes Tried to Save Capitalism

THE GREAT STOCK MARKET CRASH OF 1929 DID NOT cause the Great Depression, but it was one of the events that intensified the contractionary forces of the American economy at the time. The underlying causes of the Great Depression in the United States were created by policies and events earlier in the decade of the 1920s. Some—such as the Treaty of Versailles, which practically guaranteed a depression in Europe—took place outside of the United States. However, most causes of the Great Depression were created in the United States. Some were the result of a largely unregulated macroeconomy, and some resulted from government policies. ◆

Macroeconomic Principles

◀ One hallmark of a market economy is that nobody oversees all economic activity, or the production and consumption decisions of the millions of business firms and consumers. The relatively free decisions of independent people lead the economy in the direction that most consumers and businesses desire, but the uncoordinated actions of individual producers and consumers can also lead to cycles of boom and bust in a capitalist market economy.

◀ In macroeconomics—which refers to the analysis of an entire economy—one process at work is a multiplier, an idea pioneered by John Maynard Keynes. It's based on the simple idea that one person's spending is another person's income. If someone spends less, then someone else is making less. As that individual's income falls, spending falls again—and the process continues. So, a decrease of economic activity in one sector has repercussions across the economy.

◀ Another important idea in macroeconomics is the so-called fallacy of composition: the error of thinking that what is good, or advantageous, for one individual will also be advantageous for a group. If one farmer increases planting to get more income from the higher prices, that works. But if all farmers increase production, it's possible that all farmers will actually get less income—even from a larger crop.

◀ At the beginning of a recession or economic downturn, it's wise for individuals and households to cut back on spending and build up some cash reserves to prepare for the potential bad times. Businesses might cut back on new equipment orders or cancel some expansion plans if they think there will be a decrease in demand for their products.

In the 1920s, farm prices were high, and most farmers enjoyed rising incomes and profits. This encouraged them to plant more crops. Soon, because of the increase in production, there was a glut on the market, and farm prices plunged. That sent many farmers into bankruptcy. As farmers went bankrupt, their suppliers lost income, and some went bankrupt as well. Farm community stores, shops, businesses, and local governments all suffered.

◀ However, if the behavior is widespread, the macroeconomy will suffer. Total spending will fall, total incomes will fall, production will fall, and unemployment will rise. Keynes labeled this phenomenon the paradox of thrift: In periods of recession or depression, saving—or being thrifty—actually causes more economic hardship throughout the macroeconomy. This was especially true during the Great Depression.

◀ During the Depression, the multiplier effects of the paradox of thrift were so strong that the U.S. economy suffered from prolonged and deep deflation—meaning that most prices of goods, services, and wages were decreasing. It might seem like a good thing that prices are falling if you're a consumer, but if you're the producer or seller, declining prices are definitely bad.

◀ And deflation tends to feed on itself. If you're holding onto money, deflation makes your money worth relatively more. If you think that's going to continue, then you keep holding onto your money. And demand for goods, services, and labor will continue to decrease, leading to further declines in prices.

◀ The worst thing about deflation is what it does to those in debt. Farmers and businesspeople often must borrow before they receive the proceeds from the sale of their products. If prices fall, their incomes will fall, and their ability to repay debt decreases. This leads to the bankruptcy of farmers and businesses, and maybe even to the failure of the banks and other financial institutions that were the lenders.

Galbraith's Five Causes of the Great Depression

◀ In his book *The Great Crash, 1929,* John Kenneth Galbraith listed five principle causes of the Great Depression. For each cause, subsequent policies and institutions were developed to prevent, or at least reduce, the probability of another Great Depression.

1 The first cause was a tremendous inequality of income and wealth. An economy of extremely wealthy and extremely poor people is unstable in a capitalist economy. Those who are wealthy tend to become less aware, or fearful, of risk and

tend to have a more unstable spending pattern. In contrast, poor people have a relatively stable spending pattern. As income becomes concentrated in the hands of the rich, it doesn't have to be spent, causing a decrease in total spending. Household debt rises in low-income families, and any economic downturn—and loss of employment—causes numerous personal and business bankruptcies.

2 The second cause was the shaky state of corporate structures. Corporations were largely unregulated in the 1920s and earlier and had little government supervision of their financial information or financial practices. Additionally, a new form of investment vehicle was created, called the investment trust, which was a security created by combining into one basket the shares of stock in many individual corporations. As long as enough people were buying shares of stock, the market kept going up, but as soon as investor sentiment changed and growing numbers of people tried to sell their stock, then there was the potential for a stock market panic—and crash.

3 The third cause was the structure of the banking system. Some banks were sound; they made good loans and did not speculate in risky stocks. But banks lend to one another. When a shaky bank fails, it can't repay the good bank, and the good bank can't satisfy all of its depositors' claims either. Prior to the mid-1930s, there was very little regulation and oversight of U.S. banking activities. Although the Federal Reserve Board had been created by Congress in 1913, it was run by bankers and political appointees who tended to adopt the viewpoint of commercial bankers.

Perhaps surprisingly, Black Tuesday was a result of the Great Depression, not the cause of it.

4 The fourth cause was concentrated outside of the United States. Although the United States had few exports at the time—and therefore the country was not dependent on sales of U.S. products to foreigners—it had lent large sums of money to European governments after World War I to help rebuild Europe. Then, the United States imposed very high duties on imports under the Smoot-Hawley Tariff Act of 1930. European imports to the United States fell, and European companies and banks began to fail. A bank collapse in one European country spread to other countries, and the Great Depression took hold in Europe before it hit the United States.

5 The last major cause of the Great Depression was the profound state of ignorance about macroeconomics.

Keynesian Economics

◀ Prior to the Great Depression, classical economists assumed that a market economy—with flexible prices and competition—would never suffer from a general slump in economic activity. Therefore, the prevailing economic wisdom was to leave the economy alone and wait for it to return to health.

◀ Keynes mocked this assumption, which held that after a sufficient period of time, economies would come back to full employment and maximum production. A recession would be temporary, and suffering would be minimal.

◀ The Great Depression was not temporary—it persisted. And human suffering was immense. The Depression stimulated the analysis of Keynes and a large group of younger economists to rethink the nature of a capitalist system and its tendencies.

Mass unemployment is a breeding ground for political instability and extremist political parties. Many historians blame the rise of Nazi Germany on the effects of the Great Depression.

- Keynesian economics is primarily macroeconomics, and the modern study of macroeconomics began with the theories of Keynes and his collaborators. Keynesians are often referred to as activist economists, who believe in active macroeconomic policies by national governments and central banks.

- In some shape or form, Keynesian fiscal and monetary policies are the dominant economic programs of most major governments and central banks in the world today.

FDR's New Deal

- The reform of American capitalism as a result of the Great Depression began with the first administration of Franklin D. Roosevelt in 1933 and the beginnings of the New Deal.

- The first major policy initiative of the Roosevelt administration was FDR's March 1933 order to temporarily close all banks and decide which were healthy enough to reopen. After this, Roosevelt pressured the Federal Reserve to increase the nation's money supply and to take the United States currency off the gold standard.

◀ Many economists, especially Milton Friedman, blame the Fed for exacerbating the Depression by cutting the money supply and raising interest rates when the economy began to tighten. Until then, conventional wisdom held that inflation was a serious danger if the money supply increased at all and that a capitalist economy needed sound money above all else to function. But cutting the money supply at the beginning of an economic downturn is the exact opposite of the rational policy.

◀ To reverse the process of deflation—that is, falling prices— Roosevelt and his more progressive advisors pushed the Federal Reserve and U.S. Treasury to buy bonds and put more money into circulation.

◀ To improve the banking structure and provide more security for depositors, Congress passed the federal Banking Act of 1933, better known as the Glass-Steagall Act, which separated commercial and investment banking and created the Federal Deposit Insurance Corporation (FDIC).

◀ Galbraith maintains that the creation of the FDIC did the most to restore stability and confidence to the American banking system. There have been no systemic bank runs in the United States since. American depositors know that their deposits—up to an insured limit—are safe.

◀ To remedy the bad corporate structure leading up to the Great Depression, the New Deal created the Securities and Exchange Commission, a federal agency responsible for ensuring that publicly traded corporations produce accurate financial information and that stock markets operate in a fair and orderly manner. Its political structure, consisting of five presidentially appointed commissioners—with the party in power always holding a majority—all but ensures that many major decisions are narrow majorities in danger of being reversed next term.

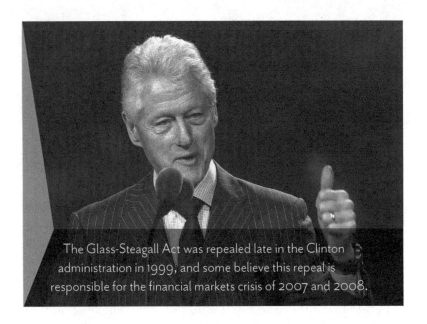

The Glass-Steagall Act was repealed late in the Clinton administration in 1999, and some believe this repeal is responsible for the financial markets crisis of 2007 and 2008.

◀ To get the economy moving again during the Great Depression, expansionary monetary policy was necessary but would not be sufficient. Fiscal policy, including direct government spending, was also necessary to revive the economy.

◀ FDR ordered public works projects at the hands of the Civilian Conservation Corps, which put young people to work in national parks and forests. The federal government also funded the Public Works Administration to reduce unemployment through the construction of highways and public buildings.

◀ The New Deal also created the Social Security Act of 1935 to counter the poverty of the American elderly, as well as widows and orphans. The Social Security Act also contained provisions for federally funded unemployment insurance.

◀ Social Security created what macroeconomists call automatic stabilizers. When the economy goes into a downturn, there is some level of spending that will not be reduced. So, the downturn is cushioned from falling any further.

◀ At the other end of the income spectrum, the federal income tax was also made much more progressive during the New Deal, starting in 1936. A progressive tax is where the tax rate goes up as income levels climb. This contrasts with a flat tax, where the rate remains the same regardless of income.

◀ A progressive tax is viewed as another automatic stabilizer, because the tax rate rises on individuals as incomes are rising and inflation becomes a more likely problem. Taking more income and spending out of the economy as inflation occurs will help reduce the demand pressures that create inflation.

◀ Conversely, when individual incomes are falling, the progressive tax automatically cuts the tax rate that individuals pay. This is exactly what you want to happen in a recession: that people get a larger share of their total income so that they will have more money to spend out of the income they receive.

In 1944, the top marginal tax rate in the United States was set at 94 percent on incomes over 200,000 dollars, which is about 2.5 million dollars today.

◄ The nature of the American capitalist system was profoundly changed by the New Deal. The U.S. capitalist system is much more regulated and managed than it was at the beginning of the 20th century, and no responsible political party, or politician, has argued for a complete repeal of New Deal policies.

In the United States, regardless of the political party in power, it has been the role of the federal government (through fiscal policy) and the Federal Reserve (through monetary policy) to stabilize the American economy and prevent a recurrence of the Great Depression.

Readings

GALBRAITH, *The Great Crash*.
KINDLEBERGER, *Manias, Panics, and Crashes*.
RAUCHWAY, *The Money Makers*.

Questions

1 According to Keynes, when businesses and consumers adopt prudent actions in advance of an expected economic downturn, this proves to be macroeconomically damaging. Why?

2 Both Keynes and Friedman placed major blame for the Great Depression in the United States on the Federal Reserve. What was the Fed doing at the beginning of the Great Depression that merited such condemnation?

Lecture 10 Transcript

How FDR and Keynes Tried
to Save Capitalism

T he great stock market crash of 1929 did not cause the Great Depression. But it was one of the events that intensified the contractionary forces of the American economy at the time. That Black Tuesday was a result—rather than cause—of this dark epoch might surprise you. But many economists of various political persuasions have come to the same conclusion: from the University of Chicago's Milton Friedman to MIT.'s Peter Temin to Harvard University's John Kenneth Galbraith, in his widely read economic history, *The Great Crash*. The underlying causes of the Great Depression in the United States were created by policies and events earlier in the decade of the 1920s. Some took place outside of the United States.

The draconian Treaty of Versailles—which ended World War I—created political conditions and economic circumstances that practically guaranteed a depression in Europe. And any economic downturn in Europe was certain to exert forces dragging down the American economy, as well, because of linkages in the global system.

Bank failures and unemployment in Europe diminished demand for American goods and services, and helped to transmit economic depression across the Atlantic.

However, most causes of the Great Depression were created in the United States. Some were the result of a largely unregulated macro-economy. And some resulted from government policies. One hallmark of a market economy is that nobody oversees all economic activity, or the production and consumption decisions of the millions of business firms and consumers. This is both blessing and a curse. It produces booms and busts. It's a blessing in the sense that the relatively free decisions of independent people lead the economy in the direction that most consumers and businesses desire. This is Adam Smith's "invisible hand" operating to produce efficiency, satisfaction, and economic growth. But the uncoordinated actions of individual producers and consumers can also lead to cycles of boom and bust in a capitalist market economy.

In the 1920s, for example, farm prices were high, and most farmers enjoyed rising incomes and profits. This encouraged them to plant more crops. Soon, because of the increase in production, there was a glut on the market, and farm prices plunged. That sent many farmers into bankruptcy. As farmers went bankrupt, their suppliers lost income, and some went bankrupt as well. Farm community stores, shops, businesses, and local governments all suffered.

One of the most important American novels, *The Grapes of Wrath* by John Steinbeck, movingly illustrates the plight of farmers suffering in the Dust Bowl of Oklahoma. The Dust Bowl was the unintentional result of farmers planting too much to take advantage of temporary higher prices, just before the Great Depression of the 1930s. Farmers in Oklahoma and Kansas plowed up grassland and forests to increase crop production. But plants and trees that held water and soil were depleted, creating the conditions for winds to sweep away topsoil, and blacken the skies.

This illustrates a couple of key principles at work in macroeconomics. Macroeconomics refers to the analysis of an entire economy, as opposed to microeconomics, which analyzes the behavior of individual consumers, businesses and markets. In macroeconomics, one process at work is something called a multiplier. The idea was pioneered by John Maynard Keynes. It's based on the simple idea that one person's spending is another person's income. If someone spends less, then someone else is making less. His or her income is cut. As that individual's income falls, spending falls again. And the process goes on and on. So, a decrease of economic activity in one sector has repercussions across the economy.

Another important idea in macroeconomics is the so-called fallacy of composition. This fallacy—or mistake in logical reasoning—is the error of thinking that what is good, or advantageous, for one individual will also be advantageous for a group. In my university classes, my first example is where a student attends a concert and stands up to get a better view of the band. If only one student person up, she will get a better view. But if everyone stands up, no one will get a better view. If one farmer increases planting to get more income from the higher prices, that works. But if all farmers increase production, it's possible that all farmers will actually get less income—even from a larger crop.

At the beginning of a recession or economic downturn, it's wise for individuals and households to cut back on spending, and build up some cash reserves to prepare for the potential bad times ahead. Businesses might cut back on new equipment orders, or cancel some expansion plans, if they think there will be a decrease in demand for their products. However, if the behavior is widespread, the macroeconomy will suffer. Total spending will fall, total incomes will fall, production will fall, and unemployment will rise. Keynes labeled this phenomenon "the paradox of thrift."

In periods of recession or depression, saving—or being thrifty—actually causes more economic hardship throughout the macroeconomy. This was especially true during the Great Depression. During the Depression, the multiplier effects of the paradox of thrift were so strong that the U.S. economy suffered from prolonged and deep deflation. Deflation means that most prices of goods and services and wages are going down. It might seem like a good thing that prices are falling, if you're a consumer. But if you're the producer or seller, declining prices are definitely bad.

And deflation tends to feed on itself. If you're holding onto money, deflation makes your money worth relatively more. If you think that's going to continue, then you keep holding onto your money. And demand for goods, and services, and labor will continue to decrease, leading to further declines in prices.

The worst thing about deflation is what it does to those in debt. Farmers and businesspeople often must borrow before they receive the proceeds from the sale of their products. If prices fall, their incomes will fall, and their ability to repay debt decreases. This leads to the bankruptcy of farmers and businesses, and maybe even to the failure of the banks and other financial institutions that were the lenders.

In his book *The Great Crash*, John Kenneth Galbraith listed five principle causes of the Depression. For each of cause, subsequent policies and institutions were developed to prevent, or at least reduce, the probability of another Great Depression. The first cause Galbraith identified was a tremendous inequality of income and wealth. An economy of extremely wealthy and extremely poor people is unstable in a capitalist economy. Those who are wealthy tend to become less aware, or fearful, of risk. Having a few risky investments isn't too dangerous if you have a lot of other wealth. In the jargon of financial economics, high-income individuals have a higher capacity, and tolerance, for risk. In other words, if you've got a lot of dough, losing a little doesn't hurt that much.

Also, rich people tend to have a more unstable spending patterns. When you have a lot of money, you don't need to buy another house if you already have three. And you don't need to buy more shoes if you already have 50 pairs in your closet. But poor people have a relatively stable spending pattern. They almost always spend 100 percent of their income—or even slightly more. So, as income becomes concentrated in the hands of the rich, it doesn't have to be spent. Take a dollar from a poor guy—who would have spent it all—and give to a rich guy who doesn't need to spend any of it, and you will decrease total spending.

On the other end, poor people might not have enough income to buy all the necessities of life. They might need to borrow to support themselves and their families. Household debt will rise in low-income families, and any economic downturn—and loss of employment—will cause numerous personal and business bankruptcies. It's a fairly universal truth that, in purely economic terms, income and wealth inequality produces much less stable market economies.

The second cause of the Great Depression, according to Galbraith, was the shaky state of corporate structures. Corporations were largely unregulated in the 1920s and earlier, and had little government supervision of their financial information or financial practices. Additionally, a new form of investment vehicle was created, called the investment trust. This was a security created by combining into one basket the shares of stock in many individual corporations. As we better understand today, bundling sound and unsound assets tends to create another unsound financial asset. This isn't always the case. You might build a portfolio of high-risk and low-risk assets, to blend your overall market exposure to upturns and downsides. But during the financial markets crisis last decade, the combination of thousands of mortgage securities into mortgage pools—

and the combination of multiple mortgage pools into even bigger securities known as collateralized debt obligations—underscored the potentially bad outcome of bundling sound and unsound assets.

During the 1920s, as long as enough people were buying shares of stock, there was no problem. The market kept going up. But as soon as investor sentiment changed, and growing numbers of people tried to sell their stock, then you got the potential for a stock market panic—and crash. During the run-up to the Great Depression, a lot of stocks were bought with borrowed money. Banks lent money to individuals for this purpose. And the banks were using their depositors' money to fund these loans, and purchase more stocks. So, the stock market crash of 1929 not only bankrupted lots of individual investors, it also led to the failure of many banks. And this leads us to the third cause of the Great Depression that Galbraith identified: the structure of the banking system itself.

Some banks were sound, and made good loans, and did not speculate in risky stocks. But banks lend to one another. When a shaky bank fails, it can't repay the good bank; and the good bank can't satisfy all of its depositors' claims either. We're getting very close to the idea of federal deposit insurance, which came into effect in the United States in 1933. That's one of the policy outcomes of the Great Depression I mentioned at the outset of this lecture. So, banks are financial intermediaries. They take customer deposits, make loans, and borrow and lend to one another, as well. They depend on the orderly flow of funds throughout the financial system. When this flow is disrupted, all banks suffer.

Prior to the mid-1930s, there was very little regulation and oversight of U.S. banking activities. Although the Federal Reserve Board had been created by Congress in 1913, it was run by bankers and political appointees who tended to adopt the viewpoint of commercial bankers. This would change with Franklin Delano Roosevelt's New Deal, but not in time to prevent the massive bank failures of the early 1930s.

Galbraith's fourth cause of the Great Depression was concentrated outside of the United States. Although the United States had few exports, at the time—and therefore the country was not dependent on sales of U.S. products to foreigners—it had lent large sums of money to European governments after World War I, to help rebuild Europe. Britain, France, and Germany all struggled at different stages during the 1920s. Then, the United States imposed very high duties on imports under the Smoot-Hawley Tariff Act of June 1930. Smoot-Hawley raised tariffs to about 50 percent on foreign goods coming into the United States. So, European imports to the U.S. fell, and European companies—and European banks— began to fail.

When I take student tour groups to Austria these days, we always visit an impressive building near the Shottentor on the Ring in Vienna. The building was the headquarters of the Creditanstalt Bank, which the Rothschild banking family founded in 1855. Creditanstalt placed deposits in German banks, and made loans to German companies. As they suffered, Creditanstalt suffered, too—and it failed in May 1931. A bank collapse in one European country spread to other countries, and the Great Depression took hold in Europe before it hit the United States.

Finally, the last major cause of the Great Depression was the profound state of ignorance about macroeconomics, according to the Galbraith. Galbraith was a brilliant Canadian-born man who earned his Ph.D. in agricultural economics at the University of California, Berkeley. He worked in the U.S. government's Office of Price Administration during World War II, and directed the U.S. Strategic Bombing Survey, at one time. He eventually became an economics professor at Harvard, and advisor to President John F. Kennedy.

Prior to the Great Depression, classical economists assumed that a market economy—with flexible prices and competition—would never suffer from a general slump in economic activity. Therefore, the prevailing economic wisdom was to leave the economy alone, and wait for it to return to health. Keynes mocked this assumption, which held that after a sufficient period of time—termed "the long run"—economies would come back to full employment and maximum production. A recession would be temporary; and suffering would be minimal. In his *Tract on Monetary Reform* in 1923, Keynes said, "This long run is a misleading guide to current affairs. In the long run we are all dead. Economists set themselves to easy, too useless a task if in tempestuous seasons they can only tell us that when the storm is long past the ocean is flat again." The Great Depression was not temporary, it persisted. And human suffering was immense. Mass unemployment is also a breeding ground for political instability and extremist political parties. Many historians blame the rise of Nazi Germany on the effects of the Great Depression.

The Depression stimulated the analysis of John Maynard Keynes and a large group of younger economists to rethink the nature of a capitalist system and its tendencies. Keynesian economics is primarily macroeconomics, and the modern study of macroeconomics began with the theories of John Maynard Keynes and his collaborators.

In the United States, the principle Keynesian theorist was Paul Samuelson of MIT, the first U.S. economist to win the Nobel Prize in economics. His 1948 primer, *Economics*, was reported to be the nation's best-selling textbook for some 30 years. Keynesians are often referred to as "activist" economists who believe in active macroeconomic policies by national governments and central banks. In some shape or form, Keynesian fiscal and monetary policies are the dominant economic programs of most major governments and central banks in the world today.

The reform of American capitalism as a result of the Great Depression began with the first administration of Franklin D. Roosevelt in 1933, and the beginnings of the New Deal. The first major policy initiative of the Roosevelt administration was FDR's March 1933 order to temporarily close all banks, and decide which were healthy enough to reopen. After this, Roosevelt pressured the Federal Reserve to increase the nation's money supply, and to take the United States currency off the gold standard.

Many economists, especially Milton Friedman, blame the Fed for exacerbating the Depression by cutting the money supply and raising interest rates when the economy began to tighten. Until then, conventional wisdom held that inflation was a serious danger if the money supply increased at all, and that a capitalist economy needed sound money above all else to function. But cutting the money supply at the beginning of an economic downturn is the equivalent of bleeding a patient who is sick. It's the exact opposite of the rational policy.

President Roosevelt was responding to the concerns of Midwestern farmers who needed higher prices to stay in business, avoid bankruptcy, and repay their loans. For this reason, too, he felt, the money supply could not be tied to something as arbitrary as the supply of gold. In Roosevelt's words: "The American people should control their money. Their money should not control them." I think it's one of the most brilliant descriptions of the nature of monetary policy ever spoken.

Monetary policy is a tool for the improvement of economic conditions and the welfare of people. It's not an end in itself. To reverse the process of deflation—that is falling prices—Roosevelt and his more progressive advisors pushed the Federal Reserve and U.S. Treasury to buy bonds, and put more money into circulation. This might stoke inflation. But, as one of Roosevelt's key economic advisors put it: "Inflation would lose bonds, deflation would lose homes and lives."

To improve the banking structure, and provide more security for depositors, Congress passed the federal Banking Act of 1933, better known as the Glass-Steagall Act. It separated commercial and investment banking, and created the Federal Deposit Insurance Corporation. Professor Galbraith maintains that the creation of the FDIC did the most to restore stability and confidence to the American banking system. There have been no systemic bank runs in the United States since. American depositors know that their deposits—up to an insured limit—are safe. So, they need not fear keeping their money in a bank rather than under a mattress.

To actually see a bank run in the United States these days, you'd have to watch a movie like *It's a Wonderful Life*; or, in Britain, *Mary Poppins*. When I was working my way through college, I had a job as an usher in a movie theater. We had *Mary Poppins* for 10 weeks, and I saw the movie about 70 times. I watched the children, Jane and Michael, visit their father at the bank where he worked, and create a panic—a bank run—when their father doesn't let them take some of their money out to buy food to feed the pigeons. They scream, "Give it back! Gimmeback my money!" Thinking the institution is alarmingly short on cash, all the other customers run to withdraw their funds. This causes the bank to collapse, and their father to lose his job.

Returning now to Washington and Congress: to remedy the bad corporate structure leading up to the Great Depression, the New Deal created the Securities and Exchange Commission, a federal agency responsible for ensuring that publicly traded corporations produce accurate financial information, and that stock markets operate in a fair and orderly manner. I should add that the Glass-Steagall Act was repealed late in the Clinton administration in 1999, and some believe this repeal is responsible for the financial markets crisis of 2007 and 2008. It's also safe to say that someone is complaining about the Securities and Exchange Commission every day of the year. Its political structure, consisting of five presidentially appointed commissioners—with the party in power always holding a majority—all but ensures that many major decisions are narrow majorities, in danger of being reversed next term.

Now, to get the economy moving again during the Great Depression, expansionary monetary policy was necessary but would not be sufficient. Keynes likened it to trying to get fat by buying a larger belt. Fiscal policy, including direct government spending, was also necessary to revive the economy. So, FDR ordered up public works projects at the hands of the Civilian Conservation Corps, which put young people to work in national parks and forests. The income they earned helped to sustain their families, and the businesses their families patronized.

Oklahoma—as John Steinbeck portrayed in *The Grapes of Wrath*— was particularly hard hit by the Depression, and it was one of the key recipients of New Deal spending. One such initiative was the Public Works Administration, or PWA, which the federal government funded to reduce unemployment through the construction of highways and public buildings. All of the sidewalks along Adams Hall—the home of the economics department at the University of Oklahoma, where I got my Ph.D.—were built by the Public Works Administration. Each day I walked to class, I was supported by the good folks of the PWA.

The New Deal also created the Social Security Act of 1935 to counter the poverty of the American elderly, as well as widows and orphans. This taxpayer-funded safety net put income into the hands of older Americans, who were pretty certain to spend it. Not only did this help the needy, but, through the multiplier process, it also helped the businesses they frequented, and the people who owned and worked in those businesses.

The Social Security Act also contained provisions for federally funded unemployment insurance. One problem with the Social Security Act is that it excluded agricultural workers and domestic workers. This was at the insistence of some Southern senators who wanted to exclude African-Americans from the benefits of the Social Security system.

Nevertheless, Social Security created what macroeconomists call "automatic stabilizers." When the economy goes into a downturn, there is some level of spending that will not be reduced. So, the downturn is cushioned from falling any further.

At the other end of the income spectrum, the federal income tax was also made much more progressive during the New Deal, starting in 1936. A progressive tax is where the tax rate goes up as income levels climb. This contrasts with a flat tax, where the rate remains the same regardless of income. In 1944 the top marginal tax rate in the U.S. was set at 94 percent on incomes over $200,000, which is about $2.5 million in today's income. So, when you hear people complaining about the high current top marginal rate today of 39.6 percent, some historical perspective might reduce their complaining. The state where I live, Illinois, has a flat rate income tax. It's 3.5 percent for me—and 3.5 percent for Michael Jordan.

A progressive tax is viewed as another automatic stabilizer, because the tax rate rises on individuals as their incomes are rising and inflation becomes more of a likely problem. Taking more income and spending out of the economy as inflation occurs will help to reduce the demand pressures that create inflation. Conversely, when individual incomes are falling, the progressive tax automatically cuts the tax rate that individuals pay. I tell my students that one good thing about living through a recession with a progressive income tax is you get an automatic tax reduction. This is exactly what you want to happen in a recession. You want people to get a larger share of their income so they will have more money to spend out of the income they receive.

The experience of World War II demonstrated that significant increases in government spending could bring a capitalist economy out of a depression very quickly. In my macroeconomics classes, I now refer to World War II as "the mother of all stimulus packages." In the United States, regardless of the political party in power, it has been the role of the federal government (through fiscal policy) and the Federal Reserve (through monetary policy) to stabilize the American economy, and prevent a recurrence of the Great Depression.

The nature of the American capitalist system was profoundly changed by the New Deal. We still have arguments about the size of government, and the proper pace of monetary expansion or contraction. But the U.S. capitalist system is much more regulated and managed than it was at the beginning of the 20th century. And no responsible political party, or politician, has argued for a complete repeal of New Deal policies—or a return to the America of the late 1920s.

Lecture 11

Social Democracy in Europe

S OCIAL DEMOCRATS BELIEVED THAT CAPITALISM could be reformed and made to work for the benefit of all members of society and that such improvements could be achieved through democratic elections and reform. Social democrats in all European countries believed that some form of planning, or state management, was essential to reform and sustain the capitalist system. But all European countries that adopted social democratic policies and developed social democratic parties implemented reforms and planning in different ways, so a discussion of European social democracy is not a description of one model of society but an exercise in comparative economic policies and institutions. ◆

Many prominent leaders of the early social democracy movement in Germany were members of the Catholic Church's Social Union movement, which emphasized the dignity of workers and their families. It supported the interests of workers being collectively represented by organized trade unions.

In the same way, progressive members of the Anglican Church in Great Britain were among the early reformers of industrial capitalism, and they shared many aims with the German social democrats.

Reforming Capitalism

◀ Some historians distinguish between ethical motives for reforming capitalism and prudential motives. Ethical motives include the belief that allowing poverty and unemployment to exist in society is immoral and contrary to Christian values of charity and love of humankind.

- Prudential motives, by comparison, are based on the idea that poverty and unemployment lead to social upheaval and class violence. Therefore, to save capitalism from violent opposition, the prudential reformer believes that it's necessary to assure some basic level of well-being for even the lowest members of society.

- Capitalist development created certain human problems in all capitalist economies. Industrial capitalism in the late 19th century led to the explosive growth of cities and large factory production. This growth and industry led to increases in production never seen in human history.

- Urban growth created by capitalism brought with it problems of pollution, crowding, crime, poverty, and disease. These problems also created ethical and moral dilemmas.

The Beginnings of Social Democracy

- The beginnings of social democracy and reform movements started with highly educated, upper-class members of Victorian society. One such person was William Beveridge, who became a member of a group of intellectual reformers that also included Sidney and Beatrice Webb, founders of the Fabian Society—a group of democratic socialist thinkers.

- The Webbs provided some of the ideas that inspired the formation in 1900 of a group known as the Labour Representation Committee. In 1906, it became the British Labour Party.

- Much later, Beveridge would author a major post–World War II report that brought substantial changes to the British capitalist system. The Beveridge Report was the blueprint for the creation of the modern British social welfare state. It called for the creation of, among other things, a national health system funded and operated by the British government.

◀ But even decades before the Beveridge Report, the Webbs and their fellow democratic socialists advocated a national insurance program that would provide pensions for older people and unemployment insurance for workers who lost their jobs. They were among the first to argue for a system of national health care—provided by the state—for all members of British society.

◀ The German social Catholics would also support a social welfare state that included government-funded health care for all families as well as support for labor unions that included all workers.

◀ The German trade union movement included not only industrial workers, but also public employees, workers in service industries, and farmers. This reflected the social Catholic value of solidarity and care for all members of society, regardless of their economic status or wealth.

Public versus Private Goods

◀ One frequent criticism of capitalist economies is that capitalism produces an excess of private goods and a shortage of public goods. Many controversies in comparative economic systems involve the definition of just what exactly is a public good and a private good and whether it is necessary for governments to produce public goods.

◀ The American economist Paul Samuelson gave the clearest definitions and distinctions between private goods and public goods. He said that private goods can be characterized as rivalrous and excludable. In this context, rivalrous refers to the idea that if someone consumes any of the good, there is less for you. A pizza is rivalrous. Excludable means that you can be prevented from consuming the good. If you don't have any money, you can't buy a pizza.

◄ Public goods are nonrivalrous and nonexcludable. One of the most famous examples economists use is a lighthouse on a rocky point in the ocean. If you're in your ship and you see a lighthouse, that doesn't mean that someone else can't see the lighthouse. Your use of the lighthouse doesn't diminish another person's ability to benefit from it. And nobody can be excluded from the benefits of the lighthouse even if they didn't pay anything to get it built.

◄ One of the problems with public goods is called the free rider problem. This problem is why public television must have so many pledge drives. Once it broadcasts, anyone can receive and enjoy the same show. Alternatively, we "pay" for most commercial television by having to put up with all the inane and intrusive commercials.

◄ Television is a public good in the Paul Samuelson sense. Other important public goods are clean air, clean water, public health research, and programs to eliminate communicable diseases.

◄ The questions of what public goods should be produced, how much should be produced, and how they should be paid for were important questions for early proponents of social democracy.

◄ Capitalism proved quite spectacular at producing private goods. But in its early days, capitalism was not so good at producing public goods.

The Rise of Social Democracy

◀ In Britain, the Labour Party began to advocate for the national government to provide public goods early last century. The origins of the National Health Service and municipal water systems are found in the early struggles against communicable diseases, such as cholera and tuberculosis.

◀ The Labour Party won its first parliamentary majority in 1924 on a platform of reforms and public-sector responses to what it portrayed as the more egregious effects of capitalism. And while the Labour Party initially advocated the replacement of capitalism with a socialist economy, it was to be achieved peacefully through the ballot box.

◀ In Germany, the beginnings of social democracy—and the reform of the capitalist system—took place somewhat earlier, under the government of 19th-century chancellor Otto von Bismarck, who created the first system of public health care and unemployment insurance in a capitalist economy. He was responding to pressures from communist, social democratic, and workers' organizations.

Otto von Bismarck was the founder and first chancellor of the German Empire, from 1871 to 1890.

◀ The rise of social democracy in Germany has an echo in the United States, in the rise of the Socialist Party of Wisconsin—especially in the city of Milwaukee, which at one time had a very large German immigrant population. The Socialist Party of Wisconsin was a reforming party, not a revolutionary one. It concentrated on municipal improvements in streets and the water and sewer systems. Socialists in Milwaukee ran successful political campaigns until the end of the 1950s.

◀ The ethical or moral basis for the rise of social democracy comes from Judeo-Christian theology concerning charity and the welfare of fellow humans. In this view, the suffering of humans, whatever its cause, requires us to try to alleviate that suffering. To some religious thinkers, permitting the continuation of suffering among one's fellow human souls could be considered immoral and sinful.

The Social Democratic Party of Germany was founded in 1863, and by 1912, it was the largest party in the German parliament, or Reichstag.

◀ Sometimes that alleviation of suffering can take the form of private charity and individual good works. But in the rapidly developing capitalist system, private acts of charity came to seem insufficient or incapable of dealing with the human consequences of industrial capitalism.

◀ The prudential reasons for social democracy come from fear. Increased numbers of working-class laborers were often underpaid, injured, poorly housed, and poorly fed at the end of the 19th century. This led to the rise of trade unions and labor-based political parties.

◀ These working-class organizations could potentially be violent and revolutionary. Revolutionary communist parties—along with socialist and social democratic parties—all attracted working-class support. Socialist and social democratic parties generally favored nonviolent and electoral means to achieve their goals.

◀ In contrast, communist parties often had no reservations about using violent means to achieve the complete overthrow of the capitalist economic system. If revolutionary communist parties garnered enough support, private property and capitalist profits would be jeopardized. In such an uncertain situation, business confidence, investment, and economic growth would deteriorate.

◀ Some thought it prudent—or moral—to create a system of public unemployment benefits, health care, housing, and pensions to pacify the radicalizing working class. Workers who were upset with their working and living conditions could join or support fascist, as well as socialist or communist, parties.

◀ Even today, one of the fears of unemployment in Europe is that it furthers the growth of fascist parties, such as the National Front in France and the Golden Dawn in Greece.

Unstable Capitalism and Stabilizing Influences

◀ A final reason for social democracy's attempts to reform capitalism is the belief among many economists and political leaders that the capitalist system is inherently unstable. Not only John Maynard Keynes in Britain but also economists in Sweden, Germany, France, and Austria developed theories about the tendency of capitalist economies to go through phases of booms and busts.

◀ It was thought that capitalism was bad for ordinary workers and citizens, as well as those who generally controlled the means of production. Capitalism would generate periodic bouts of unemployment, poverty, hunger, and homelessness.

◀ Modern capitalist enterprise—which is usually large enterprise—requires comprehensive long-run planning. Capitalist managers and their bankers need some reasonable forecast of sales to make rational financial and production plans. If the economy is radically unstable, such planning is impossible.

◀ The capitalists might be against government or public planning, but they could not survive without planning for their own individual enterprises. Even large capitalist enterprises must react to economy-wide, or macroeconomic, conditions.

◀ So, if overall business activity in the economy is diminishing, then individual capitalist enterprise managers must cut back on their production plans and purchases. Such cutbacks on purchases have a ripple effect that tends to exacerbate swings in economic activity.

◀ Somewhere, there must be a stabilizer. And the stabilizer cannot be governed by private-profit considerations. By process of elimination, that leaves only national governments to fulfill the role of stabilizer. You could say that the stabilizer function is a very important public good.

◀ Unemployment insurance and old-age pensions provide another important stabilizing mechanism. When workers lose jobs, they lose income and spending power. This is obviously bad for the workers, but it's also bad for all the merchants, landlords, and financial institutions where these workers were customers. By providing unemployment insurance—which pays a temporary cash benefit—workers retain some spending power and are able to support the businesses that depend on them. Old-age pensions do a similar thing on a more permanent basis.

◀ Central banks are another stabilizing influence on capitalist economies that are created by national governments. In the United States, the Federal Reserve System was created by an act of Congress in 1913 in response to the financial Panic of 1907. The Federal Reserve System didn't function effectively at first and made some mistakes during the Great Depression, but it has functioned well for many decades.

◀ Even so, the reforms and new public programs of the Progressive era, from the 1890s to the 1920s, didn't prevent the Great Depression of the 1930s. These public-spending and pension programs were small at first and not well funded. There was a continuing belief by many politicians and economists in the need to maintain a balanced public budget each year, in good times and bad.

◀ The adoption of a more elastic approach—most significantly in the form of Keynesian deficit-spending policies in times of economic downturns—would have to wait until after World War II. The significantly larger taxes needed to pay for these massive public-spending programs would also not come about until World War II.

◀ Progressive income taxes would provide the national income for governments to undertake historically unprecedented levels of public spending to support public works, unemployment insurance, public health policies, and old-age pensions.

Early social democrats would be astounded— and probably pleased— that many of the reforms and programs they advocated in the late 19th and early 20th centuries are widely in place today.

But all such benefits have a cost. The generous social programs in Europe mean that Europeans pay the highest tax rates in the world.

Readings

BARZINI, *The Europeans.*
CRAIG, *The Germans.*

Questions

1 The social democracy movements in both Britain and Germany had significant religious roots. What religious values inspired these movements?

2 What economists call public goods often have to be paid for with mandatory taxes on all citizens. Why is this government intervention in a market economy sometimes necessary?

Social Democracy in Europe

M any prominent leaders of the early social democracy movement in Germany were members of the Catholic Church's social union movement. This movement emphasized the dignity of workers and their families. In political terms, it supported the interests of workers being collectively represented by organized trade unions. If you believe in strong, large, and healthy families—a very Catholic belief to which I can attest as one of 18 grandchildren of German-Irish grandparents—then you might support generous public funding for such support. And support for families—that is, state aid for mothers and children—is something the Germans call *Muttergeld* and *Kindergeld*.

Of course, taxes had to be collected to pay for the expansion of this support into today's generous and substantial social safety net. And the burden on the state became very large in times of economic crises, recessions and depressions. Many leaders of the church's social union movement would eventually become the leaders of the German Social Democratic Party.

In the same way, progressive members of the Anglican Church in Great Britain were among the early reformers of industrial capitalism. And they shared many aims with the German Social Democrats. Social democrats believed that capitalism could be reformed, and made to work for the benefit of all members of society. And they believed that such improvements could be achieved through democratic elections, and reform. By comparison, revolutionary socialists believed that capitalism was inherently unjust and corrupt, and that in a communist society, capitalism should be totally replaced. The communists also believed that violent revolution might be necessary to abolish the capitalist system.

Social democrats in all European countries believed that some form of planning, or state management, was essential to reform and sustain the capitalist system. But all European countries that adopted social-democratic policies—and that developed social-democratic parties—implemented reforms and planning in different ways. There was not one blueprint for how to reform, manage, and plan a capitalist economy.

So, a discussion of European social democracy is not a description of one model of society but an exercise in comparative economic policies and institutions.

With that said, some historians distinguish between ethical motives for reforming capitalism, and prudential motives. I agree there are two types of arguments for reforming capitalism. Ethical motives include the belief that allowing poverty and unemployment to exist in society is immoral; and contrary to Christian values of charity and love of mankind. Prudential motives, by comparison, are based on the idea that poverty and unemployment lead to social upheaval and class violence. Therefore, to save capitalism from violent opposition, the prudential reformer believes it's necessary to assure some basic level of wellbeing for even the lowest members of society.

Capitalist development created certain human problems in all capitalist economies. Industrial capitalism in the late 19th century led to the explosive growth of cities, and large factory production. This growth and industry led to increases in production never seen in human history. Urban growth created by capitalism brought with it problems of pollution, crowding, crime, poverty and disease. These problems also created ethical and moral dilemmas. Just living in a big city would assault you with the stench and sights of urban squalor.

But even Karl Marx, the most-famous communist revolutionary thinker, had some positive things to say about the creations of the new capitalist economy. One of my favorite of Marx's quotes comes from *The Communist Manifesto*. In it, Marx praises the new capitalist class—the bourgeoisie— for the creation of big cities. He says: "The bourgeoisie, by the rapid improvement of all instruments of production ... has subjected the country to the rule of the towns. It has created enormous cities, has greatly increased the urban population as compared with the rural, and has thus rescued a considerable part of the population from the idiocy of rural life."

When I was in graduate school at the University of Oklahoma in Norman, Oklahoma, I would drive home to Houston at Christmas, spring break, and summer holidays. And as I drove through rural Oklahoma and Texas, Marx's words would become dramatically visible to me. Marx was a big city boy who lived most of his adult life in London.

The beginnings of social democracy and reform movements started with highly educated, upper-class members of Victorian society. One such person was William Beveridge. Born in 1879, Beveridge was the son of a British judge in imperial India. He became a member of a group of intellectual reformers that also included Sidney and Beatrice Webb, who were founders of the Fabian Society—a group of democratic socialist thinkers. The Webbs provided some of the ideas that inspired the formation in 1900 of a group known as the Labour Representation Committee. In 1906, it became the British Labour Party.

Much later, Beveridge himself would author a major post-World War II report that brought substantial changes to the British capitalist system. The Beveridge Report was the blueprint for the creation of the modern British social welfare state. This report called for the creation of, among other things, a national health system funded and operated by the British government. But even decades before the Beveridge Report, the Webbs and their fellow democratic socialists advocated a national insurance program that would provide pensions for older people, and unemployment insurance for workers who lost their jobs. They were among the first to argue for a system of national health care—provided by the state—for all members of British society.

The German Social Catholics would also support a social-welfare state that included government funded health care for all families, as well as support for labor unions that included all workers. The German trade union movement included not only industrial workers, but also public employees, workers in service industries, and farmers. This reflected the social Catholic value of solidarity and care for all members of society, regardless of their economic status or wealth.

One frequent criticism of capitalist economies is that capitalism produces an excess of private goods, and a shortage of public goods. Many controversies in comparative economic systems involve the definition of just what exactly is a public good and a private good, and whether it is necessary for governments to produce public goods.

Some explanations are in order here. The American economist Paul Samuelson gave the clearest definitions—and distinctions between—private goods and public goods. Samuelson said private goods can be characterized as "rivalrous" and "excludable." These are somewhat awkward terms. And economists are famous for creating awkward terms! But in this context, rivalrous refers to goods that—if I consume any of it—there is less for you. A cup of coffee or a pizza is rivalrous. The more I drink of the coffee, the less there is for you. The more slices of pizza I eat, the fewer slices are left for you. Excludable means you can be prevented from consuming the good.

If you don't have any money, you can't buy a cup of coffee or the pizza. If you don't buy a ticket, I won't let you into the movie theater.

Public goods are different. They are non-rivalrous and non-excludable. One of the most famous examples economists use is a lighthouse on a rocky point in the ocean. If I'm in my ship, and I see a lighthouse, that doesn't mean you can't see the lighthouse. My use of the lighthouse doesn't diminish your ability to benefit from it. And no-one can be excluded from the benefits of the lighthouse even if they didn't pay anything to get it built.

Another example of a public good is the running path on the Chicago lakeshore in winter. Chicago has an 18-mile running path along Lake Michigan, starting up north at the Foster Avenue beach and going all the way down south near Jackson Park. I love to run in the winter, if the temperature is at or just above 20 degrees Fahrenheit. Although I'm a Texas boy by birth, I hate being outside in the heat. But a sunny day with snow on the ground is great for running along the lake. But running in deep snow ain't fun, as we would say in Texas. So, the Chicago Park District plows the snow off the path, and creates a pretty nice running surface. Now, once the path is plowed, it's plowed for everybody. If I really wanted the path plowed—and there was no park district to plow it—I could pay someone to clear the path. But everybody could use it then, even though they didn't pay for it.

Here we see one of the problems with public goods. It's called the "free-rider problem." The free-rider problem is why public television must have so many pledge drives. Once it broadcasts, anyone can receive and enjoy the same show. Alternatively, we "pay" for most commercial TV by having to put up with all the inane and intrusive commercials. Television is a public good in the Paul Samuelson sense.

Some other important public goods are clean air, clean water, public health research, and programs to eliminate communicable diseases. The questions of what public goods should be produced, how much should be produced—and how they should be paid for—were important questions for early proponents of social democracy.

For instance, in cities with a booming factory economy, how should the problems of dirty air, polluted water, housing shortages, poverty, and disease be handled? To alleviate some of these problems, public goods had to be produced. Capitalism proved quite spectacular at producing private goods. But in its early days, capitalism was not so good at producing public goods.

Much later, when I was growing up in Bellaire, Texas, several of my classmate were stricken with polio. Fortunately, the American medical researchers Jonas Salk and Albert Sabin had, by then, developed vaccines against polio. And both men refused to patent their discoveries, so that the breakthroughs could be made widely available. We all benefited by reducing, and eventually eliminating, the threat of polio in America.

In Britain, the Labour Party began to advocate for the national government to provide public goods early last century. The origins of the National Health Service and municipal water systems are found in the early struggles against communicable diseases, such as cholera and tuberculosis. Cholera, especially, was a creation of polluted water supplies. If you construct a clean water supply, you create a clean water supply for everyone. Water itself might have some of the characteristics of a private good, but a clean water supply is a public good. Creating public hospitals for all persons with tuberculosis provides a much safer health environment for everyone.

The Labour Party won its first parliamentary majority in 1924, on a platform of reforms, and public-sector responses to what it portrayed as the more egregious effects of capitalism. And while the Labour Party initially advocated the replacement of capitalism with a socialist economy, it was to be achieved peacefully through the ballot box.

In Germany, the beginnings of social democracy—and the reform of the capitalist system—took place somewhat earlier, under the government of Otto von Bismarck, a 19th-century chancellor. In a life that spanned almost a century—from 1815 to 1898—Bismarck was influenced by the teachings of the Lutheran church; and, indirectly by new Catholic social thinking inspired by the encyclicals of Pope Leo XIII. Bismarck was the prime minister of Prussia from 1862 to 1873, and he became the founder and first chancellor of the German empire from 1871 to 1890. His government—supported by the Catholic Center Party—was fearful of the rise of communist parties and movements in Germany.

Let's not forget that the founder of revolutionary communism was another German, Karl Marx, and that Marx had significant influence on politics in his native land. Marx also had some impressive followers who would become leaders of revolutionary communist movements in Germany. The most important of these was Rosa Luxemburg.

Luxemburg was not only a political leader of the German Communist Party but also a prominent intellectual and writer. Her major work, *The Accumulation of Capital*, was an analysis of the capitalist system, and a political program for the overthrow of the capitalist system. She was murdered under suspicious circumstances in 1919, during a communist uprising in post-World War I Germany.

Bismarck created the first system of public health care and unemployment insurance in a capitalist economy. He was responding to pressures from communist, social democratic, and workers' organizations. To promote German industrial development, Bismarck funneled significant public funds to universities and research institutions in the sciences. The Social Democratic Party of Germany, or SPD, was founded in 1863. And by 1912, it was the largest party in the German parliament, or Reichstag.

The rise of social democracy in Germany has an echo in the United States, in the rise of a Socialist Party of Wisconsin—especially in the city of Milwaukee, which at one time had a very large German-immigrant population.

Milwaukee elected the first Socialist Party mayor, Emil Seidel, in 1910. The Socialist Party of Wisconsin was a reforming party, not a revolutionary one. It concentrated on municipal improvements in streets, and the water and sewer systems. Socialists in Milwaukee were given the nickname of "sewer socialists," and ran successful political campaigns until the end of the 1950s.

The ethical or moral basis for the rise of social democracy comes from Judeo-Christian theology concerning charity, and the welfare of your fellow-man. In this view, the suffering of humans, whatever its cause, requires us to try to alleviate that suffering. To some religious thinkers, permitting the continuation of suffering among one's fellow human souls could be considered immoral and sinful. Most of the good Jesuit fathers who taught me at Strake Jesuit high school in Houston were adherents to some form of liberation theology, and the social gospel. So, we sons of the Texas middle and upper class were exposed to quite liberal social thinking during President Lyndon Johnson's War on Poverty in the 1960s.

Sometimes, that alleviation of suffering can take the form of private charity and individual good works. But in the rapidly developing capitalist system, private acts of charity came to seem insufficient, or incapable of dealing with the human consequences of industrial capitalism. All religions are, in some sense, social movements; and collections of people to solve common problems. It's not such a large leap to go from religious social organizations to public social organizations to solve problems.

Governments are another form of social organization. In the Jeffersonian tradition, governments are created by people to protect life, liberty, and the pursuit of happiness. Sometimes the protection of life requires public action. It should not be surprising that a social movement, like social democracy, came from religious people who had moral qualms, and who experienced discomfort with the consequences of an unregulated capitalist economic system.

Two sources of social democracy—prudential and macroeconomic— might be the stronger reasons for its development. The prudential reasons for social democracy come from fear. Increased numbers of working-class laborers were often underpaid, injured, ill-housed, and ill fed, at the end of the 19th century. This led to the rise of trade unions, and labor-based political parties. These working-class organizations could be potentially violent and revolutionary.

Revolutionary communist parties—along with socialist and social democratic parties—all attracted working-class support. Socialist and social democratic parties generally favored non-violent, and electoral means to achieve their goals. In contrast, communist parties often had no reservations about using violent means to achieve the complete overthrow of the capitalist economic system. If revolutionary communist parties garnered enough support, private property and capitalist profits would be jeopardized. In such an uncertain situation, business confidence, investment, and economic growth would deteriorate.

In imperial Germany, for example, capitalist wealth and power became quite large. By 1887, Alfred Krupp's industrial enterprise employed more than 20,000 workers.

Some thought it prudent—or moral—to create a system of public unemployment benefits, health care, housing, and pensions to pacify the radicalizing working-class. Workers who were upset with their working and living conditions could join or support fascist, as well as socialist or communist parties. Many historians credit Germany's mass unemployment during the latter part of the 1920s for the rise of Hitler, and the National Socialist German Workers' Party—the Nazis. This name was rather ironic since once Hitler came to power, his policies oppressed the German workers to the benefit of the industrialists and bankers—who had been the major bankrollers of the Nazi party.

Even though communists and fascist parties were often enemies, occasionally they cooperated to challenge the capitalist system. The German Communist Party collaborated with the Nazi party in the Berlin transport strike of 1932—the year before Hitler came to power. This move turned out to be disastrous for the German Communist Party. The disruption caused by the strike was one of the reasons Germans voted for the Nazis, who promised to restore order. Soon after taking office, Hitler moved to crush and eliminate communists and socialists. Dachau—the first concentration camp in Germany—was originally established to hold communist and socialist opponents of the Nazi government.

Even today, one of the fears of unemployment in Europe is that it furthers the growth of fascist parties such as the National Front in France, and the Golden Dawn in Greece.

A final reason for social democracy's attempts to reform capitalism is the belief among many economists and political leaders that the capitalist system is inherently unstable. Not only John Maynard Keynes in Britain but also economists in Sweden, Germany, France, and Austria developed theories about the tendency of capitalist economies to go through phases of booms and busts.

Charles Kindleberger's great study of capitalist instability, *Manias, Panics, and Crashes*, gives a dramatic flavor to the study of economic ups and downs under capitalism. Kindleberger explains that financial panics and crashes are often international. He writes: "Boom and panic in one country seem to induce boom and panic in others, often through purely psychological channels. Just as one huge bubble breeds others in a country, so a host of bubbles in a financial market seems to inspire the production of others in other countries." We saw this international phenomenon in the real estate-inspired financial crash of 2007 and 2008. The real estate bubble in the United States inspired similar bubbles in Ireland, Spain, Iceland, and Greece.

It was thought that capitalism was bad for ordinary workers and citizens, as well as those who generally controlled the means of production. Capitalism would generate periodic bouts of unemployment, poverty, hunger, and homelessness. Modern capitalist enterprise—which is usually large enterprise—requires comprehensive long-run planning. An automobile coming off an assembly line today is the product of planning at least several years in the past. The construction of the factory that produces the automobile requires several years of planning and construction. The engineering, metallurgy, design, and market research are long-run processes.

Capitalist managers and their bankers need some reasonable forecast of sales to make rational financial and production plans. If the economy is radically unstable, such planning is impossible. The capitalists might be against government or public planning, but they could not survive without planning for their own individual enterprises.

Even large capitalist enterprises must react to economy-wide, or macroeconomic, conditions. So, if overall business activity in the economy is diminishing, then individual capitalist enterprise managers must cut back on their production plans and purchases. Such cutbacks on purchases have a ripple effect—something that Keynesian economists characterize as a multiplier effect. This ripple, or multiplier, tends to exacerbate swings in economic activity. Somewhere, there must be a stabilizer. And the stabilizer cannot be governed by private profit considerations. By process of elimination, that leaves only national governments to fulfill the role of stabilizer. You could say that the stabilizer function is a very important public good.

In response to the Great Depression, the Socialist Party government of Vienna created a vast public housing projects in the city's Heiligenstatt district. Public housing projects support the construction industry, and all its suppliers and workers, and do not depend on profit streams to be built, or maintained. As an economist specializing in comparative economic systems, one of my first visits in Vienna was to this public housing complex, where one of the main buildings—the Karl Marx Hof—is a tourist attraction.

Similarly, public projects for water and sewer systems, roads and bridges, schools and hospitals all provide employment and contracting opportunities for private firms. Unemployment insurance and old-age pensions provide another important stabilizing mechanism. When workers lose jobs, they lose income and spending power. This is obviously bad for the workers, but it's also bad for all the merchants, landlords, and financial institutions where these workers were customers.

By providing unemployment insurance—which pays a temporary cash benefit—workers retain some spending power. And they are able to support the businesses that depend on them. Old-age pensions do a similar thing on a more permanent basis. Workers eventually will go back to work, hopefully. But senior citizens probably won't. And seniors might not have much other income. So, a government pension provides them with a permanent source of spending power.

Even the guarantee of a pension is of great benefit. One cause of increased suicides, alcoholism, and drug abuse among older Americans has been the disappearance of many defined-benefit pension plans in America, according to a National Science Foundation paper published by Princeton University economists Anne Case and Angus Deaton.

There's similar economic disruption and unemployment in European countries. But most European countries have generous defined-benefit pension plans, and decreasing morbidity and mortality rates, rather than the increasing rates in the U.S.

Central banks are another stabilizing influence on capitalist economies, created by national governments. In the United States, the Federal Reserve System was created by an act of Congress in 1913. This was in response to the financial Panic of 1907. The Federal Reserve System didn't function effectively at first, and made some mistakes during the Great Depression. But it has functioned well for many decades, including in response to the savings and loan crash of the 1980s, and stock market crashes in 1987; the dot-com bust of 2000 and 2001; and the financial markets crisis of 2008 and 2007.

Even so, the reforms and new public programs of the Progressive era from the 1890s to the 1920s didn't prevent the Great Depression of the 1930s. These public spending and pension programs were small at first, and not well-funded. There was a continuing belief by many politicians and economists in the need to maintain a balanced public budget each year, in good times and bad.

The adoption of a more elastic approach—most significantly in the form of Keynesian deficit-spending policies, in times of economic downturns—would have to wait until after World War II. The significantly larger taxes needed to pay for these massive public spending programs would not come about until World War II, as well.

Progressive income taxes—with the taxable rate rising along with taxable income—would provide the national income for governments to undertake historically unprecedented levels of public spending to support public works, unemployment insurance, public health policies, and old-age pensions.

Early social democrats would be astounded—and probably pleased—that many of the reforms and programs they advocated in the late 19th and early 20th centuries are widely in place today. But all such benefits have a cost. The generous social-welfare programs in Europe mean that Europeans pay the highest tax rates in the world. These obligations create controversy—and financial burdens—well into the future.

Lecture 12

Sweden's Mixed Economy Model

S WEDEN IS THE BEST EXAMPLE OF AN ECONOMIC
system in between the extremes of free market
capitalism and government-owned and controlled
socialism. The modern image of Sweden is of an
egalitarian economy with a high standard of living,
a high level of social welfare spending—and a
correspondingly high level of taxes. In this lecture,
you will discover how the Swedish economic system
evolved into the mixed economy it has today. ◆

A History of Equality

◀ One of the enduring values of Swedish society is a national sense
of solidarity and equality. This has deep roots in Swedish history.
Solidarity was created, in part, by the harsh and variable climate
and by the early abolition of feudalism.

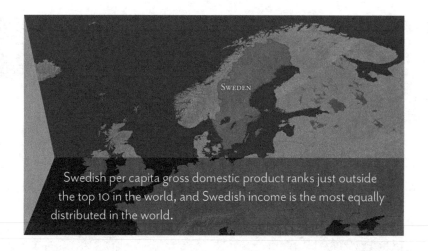

Swedish per capita gross domestic product ranks just outside the top 10 in the world, and Swedish income is the most equally distributed in the world.

◀ Sweden was one of the first European countries to create a society of independent farmers who owned their own land. This created incentives to produce as much as possible. But production was limited by the northern climate and its short growing season. The unfavorable conditions meant that Swedish farmers were compelled to rely on one another and share in the burdens and risks of farming.

◀ One of the primary forms of economic organization that Sweden created, and is still alive today, is the cooperative. Cooperatives share expenses, expertise, risks, and rewards of economic activity. By their very nature, they tend to even out the vagaries of the larger market. This promotes a rather egalitarian outcome in terms of income distribution.

◀ The abolition of feudalism—serfdom and slavery were outlawed in 1335—also eliminated one of the major class divisions in society and limited how unequal income and wealth could become. Countries that have much longer histories of feudalism, such as France and Spain, tend to have much more hierarchical social structures and much more unequal distributions of income.

One of the incorrect stereotypes about Sweden is that it is a socialist system, with predominantly government ownership of the means of production. On the contrary, Sweden is a mostly privately owned economic system with limited direct government ownership of productive enterprises. But the modern Swedish government is heavily involved in the country's economic system.

Trade and Exports

◀ Sweden is a large country geographically but quite small in terms of population. To be economically viable, Sweden has always had to rely on foreign trade for markets for its goods—and for vital imports unavailable domestically.

◀ In the 16th and 17th centuries, Sweden was one of the members of the Hanseatic League, an international organization of trading partners in the North Sea and the Baltic Sea that facilitated trade and provided a secure legal framework for trading enterprises and shippers.

◀ Sweden was primarily an exporter of wood and wood products in the Hanseatic League. Later, in the 19th century—as technology developed—Sweden became an exporter of metallurgical and engineering products.

◀ But the technological improvements to Swedish industry, and the growth of large-scale commercial forestry enterprises, created large factories in major Swedish cities and migration from the countryside by displaced farmers.

◀ The familiar result was excess labor supply in the cities and cycles of unemployment and poverty. Severe poverty in the late 19th century led to the migration of more than a million Swedes to America in search of economic opportunity. The Swedish workers who remained also began to form cooperatives for basic consumer goods and trade unions to bargain for better wages and working conditions.

◀ In World War I, Sweden was a neutral country and benefited from the demand for war goods. This foreign demand gave a boost to Swedish industry for a few years, but the end of the war brought a severe recession to the Swedish economy.

◀ Because of the postwar recession, Swedish workers began to organize and strike for higher wages and more secure working conditions. Swedish industrialists resisted the workers' demands. There were violent confrontations between the workers and the security forces of the industrialists.

◀ This left a deep impression on the Swedish people and a continuing fear of social collapse and anarchy. Ever since, the memory has contributed to relatively mild labor-management relations in contemporary Sweden. There's still conflict between workers and industrialists, but the conflict is carried out mainly in the political sphere.

◀ After Swedish workers organized into industrial trade unions, they created a political party based on the trade union movement—a practice common in other European countries, too. The trade union federation in Sweden is the LO, which stands for *Landsorganisationen,* or national organization. The political party created from this organization is the Swedish Social Democratic Party.

◀ Because Sweden is a rather small economy and modern factories are large enterprises, it was relatively easy to organize Swedish workers. Even in a small economy, factories need to be large to take advantage of economies of scale—the effect of reducing per-unit costs as the scale of output increases—to be internationally competitive.

◀ The Swedish Social Democratic Party won the office of prime minister for the first time in 1920, and—with one brief interruption—has governed Sweden ever since.

◀ Sweden has a parliamentary system with proportional voting, which means that there are many parties in the Swedish political system. There are farmers' parties, small business and professionals' parties, employer-based parties, and green parties. Such a system rewards the largest party, even if it's not a majority party.

◀ In most parliamentary systems, there's rarely a majority party. Typically, coalitions must be formed with two or more parties that can achieve a majority of votes. A government will then be formed, with the largest party choosing the head of government—usually called the prime minister or chancellor.

◀ Sweden has a prime minister, and this person has typically been a member of the Swedish Social Democratic Party. This dominance of the Swedish government by a workers' party makes it easier to understand the major objectives of most Swedish governments. They are the objectives of the workers organized in trade unions.

◀ These objectives are not always in conflict with the interests of Swedish capitalists and business leaders, although they often are. The objectives that are shared between workers and capitalists tend to be concerned with foreign trade and the necessity for Swedish exports to be competitive on the world market. This means that Swedish workers' wage demands can't be too outrageous, or Swedish goods will be too expensive for importing countries.

◀ Swedish goods must also be of high quality and reliability. This means that they must be well made and attractive. Workers, therefore, need to be concerned with the quality of their work and the quality of the products they produce.

◀ Swedish companies that are heavily dependent on exports—and almost all Swedish companies are dependent on exports—must also be very concerned with the quality and marketability of their products.

> A growing economy increases the demand for workers and creates more job security. It also provides a more favorable situation for workers to demand higher wages. Capitalists like economic growth because growth usually increases sales and profits.

Key Fiscal Policies

◀ In the Great Depression of the late 1920s and early 1930s, the Swedish government was one of the first to use active fiscal policy to counteract the effects of the depression. On a limited basis, the Swedish government initiated public works projects and increased transfer payments to pump up demand for Swedish goods and services. They were practicing Keynesian policies before Keynes had developed his theories of how to get a capitalist economy out of a depression.

◀ World War II provided another boost to the Swedish economy. Sweden was a neutral country once more and did not suffer any damage to its domestic economy. And the war once again stimulated the economy. After the war, the Swedish economy faced a problem of declining demand for war goods and the resulting decline in sales and employment. But this time, Swedish firms were able to transform their production to peacetime output.

Because it was a neutral country in both world wars, many people assume that Sweden is pacifist, with no military-industrial complex in its economy. On the contrary, Sweden is a significant producer and exporter of high-technology military hardware.

◀ The best example is the Swedish Aircraft Company, or *Svenska Aeroplan Aktiebolaget* (SAAB). In World War II, SAAB did a booming business in military aircraft. But after the war, demand for its products decreased significantly. So, with its very sophisticated industrial plants and highly skilled engineers and workers, SAAB decided to make cars. For 60 years, SAAB was an important car company, but it has since gone bankrupt.

◀ After World War II, the Social Democratic–led governments initiated several key policies to establish the Swedish economic system as a mixed economy. Because the Swedish Social Democratic Party was founded and supported by the Trade Union Federation, its most important objective was a high rate of employment. So, the government was an active user of traditional Keynesian fiscal and monetary policies to stimulate economic growth and low rates of unemployment.

◀ But to achieve high levels of employment, the Swedish governments went far beyond standard Keynesian demand management. The Swedish government pursued active labor market policies. These policies were designed to stimulate and support employment, especially when private market demand might be diminishing. Labor market polices included providing government subsidies to private employers to retain workers that might have otherwise been let go.

◀ Because Swedish workers and employers were so well organized, a feature of the Swedish labor market was consensus bargaining and comprehensive labor agreements on wages and working conditions—that every worker gets and thinks is fair. This was especially important due to the dependence of the Swedish economy on exports.

◀ One of the primary findings of labor market research in the realm of efficiency wage theory is that workers will work effectively, and well, if they think they're being treated fairly. Swedish workers are paid well, so it's essential that they should also be very productive, if their products are to remain competitive on the world market.

◀ Another key policy tool of all Swedish governments is the guidance of the exchange rate—making sure that the Swedish krona is not too expensive in relation to its trading partners. It might seem good to have a "strong" currency that is highly valued and very expensive, but if you are an exporting country, an expensive currency means expensive products. A high value for the Swedish krona means fewer exports of jet fighters, for example.

◀ For this reason, although Sweden is a member state of the European Union, it has not adopted the euro. Instead, it has kept its own currency to have another lever with which to manage the flows of exports from Swedish industries.

◀ The most controversial aspect of Swedish government policy is the country's extensive welfare state and income redistribution. Swedish citizens receive free health care, free education through university, high levels of unemployment benefits and pensions, and generous family leave for parents of newborns. The Swedish government also redistributes income in a more comprehensive way than any other government in the world.

◀ One cost of Sweden's well-developed social structure is the tax burden on the average Swedish worker. Swedes pay an average of 53 percent of their income in taxes. Sweden ranks 5th in the high-tax category; only Finland, Denmark, France, and Belgium rank ahead of Sweden.

◀ High taxes can legitimately be said to limit freedom. The Swedish government limits the freedom of Swedish citizens to spend their own money.

◀ Many Swedish employers and industrialists complain that the country's high levels of economic security and guaranteed income have diminished the work ethic of the Swedish worker—and are a drag on efforts to increase productivity in the face of globalization and foreign competition.

◀ However, the Swedes have decided democratically to give up some of their individual economic freedom to live in a more egalitarian and economically secure society. Swedish elections are fought over the size and comprehensiveness of their welfare state.

Readings

OXFAM AND DEVELOPMENT FINANCE INTERNATIONAL,
   The Commitment to Reducing Inequality Index.
RYNER, *Capitalist Restructuring, Globalization, and the Third Way.*

Questions

1 What was it about Swedish history and geography that created the strong incentives for cooperative agriculture? Where do you find traces of this in the United States?

2 Does the Swedish government own a lot of the productive enterprises in Sweden? Why do critics refer to the Swedish economy as socialist?

Sweden's Mixed Economy Model

S weden is the best example of an economic system in-between the extremes of free market capitalism and government-owned and controlled socialism. Many scholars have referred to the Swedish economic system as "The Third Way." It's a middle road. The modern image of Sweden is of a modern, egalitarian economy with a high standard of living, a high level of social welfare spending—and a correspondingly high level of taxes.

Swedish per capita GDP is about $55,040, ranking just outside the Top 10 in the world: below Denmark, and just ahead of the United States. And Swedish income is the most equally distributed in the world, according to a measure known as Gini coefficients. A Gini coefficient is a mathematical measure of income inequality that ranges in value from 0 (meaning complete equality) to 100 (meaning complete inequality). Namibia has the world's highest inequality, with a Gini coefficient of 63.9. The value of the Gini coefficient in the United States is 40. By comparison, in Sweden, it's 25.

But how did the Swedish economic system evolve over the years into the modern, mixed economy we see today? One of the enduring values of Swedish society is a national sense of solidarity and equality. This has deep roots in Swedish history. Solidarity was created, in part, by the harsh and variable climate, and by the early abolition of feudalism. Serfdom and slavery were outlawed in 1335.

Sweden was one of the first European countries to create a society of independent farmers who owned their own land. This created incentives to try and produce as much as possible. But production was limited by the northern climate, and its short growing season. These unfavorable conditions meant that Swedish farmers were compelled to rely on one another, and share in the burdens and risks of farming. One of the primary forms of economic organization Sweden created, and which is still alive today, is the cooperative.

Cooperatives exist all over the world, but they are still primarily in agriculture. They share expenses, expertise, risks and rewards of economic activity. By their very nature, they tend to even out the vagaries of the larger market. And this, obviously, promotes a rather egalitarian outcome, in terms of income distribution.

The abolition of feudalism also eliminated one of the major class divisions in society, and limited how unequal income and wealth could become. Countries that have much longer histories of feudalism—let's say France and Spain—tend to have much more hierarchical social structures, and much more unequal distributions of income.

This emphasis on wide dispersion of ownership and limited social classes was one of the brilliant insights of the American founding father Thomas Jefferson—and his idea that democracy would flourish in a system with no rigid social classes. Jefferson also believed that equal access to knowledge and opportunity was the best approach to fostering a democratic society. As we shall see, one of the incorrect stereotypes about Sweden is that it is a socialist system, with predominantly government ownership of the means of production.

On the contrary, Sweden is a mostly privately owned economic system with limited direct government ownership of productive enterprises. But as we shall also see, the modern Swedish government is heavily involved in the country's economic system. Sweden is a large country geographically but quite small in terms of population. Even today, it has a population of less than 10 million. So, to be economically viable, Sweden has always had to rely on foreign trade for markets for its goods—and for vital imports unavailable domestically. In other words, foreign trade has always played a large role in the Swedish economy.

In the 16th and 17th centuries, Sweden was one of the members of the Hanseatic League. The Hanseatic League was an international organization of trading partners in the North Sea and the Baltic Sea. It facilitated trade and provided a secure legal framework for trading enterprises and shippers. Sweden was primarily an exporter of wood and wood products in the Hanseatic League.

Later, in the 19th century—as technology developed—Sweden became an exporter of metallurgical and engineering products. But the technological improvements to Swedish industry, and the growth of large-scale commercial forestry enterprises, created large factories in major Swedish cities. And migration from the countryside by displaced farmers. The familiar result was excess labor supply in the cities, and cycles of unemployment and poverty. Severe poverty in the late 19th century led to the migration of more than a million Swedes to America, in search of economic opportunity.

When I was teaching at my first university in western Wisconsin, I lived in St. Paul, Minnesota, a state settled by Scandinavian immigrants. Every morning when my clock-radio alarm went off, I was awakened to the commercial jingle of the Cenex cooperative, known today as CHS. It's not by coincidence that this cooperative was in Minnesota.

The Swedish workers who remained also began to form cooperatives for basic consumer goods, and they formed trade unions to bargain for better wages and working conditions. In World War I, Sweden was a neutral country, and benefited from the demand for war goods. This foreign demand gave a boost to Swedish industry for a few years. Unfortunately, the end of World War I brought a severe recession to the Swedish economy.

Global connections are crucial to a capitalist economic system. Declining demand from significant trading partners can create severe economic hardship for economies that rely heavily on foreign trade for a major part of their economic activity. Smaller countries are especially vulnerable to foreign-trade repercussions, since they cannot produce a wide enough variety of goods and services to be self-sufficient.

Because of the post-war recession, Swedish workers began to organize and strike for higher wages, and more secure working conditions. Swedish industrialists resisted the workers' demands. There were violent confrontations between the workers and the security forces of the industrialists. This left a deep impression on the Swedish people, and a continuing fear of social collapse and anarchy. Ever since, the memory has contributed to relatively mild labor-management relations in contemporary Sweden. There's still conflict between workers and industrialists, but the conflict is carried out mainly in the political sphere.

After Swedish workers organized into industrial trade unions, they created a political party based on the trade union movement—a practice common in other European countries, too. The Trade Union federation in Sweden is the LO. This stands for the *Landsorganisationen*, or national organization. The political party created from this organization is the Social Democratic Workers Party of Sweden, the SAP.

Because Sweden is a rather small economy, and modern factories are large enterprises, it was relatively easy to organize Swedish workers. Even in a small economy, factories need to be large to take advantage of economies of scale to be internationally competitive. Economies of scale refers to the effect of reducing per-unit costs as the scale of output increases. Henry Ford and his massive Ford assembly line is probably the most recognized early application of economies of scale.

The Social Democratic party of Sweden won the office of prime minister for the first time in 1920, and—with one brief interruption—has governed Sweden ever since. Sweden has a parliamentary system with proportional voting, which means that there are many parties in the Swedish political system. There are farmers' parties, small business and professionals' parties, employer-based parties, and green parties.

Such a system rewards the largest party even if it's not a majority party. In most parliamentary systems, there's rarely a majority party. What usually occurs is that coalitions must be formed with two or more parties that can achieve a majority of votes. A government will then be formed, with the largest party choosing the head of government—usually called the prime minister or chancellor. Sweden has a prime minister. And this person has typically been a member of the Swedish Social Democratic party.

This dominance of the Swedish government by a workers' party makes it easier to understand the major objectives of most Swedish governments. They are the objectives of the workers organized in trade unions. These objectives are not always in conflict with the interests of Swedish capitalists and business leaders, although they often are.

The objectives that are shared between workers and capitalists tend to be concerned with foreign trade, and the necessity for Swedish exports to be competitive on the world market. This means that Swedish workers' wage demands can't be too outrageous, or Swedish goods will be too expensive for importing countries. Swedish goods must also be of high quality and reliability. This means they must be well-made, and attractive. Workers, therefore, need to be concerned with the quality of their work, and the quality of the products they produce. Obviously, Swedish companies that are heavily dependent on exports—and almost all Swedish companies are dependent on exports—must also be very concerned with the quality and marketability of their products.

A growing economy increases the demand for workers, and creates more job security. It also provides a more favorable situation for workers to demand higher wages. Capitalists like economic growth because growth usually increases sales and profits.

In the Great Depression of the late 1920s and early 1930s, the Swedish government was one of the first to use active fiscal policy to counteract the effects of the depression. On a limited basis, the Swedish government initiated public works projects, and increased transfer payments to pump up demand for Swedish goods and services. They were practicing Keynesian policies before Keynes had developed his theories of how to get a capitalist economy out of a recession.

The Second World War provided another boost to the Swedish economy. Sweden was a neutral country once more, and did not suffer any damage to its domestic economy. And the war once again stimulated the economy. After the war, the Swedish economy faced a problem of declining demand for war goods, and the resulting decline in sales and employment. But this time, Swedish firms were able to transform their production to peacetime output.

The best example is the Swedish Aeroplane Stock Company, or *Svenska Aeroplan Aktie Bolaget*. I love saying that. Its initials are S-A-A-B, SAAB. In the Second World War, SAAB did a booming business (pun intended) in military aircraft. But after the war, demand for its products decreased significantly. What to do with very sophisticated industrial plants and highly skilled engineers and workers? SAAB decided to make cars. It asked five of its engineers to come up with a design and production plan for a passenger automobile. And, according to SAAB company history, three of the engineers didn't even have driver's licenses. But design a car they did. It featured an aerodynamic shape and many safety features.

I have some personal experience to share. First, I ran the Stockholm marathon in 1996, after attending an academic conference in Russia. And here's a personal training tip: avoid extensive consumption of vodka, sour cream, and caviar; it's not the best premarathon preparation. But I was impressed with Swedish quality and design. So, my first internationally capable cell phone was an Ericsson "World Phone." Ericsson is a major communications technology firm that doesn't make cell phones anymore. It concentrates on building the infrastructure for mobile phone systems.

My furniture also came mainly from IKEA, a globally ubiquitous brand of inexpensive, well-designed furniture founded by a famous Swedish entrepreneur Ingvar Kamprad. The I and K in IKEA come from Ingvar Kamprad's name. The E and A are the first letters in the name of the farm he grew up on, and of his home town.

One of my favorite music groups was the Swedish pop of ABBA. The letters ABBA are also an acronym for the four members of the group. I love to play tennis, and at that time my tennis heroes were Bjorn Borg, Mats Wilander, and Jonas Svensson. You're beginning to get the idea: I liked Swedish products.

Finally, I decided to buy a SAAB. I got it through their European Delivery Program. It came with a trip to Trollhattan, Sweden—their headquarters and main factory location—and a factory tour, after which I picked up my car. At that time, SAAB was part of the American automaker General Motors. And for 60 years, SAAB was an important car company in Sweden, and a leader in automotive safety technology that sold most of its output outside of the country. Unfortunately, since then it has gone bankrupt. Its assets were sold to a Chinese technology firm.

Volvo, the other Swedish car brand, was previously owned by Ford Motor Co. It's now owned by a different Chinese firm, Geely. It still maintains significant production in Gothenburg, Sweden. I sometimes illustrate the narrow gap between rich and poor in Sweden by saying that you can tell a rich Swede from a poor Swede by looking at their cars. Rich Swedes drive new Volvos and poor Swedes drive old Volvos. A bit of an exaggeration, but not too far off the mark.

To finish my SAAB story, the SAAB aircraft firm is still in operation, and is a leading international supplier of small commercial aircraft and military fighter jets. This brings me to another misconception about Sweden. Because it was a neutral country in both world wars, many people assume that Sweden is pacifist, with no military-industrial complex in its economy. On the contrary, Sweden is a significant producer and exporter of high-technology military hardware.

After World War II, the Social Democratic-led governments initiated several key policies to establish the Swedish economic system as a mixed economy. Because the Swedish Social Democratic Party was founded and supported by the Trade Union Federation, its most important objective was a high rate of employment. So, the government was an active user of traditional Keynesian fiscal and monetary policies to stimulate economic growth and low rates of unemployment.

But to achieve high levels of employment, the Swedish governments went far beyond standard Keynesian demand management. The Swedish government pursued active labor market policies. These policies were designed to stimulate and support employment, especially when private market demand might be diminishing. Labor-market polices included providing government subsidies to private employers to retain workers that might have otherwise been let go. Other policies involved subsidies to public enterprises like libraries and parks departments to increase hiring, especially of young people looking for their first job.

One consistent finding of labor-market economists is that among the best ways to get a good job is to already have a job. This might sound simple-minded, but it's based on the idea that having a job teaches certain very specific skill and traits that successful employees have. Things like following a work schedule, completing assigned tasks, how to fill out time cards and work reports, and the management of a regular salary.

So, one of the keys to a successful career is getting a first job—any job—that gives you some labor-market experience. The longer younger people go without a first job, the more likely they will be unemployed or underemployed throughout their adult lives. A first job is the first rung on the employment ladder.

Because Swedish workers and Swedish employers were so well organized, a feature of the Swedish labor market was consensus bargaining, and comprehensive labor agreements on wages and working conditions. This was especially important due to the dependence of the Swedish economy on exports. In unorganized labor markets—with many different contract negotiations—you often have what may be called a "leap frog effect." One group of workers gets a 1 percent raise, another group thinks they can do better and gets a 2 percent raise. A third group, maybe better positioned and better organized, gets a 3 percent raise. And this spiral might go on quite long. For individual workers, this is a good thing. But for export industries, it could lead to price hikes and goods becoming uncompetitive. So, it's in everyone's self-interest to have a comprehensive wage agreement that every worker gets, and thinks is fair.

One of the primary findings of labor-market research under the heading of "efficiency wage theory" is that workers will work effectively, and well, if they think they're being treated fairly. Fairness is a major determinant of productivity. Swedish workers are well paid, so it's essential they should also be very productive, if their products are to remain competitive on the world market.

Another key policy tool of all Swedish governments is the guidance of the exchange rate—making sure that the Swedish krona is not too expensive, in relation to its trading partners. It might seem good to have a "strong" currency that is highly valued and very expensive. But if you are an exporting country, an expensive currency means expensive products. A high value for the Swedish krone means fewer exports of jet fighters, groovy furniture—and hip clothes from H&M. For this reason, although Sweden is a member state of the European Union, it has not adopted the euro. Instead, it has kept its own currency to have another lever with which to manage the flows of exports from Swedish industries.

The most controversial aspect of Swedish government policy is the country's extensive welfare state, and income redistribution. Swedish citizens receive: free health care, free education through university, high levels of unemployment benefits and pensions, and generous family leave for parents of newborns.

Sweden was one of the first countries to institute "papa leave." Traditionally, paid time off to care for newborns was maternity leave. Women were expected to leave work, and stay home to take care of the new baby. But Sweden has a long history of equal rights. So, to be fair, papas were also given the opportunity to leave work and stay home. Initially, not too many new fathers took advantage of this option. It remained mostly women who left to take care of new babies. So, the Swedish government increased the monetary amount of papa leave to encourage more men to stay home. That they had to do this, I think, is proof that taking care of infants is a heck of a lot harder than almost any job in the paid labor market.

The Swedish government also redistributes income in a more comprehensive way than any other government in the world. Oxfam, which is a global organization dedicated to fighting hunger, along with Development Finance International—a London firm that works with low-income countries—have issued a report entitled "The Commitment to Reducing Inequality Index." It's described as a "global ranking of governments based on what they are doing to tackle the gap between rich and poor." Of the 152 countries evaluated, Sweden comes out number one. The top five are Sweden, Belgium, Denmark, Norway, and Germany. Each one has a strong social-democratic political party, and extensive government involvement in the economy. The United States ranks number 23, just below Malta and just above the Czech Republic. Nigeria ranks 152nd and last—just below Bahrain.

The index itself is a composite measure based on three types of policies to reduce inequality: First, spending on health, education, and social protection; second, progressive structure and incidence of tax; and third, labor-market policies to address inequality.

One positive result shows up in life-expectancy data. When I was young, I didn't really think life expectancy data was all that important. Now, for obvious reasons, I consider life expectancy data to be extremely important. Sweden ranks 11th in the world life expectancy, with an average life expectancy of 81.7 years. Monaco ranks first, but it's unfair to compare a tiny principality of tax-dodgers to a regular country. The United States' life expectancy is 78.9. In that measure, America ranks 45th, just ahead of Guam and below Cuba. Now you might say that the difference between 81.7 in Sweden and 78.9 in the U.S. is rather small. Talk to me when you're 78!

Now, nothing in economics comes without a cost. One cost of Sweden's well-developed social structure is, of course, the tax burden on the average Swedish worker. Swedes pay an average of 53 percent on their income in taxes. Sweden ranks 5th in the high-tax category. Only Finland, Denmark, France, and Belgium rank ahead of Sweden.

You sometimes hear Americans complaining about high taxes. In fact, you always hear Americans complaining about high taxes. My favorite economist, John Kenneth Galbraith, often remarked that the American colonists were said to be revolting against "taxation without representation"—but they were also probably revolting against taxation. Americans pay about 38 percent of their income in total taxes. This includes federal income taxes, social security taxes, sales taxes, property taxes and so on. You might think that's too much, and you're entitled to your opinion. But relatively speaking, the United States is a low-tax country. Americans rank 27th among high income countries in the percentage of tax they pay.

High taxes can legitimately be said to limit freedom. The Swedish government limits the freedom of Swedish citizens to spend their own money. Many Swedish employers and industrialists complain that the country's high levels of economic security and guaranteed income have diminished the work ethic of the Swedish worker—and are a drag on efforts to increase productivity in the face of globalization and foreign competition. The fates of SAAB, Ericsson, and Volvo are evidence they might have an argument. However, the Swedes have decided democratically to give up some of their individual economic freedom to live in a more egalitarian and economically secure society. Swedish elections are fought over the size and comprehensiveness of their welfare state.

As in most rich countries, the Swedish population today is aging. Can the Swedish economic system continue to afford comprehensive health care and generous pensions? These are the two primary drivers of government spending as populations age. Can the Swedes afford their system of *"Krybbe to grav"*—as *The Economist* magazine has asked?

One of the most fascinating aspects of comparative economic systems is the interplay between social values, national history, and the costs and benefits of the economic system. The Swedish system clearly delivers significant benefits to its citizens. Can it still afford the costs? And if not, how will the system have to be modified to remain viable in an increasingly globalized and competitive world economy?

Lecture 13

French Indicative Planning and Jean Monnet

T HE FRENCH ECONOMIC SYSTEM TODAY REFLECTS A
history of wars, revolutions, and political battles
between right- and left-wing political parties and
is a blend of capitalist private property in industry
and agriculture along with significant state
ownership and control. The French system of
economic planning—led by the state—is known
as indicative planning. The word "indicative"
distinguishes it from the type of planning used
in communist economies, which is referred to as
command planning. ◆

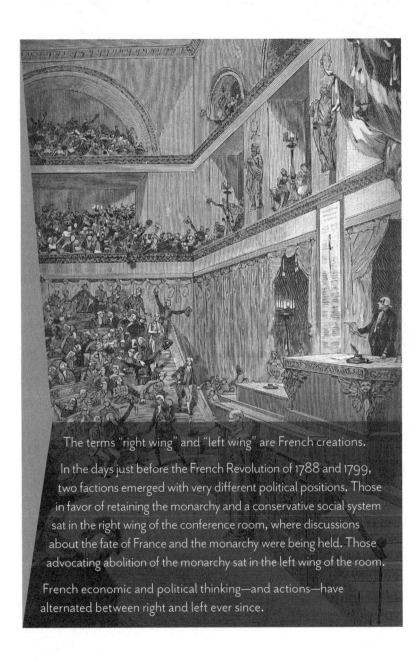

The terms "right wing" and "left wing" are French creations.

In the days just before the French Revolution of 1788 and 1799, two factions emerged with very different political positions. Those in favor of retaining the monarchy and a conservative social system sat in the right wing of the conference room, where discussions about the fate of France and the monarchy were being held. Those advocating abolition of the monarchy sat in the left wing of the room.

French economic and political thinking—and actions—have alternated between right and left ever since.

French Economy and Society

◁ Control and influence of the economy by the French government has a long history. Even in the time of the monarchy, the French state used taxes and control of foreign trade to lead economic development in the desired direction.

◁ Protection of French farmers from foreign competition was accomplished with high tariffs on imports of foreign agricultural products. As with all economic policies, this created benefits and costs—winners and losers.

◁ The winners were the French farmers, who enjoyed relatively high prices and higher incomes. The losers were the urban French workers and, indirectly, French capitalists, who had to pay higher wages to compensate their workers for higher food prices. The redistribution of incomes from workers and capitalists hindered the development of French industrial capitalism and maintained the small scale of the typical French farm.

◁ The lack of a dynamic industrial sector in France meant that it was a country of small, inefficient farms—and small-scale industry and manufacturing—for most of the 19th century. So, while Britain experienced the industrial revolution, France remained a bucolic and peasant country, outside of a few big cities, which were predominantly centers of government, education, and culture rather than of industry and large-scale manufacturing.

◁ French society suffered many conflicts and upheavals. After the French Revolution—and the abolition of the monarchy— came the Reign of Terror, the guillotine, and the dictatorship of Napoleon Bonaparte. Napoleon did bring some modernizing changes to the French economy. He created a professional military, a university system for training civil servants and administrators, and a modern legal code: the Napoleonic Code.

◀ Although France came late to industrial capitalism, French social thought led the way to the creation of socialist theories. Karl Marx credited writers such as Pierre Proudhon—author of the phrase "property is theft"—and Charles Fourier, creator of the idea of syndicalism, as inspirations for his theories of communism.

◀ The French Socialist Party achieved its first electoral victory in 1936. Coming at the height of the Great Depression, the government of Socialist Party leader Léon Blum advocated higher minimum wages, limitations on the work week, and nationalization of the railroads. However, the German Nazi army's invasion and occupation of France put an end to the reforms and policies of the Blum government.

In the United States, attorneys in Louisiana must still navigate a legal system heavily influenced by French colonial administrators of the 19th century.

◀ While the Nazis installed their own government in Paris and directly ruled the northern part of the country, a collaborationist government headquartered in the south carried out Nazi policies in the rest of France. These policies included abolition of trade unions and the suppression of workers' rights and wages, as well as rounding up Jews to be transported to Nazi labor and death camps. This history of French right-wing collaboration—to the benefit of many French capitalists—severely damaged the reputation of conservatives and industrialists in France.

◀ One of the main opposition forces in France during the Nazi occupation was the French Communist Party, which provided many leaders to the French Resistance. Socialist Party members also performed heroically in opposition to the policies of the Third Reich. This history of resistance created significant status and support for left-wing parties in French politics after World War II.

◀ The communist and socialist parties in France were either outright hostile to capitalism or in favor of significant reform and limits to capitalist economic institutions. To this day, the word "socialism"—and the role of the French Socialist Party—are still key elements of French society and politics.

Monnet's Indicative Planning

◀ The French career military officer Charles de Gaulle—a veteran of World War I and a former German prisoner of war—emerged as a hero of the French government in exile. He led French Resistance forces, who helped the Allies liberate France.

◀ De Gaulle was not a socialist or a communist. Rather, he was a French nationalist who wanted to restore France as a leading power in Europe. He also sought, somewhat unrealistically, to make France a leading power in the world again. In 1945, France was a defeated and demoralized country with a weak economy.

◀ As a politician, de Gaulle was by no means of the left-wing persuasion, but he became convinced that to redevelop the French economic system, a comprehensive approach was necessary—to include economic planning and significant government involvement.

◀ The man de Gaulle relied on was a native of Cognac named Jean Monnet, who never formally held a government position but served as a personal advisor to de Gaulle and to the French Ministry of Planning. Monnet never joined a political party, but he worked for the good of France and the world economy.

◀ His two greatest sources of support in the development of his planning initiative were the U.S. government and the French Socialist Party. To prevent World War III—and to help all of Europe rebuild after World War II—the United States created the 12-billion-dollar European Recovery Program. Also known as the Marshall Plan, it was named for George C. Marshall, the wartime U.S. Army chief of staff who would go on to become secretary of state.

◀ In France, Monnet used the funds available to his government to develop French infrastructure and industrial capability. One aim of the Marshall Plan was to aid in the development of market-oriented economies and diminish the appeal of communism.

The Marshall Plan was a creation of the Truman presidency. But Harry Truman was politically wise enough not to label it the "Truman Plan." The plan faced strong opposition from the Republicans in Congress, and Truman needed some Republican votes to get it passed.

◀ The Great Depression had been a tremendous blow to the reputation of capitalist economic systems. And the victory of the Soviet Union over the Third Reich created some sympathy and admiration for the Soviet economic system. Communist parties in western Europe—especially in France and Italy—acquired some of this appeal.

◀ The French Socialist Party was in favor of reforming the capitalist system and, maybe at some time in the future, replacing it. But the party would replace it only through democratic elections and the will of the majority of the population. Communist parties, in contrast, favored violent revolution and the immediate overthrow of the capitalist system.

◀ The French Socialist Party worked hard to distinguish itself from the French Communist Party. And it was more willing to work with Jean Monnet and his plan to make the French economic system modern and productive.

◀ The system that Jean Monnet introduced was indicative planning, which means that the government creates plans for major French industries in consultation with domestic business, labor, and government officials. The plans are not mandatory, and there's no overt coercion to fulfill the plan's objectives. The plan merely "indicates" the intentions of the French national government to modernize and develop the economy.

◀ However, the French government has many methods with which to realize its plans. And the French government, in contrast with some other European economies with socialist parties in leadership positions after World War II, carried out a significant program of nationalization, which involves government takeovers of privately owned enterprises.

◀ The French government nationalized key infrastructure enterprises—including the French telephone, water distribution, and national railway systems—to assure adequate energy and transportation for all French businesses. Additionally, the French government nationalized the banking system to give it control over the distribution of credit and loans to French business and consumers.

◀ In recent decades, a prevailing trend in world economies has been to privatize enterprises. But the French continue to maintain an economic system with a significant number of government-owned industries. For example, while British rail has been privatized, the French rail system is still government owned and operated.

◀ Added to the direct control the French government exercised over French industrial enterprises, it also used many indirect methods. Industries that were part of the government plan's broader objectives would be offered low-interest loans and easy credit conditions by government-owned financial institutions.

◀ Taxes and subsidies were also used to direct business activity. To create incentives for French private business to follow the government's economic plan, differential tax rates—and even direct payments to businesses that were part of the objectives—were also used.

◀ These direct and indirect methods gave the French government strong control over the French economic system.

French Politics and Values

◀ The French, like most electorates, switch back and forth from conservative to left-wing politics and values. Socialist-led governments alternate with more conservative governments. At times, France has been led by political parties influenced by the legacy of Charles de Gaulle. These parties tend to be more conservative. They often favor less government planning and ownership.

◀ When Ronald Reagan and Margaret Thatcher's philosophy of free market capitalism was first capturing American and British elections, it briefly also had some influence in France. Some banks were privatized, and major industrial firms were at least partially privatized.

◀ But in 1981, France elected the French Socialist Party leader François Mitterrand as president. Mitterrand was elected during a European recession and a big rise in French unemployment, and his original platform was a very left-wing one. It included such elements as the elimination of capital punishment and large increases in the minimum wage and unemployment benefits, paid for with tax increases on the rich. The government also renationalized some of the major banks and public utilities and carried out large construction projects.

◀ The Mitterrand program led to big decreases in French unemployment and generated economic growth. However, it also created large government deficits and large balance-of-payments deficits.

◀ Unfortunately, while the Mitterrand government was carrying out its expansionary fiscal and monetary policies, the British government, under Margaret Thatcher, and the German government, under Helmut Kohl, were carrying out austerity policies. They were reducing government spending and increasing interest rates.

◀ This meant that the French—who temporarily had more income—were importing more British and German products, while the British and the Germans—who temporarily had less income, under their austerity programs—were importing fewer French products.

◀ The Bank of France had to raise its interest rate to counteract the higher German interest rates and protect the value of the French franc. This eventually had a depressing effect on the French economy. A decrease in French exports to its two main trading partners also led to layoffs in French exporting enterprises. French voters blamed the Mitterrand government for these unfavorable economic outcomes.

◀ Mitterrand's leftist government was followed by the more conservative government of the Gaullist party leader Jacques Chirac. But a French conservative is still in favor of more government direction and social welfare policies by comparison with a conservative in the United States. No French president would radically change the national health-care system, which the World Health Organization has called the best in the world.

◀ After 17 years of moderate right-of-center governments under Chirac and Nicolas Sarkozy, the French elected another socialist in 2012: François Hollande. The Socialist Party manifesto, or platform, promised many things, including an increase in the minimum wage, an increase in the research budget, and the construction of 120,000 new housing units a year for the poor.

The French government plays a major role in the redistribution of income and, therefore, in reducing inequality. French citizens pay some of the highest taxes in the world: 57 percent of their income, on average. Those French who earn high incomes bear a large burden for the activities of the French state, but there are benefits for the average French worker and for middle- and lower-income French citizens.

Readings

DUCHENE, *Jean Monnet.*
JUDT, *Postwar.*

Questions

1 The French seem to like bureaucracy and complex organizations. How does this preference manifest itself in their economic system?

2 The French high-speed train network, featuring the TGVs, could be an example of the superiority of public ownership and control. Why might this be?

Lecture 13 Transcript

French Indicative Planning and Jean Monnet

The French economic system today reflects a history of wars, revolutions, and political battles between right- and left-wing political parties. Even the terms right wing and left wing are French creations. In the days just before the French Revolution of 1788 and 1799, two factions emerged with very different political positions. Those in favor of retaining the monarchy, and a conservative social system, sat in the right wing of the conference room, where discussions about the fate of France and the monarchy were being held; those advocating abolition of the monarchy sat in the left wing of the room. French economic and political thinking—and actions—have alternated between right and left ever since.

The French economic system today is a blend of capitalist private property in industry and agriculture, along with significant state ownership and control. And the French system of economic planning—led by the state— is known as indicative planning. The word "indicative" distinguishes it from the type of planning used in communist economies, which is referred to as command planning.

Control and influence of the economy by the French government has a long history. Even in the time of the monarchy, the French state used taxes and control of foreign trade to lead economic development in the desired direction. Protection of French farmers from foreign competition was accomplished with high tariffs on imports of foreign agricultural products. As with all economic policies, this created benefits and costs— winners and losers. The winners were the French farmers, who enjoyed relatively high prices and higher incomes. The losers were the urban French workers, and—indirectly—French capitalists who had to pay higher wages to compensate their workers for higher food prices. The redistribution of incomes from workers and capitalists hindered the development of French industrial capitalism, and maintained the small scale of the typical French farm.

In contrast, the English traded grain products freely. They did so under the influence of the classical British economist David Ricardo, a member of Parliament who in 1817 wrote a treatise on the benefits of free trade. This practice benefited English industrialists at the expense of English farmers and landlords.

The lack of a dynamic industrial sector in France meant that it was a country of small, inefficient farms—and small-scale industry and manufacturing—for most of the 19th century. So, while Britain experienced the industrial revolution, France remained a bucolic and peasant country, outside of a few big cities. And French big cities were predominantly centers of government, education, and culture rather than of industry and large-scale manufacturing.

Looked at another way, British cities like London, Birmingham, and Manchester were big, gray, dirty—and growing richer—in the 19th and first half of the 20th century. French cities like Paris and Lyon were centers of civil servants; students and professors; doctors and lawyers; chefs and restaurateurs; and painters and writers. Much later, by the latter part of the 20th century, London, Birmingham and Manchester were still big, gray and dirty. But they were no longer so rich, as globalization and de-industrialization wiped out big industries. Paris and Lyon remained picturesque and beautiful.

Still, French society suffered many conflicts and upheavals. After the French Revolution—and the abolition of the monarchy—came the Reign of Terror, the guillotine, and the dictatorship of Napoleon Bonaparte. Napoleon did bring some modernizing changes to the French economy. He created a professional military, as well as a university system for training civil servants and administrators, and a modern legal code: The Code Napoleon. In the United States, attorneys in the state of Louisiana must still navigate a legal system heavily influenced by French colonial administrators of the 19th century.

Although France came late to industrial capitalism, French social thought led the way to the creation of socialist theories. Karl Marx credited writers like Pierre Proudhon—the author of the phrase, "property is theft"—and Charles Fourier, the creator of the idea of syndicalism, as inspirations for his theories of communism. Marx identified three sources in his development of communist theory: English political economy, German philosophy; and French socialism.

The French Socialist Party (PSF) achieved its first electoral victory in 1936. Coming at the height of the Great Depression, the government of PSF leader Leon Blum advocated higher minimum wages, limitations on the work week, and nationalization of the railroads. However, the German Nazi army's invasion and occupation of France put an end to the reforms and policies of the Blum government.

The history of Nazi occupation is not a particularly glorious chapter in French history. While the Nazis installed their own government in Paris, and directly ruled the northern part of the country, a collaborationist government headquartered in the south—in Vichy, and led by French General Philippe Petain—carried out Nazi policies in the rest of France. These policies included abolition of trade unions, and the suppression of workers' rights and wages, as well as rounding up Jews to be transported to Nazi labor and death camps. This history of French right-wing collaboration—to the benefit of many French capitalists, including Louis Renault—severely damaged the reputation of conservatives and industrialists in France.

One of the main opposition forces in France during the Nazi occupation was the French Communist Party, which provided many leaders to the French Resistance. Socialist Party members also performed heroically in opposition to the policies of the Third Reich. This history of resistance created significant status and support for left-wing parties in French politics after World War II. The communist and socialist parties in France were either outright hostile to capitalism, or in favor of significant reform and limits to capitalist economic institutions. To this day, the word socialism—and the role of the French Socialist Party—are still key elements of French society and of French politics.

The French career military officer Charles de Gaulle—a veteran of World War I, and a former German prisoner of war—emerged as a hero of the French government in exile. And he led French resistance forces who helped the Allies liberate France. De Gaulle was not a socialist or a communist. Rather, he was a French nationalist who wanted—above all—

to restore France as a leading power in Europe. He also sought, somewhat unrealistically, to make France a leading power in the world again. In 1945, France was—for all intents and purposes—a defeated and demoralized country with a weak economy.

As a politician, de Gaulle was by no means of the left-wing. But he became convinced that to redevelop the French economic system, a comprehensive approach was necessary—to include economic planning and significant government involvement. The man de Gaulle relied upon was a shy, soft-spoken native of Cognac named Jean Monnet. Born in 1888, Monnet was the son of a wealthy brandy merchant. What would you expect of somebody from a town with such a nice name? Monnet told de Gaulle in 1945, "You speak of greatness ... but today the French are small. There will be greatness only when the French are of a stature to warrant it." And, Monnet said: "For this purpose, they must modernize—because at the moment they are not modern. Materially, the country needs to be transformed."

Monnet never formally held a government position. But he served as a personal advisor to de Gaulle, and to the French Ministry of Planning. And Monnet was far from some idealistic academic, or naïve country boy. He had extensive sales experience in Great Britain and Canada. He'd been a banker and consultant in New York—and one of the leaders in efforts to create the World Bank. He never joined a political party. But he worked for the good of France, and the world economy.

His two greatest sources of support in the development of his planning initiative were the United States government and the French Socialist Party. The U.S. government had learned from the mistakes made by the British and French governments at the end of World War I. The Versailles Treaty that ended that war had punished the Germans and their allies, and helped usher in the Great Depression. To prevent World War Three—and help all Europe rebuild—the United States created the European Recovery Program. It was known as the Marshall Plan, after George C. Marshall, the war-time Army chief of staff who afterward became secretary of State.

The Marshall Plan was a $12 billion program of resistance to help rebuild post-war Europe. It was a creation of the Truman presidency. But Harry Truman was politically wise enough not to label it the Truman plan. The plan faced strong opposition from the Republicans in Congress. And Truman needed some Republican votes to get it passed.

The genius of the Marshall Plan—besides its name—was that although this program of assistance seemed quite altruistic on the part of the United States, it was also very beneficial to the American economy—the strongest and most productive in the world.

U.S. aircraft factories, motor vehicle factories, pipelines, hydroelectric plants, steel mills, aluminum plants, food production facilities, and railroads had sprung up as a result of World War II. Without war demand, who was going to buy all the goods that the American economy was now capable of producing? All the other major economies in the world had been decimated—the winners as well as the losers. They had very little productive capability, and, therefore, nothing much to export. Furthermore, everything they could produce was needed domestically to feed, clothe, and house their own devastated populations. So how could they buy anything that America was ready to export? The only way is if the United States advanced them the money with which to buy American products. Yes, the Marshall Plan was quite generous, but it was not totally altruistic and self-sacrificing.

Another brilliant aspect of the Marshall Plan is that it was given to Europeans as a group, and necessitated collective European action. So, victors and vanquished alike were part of cooperative efforts to rebuild Europe. The losers in World War II benefited from American aid and were not punished economically, as they had been at the end of the first World War.

In France, Monnet used the funds available to his government to develop French infrastructure and industrial capability. One aim of the Marshall Plan was to aid in the development of market-oriented economies, and diminish the appeal of communism. The Great Depression had been a tremendous blow to the reputation of capitalist economic systems. And the victory of the Soviet Union over the Third Reich created some sympathy and admiration for the Soviet economic system.

Communist Parties in western Europe—especially in France and Italy—acquired some of this appeal. The French Socialist Party was in favor of reforming the capitalist system, and—maybe at some time in the future—replacing it. But would replace it only through democratic elections, and the will of the majority of the population. Communist parties, in contrast, favored violent revolution, and the immediate overthrow of the capitalist system. The French Socialist Party worked hard to distinguish itself from the French Communist Party. And it was more willing to work with Jean Monnet and his plan to make the French economic system modern and productive.

The system Jean Monnet introduced was indicative planning. This means the government creates plans for major French industries, in consultation with domestic business, labor, and government officials. The plans are not mandatory. And there's no overt coercion to fulfill the plan's objectives. The plan merely "indicates" the intentions of the French national government to modernize, and develop, the economy. However, the French government has many methods with which to realize its plans. And the French government, in contrast with some other European economies with Socialist parties in leadership positions after World War II, carried out a significant program of nationalization.

Nationalizations are government takeovers of privately owned enterprises. Some were punitive in nature. The nationalization of vehicle maker Renault was one such punitive nationalization. Louis Renault and his company had actively collaborated with the Nazi occupiers of France, and had produced more than 30,000 military vehicles for the Third Reich. Ownership of such a large industrial enterprise gave the French government direct ability to influence the production of Renault's suppliers, as well. Automobile enterprises are large consumers of steel, rubber, electrical components, and fabrics. The government—by announcing yearly production targets for Renault vehicles—signaled suppliers how to plan their output levels and resource demands.

The French government also nationalized key infrastructure enterprises to assure adequate energy and transportation for all French businesses. Electricite de France (EDF)—the French power utility—and Gaz de France, the supplier of natural gas, both were both created and nationalized, in 1946. Later, the French telephone system and water distribution system were nationalized. Even today, the French national railway system is a totally owned government enterprise, employing more than 180,000 people. Eventually the air-transport system was developed by government-owned Air France, and—even today—it remains a majority owner.

Additionally, the French government nationalized the banking system to give it control over the distribution of credit and loans to French business and consumers. In recent decades, a prevailing trend in world economies has been to privatize enterprises. But the French continue to maintain an economic system with a significant number of government-owned industries. For instance, while British rail has been privatized, and the German electricity market is private, the French rail system is still government-owned and operated. And EDF is still majority owned by the government, although private investors now own a minority interest in publicly traded shares.

Added to the direct control the French government exercised over French industrial enterprises, it also used many indirect methods. Industries that were part of the government plan's broader objectives would be offered low-interest loans, and easy credit conditions, by government-owned financial institutions. Businesses that needed to invest in capital goods were given accelerated depreciation credits on their taxes.

Depreciation is an accounting method of allocating the cost of an asset over its productive life. Favorable tax treatment that allows deductions for depreciation will reduce the tax obligations of private businesses, and thus increase their profitability. This makes those businesses more attractive to own and expand. Taxes and subsidies were also used to direct business activity.

To create incentives for French private business to follow the government's economic plan, differential tax rates—and even direct payments to businesses that were part of the objectives—were also used. These direct and indirect methods gave the French government strong control over the French economic system. To run such a comprehensive and complex planning system, well-educated and motivated personnel were essential.

And here's where we come back to Napoleon. One of Napoleon's most important creations was the Ecole Nationale d'Administration—the higher "finishing school" for French bureaucrats and politicians. A graduate of the ENA—so-called *Enarques*—usually lead major French enterprises, both public and private. And this is a rather non-partisan designation. At the top, nationalist politicians, socialist politicians, and moderate politicians are almost always graduates of the ENA. In France, a career as a politician and bureaucrat is seen as performing a valuable role in society. It does not have nearly the negative connotations that those careers sometimes signal in the United States.

If we use the example of the French railway system, we can see how French indicative planning works in practice.

If the French government decides that a new high-speed train line from Paris to Nice is necessary, a very large part of the French economy will be affected. The land for the tracks must be cleared, requiring companies and workers to perform this task. Tracks must be constructed and laid. This requires significant outputs of iron, and steel, and concrete. Furthermore, the train system in France is almost entirely electric, so the wiring, and posts for the wires—and the generating systems for the electricity—must be produced. The trains themselves must be manufactured, and this creates demand for engineering firms, metallurgy, power system, communications, and construction. In the towns, the new train line will pass through, new stations, bus connections, and retail and tourist facilities must be built. This list is by no means complete, but it gives you an idea of the scope of how the French government influences private enterprise in the French economic system.

As in any democracy, different opinions and values affect the government's direction. The French, like most electorates, switch back and forth from conservative to left-wing politics and values. Socialist-led governments alternate with more conservative governments. At times, France has been led by political parties influenced by the legacy of Charles de Gaulle. These parties tend to be more conservative. They often favor less government planning and ownership.

When Ronald Reagan and Margaret Thatcher's philosophy of free-market capitalism was first capturing American and British elections a few decades ago, it briefly also had some influence in France. Some banks were privatized, and major industrial firms were at least partially privatized, with investor stakes listed on the Paris stock exchange.

But in 1981, France elected the French Socialist Party leader Francois Mitterrand as president. And he served two seven-year terms, retiring from office in 1995. (Today, French presidents serve only five-year terms.)

Mitterrand was elected during a European recession, and a big rise in French unemployment. And his original platform was very left-wing. It included such elements as: the elimination of capital punishment (still carried out at that time by the guillotine); large increases in the minimum wage and unemployment benefits, paid for with tax increases on the rich. The government also renationalized some of the major banks and public utilities, and carried out large construction projects.

One of my favorite suggestions from the PBS host Rick Steves' TV travel show is to stand on top of the Arch de Triomphe, and look at the major construction projects of important French leaders. The Arch de Triomphe was a creation of Napoleon. If you look east, you see the Louvre Museum, originally a palace built by Louis XIV. And when you turn around and look west, you see the new business district anchored by the La Grande Arche de la Defense building constructed by the Mitterrand government. Mitterrand also built a new Paris Opera, La Bastille; and a new library, La Biblioteque Nationale. The Mitterrand program led to big decreases in French unemployment, and generated economic growth. However, it also created large government deficits and large balance of payments deficits.

Unfortunately, while the Mitterrand government was carrying out its expansionary fiscal and monetary policies, the British government under Margaret Thatcher—and the German government, under Helmut Kohl—were carrying out austerity policies. They were reducing government spending, and increasing interest rates. This meant that the French—who temporarily had more income—were importing more British and German products, while the British and the Germans—who temporarily had less income, under their austerity programs—were importing fewer German products.

The Bank of France had to raise its interest rate to counteract the high German interest rates, and protect the value of the French franc. This increase in interest rates eventually had a depressing effect on the French economy. A decrease in French exports to its main two trading partners also led to layoffs in French exporting enterprises. French voters blamed the Mitterrand government for these unfavorable economic outcomes. But the economic outcome was inevitable in an age of increased international trade and interconnections.

What happens in one country affects other countries too, especially if they are close geographically, and major trading partners. Mitterrand's leftist government was followed by the more conservative government of the Gaullist party leader, Jacques Chirac. But a French conservative is still in favor of more government direction and social-welfare policies by comparison with a conservative in the United States. No French president would radically change the national health care system, which the World Health Organization has called the best in the world.

After 17 years of moderate right-of-center governments under Chirac and Nicolas Sarkozy, the French elected another socialist in 2007: Francois Hollande. The Socialist Party manifesto, or platform, promised many things.

Among them was the renationalization of Electricite de France; an increase in the minimum wage; an increase in the research budget (by 10 percent); and the construction of 120,000 new housing units a year for the poor.

The nature of the French minimum wage—realistically, it's better to call it a minimum income—is radically different from the U.S. minimum wage. The U.S. approach covers only hourly employment. It doesn't necessarily do anything to provide a basic monthly income, with significant implications for lower-income members of society.

The French government, by comparison, plays a major role in the redistribution of income. French citizens pay some of the highest taxes in the world—57 percent of their income, on average. This ranks third in the world, behind only the Finns and the Danes.

Obviously, those French who earn high incomes bear a large burden for the activities of the French state. This might lead to the out-migration of French entrepreneurs and business professionals, and stifle innovation. Economic growth could suffer. And the French economy may lag behind more dynamic and less egalitarian economic systems.

But there are benefits for the average French worker, and for middle- and lower-income French citizens.

According to the non-governmental organization Oxfam, the French government ranks 8th out of 152 countries covered in the commitment to reducing inequality. The index is based on: spending on health, education and social protection; its progressive structure; and labor market policies to address inequality. The United States ranks 23rd in the same assessment. In another study of inequality, the economists Thomas Piketty, Emmanuel Saez, and Gabriel Zucman found that the average pretax income of adults in the bottom half of income distribution in France was $18,000. In United States, it was $16,000. And this was in spite of the fact that the U.S. had a higher average income overall. In the United States, increases in national income have increasingly gone to the top 10 percent of income receivers. And since the French tax system is much more progressive, the bottom 50 percent of French citizens have an even higher net income than U.S. citizens in the bottom half.

Piketty and his colleagues attribute some of the differences in income distribution between France and the United States to differences in their approaches to college admission and tuition finance. By this he means that a French family does not have to worry about how it will pay for tuition if daughter Marie or son Pierre is admitted to the University of Paris. There is no tuition. The major worry of a French family is how Marie or Pierre will do on the national examinations given at the end of high school that determine admission to university. Now, obviously, wealthy families that can afford tutors, books, and test preparation courses might have an advantage. But poor families with bright children have a better chance of going to the best universities in contrast to the United States.

Other factors in the more equal distribution of income in France are French labor-market institutions that give workers more bargaining power; and, as I've mentioned, the relatively progressive nature of the French tax system.

One of the recent developments that worries me, as a college professor—and an economics professor, at that—is the steep increases in tuition at public and private colleges in the United States. Unequal access to higher education in the United States is potentially bad for economic growth and efficiency—and bad for democracy.

Lecture 14

British Labour Party and National Health

FOR DECADES, THE ECONOMY OF GREAT BRITAIN HAS alternated between periods of nationalization and of privatization. This coincided with the political battles unfolding at the same time between the left-wing British Labour Party and the right-of-center British Conservative Party. The British Labour Party was founded in 1900 as part of the reform-minded social democratic movement that swept much of Europe and parts of the United States. The Labour Party occasionally carried parliamentary majorities before World War II, but the party's real power to change the system emerged in the aftermath of World War II. ◆

The Labour Party and the Beveridge Report

◀ Prime Minister Winston Churchill's wartime government had been an all-party coalition that successfully led Britain during the fight against Nazi Germany. Churchill followed the inept, and failed, Conservative Party government of Neville Chamberlain.

◀ It was Chamberlain who signed the Munich Agreement with Adolf Hitler that ceded Czechoslovakia to the Third Reich. This betrayal colored British opinion of Conservative parliamentarians and gave the Labour Party a significant political advantage in the postwar period.

◀ Additionally, Britain's experience of fighting a successful war—and making all the sacrifices necessary for victory—instilled in the average citizen a sense of entitlement at war's end. No more big sacrifices by the average working-class family for the good of the empire and the king.

◀ Still, in a rather ironic development right after the war's end, the government of Prime Minister Winston Churchill was replaced by a Labour Party government led by Clement Attlee. The Labour Party was the beneficiary of renewed working-class political demand and power, and the party's victory would usher in profound and far-reaching changes to the British economy.

◀ But first, the Potsdam Conference to decide the postwar settlement of Germany convened on July 17, 1945, just outside of Berlin. Josef Stalin, the leader of the Soviet Union, was met by two new national leaders: Great Britain's Attlee and U.S. President Harry Truman.

◀ While Clement Attlee was the official head of government, the leading figure in the transformation of the British economic system was William Beveridge. As World War II turned in the Allies' favor, Beveridge was asked to form a commission to propose social policies for Britain after the war. He produced a study called "Social Insurance and Allied Services," commonly known as the Beveridge Report.

◀ The Beveridge Report was a blueprint for a Labour Party program of social welfare policies proposed and passed in 1948. It called for comprehensive unemployment insurance, old-age pensions, and—most dramatically—free, universal, public health care.

The National Health Service

◀ The British National Health Service (NHS) would be universal in that all residents of the United Kingdom would be covered. It would be free in the sense that there would be no payments for services or medical bills after treatment. And it would be public in the sense that all hospitals and medical specialists would be employees of the government.

◀ Naturally, this raised strenuous objections from doctors organized by the British Medical Association. One of the tactics that the Labour government employed was to allow general practitioners to remain private professionals, who would be paid by the NHS.

◀ Like any complex economic institution—especially one that contains principles of socialism or public ownership—there were both costs and benefits to the creation of the NHS.

◀ About 47 percent of British income is paid to the government, and sales taxes on all goods and services in Britain average about 20 percent. The British also pay higher income taxes than income earners in the United States. Another cost is measured in the waiting times for nonemergency treatments and the NHS's refusal to pay for some procedures.

◀ Because the NHS covers all United Kingdom residents and charges nothing at the point of service, it must implement many cost-reducing policies. One of the most effective is called the capitation payment system.

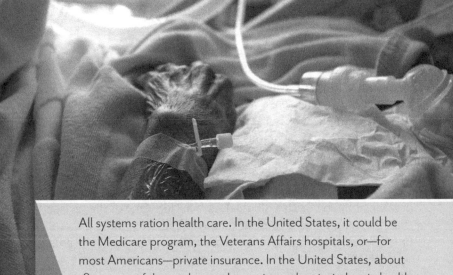

All systems ration health care. In the United States, it could be the Medicare program, the Veterans Affairs hospitals, or—for most Americans—private insurance. In the United States, about 18 percent of the total gross domestic product is tied up in health care. No other country dedicates nearly as much of its total income to health care. The British spend about half of that, at 9.4 percent. And even so, the British live slightly longer than Americans, at 80.4 years compared to 78.9 years.

◀ Although British general practitioners are private professionals, most receive almost all of their income from the NHS. They are paid for each person that registers with their office. And it's a set amount, no matter what kind of treatments or procedures the person receives. The healthier the person, the less expense for the general practitioner and the greater the physician's net income.

◀ General practitioners do basic services, such as flu shots—which are free. An enormous public benefit to having everyone in a society covered by flu vaccines is that because less work time is lost, there's more time left over for production of goods and services. There's also a tremendous cost savings due to minimizing doctors' bills, insurance forms, and insurance claims processing.

◀ Another component of the British social welfare system that reduces medical costs is the low tuition at British medical schools. British physicians don't graduate with the tremendous

One of the biggest drivers of American health costs is the huge amount of paperwork associated with it.

debt burdens common to American medical students, which push many into medical specialties that promise high incomes, such as plastic surgery and cardiac surgery. British specialists are government employees and live on a fixed salary.

◀ British general practitioners are private practitioners who earn more as they accept more clients, so Britain has twice as many general practitioners per capita as in the United States. And most health-care economists conclude that general practitioners who treat symptoms early are a much more effective method of health-care cost control.

◀ The most controversial aspect of the NHS goes by the acronym NICE—the National Institute for Health and Care Excellence—which is the gatekeeper for medical practices and procedures in the NHS system. NICE refuses to fund procedures and tests that it deems unnecessary or too costly for the benefits derived. But NICE does play a role in reducing the prevalence and costs of malpractice claims.

◀ While the Beveridge plan to create the NHS initially was met with skepticism in the medical community, employers were generally supportive for self-interested reasons. British industry had to compete with other high-income countries on quality as well as price. As the medical expense of providing health insurance was shifted to the national government, employers benefited financially while employing healthier, more productive workers.

◀ Business leaders also expressed little objection to the parts of the Beveridge Report that called for universal unemployment insurance and old-age pensions. This arose from the realization that minimum levels of personal income would support consumer demand for goods and services and act as a stabilizer, even amid economic downturns.

◀ The Labour governments also introduced a more progressive income tax to redistribute income from the rich to the poor. While income redistribution served to benefit the working-class base of the Labour Party, moving income from the rich to the poor also increases total spending, because lower-income individuals tend to spend a higher percentage of their incomes than higher earners do. Keynes referred to this as a higher marginal propensity to consume. He maintained that differential incomes—income inequality—explains most differences in the tendency to spend.

Industry Nationalizations

◀ The Labour Party initiated a wave of industry nationalizations in the early post–World War II era. At Labour Party urging, the British government nationalized the railroads, coal mines, steel mills, shipyards, electric utilities, and airlines.

◀ The goal was to promote employment, high wages, and stable economic activity. The stability argument arose from the Labour Party's belief that unbridled competition among major industrial firms was a key source of prewar economic instability, leading to recessions and the Great Depression.

◀ The British were much less interested in economic planning than the French were, with their system of indicative planning. The French government, in consultation with business and labor interests, created a unified economic plan for the country and signaled, or indicated, its preferences through a series of policy prescriptions, including tax incentives and subsidies.

◀ The British maintained greater faith in competition and in market pricing than continental Europeans did. British industry and labor typically wanted to retain the freedom to set higher prices and strike for higher wages. These freedoms tend to be more restricted in the French system of indicative planning—and in other forms of national planning, even by democratic governments.

◀ The Labour Party's vision of the British social welfare system went largely unchanged in the 1950s and 1960s, except the NHS was modified so that people had to make small copayments for glasses, contact lenses, false teeth, and prescription drugs. Children, the elderly, and the poor were exempt from these charges.

◀ The last Labour government of the 1970s engaged in one last round of industry nationalizations. British Petroleum and Rolls Royce were nationalized—not for planning or stabilization reasons, but mainly because they were on the verge of bankruptcy at the time. Government bailouts in the form of nationalization was a way to save the companies and the jobs of the people who worked there.

Economic Distress

◀ In most industrial democracies, the 1970s was a time of stagflation, which refers to the combination of economic stagnation—that is, a lack of growth—occurring at the same time as inflation drives costs and prices higher.

◀ Most economists believe that inflation occurs as a result of rapid growth, low unemployment, and high demand for goods, services, and workers. If the economy is stagnating, or declining, the level of prices should be dropping as people and businesses spend less.

◀ The major cause of the economic stagflation of the 1970s was the oil embargo imposed on the United States and some other Western nations by the Organization of Arab Petroleum Exporting Countries. These Middle Eastern members of OPEC (Organization of the Petroleum Exporting Countries) relied almost entirely on petroleum sales to finance their national economies. The effect was to significantly restrict the supply of oil to industrial countries and, therefore, to drive up the prices of gasoline and everything else.

◀ Gasoline prices in the United States doubled in 1973, and doubled again in 1979. For industries and households in industrial democracies, the effects of the oil shock were devastating. Any manufactured product that took energy to produce became much more expensive. Anything shipped by air, rail, or truck cost much more to transport.

◀ British industries were older—and energy inefficient—and therefore at a severe competitive disadvantage. Prices in Britain increased by as much as 17 percent per year in the late 1970s. British factories, mines, and shipyards laid off workers by the hundreds of thousands.

◀ In response, two competing explanations—and suggested cures—were offered to address Britain's economic distress.

◇ The Labour Party blamed the capitalist system and argued for more Keynesian-style fiscal and monetary stimulation. They wanted to increase the money supply and expand government spending to put Britain back to work.

◇ The Conservative Party blamed the welfare state: high taxes and inefficient publicly owned enterprises. Conservatives believed that high taxes led to elevated prices while also reducing incentives to invest in new ideas. They argued that inefficient state-owned enterprises produced substandard goods and services that were uncompetitive in world markets.

The Thatcher Government

◀ The 1979 election was a contest between these two vastly different visions. The Conservative Party, led by Margaret Thatcher, won the election and radically remade the British welfare state that William Beveridge and the Labour Party had created.

◀ The Thatcher government significantly reduced taxes, especially on higher-income Brits. Thatcher broke a strike of the miner's union and reduced the powers of trade unions in general. She also pushed through deregulation of the financial industry, which led to booming business in the London financial sector and high incomes for British financial professionals. The Thatcher government also privatized many government-owned enterprises.

◀ Many Brits became quite wealthy and successful as a result of Thatcher's policies. London became a magnet for entrepreneurs and businesspeople. One negative result of the Thatcher years was a large increase in income inequality in Britain.

WORLD GINI INDEX SCORES

GREAT
BRITAIN: 32.6

SWEDEN: 27.3

UNITED STATES
OF AMERICA: 41.1

Sweden is at the low end of income inequality, with a Gini
index value of 27.3, according to the World Bank. Great Britain's
Gini index score is 32.6—more unequal than social democratic
Sweden but less unequal than the United States' 41.1.

◀ The one sector of the British social welfare system that the
Thatcher government didn't touch was the NHS. The NHS
had such strong public support that even in the midst of free
enterprise euphoria and mass privatizations, William Beveridge's
prize creation remained a publicly owned institution.

◀ The Conservative Party ruled Britain from 1979 to 1997. Near
the end of its reign, the British electorate became less enchanted
with the free market direction of Thatcherite policies and elected
a Labour Party government in 1997 led by Tony Blair.

◀ Blair ran as a candidate from "New" Labour. He didn't reverse
any of the Thatcher nationalizations. But his government did
raise minimum wages, unemployment benefits, and old-age
pensions. The Labour Party won three elections and governed
until 2010, when a new Conservative government led by David
Cameron took over.

BEVERIDGE, *Full Employment in a Free Society*.
WEBSTER, *The National Health Service*.

Questions

1   After World War II, the British voters threw out the government of Winston Churchill and elected a Labour Party government. What did the voters want?

2   The British have a system of national health care that is almost completely government owned and controlled. What are the advantages and disadvantages of this system compared to the American health-care system?

Lecture 14 Transcript

British Labour Party and National Health

F or decades, the economy of Great Britain has alternated between
periods of nationalization and of privatization. This coincided with
the political battles unfolding at the same time between the left-wing
British Labour Party and the right-of-center British Conservative Party.
The British Labour Party was founded in 1900 as part of the reform-
minded, social democratic movement that swept much of Europe and parts
of the United States. The Labour Party occasionally carried Parliamentary
majorities before World War II—mainly during the Great Depression,
which hit Britain in the late 1920s. But the Labour Party's real power to
change the system emerged in the aftermath of the Second World War.

Prime Minister Winston Churchill's war-time government had been an
all-party coalition that successfully led Britain during the fight against
Nazi Germany. Churchill followed the inept, and failed, Conservative
Party government of Neville Chamberlain. It was Chamberlain who signed
the Munich Agreement with Adolf Hitler that ceded Czechoslovakia to
the Third Reich. This betrayal colored British opinion of Conservative
parliamentarians, and gave Labour a significant political advantage in
the post-war period.

Additionally, Britain's experience of fighting a successful war—and
making all the sacrifices necessary for victory—instilled in the average
citizen a sense of entitlement at the war's end. No more big sacrifices
by the average working-class family for the good of the empire and the
king. Still, in a rather ironic development right after the war's end, the
government of Prime Minister Winston Churchill was replaced by a
Labour Party government led by Clement Attlee. Churchill the war hero
giving way to the rather non-descript Attlee.

It was a time for the average worker to get some benefit from the British
economy. The Labour Party was the beneficiary of renewed working-class
political demands and power. And the British Labour Party victory would
usher in profound, and far-reaching, changes to the British economy.

But first, the Potsdam Conference to decide the post-war settlement of Germany convened on July 17, 1945, just outside of Berlin. Josef Stalin, the leader of the Soviet Union, was met by two new national leaders: Great Britain's Attlee, whose party had won its parliamentary majority that month, and the U.S. President Harry Truman, who'd been on the job for just five months.

The previous Allied conference had taken place in February in Yalta on the Crimean Peninsula of the Soviet Union. At that time, Stalin had been joined by Churchill and the American President Franklin Delano Roosevelt, who would die two months later. Each of the three leaders had their own palace—the palaces having been built for the vacationing Russian czars and their court. But the Allied leaders met in Roosevelt's palace, because he was in failing health, and suffering from the effects of his life-long battle with polio. Roosevelt stayed in the Livadia Palace, which the Tsar Nicholas II had built as an Italian-style spring and summer residence for the last royal Romanovs. I once had the opportunity to visit it.

The Allied leaders at the Potsdam conference in Germany also stayed in palaces built for nobility. The Potsdam palace was built for the 18th century Prussian ruler Frederick the Great. Stalin understood the kind of political succession that had brought Truman in place of the late Roosevelt. But he was baffled by how Churchill—a wartime leader and victor—could be replaced while he was still alive, and capable of governing.

Now, while Clement Attlee was the official head of government, the leading figure in the transformation of the British economic system was a colorful and fascinating man named William Beveridge. Beveridge was born in India in 1879 to a wealthy British government official. His mother, Annette Akroyd Beveridge—a prominent Unitarian social activist in Britain—went to India to open a school for poor Indian girls. There, she met Beveridge's father, Henry, a judge in the Indian Civil Service. Their son—like most upper-class English youths—was sent to an English boarding school to prepare for a university education. He attended Oxford University, where he majored in mathematics and the classics. This is an interesting combination that speaks of elite British higher education.

Beveridge was undecided about a career. He dabbled in law and business before a former professor suggested he go to work in a London settlement house in the poor East End. A settlement house is a place for the poor and homeless to live when they have no other alternatives. This settlement house was a project of Sidney and Beatrice Webb—prominent British socialist economists, who were instrumental in the founding of the Labour Party through the Fabian Society. The Fabians believed in gradual progress toward socialism rather than radical revolution. They'd adopted the name of the Roman general Fabius Cunctator, who patiently secured victory while avoiding pitched battles.

Beveridge's connection to the Webbs led to his appointment as the director of the London School of Economics from 1919 to 1937. The LSE today is one of the leading universities in the world, devoted to economics and politics.

The Webbs founded it in 1895 as a left-wing counterweight to the conservative economic thinking that came out of Oxford and Cambridge.

At the London School, Beveridge devoted himself to the study of unemployment, poverty, and illness. He wrote many books, pamphlets, and newspaper articles on the need for a national system of unemployment benefits, old-age pensions, and health care. He also created the Academic Assistance Council, which provided a home for academics who were persecuted—and forced out of Germany by the Nazis—because they were Jewish, or left-wing, or simply opposed to the policies of Adolf Hitler.

As the Second World War turned in the Allies' favor, Beveridge was asked to form a commission to propose social policies for Britain, after the war. He produced a study called, "Social Insurance and Allied Services." It might be hard to believe but it was a best seller in Britain and even sold 50,000 copies in the United States. Ever since, it has been known as *The Beveridge Report. The Beveridge Report* was a blueprint for a Labour Party program of social welfare policies proposed and passed in 1948. It called for comprehensive unemployment insurance, old-age pensions, and, most dramatically, free, universal, public health care.

The British National Health Service would be comprehensive in that all residents of the United Kingdom would be covered. It would be free in the sense that there would be no payments for services or medical bills after treatment.

And it would be public in the sense that all hospitals and medical specialists would be employees of the government.

Naturally, this raised strenuous objections from doctors organized by the British Medical Society. One of the tactics the Labour government employed was to allow general practitioners to remain private professionals, who would be paid by the National Health Service. Like any complex economic institution—especially one that contains principles of socialism or public ownership—there were both costs and benefits to the creation of the NHS.

Although the British do not pay taxes as high as in Sweden or France, about 47 percent of their income is paid to the government. Sales taxes on all goods and services in Britain average about 20 percent. Americans complain when sales taxes get close to 10 percent. The British pay higher income taxes than income earners in the U.S., as well.

Another cost is measured in the waiting times for non-emergency treatments, and the NHS's refusal to pay for some procedures.

The American author T.R. Reid has written an excellent book about different health systems around the world. It's called, *The Healing of America: A Global Quest for Better, Cheaper, and Fairer Health Care.* In it, Reid complains about living as a foreign correspondent in London, and the NHS refusing shoulder surgery to alleviate the discomfort in his shoulder when he swung a golf club. All systems ration health care. In the United States, it could be the Medicare program, the Veterans Administration hospitals, or—for most Americans—private insurance. In the United States, about 18 percent of our total gross domestic product is tied up in health care. No other country dedicates nearly as much of its total income to health care. The British spend about half of that at 9.4 percent. And even so, the British live slightly longer than Americans, at 80.4 years compared to 78.9.

Because the NHS covers all United Kingdom residents, and charges nothing at the point of service, the NHS must put in place many cost-reducing policies. Maybe one of the most effective is something called the capitation payment system. Although British general practitioners are private professionals, most receive almost all their income from the NHS. They are paid for each person that registers with their office. And it's a set amount, no matter what kind of treatments or procedures the person receives. The healthier the person, the less expense for the GP, and the greater the physician's net income. So, for instance, GPs do basic services such as flu shots—which are free.

There's an enormous public benefit to having everyone in a society covered by flu vaccines. Because less work time is lost, there's more time left over for production of goods and services. There's also a tremendous cost savings due to minimalizing doctors' bills, insurance forms, and insurance claims. One of the biggest drivers of American health costs is the huge amount of paperwork associated with it. Surely, I'm not the only one constantly inundated by pages and pages of health forms, claims forms, and explanation-of-benefit forms that regularly clog up my mail box.

Another component of the British social-welfare system that reduces medical costs is the low tuition at British medical schools. British physicians don't graduate with the tremendous debt burdens common to American medical students. Consider this: in the United States, young physicians start out their careers about a half-million dollars behind the average college graduate in terms of tuition expense and debt, according to the Association of American Medical Colleges. This pushes many American physicians into medical specialties that promise high incomes, such as plastic surgery and cardiac surgery. By comparison, British specialists are government employees, and live on a fixed salary.

Turning the equation around: British GPs, in contrast, are private practitioners who earn more as they accept more clients. So, Britain has twice as many GPs per capita as in the United States. And most health-care economists conclude that GPs who treat symptoms early are much more effective in reducing health-care costs overall.

The most controversial aspect of the British National Health Service goes by the acronym NICE. This stands for the National Institute for Health and Clinical Excellence. NICE is the gatekeeper for medical practices and procedures in the National Health Service system. NICE refuses to fund procedures and tests that it deems unnecessary, or too costly, for the benefits derived. For instance, NICE has recently decided that the PSA screening-test for prostate cancer is not an accurate indicator, and, therefore, not cost effective. Just recently, my own private physician has come to the same conclusion.

The other rather nice thing about NICE is its role in reducing the prevalence and costs of malpractice claims. If a specialist's treatment or procedure is approved by NICE, then the doctor is not subject to malpractice claims for that procedure. NICE also significantly reduces so-called defensive medicine practices, where doctors perform elaborate tests and x-rays to further protect themselves from malpractice claims. I doubt it's coincidental that British doctors pay less than 10 percent of what American doctors do for malpractice insurance.

While the Beveridge plan to create the NHS initially met with skepticism in the medical community, employers were generally supportive for self-interested reasons. British industry had to compete with other high-income countries on quality as well as price. As the medical expense of providing health insurance was shifted to the national government, employers benefited financially while employing healthier and more productive workers.

Business leaders also expressed little objection to the parts of the Beveridge report that called for universal unemployment insurance and old age pensions. This did not arise from Christian charity but rather from the realization that minimum levels of personal income would support consumer demand for goods and services, and act as a stabilizer, even amid economic downturns.

The Labour governments also introduced a more progressive income tax. This was done to redistribute income from the rich to the poor. It was often referred to as "Robin Hood economics"—after another famous Englishman. While income redistribution served to benefit the working-class base of the Labour Party, it's also true that moving income from the rich to the poor increases total spending. This follows from the regularly observed tendency of lower-income individuals to spend a higher percentage of their incomes than higher earners do. Keynes referred to this as a higher "marginal propensity to consume."

I always tell my students that this is a good ice-breaker to use as a pick-up line in a bar: MPC. Much more useful than asking someone their astrological sign. I don't really believe in astrology, but I have noticed that couples with similar marginal propensities to consume seem to have a better chance of staying together. In my experience, people with high MPCs get along with others with similarly high MPCs. People with low marginal propensities to consume—a thriftier sort of person—have a much better chance of a long relationship with a fellow thrifty person.

In this view, one might theorize that divorce is often a function of radically different MPCs! Keynes did talk about psychological differences. But he maintained that differential incomes—income inequality—explains most differences in the tendency to spend.

So, the Labour Party adopted many of the Beveridge report recommendations. It also initiated a wave of industry nationalizations in the early post-World War II era. At Labour Party urging, the British government nationalized the railroads, coal mines, steel mills, shipyards, electric utilities, and the airlines. The goal was to promote employment, high wages, and stable economic activity. The stability argument arose from Labour's belief that unbridled competition among major industrial firms was a key source of prewar economic instability, leading to recessions and the Great Depression.

The British were much less interested in economic planning than the French were, with their system of indicative planning. That is to say that the French government, in consultation with business and labor interests, created a unified economic plan for the country, and signaled—or indicated—its preferences through a series of policy prescriptions, including tax incentives and subsidies. The British maintained greater faith in competition and in market pricing than continental Europeans did. Maybe this reflected the economic thinking of classical British economists like Adam Smith and David Ricardo. And so, British industry and labor typically wanted to retain their freedom to set higher prices, and strike for higher wages. These freedoms tend to be more restricted in the French system of indicative planning—and in other forms of national planning, even by democratic governments. The Labour Party's vision of the British social welfare system went largely unchanged in the 1950s and 1960s, except the NHS was modified so that people had to make small co-payments for glasses, contact lenses, false teeth, and prescription drugs. Children, the elderly, and the poor were exempt from these charges.

The last Labour government of the 1970s engaged in one last round of industry nationalizations. British Petroleum, British Leyland Motors, and Rolls Royce all were nationalized—not for planning, or stabilization reasons, but mainly because they were on the verge of bankruptcy, at the time. Government bailouts in the form of nationalization was a way to save the companies, and the jobs of the people who worked there. This is sometimes referred to this as "lemon socialism"—the government taking over lemons that nobody else wanted.

The 1970s was a time of "stagflation" in most industrial democracies. Stagflation is an ugly word made up by economists. It refers to the unusual combination of economic stagnation—that is, a lack of growth—occurring at the same time as inflation drives costs and prices higher. Most economists believe that inflation occurs as a result of rapid growth, low unemployment, and high demand for goods, services and workers. If the economy is stagnating—or declining—the level of prices should be dropping, as people and businesses spend less.

The major cause of the economic stagflation of the 1970s was the oil embargo imposed on the United States and some other Western nations by the Organization of Arab Petroleum Exporting Countries. These Middle Eastern members of OPEC relied almost entirely on petroleum sales to finance their national economies. The effect was to significantly restrict the supply of oil to industrial countries, and, therefore, to drive up the prices of gasoline and everything else. Gasoline prices in the United States doubled in 1973, and doubled again in 1979.

I was an undergraduate at the University of Houston in 1970. My car was a 1966 Ford Galaxie 500 XL. What a great car! It had a 452-cubic inch V-8 engine, power steering, power brakes, air conditioning—a necessity in south Texas—and an automatic transmission. Going downhill, it probably got about eight miles to a gallon. It had a 20-gallon gas tank and it cost about $4.00 to fill my tank. Gas was about 20 cents a gallon, at the time. After the first OPEC embargo in 1973, gas prices shot up to the unheard-of level of about 50 cents a gallon. And then in 1979, the gas price jumped again to about $1 a gallon. It cut down my driving a little bit. So, I got rid of my Ford Galaxie 500 XL, and bought a little red Toyota that could have fit in the front seat of my Ford.

More broadly—for industries and households in industrial democracies—the effects of the oil shock were devastating. Any manufactured product that took energy to produce got much more expensive. Anything shipped by air, rail, or truck cost much more to transport. British industries then were older—and energy inefficient—and so at a severe competitive disadvantage. Prices in Britain increased by as much as 17 percent a year, in the late 1970s.

British factories, mines, and shipyards laid off workers by the hundreds of thousands.

In response, two competing explanations—and suggested cures—were offered to address Britain's economic distress. The Labour Party blamed the capitalist system, and argued for more Keynesian-style fiscal and monetary stimulation. They wanted to increase the money supply, and expand government spending, to put Britain back to work. The Conservative Party blamed the welfare state: high taxes, and inefficient publicly owned enterprises. Conservatives believed that high taxes led to elevated prices while also reducing incentives to invest in new ideas. They argued that inefficient state-owned enterprises produced substandard goods and services that were uncompetitive in world markets.

The 1979 election was a contest between these two vastly different visions. The Conservative Party, led by Margaret Thatcher, won the election and radically remade the British welfare state that William Beveridge and the Labour Party had created. Margaret Thatcher was the daughter of a small-town grocer. She wasn't the typical Oxford-educated, upper class Conservative politician. She was strongly influenced by the writings of the Austrian economist, Friedrich Hayek, and the American economist, Milton Friedman.

The Thatcher government significantly reduced taxes, especially on higher income Brits. She broke a strike of the miner's union, and, like her American counterpart, Ronald Reagan, reduced the powers of trade unions in general. She also pushed through deregulation of the financial industry, which led to booming business in the London financial sector, and high incomes for British financial professionals.

And the Thatcher government privatized many government-owned enterprises. The British automakers Jaguar and Land Rover were sold to Ford Motor Co., and, subsequently, to India's Tata Motors. Rolls Royce and Mini Cooper were sold to BMW. The aircraft engine component of Rolls Royce was privatized as a separate corporation. British Petroleum was privatized—as was British Airways. British Telecom was privatized, and the national rail system was broken up and sold to private firms in pieces. One purchaser of a part of British Rail was Richard Branson, the founder of Virgin Records and Virgin Airlines. There's now a Virgin Rail, as part of the privatized British railroad industry.

Many Brits became quite wealthy and successful as a result of Margaret Thatcher's policies. London became a magnet for entrepreneurs and business people. One unexpected effect of Thatcher-era deregulation was the arrival of hundreds of young French chefs in London. Drawn by lower taxes and the Channel Tunnel, or Chunnel—which connects London and Paris by rail—young enterprising chefs flocked to suddenly cool London, and the promised land of less red tape and restrictions, to open restaurants. As a consequence, London became a much better place to dine.

The British motor industry also grew, as Japanese, German, and Indian capitalists built—or modernized—it. Britain is also now the headquarters, and main testing area, for many Formula One motor racing teams.

One negative result of the Thatcher years was a large increase in income inequality in Britain. Sweden is at the low end of income inequality, with a Gini index value of 27.3, according to the World Bank. Certain South American countries usually have the highest world's Gini index co-efficient. Colombia and Brazil, two highly unequal societies, are at

53.5 and 52.9. Great Britain's Gini index score is 32.6—more unequal than social democratic Sweden but less unequal compared to the United States' at 41.1.

The one sector of the British social-welfare system that the Thatcher government didn't touch was the National Health Service. The NHS has such strong public support that even in the midst of free-enterprise euphoria, and mass privatizations, William Beveridge's prize creation remained a publicly owned institution.

The Conservative Party ruled Britain from 1979 to 1997. Near the end of its reign, the British electorate became less enchanted with the free-market direction of Thatcherite policies and elected a Labour Party government in 1997 led by Tony Blair. But it was not your grandmother's Labour Party. Blair ran as a candidate from "New" Labour. He didn't reverse any of the Thatcher nationalizations. But his government did put more money into the National Health System. And it raised minimum wages, unemployment benefits, and old-age pensions.

The Blair government seemed to want to minimize the pain and loss associated with a deregulated market economy. The Labour Party won three elections, and governed until 2010, when a new Conservative government led by a young, dynamic David Cameron took over. And so, the pendulum of Labour and Conservative party politics goes on.

Still, the NHS remains such a popular British institution that at the opening ceremony of the London Olympics a few years ago, one of the parade floats was a mockup of a NHS clinic. William Beveridge would have been proud to be in the stadium, watching his creation cheered.

Lecture 15

Social Welfare in Germany: Bismarck to Kohl

THE OCCUPATION OF GERMANY AFTER WORLD WAR II had profound effects on the country's postwar development, beginning with the creation of two new countries: the German Democratic Republic (East Germany) and the Federal Republic of Germany (West Germany). This division, at least temporarily, undid the unification of Germany that Otto von Bismarck had accomplished less than a century earlier. Bismarck combined 39 independent states under his leadership in Berlin. He was also the founding father of the German social welfare system. In fact, he was the first political leader in the world to create national systems of unemployment insurance, old-age pensions, and health care. ◆

Bismarck's Health-Care System

◀ Otto von Bismarck believed in German development and German power. He was a driver of German industrialization and technological development. He understood that modern military power is based on industrial capability and advanced technology. Additionally, he was motivated by his Lutheran beliefs and the duty of the rich to help the poor.

◀ Bismarck understood that any worker who feared losing his or her job—and income—would not be the most productive employee. Furthermore, workers who were unhealthy and had no care when they were sick would hold back national economic development. And when workers retired, they would need incomes to support themselves in old age. So, Bismarck devised systems of worker protection and worker development in the German Reich. These policies also helped diminish the appeal to workers of the rival Social Democratic Party.

◀ Bismarck was an enemy of all political parties, because they challenged his hold on power. He was also an enemy of the Catholic Church, which he saw as too reactionary and conservative. The Catholic Church promoted a quiet rural life of obedience, but Bismarck needed Germans to move to the cities and take up jobs in the new factories of industrializing Germany.

◀ Bismarck's health-care system, created in 1883, required all employees to contribute a share of their wages to pay for workers' health insurance. And he required employers to pay an equal amount into the system for each employee. If a German worker loses his or her job, unemployment benefits take over the burden of making the health insurance contributions. So, a German worker doesn't lose health care when a job is lost.

In the present-day German health-care system, employees and employers each contribute the equivalent of 7.5 percent of the worker's wage.

◀ The premiums are paid to so-called sickness funds, which are nonprofit organizations required to accept all applicants. They earn no profits, but their executives are compensated based on the number of their members, so there is some incentive to compete for new members.

◀ The Bismarck system of health care and social welfare lasted through two world wars as well as through political upheavals and the dictatorship of the Third Reich. And it remains the basis for unified Germany's system of social welfare.

Development of the New Federal Republic

◀ Today's Germany went through an uncertain and difficult division after World War II. Once fighting stopped, the Allied military commands were the supreme powers in Germany. And between the end of the war in 1945 and the establishment of the Federal Republic in May 1949, several different scenarios were advanced by the Allied powers and German politicians.

◀ There was strong sentiment in both the United States and the Soviet Union to deindustrialize Germany and return it to the rural and agricultural land it had been before Bismarck. But there were also major factors militating against this plan. France, Britain, and other economies in western Europe needed German industrial goods to rebuild their economies. They also needed German consumers and businesses to buy their exports.

◀ Although the United States and the Soviet Union had been allies in World War II, differences and disputes developed almost as soon as the war ended. Not only was Germany divided into four zones of occupation, but Berlin—the capital, deep inside the Soviet zone—was itself divided into four zones of occupation and administration. And the Soviets wanted the other three Allied powers—Britain, France, and the United States—to leave Berlin under direct and total Soviet control.

◀ The United States and the Soviet Union also disagreed about the nature of governments and economic systems in eastern Europe, which were now under the complete control of the Red Army. The Cold War was developing, and the Soviet Union and the United States were becoming adversaries rather than allies.

◀ Political parties and movements inside Germany had very different opinions and political platforms than those expressed by their occupiers. The Social Democratic and Communist Parties wanted an untied, neutral, and socialist Germany. Conservative parties, businesspeople, and professionals wanted a market-based liberal democracy.

◀ Trade unions wanted a market economy, but one in which there were highly developed social welfare policies and regulations. And there were some who wanted a return to the militaristic and dictatorial system of the Third Reich.

◀ For the three Allied powers governing in the west, there were immediate and serious short-term problems to be overcome. There were millions of hungry, unemployed, and homeless Germans. Additionally, there were millions of displaced Germans streaming into the western zones of the country from eastern Europe.

◀ In addition, there was a money problem. The old reichsmark of the defeated Germany was becoming more and more worthless as prices rose. To counter postwar inflation, the Allied powers and the interim western German government carried out an overnight currency reform. Old reichsmark—up to 400 of them—could be traded in for the new deutschmark at a ratio of 10 old marks to one new mark. This wiped out lots of paper financial wealth. But it had a galvanizing effect on the western German economy.

◀ The Soviets objected mightily. More than any other factor, the new currency led to the establishment of a formal government, and national state, in western Germany. The Soviets countered by founding the German Democratic Republic in their zone. This two-state system was to last until 1989, and the fall of the Berlin Wall.

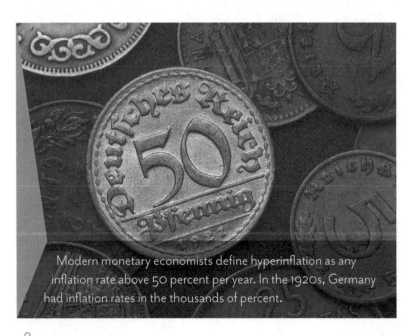

Modern monetary economists define hyperinflation as any inflation rate above 50 percent per year. In the 1920s, Germany had inflation rates in the thousands of percent.

> The rapid development of West German capitalism had some unsavory aspects. Many business leaders and industrialists who had actively supported—and profited from—the Nazi regime were not prosecuted for war crimes. Others were let out of prison early and allowed to reestablish themselves as business leaders in the new republic.

◀ The other major factor in the rapid development of the new Federal Republic was the Marshall Plan. Formally known as the European Recovery Program, it's better known today for its association with U.S. Secretary of State George C. Marshall.

◀ With the Marshall Plan aid and a stable currency, the West German economy took off and was the fastest-growing economy in Europe. It also had an unexpected benefit as the result of its wartime destruction: West German factories were now rebuilt with the most modern and up-to-date equipment. German industry had an advantage over British and French industry, which still worked with older equipment.

◀ West German industry received a great deal of investment funding from its large banks. German citizens tended to be rather conservative and risk averse. Therefore, they preferred the safety of banks, which guaranteed set—if low—interest rates to the relative risk of investing their savings in stocks. In turn, the banks lent depositors' savings to German businesses. This relative freedom from short-term pressure gave German business leaders a greater chance to pursue longer-term strategies and growth projects.

- Even though the West German economy was based on a laissez-faire market system, the German government still played a large role. Some German industries—such as the German rail system and German utilities—were dominated by publicly owned enterprises. Additionally, some firms, such as Volkswagen, were owned primarily by private stockholders but with some additional stake held by the government.

- All large German enterprises with more than 500 employees were required to have members of the relevant trade union, representing workers in its industry, on its board of directors. This principle—called *Mitbestimmung*, or codetermination—gives German workers a voice, and a stake, in the long-term success of their employer.

- German workers typically are well paid. Germany also typically has among the largest trade surpluses of any country in the world. To simultaneously have high labor costs and a large trade surplus means that German workers are highly productive. And productivity depends on education and skills.

Modern labor market theory—known as the theory of efficiency wages—contends that worker productivity is improved by higher wages and by a feeling of being treated fairly.

German Education and Business

◀ The German educational system does an excellent job of preparing students for the workforce. Moreover, hiring firms frequently are subsidized by the federal government, which bears some of the expense of employing younger and less skilled workers. As a result, youth unemployment rates in Germany are among the lowest in the world. This early connection to the labor force builds lifetime skills and ever-higher productivity.

◀ German labor law is also much different than U.S. labor law. In the United States, many jobs in the private workforce are let under a system that allows employers to hire and fire at will. U.S. employers typically have few regulations that constrain them from terminating individual workers.

◀ In Germany, by comparison, firms that intend to lay off workers undergo a long process of notification, appeal, and generous severance payments. This typically makes German firms reluctant to fire workers, but also quite conservative in taking on new ones.

◀ So, the typical German firm's labor-turnover ratio is much lower than for a U.S. firm. This longer attachment to a single employer means that the typical German firm enjoys the benefits of the training and education it provides to its workers longer than a U.S. firm does.

◀ This internalization of the growth of human capital is among the secrets of high German labor productivity. Because a German firm expects its worker to remain with it for a longer period of time—to the firm's benefit—it's more willing to train its workers.

◀ German workers also get a lot of time off. There's some evidence that a generous vacation and leave policy tends to create more rested, healthier, motivated, and productive workers. German workers aren't too stressed out about unemployment, old-age incomes, or bouts of illness and injury, and less stress tends to promote better health and longer life expectancy.

◀ Germans who attend a university tend to stay in school longer. There's no tuition, and university students get payments either from their parents or from the government. German university students enjoy highly subsidized meals, transportation, housing, and entertainment, so it's not unusual for German students to remain in university full time until their late twenties.

◀ Helmut Kohl—who was the chancellor of West Germany and then reunited Germany for 16 years, from 1982 to 1998—often complained that Germany was becoming a *kollektive Freizeitpark*: a collective amusement park, where nobody worked. However, attempts to impose tuition charges and maximum lengths of study have met with furious resistance from students' unions as attacks on academic freedom.

◀ Although the German government regulates employment and prices and subsidizes health care and education on a large scale, it does not tell German businesses what to produce. Planning in Germany has too many echoes and negative connotations from the Nazi period, when industry was tightly planned to provide for the war machine of the Third Reich. Long-range economic planning—to the extent that it exists at all—is done by the larger German banks and large industrial conglomerates.

- Even though Germany has many large world-class firms, it also has a large and thriving sector of small- and medium-size firms. This is the so-called *mittelstand*. It consists mainly of family-owned firms that specialize in specific high-quality consumer and industrial products. They benefit from the vocational education and apprenticeship programs.

- All German firms, whether large or small, must belong to some business federation. Very large companies belong to the Federation of German Industries. Others belong to the Association of German Chambers of Industry and Commerce, which has affiliates all over the world.

- The German business chambers are the main organizations that supervise the country's student-worker apprentice programs and establish the criteria for professional exams and licensure. Almost all German workers—whatever their trade or occupation—have a professional license, or permit, that was obtained through specific education, training, and examinations.

- There are some hidden characteristics, or costs, to the Germans educational system, too. One criticism is that early placement into a vocational track tends to reinforce social-class distinctions and income inequality. Students from upper-class families tend to track into academic secondary education, in college preparatory schools. Working-class young people tend to track into vocational schools and blue-collar occupations.

- Another major cost is that German tax revenues pay for the employer subsidies. Partly as a result, Germans pay significantly higher taxes than Americans. The overall tax rate in Germany is about 45 percent, compared with about 32 percent in the United States.

BERGHOFF, KOCKA, AND ZIEGLER, EDS.,
   Business in the Age of Extremes.
CRAIG, *The Germans.*

Questions

1 Why was the Marshall Plan good for the post–World War II
   West German economy and good for the U.S. economy?

2 How do German labor market laws and institutions
   create incentives for German businesses to improve their
   workers' skills and productivity?

Social Welfare in Germany: Bismarck to Kohl

The occupation of Germany after the Second World War had profound effects on the country's post-war development—beginning with the creation of two new countries. In the war's immediate aftermath, the defeated Third Reich was divided into four zones of occupation. The area that once had been the Kingdom of Prussia—the northeastern part—became the Soviet zone of occupation. And soon, it was transformed into the German Democratic Republic, GDR—better known to most of us as East Germany. The other three areas—the British Zone of Occupation in the north, the French zone in the Rhineland, and the American zone in the southern areas of Bavaria and Baden-Wurttemberg—were transformed into the Federal Republic of Germany, familiarly known as West Germany. This division—at least temporarily—undid the unification of Germany that Otto von Bismarck, had accomplished less than a century earlier. Bismarck, the conservative statesman and former prime minister of Prussia, combined 39 independent states under his leadership in Berlin.

Bismarck was one of the big men in German history. By big I not only mean important but also physically big. A bit later, we'll meet another very big man in modern German history—the post-war Chancellor Helmut Kohl. Both big men weighed more than 300 pounds. Each summer, Chancellor Kohl took a vacation known as a *diat kur*. Translated literally from the German, that means "diet regimen." In contrast, Otto Von Bismarck was quite proud of his monumental stature.

Bismarck is important to our discussion today because he was the founding father of the German social-welfare system. In fact, he was the first political leader in the world to create national systems of: unemployment insurance, old age pensions, and health care. Today's German health-care system is not much different than the one that Bismarck created in 1883. Before Bismarck gave Germany this system, he was instrumental in creating a unified nation through military campaigns and threats. The German Reich came into existence in 1871. And Bismarck became known as the Iron Chancellor for his authoritarian rule.

Bismarck was not a democrat, nor a believer in representative government. He believed in German development, and German power. He was a driver of German industrialization and technological development. He understood that modern military power is based on industrial capability, and advanced technology. Additionally, he was motivated by his Lutheran beliefs, and the duty of the rich to help the poor.

Nobody's motivations have merely one basis. Human beings are complicated beings, and have many different drives and impulses. Bismarck was no different. Bismarck understood that any worker who feared losing his or her job—and income—would not be the most productive employee. Further, workers who were unhealthy, and had no care when they were sick, would hold back national economic development. And when workers retired, they would need incomes to support themselves in old age. So, Bismarck devised systems of worker protection and worker development in the German Reich.

These policies also helped to diminish the appeal to workers of the rival Social Democratic Party. Bismarck was an enemy of all political parties, because they challenged his hold on power. He was also an enemy of the Catholic Church, which he saw as too reactionary and conservative. The Catholic Church promoted a quiet, rural life of obedience. But Bismarck needed Germans to move to the cities, and take up jobs in the new factories of industrializing Germany.

The German industrial capitalist Alfred Krupp was the heir to a family manufacturing fortune that specialized in cast-steel cannons and other war-making armaments, and which became known to history as "The Arms of Krupp." He didn't need illiterate farmers in his country. He needed urban, educated, and skilled factory workers.

Bismarck's health-care system required all employees to contribute a share of their wages to pay for workers' health insurance. And he required employers to pay an equal amount into the system for each employee. Bismarck's system was mandatory. It's pretty clear that all efficiently run health-care systems require some type of mandates. In the present-day German health-care system, employees and employers each contribute the equivalent of 7.5 percent of the worker's wage.

If a German worker loses his or her job, unemployment benefits take over the burden of making the health-insurance contributions. So, a German worker doesn't lose health care when a job is lost. The premiums are paid to so-called sickness funds. These are non-profit organizations required to accept all applicants. They earn no profits. But their executives are compensated based on the number of their members. So, there is some incentive to compete for new members.

The Bismarck system of health care and social welfare lasted through two world wars, as well as through political upheavals, and the dictatorship of the Third Reich. And it remains the basis for unified Germany's system of social welfare. But today's Germany went through an uncertain and difficult division after World War II.

The Allied military commands were the supreme powers in Germany, once fighting stopped. And between the end of the war in 1945, and the establishment of the Federal Republic in May 1949, several different scenarios were advanced by the Allied powers and German politicians. There was strong sentiment in both the United States and the Soviet Union to de-industrialize Germany, and return it to the rural and agricultural land it had been before Bismarck. The Soviets were particularly in favor of this scenario, as they had been the victims of German aggression and slaughter twice in the first half of the 20th century. Some estimates of Soviet casualties in Second World War alone run as high as 30 million people. In the Battle of Stalingrad in 1942-1943, the Soviets lost more than a million dead. That's twice the number of U.S. war dead in Europe and the Pacific combined.

There was also some support in the administration of President Franklin D. Roosevelt for a de-industrialization program in Germany. It was vigorously supported by Roosevelt's Treasury secretary, Henry Morgenthau. And it got the name the Morgenthau Plan. But there were also major factors militating against this plan. France, Britain, and other economies in Western Europe needed German industrial goods to rebuild their economies. They also needed German consumers and businesses to buy their exports.

Although the United States and the Soviet Union had been allies in World War II, differences and disputes developed almost as soon as the war ended. Not only was Germany divided into four zones of occupation, but Berlin—the capital, deep inside the Soviet zone—was itself divided into four zones of occupation and administration. And the Soviets wanted the other three allied powers—Britain, France, and the United States—to leave Berlin under direct and total Soviet control. The United States and the Soviet Union also disagreed about the nature of governments and economic systems in Eastern Europe, which were now under the complete control of the Red Army. So, the Cold War was developing, and the Soviet Union and the United States were becoming adversaries rather than allies.

Political parties and movements inside Germany had very different opinions and political platforms than those expressed by their occupiers. The Social Democratic and Communist Parties wanted an untied, neutral, and socialist Germany. Conservative parties, businesspeople, and professionals wanted a market-based liberal democracy. Trade unions—especially in the western part of the country—wanted a market economy, but one in which there were highly developed social-welfare policies and regulations. And there were some—not always overtly—who wanted a return to the militaristic and dictatorial system of the Third Reich.

For the three Allied powers governing in the west, there were immediate and serious short-term problems to be overcome. There were millions of hungry, unemployed, and homeless Germans. Additionally, there were millions of displaced Germans streaming into the western zones of the country from Eastern Europe. They had either been thrown out of their native countries—like the Sudeten Germans displaced from Czechoslovakia—or were Germans fleeing the Soviet Red Army as it established its hold on eastern Europe.

In addition, there was a money problem. The old reichsmark of the defeated Germany was becoming more and more worthless as prices rose. Rapid inflation was reviving memories of German hyperinflation of the 1920s. Nowadays, monetary economists define hyperinflation as any inflation rate above 50 percent per year. In the 1920s, Germany had inflation rates in the thousands of percent.

When I was an undergraduate at the University of Houston in the 1960s, there was an old German carpenter who worked on campus, and came to a lot of student discussions. My favorite story of his was his experience as a carpenter in Germany during the 1920s. Fred told us that he had to get paid twice a day, because he couldn't carry home all the money he earned if he waited until the end of the day. He would give the money to his wife, and she would quick run to the store to buy bread before the prices went up.Germans, to this day—if they are older, or have some historical knowledge—have a visceral fear of inflation coming back. This fear manifested itself in the 1990s, when Germany was debating giving up the deutschmark in favor of the new and untried euro.

To counter post-war inflation, the Allied powers and the interim western German government carried out an overnight currency reform. Old reichsmark—up to 400 of them—could be traded in for the new deutschmark at a ratio of 10 old marks to 1 new mark. This wiped out lots of paper financial wealth. But it had a galvanizing effect on the western German economy.

The Soviets objected mightily. And more than any other factor, the new currency led to the establishment of a formal government, and national state, in western Germany. The Soviets countered by founding the German Democratic Republic in their zone. This two-state system was to last until 1989, and the fall of the Berlin Wall.

The other major factor in the rapid development of the new federal republic was the Marshall Plan. Formally known as the European Recovery Program, it's better known today for its association with U.S. Secretary of State George Marshall. Political and economic leaders in the United States had learned the lessons of the disastrous Versailles Treaty that ended World War I. Making defeated enemies poorer and bitter was a recipe for potential economic depression, and also warlike sentiments and hostilities.

In the United States, as plan sponsor, the Marshall Plan is sometimes viewed as pure charity. But it had several beneficial effects for the U.S. economy. First, it stimulated foreign demand for American consumer and industrial goods. Secondly, by helping to reestablish a market economy in western Europe, it diminished the appeal of Soviet-style communism. With that said, the rapid development of West German capitalism had some unsavory aspects.

Many business leaders and industrialists who had actively supported—and profited from—the Nazi regime were not prosecuted for war crimes. Others were let out of prison early, and allowed to reestablish themselves as business leaders in the new republic. Dr. Ferdinand Porsche—who had developed the Volkswagen for Hitler, and also the Panzer battle tank for the Wehrmacht—was let out of prison after a very short time, and allowed to run his automobile empire once again. Many ex-Nazis found their way to become prominent again in German business and politics. This was to create friction and estrangement between older Germans and younger Germans, some of whom felt more shame for their country's history.

Not all ex-Nazis who rose to power were West German. Many ex-members of the Third Reich police and SS found employment with the police and spy services of East Germany—especially in the Stasi, the East German secret police. When the creation of the European Union and the euro were being debated in reunited Germany in the 1990s, I was spending some time teaching in Austria—and watching a good bit of German television. As an economist, I was fascinated by the debates about a single currency and an economic union. Conservative Chancellor Helmut Kohl was a big supporter—pun intended.

Once, when a news reporter for a German television network asked him why he supported the EU and the euro, Mr. Kohl glared, and asked the reporter, "Was ist die Alternative?" What is the alternative? The reporter didn't have an answer. But Chancellor Kohl did: "Sechzig Millionen tod!" Sixty million dead! That's the number of total casualties in Europe during the first and second world wars. The chancellor didn't need to say that Germany bore a large part of the blame for those casualties.

With the Marshall Plan, aid and a stable currency, the West German economy took off, and was the fastest-growing economy in Europe. It also had an unexpected benefit as the result of its wartime destruction. West German factories were now rebuilt with the most modern, and up-to-date, equipment. So, German industry had an advantage over British and French industry, which was still working with older, less damaged equipment.

West German industry received a great deal of investment funding from its large banks. German citizens tended to be rather conservative and risk averse. Therefore, they preferred the safety of banks, which guaranteed set—if low—interest rates to the relative risk of investing their savings in stocks. In turn, the banks lent depositors' savings to German businesses. This relative freedom from short-term pressure gave German business leaders a greater chance to pursue longer-term strategies and growth projects.

Even though the West German economy was based on a laissez-faire market system, the German government still played a large role. Some German industries were dominated by publicly owned enterprises. For instance, the German rail system, German utilities, and the West German airline Lufthansa were publicly owned. Additionally, some firms were owned primarily by private stockholders but with some additional stake held by the government.

The ownership of Volkswagen was primarily private. But the state government of Lower Saxony owned a minority share of locally headquartered Volkswagen, and thus was entitled to put some representatives on the Volkswagen board of directors.

All large German enterprises with more than 500 employees were required to have members of the relevant trade union, representing workers in its industry, on its board of directors. This principle—called *mitbestimmung* in German, and co-determination in English—gives German workers a voice, and a stake, in the long-term success of their employer.

Modern labor-market theory—known as "the theory of efficiency wages"—contends that worker productivity is improved by higher wages, and by a feeling of being treated fairly. German workers typically are well paid. For comparison purposes, Germany's hourly compensation costs in manufacturing was $45.79 one recent year. In the United States, by comparison, hourly compensation costs in manufacturing were $35.67— $10 an hour cheaper.

A point I make in my international economics classes is that low wages are not the most important determinant of high levels of exports—and a high-wage economy does not necessarily lead to balance-of-trade deficits.

People in the United States who argue that the reason we have chronic deficits is that our wages are too high don't understand international economics, very well. If high wages lead to low exports—and high imports, and thus large trade deficits—then Germany should have a much bigger trade deficit than the United States does.

That's one logical outcome based on Germany's relatively high labor costs. But astonishingly enough, Germany typically has among the largest trade surpluses of any country in the world. In one recent year, Germany's trade surplus was more than $270 billion—the highest in the world—and significantly higher than China, in second place, with a $194 billion trade surplus. To simultaneously have high labor costs and a large trade surplus means that German workers are highly productive. And productivity depends upon education and skills.

This is another logical premise. And I have an example to support it: German secondary schools have extensive vocational educational programs that directly feed students into businesses that take them on as apprentices. So, the German educational system does an excellent job of preparing students for the workforce. Moreover, hiring firms frequently are subsidized by the federal government, which bears some of the expense of employing these younger and less-skilled workers. As a result, youth unemployment rates in Germany are among the lowest in the world.

This early connection to the labor force builds lifetime skills and ever-higher productivity.

German labor law is also much different than U.S. labor law. In the United States, many jobs in the private work force are let under a system known as "at will." In essence, it means hire and fire at will. U.S. employers typically have few regulations that constrain them from terminating individual workers. In Germany, by comparison, firms that intend to lay off workers undergo a long process of notification, appeal, and generous severance payments. This typically makes German firms reluctant to fire workers, but also quite conservative in taking on new ones. So, the typical German firm's labor-turnover ratio is much lower than for a U.S. firm. This longer attachment to a single employer means that the typical German firms enjoys the benefits of the training and education its provides to its workers longer than a U.S. firm does.

This internalization of the growth of human capital is among the secrets of high German labor productivity. Because a German firm expects its worker to remain with it for a longer period of time—to the firm's benefit—it's more willing to train its workers. German workers also get a lot of time off. I always tell my students that an employee who works full-time for a firm in Germany is guaranteed five weeks of paid vacation after one year. That's a German federal law, and applies to nearly all German workers.

I then ask my students what U.S. federal law is regarding minimum mandatory paid vacations for full-time workers.

After a few minutes and guessing—one week, two weeks, 10 days—I tell them the answer to the question; it's a trick question. There is no federal law governing minimum paid vacations in the United States; or, for that matter, mandatory paid maternity or paternity leave.

German employers also observe quite a few mandatory holidays. Northern Germany tends to be Protestant, religiously, whereas southern Germany is predominantly Catholic. So, the federal government mandates Protestant and Catholic holidays for everyone. There's some evidence that generous vacation and leave policy tends to create more rested, healthier, motivated, and productive workers. German workers aren't too stressed out about unemployment, old-age incomes, or bouts of illness and injury.

And less stress tends to promote better health and longer life expectancy. Germans live about two years longer than Americans do, on average. Not as long as the French or the Japanese—but an average life expectancy close to 81 years. By the way, this doesn't mean that Germans work longer. Germany still has a low mandatory retirement age.

And Germans who attend a university tend to stay in school longer. There's no tuition, and university students get payments either from their parents or from the government. German university students enjoy highly subsidized meals, transportation, housing, entertainment, and so on. So, it's not unusual for German students to remain in university full-time until their late twenties.

Helmut Kohl—who was the chancellor of West Germany, and then reunited Germany for 16 years, from 1982 to 1998—was often complaining that Germany was becoming a *kollektive freizeitpark*—a collective amusement park, where nobody worked. However, attempts to impose tuition charges—and maximum lengths of study—have met with furious resistance, from students' unions, as attacks on academic freedom.

Although the German government regulates employment and prices, and subsidizes health care and education on a large scale, one thing it does not do is tell German businesses what to produce. Planning in Germany has too many echoes, and negative connotations, from the Nazi period when industry was tightly planned to provide for the war machine of the Third Reich. Long-range economic planning—to the extent that it exists at all—is done by the larger German banks and large industrial conglomerates.

Now, even though Germany has many large world-class firms, it also has a large and thriving sector of small and medium-size firms. This is the so-called *mittelstand*. It consists mainly of family owned firms that specialize in specific, high-quality consumer and industrial products. They benefit from the vocational education and apprenticeship programs.

All German firms, whether large or small, must belong to some business federation. Very large companies belong to the Federation of German Industries. Others belong to the German Chambers of Industry and Commerce. The Chambers of Industry and Commerce have affiliates all over the world. In Chicago, for instance, we an active and important German American Chamber of Commerce. And I'm proud to be an academic member of this organization.

It spends most of its time facilitating trade and partnerships between American firms doing business in Germany, and German firms doing business in the United States. Its most famous—and fun activity— is the annual Christkindlmarket during the winter holiday season in downtown Chicago's Daley Plaza, famous for its Picasso sculpture. The Christkindlmarket is inspired by a holiday tradition dating to 16th-century Nuremberg. From mid-November to late December, German companies specializing in German goods and food sell their wares in wooden booths and food stalls in the city center. You can almost smell the gluhwein and bratwurst now.

The German business chambers are the main organizations that supervise the country's student-worker apprentice programs, and establish the criteria for professional exams and licensure. Almost all German workers—whatever their trade or occupation—have a professional license, or permit, that was obtained through specific education, training, and examinations. So, students come out of the vocational tracks very well-prepared for a particular occupation.

There are some hidden characteristics, or costs, to the Germans educational system, too. One criticism is that early placement into a vocational track tends to reinforce social class distinctions, and income inequality. Students from upper-class families tend to track into academic secondary education, in the *gymnasium*—or college preparatory—schools. Working-class kids tend to track into vocational schools, and blue-collar occupations.

Another major cost is that German tax revenues pay for the employer subsidies. Partly as a result, Germans pay significantly higher taxes than Americans. The overall tax rate in Germany is about 45 percent compared with about 32 percent in the U.S.

Today, Germany's aging population—and industrial competition from eastern Europe—are important challenges. Like most high-income societies, the German population is getting older. This places a heavier burden on the German health-care system, and its generous old-age pensions. Germany is a country that has not always welcomed immigrants happily. But it might increasingly need immigrants to staff its hospitals, old folks' homes, and schools.

Lecture 16

Soviet Bloc: Conformity and Resistance

A S WORLD WAR II WAS ENDING, THE ALLIED VICTORS began to negotiate the postwar fate of Europe. The two major triumphant powers—the United States and the Soviet Union—were advancing toward Germany and ultimate victory over the Nazi regime. Yet the United States and the Soviet Union had very different histories in this war. The United States had begun its most important military offensive in Europe as recently as June 1944. By comparison, the Soviet Union had borne the brunt of German attacks, beginning three years earlier. ◆

Estimates of Soviet losses in World War II range from 20 million to 30 million human lives lost.

Soviet Communism

◀ Because of Soviet sacrifices at the hands of the German army—and Soviet victories over the Germans—the Soviet Union felt entitled, at the end of the fighting in Europe, to dictate the nature of economic and political systems in the territories that the Soviets occupied. In addition, the Soviet Union and communist parties elsewhere in Europe could count on large numbers of voters in postwar elections, in part due to Soviet resistance to the Nazis.

◀ In the Czechoslovakian elections of 1946—the last free elections in Czechoslovakia for decades to come—the Czechoslovak Communist Party got almost 40 percent of the vote. Similarly, in eastern Germany, the socialist and communist parties enjoyed significant support. In short order, Stalin and his proxies across eastern Europe would cynically use this support to consolidate political power in eastern Europe and eliminate democratic opposition.

◀ By the end of the 1940s, they had quashed all open opposition, with one exception. In Yugoslavia, Marshal Tito had led an independent army of national liberation against the Nazi army during wartime. As the leader of his own independent military force, Tito was now able to develop a fairly independent political base of power and strategy for governing Yugoslavia.

◀ So, of all the eastern European countries that subsequently were organized as communist economies, Yugoslavia was the most independent—and most different—of the bloc nations. Its economy was the most decentralized, and its foreign policy was the most self-directed.

◀ The Soviets ceded control in most other areas of the Balkans. The British were granted hegemony in Greece, where large socialist and communist parties had led the fight against Germany. Now, on Stalin's orders, they gave up their opposition to a British-installed capitalist government and economic system there.

◀ The remaining nations of eastern Europe—Poland, East Germany, Czechoslovakia, Hungary, Rumania, and Bulgaria—came to be completely dominated by the Soviet Union. Their Soviet-style political and economic systems were enforced by the Red Army, on orders from the Soviet government and their proxies, in the form of carefully chosen national political leaders.

◀ The leading communist parties in the various eastern European communist countries went by different names, but they were all carbon copies of the Soviet Communist Party in structure and style and in the complete control they exercised over the countries they governed.

The Soviet Economic Model

◀ Every eastern European country under Soviet domination not only adopted one-party authoritarian states, but they also adhered to the basic Soviet economic model. This model had several common components, including state ownership of all major economic sectors, collective or state-owned agriculture, comprehensive planning, and an emphasis on industrial development.

◀ There would be no scope for private ownership or market-directed economic incentives. No profit or dividend income would be allowed. No independent financial sector or financial markets were tolerated. All labor would be allocated by state planning agencies. And foreign trade was under direct state control.

◀ While the Soviet Union gradually consolidated its command over the eastern European communist economies, the Western allies—led by the United States—rebuilt market-oriented economic systems that had frayed as a result of the Great Depression and World War II.

◀ They also created new international economic and financial institutions to help coordinate international relations. The recently created International Monetary Fund (IMF) would facilitate and supervise the international movements of money and financial capital. The World Bank would lend money to finance the reconstruction of Europe.

◀ The Organisation of European Economic Co-operation (OEEC) was established to coordinate the distribution of U.S. financial aid. This aid was formulated under the congressionally approved European Recovery Program of 1948, better known as the Marshall Plan, named for U.S. Secretary of State George C. Marshall. The OEEC laid the groundwork for the European Economic Community, or Common Market, that came into existence in 1957.

◀ Although eastern European countries such as Poland, Czechoslovakia, and Hungary were receptive to receiving much-needed American financial assistance—and were eligible for it under the Marshall Plan—the Soviets feared U.S. influence and the strings that would be attached to such aid. So, the Soviets blocked its extension to communist allies in eastern Europe.

◀ Another post–World War II organization—the North Atlantic Treaty Organization (NATO), founded in 1949—was formed to defend western Europe from future aggression. And the United Nations, founded in October 1945, would try to settle international conflicts peacefully.

◀ The Soviet Union was initially invited to join the IMF and the World Bank, but declined membership—again, for fear of U.S. influence and domination. The only one of the new international organizations the Soviets decided to join was the United Nations.

◀ After NATO's founding, the Soviets created a competing military alliance, the Warsaw Treaty Organization, as a counterweight. The Soviets also established a competing international economic body, the Council for Mutual Economic Assistance, known as Comecon and headquartered in Moscow, that directed trade among the Soviet-dominated economic systems of eastern Europe.

◀ Comecon claimed to be the eastern equivalent of the Common Market being developed in western Europe. But it was not a facilitator of private trade based on comparative advantage. Instead, Comecon served as a planning agency that oversaw essentially a barter system of trade among the countries of eastern Europe and the Soviet Union. This trade was based primarily on Soviet needs and the political decisions of the leadership of the Communist Party of the Soviet Union.

◀ Each eastern European communist economy was oriented to emphasize heavy industry, just as the Soviets had done in their initial five-year plans. Consumer goods and services were given very low priority. Labor, raw materials, and capital goods were to be devoted, instead, to building up large-scale industrial enterprises that would be directed by a planning bureaucracy that answered to the political leadership of the country—the Communist Party.

◀ Each eastern European economy was also directed to concentrate on specific industrial sectors. East Germany, for example, had the task of producing railroad rolling stock for the Soviet Union. Poland was given the task of producing coal and steel. Hungary was assigned the task of producing buses.

Revolt against Soviet Domination

◀ An authoritarian state that suppresses all dissent is required to also suppress the production of consumer goods and services and eliminate political opposition. In the Soviet Union and much of eastern Europe during the late 1940s and early 1950s, there were show trials, imprisonments, and executions of political oppositionists who did not follow strict party orders. Many refugees fled from the oppression and lack of freedom.

◀ A solid border formed between eastern and western Europe to stem the flow of refugees. Winston Churchill, having only recently been voted out as the British prime minister, described—in his famous 1946 speech in Fulton, Missouri—an "iron curtain" that had descended on Europe. This Iron Curtain was to divide Europe for more than 40 years.

◀ On one side would be the rapidly recovering economies of western Europe, with their increasing abundance of consumer goods. On the other side would be the gray and much poorer economies of eastern Europe, cut off from their neighbors—not only economically, but culturally and politically.

◀ While the Soviet economy and its eastern European satellite states were inefficient and not very dynamic, significant disruption was bubbling up from time to time. These sporadic protests and internal dissent were driven by the dissatisfaction of the general population with their standards of living and the lack of political and cultural freedom.

◀ There were violent uprisings and protests in all eastern European states. The first was East Germany's in 1953. Economic authorities in East Berlin—to speed up economic development and industrial production there—had mandated increased production quotas for industrial workers without any corresponding increase in pay. Not surprisingly, workers in East Berlin revolted, and were put down with military force.

◀ The next major uprising against Soviet domination and control came in Hungary in 1956. This revolt was much more violent, bloody, and prolonged. It began as a student protest for greater political and cultural freedom. Tens of thousands of students took to the streets of Budapest, and they were fired on by state security forces. This inflamed the population. The revolt spread throughout Hungary. Eventually, Soviet troops were called in to put down the revolt. More than 2,000 Hungarians and 700 Soviet soldiers were killed. Thousands of Hungarians subsequently fled west and flooded refugee camps in Austria, Germany, and Switzerland.

◀ Meanwhile, a worker uprising centered in the Polish city of Poznan also unfolded in 1956. The spark was similar to that of the East Berlin uprising in 1953. Workers were given orders to

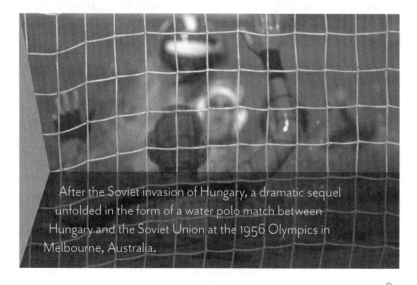

After the Soviet invasion of Hungary, a dramatic sequel unfolded in the form of a water polo match between Hungary and the Soviet Union at the 1956 Olympics in Melbourne, Australia.

increase production with no corresponding increase in pay. The Polish United Workers' Party—the name of the communist party there—responded by calling out troops. But, in a tacit challenge to Soviet hegemony, it also replaced the political leadership with a reformer named Władisław Gomułka. This uprising was put down relatively peacefully, but only after Gomułka personally assured Soviet leader Nikita Khrushchev that Poland would remain a loyal Soviet ally.

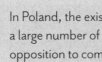

In Poland, the existence of a powerful Catholic Church and a large number of independent peasant farmers created an opposition to communist rule that was unique in eastern Europe.

◄ The next major revolt against Soviet domination and the authoritarian system of government came in Czechoslovakia during 1968, when the Czechoslovak Communist Party was under the direction of First Secretary Alexander Dubček, who now allowed significant freedom of expression in the form of novels, plays, and especially films. This wave of creativity and criticism was called the Prague Spring.

◄ In response to some films that were overtly critical of the Stalinist economic and political system imposed on Czechoslovakia, the new Soviet communist leader, Leonid Brezhnev, proclaimed the Brezhnev Doctrine, which asserted a right to intervene in the domestic affairs of Warsaw Pact member states if the existence of communism there were threatened. Under this pretext, Warsaw Pact forces led by the Soviet army invaded Czechoslovakia in August 1968 and crushed the Prague Spring. For more than 20 years to come, Czechoslovakia was a relatively grim and oppressive country that suffered the loss of many of its citizens, who fled west to freedom.

◀ Another reform movement in 1968 was launched in Hungary. Unlike Czechoslovakia's Prague Spring, which had a political emphasis, the New Economic Mechanism in Hungary concentrated on economic reform. And it permitted no independent cultural or political criticisms. It did, however, allow for some small private enterprise activity, mainly in the consumer goods and services sector. The Hungarian economic reforms—despite some success—failed to arrest a decline in the living standards of Hungarians relative to the living standards in neighboring Austria.

The ultimate consumer good that communist Hungary produced was a color-coded puzzle created by the amateur mathematician Erno Rubik known as the Rubik's cube.

DRAKULIC, *A Guided Tour through the Museum of Communism.*
——, *How We Survived Communism & Even Laughed.*
PLOKHY, *Yalta.*

Questions

1 How did the communist economies of eastern Europe
   mimic the economic system of the Soviet Union? What
   problems did this imitation create in eastern Europe?

2 Were eastern European communist countries always quiet
   and peaceful? Were they unchanging, static societies under
   Soviet domination?

Soviet Bloc: Conformity and Resistance

A s World War II was ending, the Allied victors began to negotiate the post-war fate of Europe. The two major triumphant powers—the United States and the Soviet Union—were advancing towards Germany, and ultimate victory over the Nazi regime. Yet the United States and the Soviet Union had very different histories in this war.

The United States had begun its most important military offensive in Europe as recently as June 1944. By comparison, the Soviet Union had borne the brunt of German attacks beginning three years earlier. Estimates of Soviet losses in World War II are many and conflicting, but the estimates range from 20 million to 30 million human lives lost.

In one engagement alone—the Battle of Stalingrad, which lasted from July 1942 until the Germans surrendered in February of 1943—the Soviets counted 1.1 million Russian deaths, wounded, missing, and captured, along with more than 800 thousand Axis dead, wounded, missing or captured. Among the most moving war memorials I've ever visited is in Volgograd, Russia, in the southwest part of the country. Volgograd is the name today of the former Stalingrad. There, atop Mamayev Hill, is a huge statue almost 300 feet tall, titled, *The Motherland Calls*. The names of all the Soviet soldiers buried under the hill are recorded there. And a recording of the German composer Robert Schumann's sober and evocative piano composition, *Traumerei*, plays to the light of an eternal flame.

On a personal note, I owe my own existence in a real sense to the Red Army. My dad was a navigator on a B-17 in the 8th Army Air Corps. He flew bombing missions out of Southampton, England. And he was shot down over Munich in July 1944. He would spend the remainder of the war in a Luftwaffe prison camp. Stalag Luft 1 was located in Barth, Germany—on the Baltic Sea near Peenemunde. Dad told stories about watching—along with his fellow prisoners—the test rockets of the scientist Wernher von Braun and his team fired in anticipation of the V1 and V2 attacks on Britain. At the end of the war, Hitler gave an order that all prisoners of war should be executed.

The Luftwaffe command at dad's prison camp did not carry out this order before the Red Army—in the form of a brigade of Mongolian soldiers, traveling with ox carts that carried their artillery pieces—liberated the camp. Dad said it was rather comical to look at the faces of the German soldiers as they met their rather pitiful conquerors.

So, it's not much of a stretch to say that here I'm today thanks to the Red Army's advance against the common German enemy during World War II!

Because of Soviet sacrifices at the hands of the German army—and Soviet victories over the Germans, as well—the Soviet Union felt entitled, at the end of the fighting in Europe, to dictate the nature of economic and political systems in the territories that the Soviets occupied. In addition, the Soviet Union and communist parties elsewhere in Europe could count on large numbers of voters in post-war elections, in part due to Soviet resistance to the Nazis. In the Czechoslovakian elections of 1946—the last free elections in Czechoslovakia for decades to come—the Czech Communist Party got almost 40 percent of the vote. Similarly, in eastern Germany, the socialist and communist parties enjoyed significant support.

In short order, Stalin and his proxies across eastern European would cynically use this support to consolidate political power in Eastern Europe, and eliminate democratic opposition. By the end of the 1940s, they'd quashed all open opposition with one exception. In Yugoslavia, Marshal Tito had led an independent army of national liberation against the Nazi army during wartime. As the leader of his own independent military force, Tito was now able to develop a fairly independent political base of power and strategy for governing Yugoslavia. So, of all the eastern European countries that subsequently were organized as communist economies, Yugoslavia was the most independent—and most different—of the bloc nations. Its economy was the most decentralized, and its foreign policy the most self-directed.

Additionally, the Soviets ceded control in most other areas of the Balkans. The British were granted hegemony in Greece, where large socialist and communist parties that had led the fight against Germany. Now, on Stalin's orders they, they gave up their opposition to a British-installed capitalist government and economic system there.

The remaining nations of Eastern Europe, however, came to be completely dominated by the Soviet Union. Their political and economic systems were dictated from Moscow. So, Poland, East Germany, Czechoslovakia, Hungary, Romania, and Bulgaria all had Soviet-type economies and political systems imposed on them. This was enforced by the Red Army, on orders from the Soviet government, and their proxies, in the form of carefully chosen national political leaders.

In East Germany, for example, the two leading left wing parties—the communist party and the social democratic party—were forced to merge into the *Sozialistische Einheitspartei Deutschlands*, or the Socialist Unity Party—the SED. The leading communist parties in the various eastern European communist countries went by different names. But they were all carbon copies of the Soviet Communist Party in structure and style, and in the complete control they exercised over the countries they governed.

Every eastern European country under Soviet domination not only adopted one-party authoritarian states, they also adhered to the basic Soviet economic model. This model had several common components. Chief among them were: state ownership of all major economic sectors; collective or state-owned agriculture; comprehensive planning; and an emphasis on industrial development.

There'd be no scope for private ownership, or market directed economic incentives. No profit or dividend income would be allowed. No independent financial sector or financial markets were tolerated. All labor would be allocated by state planning agencies. And foreign trade was under direct state control.

While the Soviet Union gradually consolidated its command over the eastern European communist economies, the Western allies—led by the United States—rebuilt market-oriented economic systems that had frayed as a result of the Great Depression and World War II. And they created new international economic and financial institutions to help coordinate international relations. They created International Monetary Fund, which would facilitate and supervise the international movements of money and financial capital. The World Bank would lend money to finance the reconstruction of Europe.

The Organization of European Economic Cooperation, or OEEC, was established to coordinate the distribution of U.S. financial aid. This aid was formulated under the congressionally approved European Recovery Plan of 1948, better known as the Marshall Plan, named for the war-time general George C. Marshall, who was now. U.S. secretary of State. Although eastern European countries such as Poland, Czechoslovakia, and Hungary were receptive to receiving much-needed American financial assistance—and were eligible for it under the Marshall Plan—the Soviets feared U.S. influence, and the "strings" that would be attached to such aid. So, the Soviets blocked its extension to communist allies in Eastern Europe.

The Organization of European Economic Cooperation today is a worldwide body known as the Organization for Economic Co-operation and Development, or OECD. It laid the groundwork for the European Economic Community, or common market, that came into existence in 1957.

Another post-World War II organization—the North Atlantic Treaty Organization, founded in 1949—was formed to defend Western Europe from future aggression. And the United Nations, founded in October 1945, would try to settle international conflicts peacefully.

The Soviet Union was initially invited to join the IMF and the World Bank, but declined membership—again, for fear of U.S. influence and domination. The only one of the new international organizations the Soviets decided to join was the U.N. Instead, after NATO's founding, the Soviets created a competing military alliance, the Warsaw Treaty Organization, as a counterweight. The Soviets also established a competing international economic body, the Council for Mutual Economic Assistance—known as COMECON, and headquartered in Moscow. It directed trade among the Soviet dominated economic systems of Eastern Europe.

COMECON claimed to be the eastern equivalent of the common market being develop in Western Europe. But it was not a facilitator of private trade based upon comparative advantage. Instead, COMECON served as a planning agency that oversaw essentially a barter system of trade among the countries of Eastern Europe and the Soviet Union. This trade was based primarily on Soviet needs, and the political decisions of the leadership of the communist party of the Soviet Union.

Each eastern European communist economy was oriented to emphasize heavy industry, just as the Soviets had done in their initial five-year plans. Consumer goods and services were given very low priority. Labor, raw materials and capital goods were to be devoted, instead, to building up large-scale industrial enterprises. These industrial enterprises would be directed by a planning bureaucracy that answered to the political leadership of the country. And the political leadership would be the leadership of the communist party.

Each Eastern European economy was also directed to concentrate on specific industrial sectors. East Germany, for example, had the task of producing railroad rolling stock for the Soviet Union. When I would take trains in the Soviet Union, I always looked to see if the equipment—the engines and the railcars—came from East Germany. Almost always they did.

Poland was given the task of producing coal and steel. The mammoth Lenin Steel Works in Nowa Huta, outside of Krakow, is a prime example of this industrial gigantism. Although spectacularly inefficient and grossly polluting, it employed tens of thousands of workers, and provided much of the steel to rebuild Eastern Europe.

Hungary was assigned the task of producing buses. On my first trip to the Soviet Union, all the tour buses that my students and I were transported in were Ikarus buses built in Hungary. On any given day in Red Square, there would be 40 or 50 bright red Ikarus buses transporting visitors to the center of Moscow—to see Lenin's tomb, St. Basil's Cathedral, and the Kremlin.

An authoritarian state that suppresses all dissent is required to also suppress the production of consumer goods and services, and eliminate political opposition. In the Soviet Union and much of Eastern Europe during the late 1940s and early 1950s, there were show trials, imprisonments, and executions of political oppositionists who did not follow strict party orders. Many refugees fled from the oppression and lack of freedom. A solid border formed between Eastern and Western Europe to stem the flow of refugees.

Winston Churchill, having only recently been voted out as the British prime minister, described—in his famous speech at Fulton, Missouri in 1946—an Iron Curtain that had descended on Europe. This "Iron Curtain" was to divide Europe for over 40 years. On one side would be the rapidly recovering economies of Western Europe, with their increasing abundance of consumer goods. In the other side, would be the gray and much poorer economies of Eastern Europe, cut off from their neighbors. Cut off not only economically, but culturally and politically.

In the 1970s, many of my fellow graduate students were puzzled by my decision to study the economies of the Soviet Union and Eastern Europe. Some of them asked why I wanted to study a part of the world that was static—frozen in time—with an economic structure that was inefficient and seemed incapable of change. While it's true that the Soviet economy and its eastern European satellite states were inefficient and not very dynamic, significant disruption was bubbling up from time to time. These sporadic protests and internal dissent were driven by the dissatisfaction of the general population with their standards of living, and the lack of political and cultural freedom.

One of the really interesting areas of contention was music—particularly rock and roll. American rock and roll—initially based on black jazz and rhythm and blues, and popularized by Elvis Presley, Chuck Berry, Little Richard, and others—was seen by communist cultural authorities as a capitalist plot to undermine socialist culture and solidarity. And rock and roll was not only cultural—it was also economic. Popular music was an industry, driven by consumer demand and profits. It produced records, concerts, radio and television shows. It was a capitalist phenomenon created almost entirely by private enterprises. Rock and roll made lots of money—in contrast to state-sponsored cultural productions that did not respond to consumer demand—and it wasn't controlled by the government!

One of the more ironic aspects of rock-and-roll's rise in the United States was the opposition that came from some of America's cultural conservatives. Political and religious conservatives sometimes demonized rock music as either a tool of the devil or of the communists—the devil and communists being one and the same thing in the United States of the 1950s. There was more than a touch of racism in this viewpoint, too. But rock and roll was most definitely not a tool of the communists.

Economists who specialize in cultural economics maintain that the worldwide popular success of American rock music is due primarily to the fact that it is market driven, based on purely private demand. That is, it's precisely unlike much classical symphonic music and opera that rely on state subsidies or state ownership. Rock and roll is pure capitalism! And rock and roll would turn out to be one of the driving forces that eventually brought down communist societies throughout eastern Europe. So, communist authorities who saw rock and roll as a capitalist threat to their planned economies and authoritarian political systems were more perceptive than reactionaries in the U.S. who thought Little Richard was a communist agent. Good golly Miss Molly! They were wrong!

To that I'll add: the communist societies of Eastern Europe were never truly static and unchanging. There were violent uprisings and protests in all eastern European states. The first was East Germany's in 1953. Economic authorities in East Berlin—to speed up economic development and industrial production there—had mandated increased production quotas for industrial workers without any corresponding increase in pay. Not surprisingly, workers in East Berlin revolted—and were put down with military force. In West Berlin, this uprising of June 17, 1953, was commemorated with the renaming of the major boulevard that leads west from the Brandenburg Gate. It became known as The Street of the 17th of June.

The next major uprising against Soviet domination and control came in Hungary in 1956. This revolt was much more violent, bloody, and prolonged. It began as a student protest for greater political and cultural freedom. Tens of thousands of students took to the streets of Budapest. They were fired upon by state security forces. And this inflamed the population. The revolt spread throughout Hungary.

Eventually, Soviet troops were called in to put down the revolt. More than 2,000 Hungarians and 700 Soviet soldiers were killed. Thousands of Hungarians subsequently fled west, and flooded refugee camps in Austria, Germany, and Switzerland. In the United States, the television impresario

Ed Sullivan asked the public for donations to help Hungarian refugees. And a 21-year old Elvis Presley joined the effort, singing "Peace in the Valley" on *The Ed Sullivan Show*, and promising to donate himself.

After the Soviet invasion of Hungary, a dramatic sequel unfolded in the form of a water polo match between Hungary and the Soviet Union at the 1956 Olympics in Melbourne, Australia. It was called the "blood in the water match" because of the violent nature of the contest. Many Hungarians are world-class swimmers and water polo players, by the way. On a visit to Budapest in 2007, I visited Margaret Island in the middle of the Danube River. It has a lovely swimming complex. And while I was there, the Hungarian national water polo team was practicing. They were some very big, muscular dudes whom I wouldn't want to tackle anywhere, especially in the water.

Meanwhile, a worker uprising centered in the Polish city of Poznan also unfolded in 1956. The spark was similar to that of the East Berlin uprising in 1953. Workers were given orders to increase production with no corresponding increase in pay. The Polish United Workers' Party—which was the name of the communist party there—responded by calling out troops. But—in a tacit challenge to Soviet hegemony—it also replaced the political leadership with a reformer named Wladislaw Gomulka. This uprising was put down relatively peacefully, but only after Gomulka personally assured Soviet leader Nikita Khrushchev, that Poland would remain a loyal Soviet ally.

Poland was different than the other eastern European communist states in at least two important respects. First, it had a powerful Catholic Church that was separate from the state bureaucracy. In no other eastern European country did any religious organization hold such independent power and influence. The other difference was the existence of extensive private farm property in Poland. Polish peasants were allowed to hold onto their small farms after World War II, and the farmland of former German owners was redistributed.

Geographically, Poland also shifted westward after World War II. Parts of what had been Prussian Germany were now western Poland, and what had been eastern Poland and Lithuania was now the eastern part of the Soviet Union.

This shift—combined with the expulsion of ethnic Germans, and the elimination of most of Poland's Jewish population due to the Holocaust—created a demographically homogeneous population in this newly constituted country. So, the existence of a powerful Catholic Church and a large number of independent peasant farmers created an opposition to communist rule that was unique in Eastern Europe.

The next major revolt against Soviet domination and the authoritarian system of government came in Czechoslovakia during 1968. That was a revolutionary year in many parts of the world. Student riots paralyzed France, and challenged the grip on power of the 78-year-old Charles de Gaulle. Mass protests rolled across the globe—from Chicago to London, Mexico City and elsewhere. In the United States, these protests centered principally on the war in Vietnam, and erupted in the form of violent protests during the Democratic political convention in Chicago.

Back in Czechoslovakia, the protest movement began with new leadership of the Czechoslovak communist party under the direction of First Secretary Alexander Dubcek. Dubcek now allowed significant freedom of expression in the form of novels, plays, and especially films. This wave of creativity and criticism was given the name, "The Prague Spring." And dissident political thinkers began to advocate for something they called, "Socialism with a Human Face." The Czech Writers Union was allowed to elect an independent and critical president. New novels and plays could be published and produced.

Some of the best Czech writers and playwrights—authors such as Milan Kundera, Vaclav Havel, and my personal favorite, the novelist and short story writer Ivan Klima—achieved international fame. Milan Kundera's novel, *The Unbearable Lightness of Being*, became a hit film internationally, and depicted the rise and fall of the Prague Spring. Indeed, a wave of world-renowned Czech films were made in 1960s, directed by famous directors such as Milos Forman and Jiri Menzel. And films like, *The Firemen's Ball* directed by Forman, and *Closely Watched Trains* by Menzel, were overtly critical of the Stalinist economic and political system that had been imposed on Czechoslovakia.

In response, the new Soviet communist leader, Leonid Brezhnev proclaimed the Brezhnev Doctrine, which asserted a right to intervene in the domestic affairs of Warsaw Pact member-states if the existence of communism there were threatened. Under this pretext, Warsaw Pact forces led by the Soviet army invaded Czechoslovakia in August 1968, and crushed the Prague Spring. For more than 20 years to come, culminating in the "Velvet Revolution" of 1989, Czechoslovakia was a relatively grim and oppressive country that suffered the loss of many of its citizens who fled west to freedom.

I took a group of students to visit Ceske Budejovice and Prague, Czechoslovakia, in 1983. Ceske Budejovice is an important brewing city in the Bohemian region of the Czech lands. Its German name is Budweis, and the local beer had the name of Budweiser. Much later, after the reestablishment of a market economy in Czechoslovakia, there was a protracted legal fight with the Anheuser-Busch corporation over the right to use the word Budweiser.

Prague was rather forlorn looking place in 1983. Most of the buildings needed paint, plaster, and new windows, and there was only a very limited amount of consumer goods and services. In the evening, the center of Prague was mostly dark and deserted. What few people appeared on the streets were usually tourists from other Eastern European countries.

Of course, when we crossed the border into Czechoslovakia, we were required to change a certain number of Austrian schillings into Czech crowns. This was standard practice in all communist countries, as it was one of the main sources of hard currency for the local regime. In an attempt to spend some of my Czech money—you couldn't take it out of the country—I went into a dark and gloomy bookstore on Wenceslas Square. All the books were behind the counter, and locked in glass cases. You had to ask the salesperson to look at a book you wished to see. And she could refuse to show you the book, if she thought you were not permitted to look at it. I managed to buy a book of Czech photography, and a collection of short-stories by the Russian writer Anton Chekhov.

Another reform movement in 1968 was launched in Hungary. Unlike Czechoslovakia's Prague Spring, which had a political emphasis, the New Economic Mechanism in Hungary concentrated on economic reform. And it permitted no independent cultural or political criticisms. It did, however, allow for some small private-enterprise activity.

These private businesses were mainly in the consumer goods and services sector. Budapest, Hungary, had several independent restaurants that were pretty good, at the time. I ate in a few, and enjoyed some pretty good chicken paprikash while listening to Hungarian gypsy music. The musicians demanded and could accept tips—preferably in Austrian schillings or German deutschemarks.

There were independent bookstores, too, where you could browse and pull books off the shelves yourself. The range of titles was limited by government censorship. But there were books on economic problems, and acceptable reforms by respected Hungarian economists such as Janos Kornai.

The ultimate consumer good that communist Hungary produced was a color-coded puzzle created by the amateur mathematician Erno Rubik, and known as the Rubik's Cube. The Hungarian government erected a small statue of a Rubik's Cube on the banks of the Danube. I think their motivation was to counter the mistaken assertion by U.S. President Ronald Reagan that the Rubik's Cube was an excellent example of American ingenuity. Even though Erno Rubik was a small-scale capitalist, the communist leaders of Hungary wanted it known they had produced this world-renowned gadget.

The Hungarian economic reforms—despite some success—failed to arrest a decline in the living standards of Hungarians relative to the living standards in neighboring Austria. And to that I will add: the challenge of how to make Hungary's predominantly Soviet-style economy perform like a Western market economy was a puzzle that even a brilliant inventor like Erno Rubik couldn't solve.

Two Germanies: A Laboratory in Economics

AT THE END OF WORLD WAR II, THE VICTORIOUS Allies had no clear idea of what kind of postwar Germany they wanted to create. Above all, the United States didn't want to repeat the mistakes of the Versailles Treaty, which had ended World War I by imposing harsh financial reparations and major territorial realignments. Yet three major conferences of Allied powers, taking place near the end of the war and afterward, left the German question unresolved. ◆

Postwar Germany

◀ The Allied armies of the Soviet Union and the United States concluded World War II deep inside German territory and facing each other fairly close to the Elbe River. This would prove to be the eventual border between East and West Germany. Initial conceptions for the conquered European power included a united but neutral Germany.

◀ The original U.S. proposal was to deindustrialize, and de-Nazify, Germany and turn it into an agricultural and rural country. This was the Morgenthau Plan, proposed by President Franklin D. Roosevelt's secretary of the treasury, Henry Morgenthau. The plan was a punitive approach to Germany's postwar development.

◀ The major problem was that Germany had to feed, clothe, and house itself. And the population was swelling with the arrival of millions of refugees fleeing from the Soviets in the east or being displaced by Czechs and Poles in formerly German-occupied lands.

◀ Germany's occupying powers—the United States, the Soviet Union, France, and Great Britain—now divided Germany into four postwar occupation zones.

1 The U.S. Army occupied the southern half of the country, including the federal states of Bavaria, Rhineland-Palatinate, Baden-Württemberg, and Hessen.

2 The French occupied the far western part, along the Rhine river.

3 The British occupied the northwestern quarter, including the cities of Hamburg and Bremen.

4 The Soviets occupied the northeastern quarter, including the former capital of Berlin, which itself was divided into four zones of occupation under a combined military command.

◀ The location of Berlin deep inside the Soviet zone was to prove problematic, significantly as the Soviets demanded huge war reparations from Germany in the form of money, industrial equipment, and other resources; and as the United States, in early 1946, halted the movement of these reparations to the Soviets across the American occupation zone. Shortly after this, the United States, France, and Germany consolidated the three western zones of occupation.

◀ As negotiations with the Soviets broke down, in June 1948 the Soviet Union imposed a blockade on Berlin of all road, railway, and canal movement into Berlin, including into parts of the city that remained under the occupation and control of the other Allied powers.

◀ Consequently, the combined U.S., British, and French zone became the Federal Republic of Germany—that is, West Germany—in May 1949, with the Rhineland city of Bonn as its provisional capital. In October 1949, the Soviets responded by creating the German Democratic Republic—East Germany— with its capital in the Soviet zone of Berlin: East Berlin.

◀ The Soviets still held out the possibility of creating a neutral, nonaligned, united Germany. But as the Cold War developed, and as West Germany was incorporated into the North Atlantic Treaty Organization, the existence of two Germanies became more and more of a reality.

The Economy of West versus East Germany

◀ West Germany (the Federal Republic) benefited economically in several ways, in contrast to East Germany, sometimes known by its German initials as the GDR.

◀ West Germany benefited from the presence of American troops in a large part of the country. Although the Europeans sometimes complained about American soldiers, the soldiers did have money to spend. This spending—by individual GIs and the U.S. military—was a significant stimulus to West German agriculture, its consumer goods makers, and workers employed on U.S. bases.

◀ Additionally, the Federal Republic began to receive redevelopment aid under the congressionally approved Marshall Plan. In comparison, postwar France and England were destitute countries with scarcely enough resources to feed, clothe, and house their citizens.

◀ Neither the British nor the French had resources to provide more than basic relief for the German populations under their control. And the Soviets were dismantling East German industrial capacity and taking it back home. In effect, the Red Army was "undeveloping" East Germany.

◀ Furthermore, because Joseph Stalin did not allow Soviet-allied countries to receive Marshall Plan assistance, the GDR was all the more handicapped in its attempts to recover from the war.

◀ A final brake on East German economic development was the occupying Soviet administration's intent to create an economy in the GDR that nearly exactly replicated the Soviet system. This meant the collectivization of agriculture, with all the disincentives that created.

◀ In every country that adopted a Soviet-type agricultural system, food-production problems were chronic. Collectivized and state-owned agriculture has been a failure everywhere it's been tried, without exception. Farmers produce more efficiently when they own their own land and reap the economic rewards of their efforts.

◀ The Soviets also demanded that the GDR government nationalize all enterprises with more than 50 employees and create comprehensive plans for production and distribution. In state-owned economies devoid of economic incentives, large-scale enterprises tend to be grossly inefficient.

◀ So, the relative deprivation of East Germany—and especially the formerly rich cities of Berlin, Leipzig, and Dresden—was cruelly ironic. Along with Hamburg, these cities had been the centers of opposition to Hitler and the Nazi regime. Hitler despised the big German cities of the north. He thought they were full of socialists, Jews, homosexuals, foreigners, creative modern artists, and musicians—so-called undesirables.

◀ Hitler's support was mainly in the south, closer to his native Catholic Austria. So, just as the cities of Berlin, Leipzig, and Dresden were punished the most severely for the crimes of Hitler and the Nazi regime, it's doubly ironic that southern and southwestern Germany enjoyed the biggest postwar benefits.

The Berlin Wall

- After the Berlin wall fell in November 1989 and West Germans began to lecture their eastern brethren on some of their failings (and also look down on them for their relatively low standards of living), East Germans with a stronger historical foundation reacted with anger and outrage at the smugness and historical ignorance of their western cousins.

- There were large differences in the productive efficiency of East versus West German enterprises, and the gap between West and East German productivity continually widened through East Germany's 40-year history.

- The GDR economy was the most productive in the Soviet bloc. East Germany tended to be the most technology-intensive producer. It manufactured railroad equipment, telephone equipment and systems, and office equipment, among other industrial goods. East Germany was also the Soviet bloc's principal producer of chemical products.

- To control East Germany's population and prevent outright opposition, the Red Army posted more than 10 percent of its total eastern Europe troop deployments in the GDR. The governing party of the GDR, the Socialist Unity Party, depended on the presence of large numbers of Soviet soldiers to maintain its hold on power. The Soviet Union needed the GDR to be a model communist state and a dependable buffer against the West.

- The absence of private enterprise and ownership in the GDR was accompanied by rigid censorship of the arts and culture. Dissident writers, poets, and singers were harassed, denied ration cards, and often jailed. There was even an attempt to create appropriate popular music—socialist music—in contrast to the decadent and subversive jazz and rock and roll coming from the West. This absurd, and unsuccessful, attempt to turn East German citizens away from Western pop music ultimately played a key role in the GDR's collapse.

◀ In June 1953, East German workers spilled out onto the streets of East Berlin, and hundreds of other towns and cities, to protest orders to increase production with no increase in pay. This was the first postwar uprising in any of the Soviet bloc countries against the new economic and political system imposed on them by the Red Army.

◀ The GDR government had to call on Soviet troops to put down the revolt. More than 20 demonstrators were killed, and thousands were put in prison. As a result, thousands of East Germans began to flee west.

◀ By the middle of the 1950s, the West German economy was producing abundant amounts of food, clothing, and other consumer goods. This was the beginning of the West German economic miracle: the *Wirtschaftswunder*.

◀ More than 2.5 million East Germans fled to the West between 1949 and 1961, and they tended to be younger, more educated workers—the ones most needed to develop the economy.

◀ In August 1961, the East German government began to build a barrier that eventually would enclose the people of East Berlin inside a solid wall: the Berlin Wall. It was actually two sets of barriers. One was built between East and West Berlin, and the other was erected all the way around the city of West Berlin to separate Western territory from the Soviet bloc GDR. West Berlin was, thus, established as an island of democracy and freedom deep inside East Germany.

West Berlin
FEDERAL REPUBLIC OF GERMANY
(WEST GERMANY)
East Berlin
GERMAN DEMOCRATIC REPUBLIC
(EAST GERMANY)

Not knowing geography very well, some American GIs stationed in West Berlin were shocked to find it in the middle of East Germany, far from West Germany.

◁ The East German government and the Soviet military tightly controlled transit between West Berlin and West Germany. Western aircraft were granted only three flight paths, and only three Western airlines were allowed to fly through East German airspace into West Berlin. No West German airlines were given such access. The communists also tightly controlled road and rail access to West Berlin, and sometimes they stopped it entirely.

A Divided Germany

◁ With the construction of the Berlin Wall, the two Germanies— and divided Berlin—existed as distinct and opposing systems. In turn, the citizens trapped in the GDR set about trying to make the best of the situation.

◀ At first, the conservative West German governments of the Christian Democratic Union adopted a hostile and confrontational attitude. This became formalized as the Hallstein Doctrine, named after a West German state secretary for foreign affairs, Walter Hallstein. The doctrine refused to recognize the GDR as a sovereign state and declared that there was only one legitimate Germany: the Federal Republic to the west.

◀ In time, Bonn changed its approach to dealing with the "other" Germany to the east, as the construction of the Berlin Wall—and the stabilization of the East German population—inevitably led to the recognition that the GDR was more durable than anticipated.

◀ In 1969, West Germany's Social Democratic Party came to power, along with the election of former West Berlin mayor Willy Brandt as federal chancellor. The Brandt government extended full diplomatic relations to East Germany, along with the recognition that two independent nations coexisted on German soil.

◀ The Brandt government also extended loans and other aid to assist GDR development. In return, the Federal Republic in the west gained the release of some dissidents and some migration of East Germans to the West.

◀ The Federal Republic also secured rights to broadcast West German radio and television into East Germany without its signals being jammed or blocked. The ability of many East Germans to now watch West German television affected them quite profoundly.

◀ While East Germans had a higher standard of living relative to other eastern Europeans in communist economies, this was not the case in comparison to the West. And East Germans typically did not compare themselves to their socialist brothers and sisters in Bulgaria or Romania but rather to their cousins, aunts, and uncles in West Germany.

◀ The East Germans watching West German television could now watch and listen to West German news reports and documentaries. This uncensored news and information, along with the alternative view of life in the capitalist West, was unique among the countries of the Soviet bloc. And it was one of the main reasons that the revolts against communism, culminating in the collapse of the Soviet bloc, would begin in the GDR.

◀ At the same time, the Berlin Wall—and the comprehensive border between East and West Germany—constituted some of the most solid and technologically sophisticated barriers to human movement ever created up until that time.

The Berlin Wall was eventually so thick that cars and trucks could drive on top of it. It was often 10 feet wide and made of the densest concrete. There was a no-man's-land for 20 or 30 feet on either side of the wall, monitored by East German police with orders to shoot and kill anyone attempting to escape.

Readings

SCHNEIDER, *The Wall Jumper.*
WOLF, *Man without a Face.*

Questions

1 Who did East German citizens compare their lives and standard of living to? Why did this create problems for the East German communist leadership?

2 Did West German engagement with East Germany make the East German government stronger? Did East German access to West German media and economic relations between the two Germanies solidify the East German Communist Party's hold on its citizens?

Two Germanies: A Laboratory in Economics

A t the end of World War II, the victorious Allies had no clear idea of what kind of post-war Germany they wanted to create. Above all, the United States didn't want to repeat the mistakes of the Versailles Treaty, which had ended World War I by imposing harsh financial reparations, and major territorial realignments. Herbert Hoover, the former American president, is reported to have told his successor, President Franklin Roosevelt: "You can have revenge or you can have peace. You can't have both!" Yet three major conferences of Allied powers—taking place near the end of the war, and afterwards—left the German question unresolved.

The Allied armies of the Soviet Union and the United States concluded World War II deep inside German territory, and facing each other fairly close to the Elbe River. This would prove to be the eventual border between East and West Germany. Initial conceptions for the conquered European power included a united but neutral Germany. The original U.S. proposal was to de-industrialize, and de-Nazify, Germany; and turn it into an agricultural and rural country.

This was the "Morgenthau Plan" proposed by Roosevelt's secretary of the Treasury, Henry Morgenthau. Although fairly gentle-sounding, it was a punitive approach to Germany's post-war development. The major problem was that Germany had to feed, clothe, and house itself. And the population was swelling with the arrival of millions of refugees fleeing from the Soviets in the east, or being displaced by Czechs and Poles in formerly German occupied lands.

Germany's occupying powers—the United States, the Soviet Union, France, and Great Britain—now divided Germany into four post-war occupation zones. The U.S. army occupied the southern half of the country. This included the federal states of Bavaria, Rhineland-Palatinate, Baden-Wurttemberg, and Hessen. The French occupied the far western part, along the Rhine river. The British occupied the northwestern quarter, including the cities of Hamburg and Bremen. And the Soviets occupied the northeastern quarter, including the former capital of Berlin, which itself was divided into four zones of occupation under a combined military command.

The location of Berlin deep inside the Soviet zone was to prove problematic, significantly as the Soviets demanded huge war reparations from Germany in the form of money, industrial equipment, and other resources; and as the United States—in early 1946—halted the movement of these reparations to the Soviets across the American occupation zone. Shortly after this, the United States, France, and Germany consolidated the three western zones of occupation.

And as negotiations with the Soviets broken down, in June 1948 the Soviet Union imposed a blockade on Berlin of all road, railway, and canal movement into Berlin—including into parts of the city that remained under the occupation and control of the other Allied powers. Consequently, the combined U.S., British, and French zone became the Federal Republic of Germany—that is, West Germany—in May 1949, with Rhineland city of Bonn as its provisional capital. In October 1949, the Soviets responded by creating the German Democratic Republic—East Germany—with its capital in the Soviet zone of Berlin: East Berlin.

The Soviets still held out the possibility of creating a neutral, non-aligned, united Germany. But, as the Cold War developed—and as West Germany was incorporated into North Atlantic Treaty Organization, or NATO, the existence of two Germanies became more and more of a reality.

West Germany (the Federal Republic) benefited economically in several ways, in contrast to the example of East Germany, sometimes known by its German initials as the GDR. First, West Germany benefited from the presence of American troops in a large part of the country. Although the Europeans sometimes complained about American troops being overpaid, oversexed, and "over here," the good news is that they had money to spend. This spending—by individual GI's and the U.S. military—was a significant stimulus to West German agriculture, its consumer goods makers, and workers employed on U.S. bases. Additionally, the Federal Republic began to receive redevelopment aid under the congressionally approved Marshall Plan.

In comparison, post-war France and England were destitute countries with scarcely enough resources to feed, clothe, and house their citizens. Great Britain rationed bread from 1946 to 1948. It was able to feed itself only thanks to loans from the United States.

To remind ourselves that the Marshall Plan and other forms of assistance to the Europeans was not pure altruism on the part of the Americans, it's worth recalling that foreign demand for U.S. grain was a positive stimulus to American farm incomes. Meanwhile, neither the British nor the French had resources to provide more than basic relief for the German populations under their control. And the Soviets were dismantling East German industrial capacity, and taking it back home. In effect, the Red Army was "undeveloping" Eastern Germany.

Furthermore, because Joseph Stalin did not allow Soviet-allied countries to receive Marshall Plan assistance, the GDR was all the more handicapped in its attempts to recover from the war. A final brake on East German economic development was the occupying Soviet administration's intent to create an economy in the GDR that nearly exactly replicated the Soviet system itself. This meant the collectivization of agriculture, with all the disincentives that created.

In every country that adopted a Soviet-type agricultural system, food-production problems were chronic. Collectivized and state-owned agriculture has been a failure everywhere it's been tried, without exception. Farmers produce more efficiently when they own their own land, and when they reap the economic rewards of their efforts.

The Soviets also demanded that the GDR government nationalize all enterprises with more than 50 employees, and create comprehensive plans for production and distribution. Now, in some cases, large-scale enterprise is appropriate and efficient—but not in most. And in state-owned economies devoid of economic incentives, large-scale enterprises tend to be grossly inefficient.

So, the relative deprivation of East Germany—and especially the formerly rich cities of Berlin, Leipzig, and Dresden—was cruelly ironic. Along with Hamburg, these cities had been the centers of opposition to Hitler and the Nazi regime. Hitler despised the big German cities of the north. He thought they were full of socialists, Jews, homosexuals, foreigners, creative modern artists and musicians.

Jazz music was a particular target of Nazi condemnation. This was due to the African-American roots of jazz, and the inherent racism of the Nazi regime. Many of these so-called undesirables ended up in concentration camps. Some lucky ones were able to escape. Many prominent scientists, architects, writers, intellectuals, and filmmakers came to the United States, and are some of the best examples of the benefit to America of accepting these refugees, including Albert Einstein, Mies van der Rohe, and Billy Wilder. Yet America's shame was turning away other ships loaded with escaping Jews. Some of these vessels found no welcoming ports, and had to return to Germany, where many of the passengers met tragic ends.

Hitler's support was mainly in the south, closer to his native Catholic Austria. Hitler's big rallies were in Munich, Nuremberg, and Stuttgart. And so, just as the cities of Berlin, Leipzig, and Dresden were punished the most severely for the crimes of Hitler and the Nazi regime, it's doubly ironic that southern and southwestern Germany enjoyed the biggest post-war benefits.

Much later, after the Berlin wall fell in November 1989—and West Germans began to lecture their eastern brethren on some of their failings, and also to look down on them for their relatively low standards of living. East Germans with a stronger historical foundation reacted with anger and outrage at the smugness and historical ignorance of their western cousins.

One of my graduate school colleagues at the University of Oklahoma did his Ph.D. dissertation on comparative production in West and East Germany. Basically, Andy tried to find similar-size enterprises in both East and West Germany. His idea was to see if capitalist enterprises were different from communist enterprises in the same industry. If everything else were the same—except for the nature of the economic system in which each enterprise was located—then this might say something about the relative effects of capitalism versus communism. Andy often joked—somewhat politically incorrectly—that if even efficient and hard-working Germans couldn't make communism work, then what hope was there for the poor Hungarians, Czechs, Poles, etc. But, as it turned out, Andy recorded large differences in the productive efficiency of East versus West German enterprises. Sometimes, West German firms produced on the order of 50 percent more output, with the same amount of resources. And this gap between West and East German productivity continually widened through East Germany's 40-year history.

In drawling this conclusion, let's also keep in mind that the GDR economy was the most productive in the Soviet bloc. And the GDR produced most of the "high-tech" goods of the Comecon countries. Comecon was the Soviet-led Council for Mutual Economic Assistance among East bloc nations. It directed the various satellite states as to what each should specialize in. East Germany tended to be the most technology-intensive producer. It manufactured railroad equipment, telephone equipment and systems, and office equipment, among other industrial goods. East Germany was also the Soviet bloc's principal producer of chemical products.

That the East Germans had a higher standard of living compared to other eastern Europeans was clear to me on my first trip to the Soviet Union. Walking around Moscow—or traveling by river taxi on the Moscow River—I often saw comparatively prosperous looking groups of tourists. And invariably, these folks were from the GDR.

One evening in Yalta, some of my students and I went up to the bar on the top of the tourist hotel where we were staying. There was a nice-looking group of older German-speaking folks. They were at a table drinking beer, and having a pretty good time. Being the friendly Texan I am, I moseyed over to the group to say howdy in German. One of the members of the group—a man named Erich Kaatz, who would become my friend— introduced himself. He and his fellow pensioners were from East Berlin, and he could speak English quite well. I asked Erich how he had learned the language. He politely told me he had been in the German army during World War II, and had been captured and sent to a military prison camp in Texas. He'd worked as a cook in the officers' club there, and learned English in classes for prisoners.

One less-inviting result of East German ingenuity is that its Soviet-style chemical industry became responsible for some of the worst pollution in all of Europe. The ground, air, and water around the East German city of Bitterfeld—known today as Bitterfeld-Wolfen, 100 miles south of Berlin—

was notoriously noxious and foul. West German mothers who scolded their children for being dirty and messy would sometimes accuse them of creating areas *schmutzig wie Bitterfeld*—dirty as Bitterfeld.

To control East Germany's population, and prevent outright opposition, the Red Army posted more than 10 percent of its total eastern Europe troop deployments in the GDR. The governing party of the GDR, the Socialist Unity Party—known by its German initials as SED—depended on the presence of large numbers of Soviet soldiers to maintain its hold on power. The Soviet Union needed the GDR to be a model communist state, and a dependable buffer against the West.

Ultimately, East Germany would establish the most comprehensive institution of domestic spying in the world. The state security service— the *Staatssicherheitsdienst*, known as the Stasi—employed hundreds of thousands of official domestic spies, and recruited millions of accomplices among the population to keep an eye on their fellow workers, students, professors, and family members. One of the most painful revelations after the fall of the Berlin Wall, and the collapse of the GDR, was the opening up of the Stasi files to the East German public. Husbands found out that wives had reported on them; teachers discovered that colleagues and students had shared with the secret police revelations of their critical lectures or comments; workers informed on their bosses, and vice versa. More than three million East German citizens—nearly one in five, out of a total population of about 16 million—are estimated to have co-operated with the secret police, and informed on others.

The absence of private enterprise and ownership in the GDR was accompanied by rigid censorship of the arts and culture. Dissident writers, poets, and singers were harassed, denied ration cards, and often jailed. There was even an attempt to create appropriate popular music—socialist music—in contrast to the decadent and subversive jazz and rock-and-roll coming from the West. This absurd, and unsuccessful, attempt to turn East German citizens away from Western pop music—especially the young—ultimately played a key role in the GDR's collapse.

In June 1953, East German workers spilled out onto the streets of East Berlin, and hundreds of other towns and cities, to protest orders to increase production with no increase in pay. This was the first post-war uprising in any of the Soviet bloc countries against the new economic and political system imposed upon them by the Red Army. The GDR government had to call on Soviet troops to put down the revolt. More than 20 demonstrators were killed, and thousands were put into prison. As a result, thousands of East Germans began to flee west.

By the middle of the 1950s, the West German economy was producing abundant amounts of food, clothing, and other consumer goods. This was the beginning of the west German economic miracle— the *Wirtschaftswunder*.

More than 2.5 million East Germans fled to the West between 1949 and 1961, peaking at close to 400,000 a year, by the end of that period. The GDR government recognized that something had to be done. Not only were large numbers of East Germans leaving, but they tended to be younger, more educated workers: the ones most needed to develop the economy.

In August 1961, the East German government began to build a barrier that eventually would enclose the people of West Berlin inside a solid wall. The Berlin Wall. It was actually two sets of barriers. One was built between East and West Berlin. The other was erected all the way around the city of West Berlin itself to separate Western territory from the Soviet-bloc GDR. West Berlin was, thus, established as an island of democracy and freedom deep inside East Germany.

Not knowing geography very well, some American GIs stationed in West Berlin were shocked to find it in the middle of East Germany, far, far from West Germany.

The East German government and the Soviet military tightly controlled transit between West Berlin and West Germany. Western aircraft were granted only three flight paths. And only three western airlines were allowed to fly through East German airspace into West Berlin: British Airways, Air France, and Pan American. No West German airlines were given such access. The communists also tightly controlled road and rail access to West Berlin, and sometimes they stopped it entirely. The Berlin blockade of 1948-49 is the most famous instance.

In an attempt to force the Allies out of West Berlin, the East German government blocked all road and rail traffic into West Berlin, thinking that without food and fuel from the west, the West Berliners would eventually starve or freeze to death. The western military powers, including the Americans, French, British, Canadian, and Australian air forces organized the famous Berlin Airlift, and flew in hundreds of aircraft loaded with basic foodstuffs and coal.

One American flyer was nicknamed *der Rosinenbomber*—the Candy Bomber—because, as he approached Tempelhof Airfield, he would open his window, and throw candy to the children of West Berlin who lived below.

Tempelhof Airbase is closed now, and it's turned into a housing development. But there's a large monument to the flyers of the Berlin Airlift. Whenever I take students to Berlin, I drag them to this memorial so that I can tell them this story about this Cold War event.

With the construction of the Berlin Wall, the two Germanies—and divided Berlin—existed as distinct and opposing systems. In turn, the citizens trapped in the GDR set about trying to make the best of a bad situation. At first, the conservative West German governments of the Christian Democratic Union adopted a hostile and confrontational attitude. This became formalized as the Hallstein Doctrine, named after a West German state secretary for foreign affairs, Walter Hallstein. The Hallstein Doctrine refused to recognize the GDR as a sovereign state, and declared that there was only one legitimate Germany: the federal republic in the west.

In time, Bonn changed its approach to dealing with the "other" Germany to the east, as the construction of the Berlin Wall—and the stabilization of the East German population—inevitably led to the recognition that the GDR was more durable than anticipated. In 1969, West Germany's Social Democratic Party came to power, along with the election of former West Berlin mayor Willy Brandt as federal chancellor. It had been Brandt, as mayor, who'd welcomed President John F. Kennedy to West Berlin during the wall's construction.

Now, West Germany was ready for a radical change in policy towards the GDR. Under the label of *Ostpolitik*, the Brandt government extended full diplomatic relations to East Germany, along with the recognition that two independent nations co-existed on German soil. The Brandt government also extended loans and other aid to assist GDR development. In return, the federal republic in the west gained the release of some dissidents, and some migration of East Germans to the west. The Federal Republic also secured rights to broadcast West German radio and television into East Germany without its signals being jammed or blocked.

Since this was before cable or satellite or Internet TV, broadcast signals were transmitted via broadcast towers. Yet if the signals were interrupted by hills or valleys, then some East German residents would be unable to receive the programming. In fact, there was such a region in East Germany. It was a deep valley near the city of Dresden. This valley came to be referred to as the *Tal der Ahnungslosen*, which translates as the Valley of the Clueless. Now, these poor folks weren't totally clueless. They could get information about the broadcasts from friends and relatives in other areas. But this highlights the key role of information in the lives of the West Germans.

The ability of many East Germans to now watch West German television affected them quite profoundly. For while it was true that East Germans had a higher standard of living relative to other eastern Europeans in communist economies, this was not the case in comparison to the west. And East Germans typically did not compare themselves to their socialist brothers and sisters in Bulgaria or Romania but rather to their cousins, aunts, and uncles in West Germany.

The East Germans watching West German television now saw the clothes, cars, houses, and workplaces in the Federal Republic. They could also watch and listen to West German news reports and documentaries. This uncensored news and information, along with the alternative view of life in the capitalist West, was unique among the countries of the Soviet bloc. And it was one of the main reasons that the revolts against communism, culminating in the collapse of the Soviet bloc, would begin in the GDR.

At the same time, the Berlin Wall—and the comprehensive border between East and West Germany—constituted some of the most solid, and technologically sophisticated, barriers to human movement ever created up until that time. The Berlin Wall was eventually so thick that cars and trucks could drive on top of it. It was often 10 feet wide and made of the densest concrete. There was a no-man's land for 20 or 30 feet on either side of the wall, monitored by East German police with orders to shoot to kill anyone attempting to escape.

A wide swath of cut forest also ran north to south between the two Germanies. All along it, you would find guard towers, wall-monitoring roads, and automatic firing trip wires. Even so, daring escapes were sometimes attempted; and sometimes they were successful. These escapes were accomplished by digging tunnels under the wall; or by flying hot air balloons over it; or even by assembling miniature submarines to slip across the rivers (and under the fences) that separated East and West Berlin. There is a fascinating private museum today in Berlin near the former border crossing known as Checkpoint Charlie. The Checkpoint Charlie museum has some of the actual escape vehicles or models used to flee the GDR.

My strongest memory of crossing from West to East Germany comes from a trip I made by train, coming up from Munich. We crossed several borders along the way. The first border was leaving Bavaria in West Germany to cross into the GDR. I remember hearing dogs barking. The border guards all had German shepherds: *Schaeferhunds*. On the way in, the East German guards would be looking for banned books, pictures, magazines—and also for dissidents who might be trying to sneak back in for some illegal political meeting or contact. When the dogs heard a train coming, they knew it was time to get out of their kennels and go to work. When the two Germanies were reunited on October 3, 1990, I wondered about unemployment for thousands of dogs who had just lost a border to patrol.

I happened to be sitting in a compartment on the train with some rather well-to-do and conservative West Germans who were happy to tell me about all the bad things about the GDR. They said I would be able to tell when the train had entered the GDR because the tracks would be worse, and the train would start to wobble. They said the air would get dirtier, and begin to smell bad. And the houses would not be well cared for and kept up. Even though I was trying to keep an open mind, and look for some positives in the GDR, they were totally correct. The train had to slow down, because of the bad condition of the tracks. The air had a funny color, and it smelled bad. And the houses, factories, and stores were all in much worse condition than the spic-and-span, neat, brightly painted West German structures we'd just left behind.

So, the superiority of the West German economic system was observable by sight, sound, and smell. The citizens of East Germany clearly felt inferior and unlucky. The two Germanies were too unequal to sustain. It would be only a matter of time before millions of them took to the streets of Dresden, Leipzig, Berlin, and other East German cities to demand radical change.

Lecture 18

The Soviet Union's Fatal Failure to Reform

NIKITA KHRUSHCHEV, A FORMER GENERAL secretary of the Communist Party of the Soviet Union, correctly predicted that the Soviet Union would outproduce the United States in concrete, steel, iron, and coal—and by such a degree that the USSR would essentially bury the United States in these products. But by the time this happened, the United States had moved on to create aluminum alloys, plastics, structural glass, and other advanced technological products that replaced many uses for coal, iron, and concrete. This American advance—and Soviet stagnation—gives a hint of why, over time, the Soviet Union fell further and further behind U.S. ingenuity and prosperity. ◆

From Khrushchev to Gorbachev

◀ Nikita Khrushchev was a complicated—and contradictory—man, and the Soviet politburo (the principal policy-making committee of the Communist Party of the Soviet Union) ousted him from his leadership position in October 1964. Prior to this, Khrushchev had brought some openness to one of the world's most closed political and economic systems.

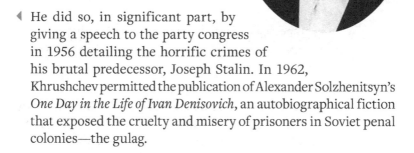

◀ He did so, in significant part, by giving a speech to the party congress in 1956 detailing the horrific crimes of his brutal predecessor, Joseph Stalin. In 1962, Khrushchev permitted the publication of Alexander Solzhenitsyn's *One Day in the Life of Ivan Denisovich*, an autobiographical fiction that exposed the cruelty and misery of prisoners in Soviet penal colonies—the gulag.

◀ After Khrushchev was deposed, Leonid Brezhnev became the new leader. And he swiftly escalated the Cold War arms race with the United States.

◀ From 1964 until March 1985, when Mikhail Gorbachev assumed power, the Soviet Union was led by a succession of older, and sometimes ailing, men whose preoccupation was maintaining the status quo domestically and achieving military parity with the United States.

Nikita Khrushchev's son Sergei told the story about how his father had ordered the release of millions of Soviet prisoners and therefore had to initiate a mass-housing program. Today, these blocks of concrete can be found in all Russian cities, and in most other countries of eastern Europe.

Sergei said that the original plan was for these blocks to be torn down and replaced with more modern, and aesthetically pleasing, structures in about 20 years. That never happened.

◀ Brezhnev's last years—before he died in 1982—were marked by physical and mental decline. He was replaced by Yury Andropov, the former head of the Soviet secret police, or KGB, who had some ideas about reform but suffered from a fatal liver disease and died in February 1984. He was replaced by Konstantin Chernenko, who was also in failing health and died in March 1985.

◀ Gorbachev was elected general secretary of the Central Committee of the Communist Party of the Soviet Union on March 11, 1985. The electors were members of the Soviet politburo in Moscow: a committee of nine men at the top of the party. At the time, the average age of a Soviet politburo member was over 70. Gorbachev cut quite the contrasting figure; he had just turned 54. And he was acutely aware of the stagnation, lack of freedom, isolation, and bankruptcy of the Soviet system.

The Soviet Economy

◀ As Soviet general secretary, Gorbachev inherited several serious problems. Military spending, and actions such as the invasion of Afghanistan, were a tremendous drain on the state budget.

◀ Soviet soldiers were suffering heavy casualties in the mountains of Afghanistan, and mothers were calling for their boys to be brought home. Additionally, more than half of a million Soviet troops were stationed in eastern Europe, adding to the economic burden on the economy.

◀ There were also substantial technological costs, such as maintaining the readiness of Soviet nuclear weapons and its intercontinental ballistic missiles, which weighed on the economy. Some of Gorbachev's key foreign policy decisions would arise from this burden.

◀ One of Gorbachev's first priorities became to extricate the Soviet army from what he referred to as the "hopeless military adventure in Afghanistan." On July 28, 1986, he announced the beginning of troop withdrawals, culminating in February 1989. His next foreign policy move was to begin disengaging from direct Soviet control over eastern Europe and reducing the numbers of Soviet troops in all of the Warsaw Pact countries.

◀ The withdrawal from Afghanistan and pullback from eastern Europe were also intended to signal interest to the United States and other NATO countries in negotiating reductions in the nuclear arms race. This competition was something that the Soviet Union could no longer afford if it were to use its scarce scientific and technological resources to improve the lives of its people.

◀ The Soviet economy was much smaller than that of the United States, even though the two countries had populations of roughly the same size. In fact, the American economy was at least twice as large as the Soviet economy. With comparably lesser resources available to the Soviet economy, distributing that smaller output resulted in a much smaller amount of goods and services for each Soviet citizen compared to in the United States.

◀ The Cold War arms race also cost the United States substantially; defense-related production took a large share of U.S. scientific and technological resources. But the American entrepreneurial spirit took many defense-related products and technologies and turned them into modern consumer tech goods and services.

◀ In his memoirs, Gorbachev laments the fact that Soviet military factories always had the latest equipment, the most talented engineers, and first claim on economic resources—compared with the outdated equipment and scarce resources available to agriculture and food.

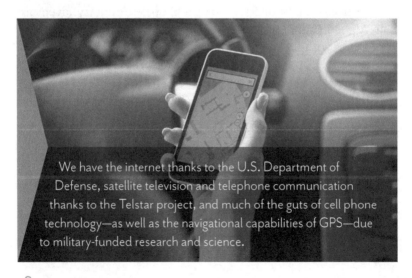

We have the internet thanks to the U.S. Department of Defense, satellite television and telephone communication thanks to the Telstar project, and much of the guts of cell phone technology—as well as the navigational capabilities of GPS—due to military-funded research and science.

◀ As the son of collective farmers, Gorbachev had a deep appreciation for the need in agriculture for suitable tractors, harvesters, and trucks to produce and transport the crops that feed a nation. Yet Soviet farm tractors tended to be obsolete, in bad repair, and lacking in the spare parts to repair them when they broke down, which was very often.

◀ Furthermore, the Soviet Union was woefully behind in food processing and storage. Milk and cheese often rotted from lack of refrigeration. Bread grew moldy from lack of rapid delivery to retail stores. This also contributed to a shorter life expectancy for the average Soviet citizen.

Problems with Soviet Planning

◀ Gorbachev and his wife Raisa understood that the totalitarian system had limited people's possibilities and imaginations. The conservative mentality had its origins in the nature of Soviet planning. Each person in the Soviet system owed his or her standard of living to the position he or she held. If the person lost that position, he or she could lose his or her home, places to shop, school for his or her children, recreational and cultural opportunities, and medical care.

◀ All of this was tied to your position in life. As you went higher up, your standard of living improved. You were eligible for a nicer and bigger apartment. You had more options for vacations. You had access to better food, clothes, furniture, and appliances. So, nobody wanted to lose status in the Soviet system.

◀ In market economies, people also lose jobs and their position. But when they lose their job, they don't automatically lose everything else, especially if they can get a job at a different company or organization.

◀ But in the Soviet Union, there was no other company or organization. There was no other place to go. The loss of position and status was usually permanent. You would be assigned to a lower position in the same enterprise or moved to a less prestigious place. This was especially true for Soviet managers.

◀ The basic operating unit in the Soviet economy was the enterprise. A Soviet enterprise was the equivalent of a single plant, or firm, in a market economy. Unlike General Electric, which has factories all over the world, a Soviet enterprise typically had a single location. And associated with the enterprise were enterprise-linked schools, cultural centers, shops, and apartments.

◀ The enterprise manager and his family—it was almost always a man—would get the best and biggest apartment, with access to shops selling Western goods and priority for medical treatment. At the same time, the enterprise manager was given production targets, or objectives, generated by central planning. These targets were always stated in terms of physical quantities and numerical values and would be given in monthly, yearly, and five-year totals.

◀ The basic planning tool in the Soviet system was the five-year plan, as instituted by Stalin at the end of the 1920s. Early on, plan targets were pretty simple: so many tons of coal to be mined, so many tons of steel to be produced, and so on. The enterprise manager would be rewarded for meeting the targets or punished for failing to meet the objective.

◀ In the Stalin period, not meeting your goal might mean exile to Siberia or worse—although after Stalin died, the major loss for an enterprise manager who did not meet his target would simply be the loss of the job and all the perks that went with that position.

◀ Because the targets for an enterprise manager were always set in physical terms, this led to some pretty dysfunctional behavior. For example, if a turbine enterprise manager was given a target of 100 turbines for the month, the incentive would be to produce the smallest turbines possible, even if larger ones were needed.

◀ The system of targets produced a strong tendency in enterprise managers to maintain the status quo. If they tried new techniques of production that might possibly be more efficient—and if the new approach failed—then they could lose their jobs.

◀ One of the chief criticisms of the Soviet economy was its lack of innovation—in terms of production methods and in range of new products. The typical Soviet manager was not focused on minimizing costs or maximizing sales revenues.

◀ In part, that's because Soviet-era managers had every incentive to hire as many workers as possible. More workers meant an easier task of meeting production targets. This created excess demand for labor and was a main reason that there was always full employment in the Soviet Union.

◀ Full employment didn't mean efficient use of labor, of course. Often, enterprises would employ workers who didn't do anything but were around in case production needed to be increased quickly to meet the target as the month came to a close. This practice of feverishly rushing to meet the target at the end of each month was called storming, and it's a pretty inefficient way to get the job done.

◀ Storming leads to shoddy quality of products and exhaustion of the workers. Afterward, the workers might need to rest a bit at the beginning of the next month. And if they rest too long, they will need to storm again. As the Soviet economy developed throughout the 20th century, this situation of shoddy and old-fashioned products became worse and worse. People in the West heard stories of Soviet citizens hounding visiting tourists for jeans, portable radios, and makeup.

◀ As bad as Soviet consumer goods were, the problem was surpassed by the problem of consumer services. In part, that's because in the Soviet planning system, if you couldn't weigh or measure something, it wasn't counted in the total production figures. So, services didn't get counted as something valuable. Repair services, communication, personal care, restaurants, and retail sales were almost nonexistent in the Soviet economy.

Raisa Gorbachev, the secretary general's wife, was the first spouse of a Soviet leader to have a public persona of her own and to dress in a modern style. Previously, all wives of the general secretary were either completely unknown or photographed just once—in old-fashioned clothes.

Soviet Failure

◄ Gorbachev set out to reform the Soviet system. And that meant giving enterprise managers more freedom to decide output and prices. But because the managers had little or no experience in this kind of decision making, the system became even less efficient and more chaotic. The freedom to set prices touched off rapid inflation.

◄ Goods became available, but only at prices that most Soviets couldn't afford. And the ruble itself became worth less and less. Some enterprises even paid their workers in whatever they produced. The entire system of enterprise supply and production broke down, and the scarcity of many goods became chronic.

◄ Amid such difficulties, Gorbachev began to allow other Soviet republics—especially the Baltic republics of Estonia, Latvia, and Lithuania—greater latitude. Soon, these republics and the Ukraine and Belarus began to demand complete independence.

◄ Finally, on Christmas Day 1991, Mikhail Gorbachev signed the documents that officially ended the Union of Soviet Socialist Republics. Six years after Gorbachev had been appointed the last general secretary, the Soviet Union disappeared off the map of the world.

Readings

GORBACHEV, *Memoirs*.
MALIA, *The Soviet Tragedy*.
REMNICK, *Lenin's Tomb*.

Questions

1 What were the initial moves made by Mikhail Gorbachev to improve the functioning of the Soviet economy? What were the reasons that he wanted the Soviet Union to change?

2 Why did the Soviet Union need to pull its troops out of Afghanistan and eastern Europe? And why did Gorbachev need to negotiate reductions in armaments with President Ronald Reagan?

The Soviet Union's Fatal Failure to Reform

W ho knew the Soviet Union would collapse on Christmas Day in December 1991? Until then, most experts had assumed that the world's other superpower would go on indefinitely. And not without reason. Nikita Khrushchev, a former general secretary of the Soviet Communist Party, once boasted that the Soviet Union would bury the United States. And although many Americans took this as a threat, Khrushchev actually predicted that the Soviet Union would out-produce the United States in concrete, steel, iron, and coal—and by such a degree that the USSR would eventually bury the U.S. in these products.

This pledge took place during the famous "Kitchen Debate" between Khrushchev and Vice President Richard Nixon—at an exhibition of American consumer culture in Moscow—in July 1959. As it turns out, the Soviet Union did surpass the United States in coal, iron, and concrete production. But by the time this happened, the U.S. had moved on to create aluminum alloys, plastics, structural glass, and other advanced technological products that replaced many uses for coal and iron and concrete. This American advance—and Soviet stagnation—gives a hint of why, over time, the Soviet Union fell further and further behind U.S. in ingenuity and prosperity.

Khrushchev was a complicated—and contradictory—man. And the Soviet Politburo (the principal policymaking committee of the Communist Party) ousted him from his leadership position in October 1964. Prior to this, Khrushchev had brought some openness to one of the world's most closed political and economic systems. He did so, in significant part, by giving a speech to the party congress in 1956 detailing the horrific crimes of his brutal predecessor, Joseph Stalin. In 1962, Khrushchev permitted the publication of Alexander Solzhenitsyn's slender novel, *One Day in the Life of Ivan Denisovich*. Solzhenitsyn's autobiographical fiction exposed the cruelty and misery of prisoners in Soviet penal colonies—the gulag. This was the first Solzhenitsyn novel I read; and, as for many, it had a profound impact on my thinking about the Soviet Union.

Nikita Khrushchev's son, Sergei, later told the story—at a very interesting presentation to the Art Institute of Chicago—about how his father had ordered the release of millions of Soviet prisoners, and therefore had to initiate a mass-housing program. Today, these blocks of concrete can be found in all Russian cities, and in most other countries of Eastern Europe. The apartment blocks were ugly. But during a tour some years ago, one of the guides told me, "We could build them fast or we could build them pretty, but not both." Khrushchev's son, Sergei, said the original plan was for these blocks to be torn down and replaced with more modern, and aesthetically pleasing, structures in about 20 years. That never happened.

After Khrushchev was deposed, Leonid Brezhnev became the new leader. And he swiftly escalated the Cold War arms race with the United States. Of course, the production of more Soviet military goods meant fewer resources would be available to produce housing. From 1964 until March 1985, when Mikhail Sergeyevich Gorbachev assumed power, the Soviet Union was led by a succession of older, and sometimes ailing, men whose preoccupation was maintaining the status quo domestically, and achieving military parity with the United States. Brezhnev's last years— before he died in 1982—were marked by physical and mental decline. He was replaced by Yuri Andropov, the former head of the Soviet secret police, or KGB, who had some ideas about reform but suffered a fatal liver disease, and died in February 1984. He was replaced by Konstantin Chernenko, also in failing health. Chernenko died in March 1985. One scholar quipped, "the Soviet Union does not have elections, they have funerals."

President Ronald Reagan made something of the same joke. Answering his critics who accused him of being reluctant to engage with the Soviet leadership, he said: "I try but they keep dying on me!"

Gorbachev was elected general secretary of the Soviet Communist Party's central committee on March 11, 1985. Admittedly, this was not a national election like many of us are accustomed to—with several candidates vying for the public's vote. Instead, the electors were members of the Soviet Politburo in Moscow: a committee of nine men at the top of the party. At the time, the average age of a Soviet Politburo member was over 70. Gorbachev cut quite the contrasting figure. He'd just turned 54 a week and a half earlier. In his *Memoirs*, Gorbachev recounts telling his wife

Raisa—on the night of the election—"We cannot go on living like this." He was acutely aware of the stagnation, lack of freedom, isolation, and bankruptcy of the Soviet system.

Gorbachev was something of a country boy, born in the Stavropol region of southern Russia. It was wheat country. His father and grandfather had worked on collective farms. But Mikhail was an extremely diligent and brilliant student, as indicated by his admission to Moscow State University—which was at the top of the higher education pyramid. Its students usually came from big cities, like Moscow and Leningrad. But Gorbachev won admission due to his high scores in school, and his personal background, coming from an agricultural family. This was a type of Soviet "affirmative action" to diversify the country's educated population.

Moscow State University students had some choice of academic major, and Gorbachev chose to study law. This was during the time of the so-called Khrushchev thaw in Soviet culture and politics. And so, students had some freedom to criticize and consider reforms of the system. Gorbachev met his wife, Raisa—a philosophy and sociology major—at Moscow State University. She continued her academic interests even as they had children, and as Mikhail moved up the communist party ladder. Raisa was Mikhail's closest confidant, and she would play a key role in the relationships between her husband and Presidents Reagan and George H.W. Bush.

As Soviet General Secretary, Gorbachev inherited several serious problems. Military spending—and actions such as the invasion of Afghanistan—were a tremendous drain on the state budget. Soviet soldiers were suffering heavy casualties in the mountains of Afghanistan, and mothers were calling for their boys to be brought home. Additionally, more than a half-million Soviet troops were stationed in Eastern Europe, adding to the economic burden on the economy. There were also substantial technological costs—like maintaining the readiness of Soviet nuclear weapons and its intercontinental ballistic missiles, which weighed on the economy. Some of Gorbachev's key foreign policy decisions would arise from this burden.

So, one of Gorbachev's first priorities became to extricate the Soviet army from what he referred to as "the hopeless military adventure in Afghanistan." On July 28, 1986, he announced the beginning of troop withdrawals, culminating in February 1989. His next foreign policy move was to begin disengaging from direct Soviet control over Eastern Europe, and reducing the numbers of Soviet troops in all of the Warsaw Pact countries. The withdrawal from Afghanistan, and pullback from Eastern Europe, was also intended to signal interest to the United States and other NATO countries in negotiating reductions in the nuclear arms race. This competition was something the Soviet Union could no longer afford if it were to use its scarce scientific and technological resources to improve the lives of its people.

The Soviet economy was much smaller than that of the United States, even though the two countries had roughly the same size populations. In fact, the American economy was at least twice as large as the Soviet economy. With comparably lesser resources available to the Soviet economy, distributing that smaller output resulted in a much smaller amount of goods and services for each Soviet citizen compared to in the U.S.

I'm not saying that the Cold War arms race didn't also cost the United States substantially. Defense-related production took a large share of U.S. scientific and technological resources. But the American entrepreneurial spirit took many defense-related products and technologies, and turned them into modern consumer tech goods and services. We have the U.S. Department of Defense to thank for the Internet; satellite television and telephone communication thanks to the Telstar project; and much of the "guts" of cell phone technology—as well as the navigational capabilities of GPS—due to military-funded research and science.

In his *Memoirs*, Gorbachev laments the fact that Soviet military factories always had the latest equipment, the best-talented engineers, and first claim on economic resources, compared with the outdated equipment and scarce resources available to agriculture and food production. As the son of collective farmers, Gorbachev had a deep appreciation for the need in agriculture for suitable tractors, harvesters, and trucks to produce and transport the crops that feed a nation. Yet Soviet farm tractors tended to be obsolete, in bad repair, and lacking in the spare parts to repair them when they broke down, which was very often.

Furthermore, the Soviet Union was woefully behind in food processing and storage. Milk and cheese often rotted from lack of refrigeration. Bread grew moldy from lack of rapid delivery to retail stores. This also contributed to a shorter life-expectancy for the average Soviet citizen. One of the perks of being a high Soviet official was that you had access to special grocery stores supplied by special greenhouses and dairies with modern—often foreign-bought—equipment and technology. Two examples illustrate this problem.

The first was the overwhelming attraction of McDonald's fast-food restaurants to Soviet citizens. When the initial McDonald's in the Soviet Union opened in Moscow on Pushkin Square, Moscow residents lined up for blocks to get in. There were two separate entrances. One side was for customers who had only Soviet rubles—a currency without a great deal of convertibility into foreign exchange, at the time. That first McDonald's opened before the collapse of the Soviet Union, and pretty much the only money Soviet citizens were allowed to have was denominated in rubles, which, in some respects, was pretty much worthless. The line for Soviet ruble holders was long—with maybe 200 people in it. They were dressed in their best clothes; men in suits and ties, women in dresses and heels. It was fine dining to them.

The other entrance was for foreigners and Soviet bureaucrats with western money: U.S. dollars, German marks, French francs. There was no line to get in on this side. I felt a bit guilty about this—probably my Catholic school sense of undeserved privilege was kicking in. But once, upon entering to Moscow—and detraining from the Trans-Siberian Express—the first place I went to eat was at a McDonald's on Smolensk Square near my hotel. The milk in the McDonald's restaurants was fresh and healthy. The meat for the "Bolshoi Mak" was hearty and tasty. And the employees smiled at the customers as they served their food. I was told that one of the most important requirements for being hired at the new McDonald's on Pushkin Square was that you had never worked in Soviet food service. I've often debated with myself about what was the greater attraction: Was it McDonald's fresh and healthy food, to the Russian way of thinking? Or was it the pleasant demeanor of the staff?

My second example about the perks of the Soviet system—and the selective availability of its consumer goods, and their quality—is the milk store on the first floor of my apartment building when I lived and was teaching in Ekaterinburg—Russia's fourth-largest city—in the fall of 1994. Ekaterinburg is 1100 miles, or nearly 1800 kilometers, east of Moscow, in central Eurasia. One of my first days in the apartment, I was pleased to find a milk store on the first floor of my building. Earlier, I'd managed to find a box of Cocoa Krispies cereal in one of the little stores in the neighborhood. Visions of Cocoa Krispies cereal with milk for breakfast danced in my head. I went into the store and bought a bottle of milk. I took the thick clear glass bottle back to my little apartment, and put it in my little refrigerator. The next morning, I jumped out of bed in anticipation of breakfast, just like at home. When I opened the refrigerator door, my heart sank. The milk had coagulated into a green solid at the bottom of the bottle. And some yellow liquid floated at the top. I emptied the bottle down the sink, and had a few handfuls of dry Cocoa Krispies for breakfast.

For the typical Soviet citizen, this was the relative quality of almost everything available to them. And the backwardness was not just in material goods and consumer services. Gorbachev and his wife Raisa understood the totalitarian system had limited people's possibilities and imaginations. The conservative mentality had its origins in the nature of Soviet planning. Each person in the Soviet system owed his or her standard of living to their position they held. If they lost that position, they could lose their home, places to shop, school for their children, recreational and cultural opportunities, and medical care. All of this was tied to your position in life. As you went higher up, your standard of living improved. You were eligible for a nicer and bigger apartment. You had more options for vacations. You had access to better food, clothes, furniture and appliances. So, no-one wanted to lose status in the Soviet system.

Now, in market economies, people lose jobs and position as well. But when you lose your job, you don't automatically lose everything else, especially if you can get a job at a different company or organization. But in the Soviet Union, there was no other company or organization. There was no other place to go. The loss of position and status was usually permanent. You would be assigned to a lower position in the same enterprise, or moved to a less prestigious place. This was especially true for Soviet managers. I'll explain more about this in a minute.

The basic operating unit in the Soviet economy was the enterprise. A Soviet enterprise was the equivalent of a single plant, or firm, in a market economy. When my Illinois State University students visited the Red Banner turbine enterprise in Zaporozhe, Ukraine, we were surprised to find all the production was in one location. Unlike General Electric Corporation—which builds turbines, and has factories all over the world—a Soviet enterprise typically had a single location.

So, associated with the turbine enterprise in Zaporozhe were enterprise-linked schools, cultural centers, shops, and apartments. The enterprise manager and his family would get the best and biggest apartment, with access to shops selling Western goods, and priority for medical treatment. At the same time, the enterprise manager was given production targets, or objectives, generated by central planning. These targets were always stated in terms of physical quantities and numerical values. For example, the turbine enterprise would be given targets in terms of the number of turbines. These numerical target objectives would be given in monthly, yearly and five-year totals.

The basic planning tool in the Soviet system was the five-year plan, as instituted by Stalin at the end of the 1920s. Early on, plan targets were pretty simple. So many tons of coal to be mined, so many tons of steel to be produced, so many bushels of wheat, and so on. The enterprise manager would be rewarded for meeting the targets, or punished for failing to meet the objective.

In the Stalin period, not meeting your goal might mean exile to Siberia or worse, though after Stalin died, the major loss for an enterprise manager who did not meet his target—and it was almost always a man—would simply be the loss of the job, and all the perks that went with that position. Because the targets for an enterprise manager were always set in physical terms, this led to some pretty dysfunctional behavior. For example, if the turbine enterprise manager was given a target of 100 turbines for the month, the incentive would be to produce the smallest turbines possible, even if larger ones were needed.

If you were the enterprise manager of a shoe factory, and you were given a target to produce 1,000 pairs of shoes this month, it would be easier to produce one size and one color for all 1,000 shoes. In the early Soviet period, when many people didn't have any shoes, a size too big or in a color you didn't like would not be enough reason to not buy the shoes. But once Soviet citizens had at least a pair of shoes, they could be a bit pickier about the next pair. Seeing only black shoes in size 12 at their local store might not be very satisfying. It might also diminish a worker's desire to work hard, and earn bonuses.

Yet the system of targets produced a strong tendency in enterprise managers to maintain the status quo. If they tried new techniques of production that might possibly be more efficient—and if the new approach failed—then they could lose their jobs. One of the chief criticisms of the Soviet economy was its lack of innovation—innovation in terms of production methods, and in range of new products. The typical Soviet manager was not focused on minimizing costs, or maximizing sales revenues.

Much later, I would run into many foreign investors who came to Russia to look for possible business projects. Many of them would lament that when they visited a factory, nobody in charge would have any idea of its costs of production. In part, that's because Soviet-era managers had every incentive to hire as many workers as possible. More workers meant an easier task of meeting production targets. This created excess demand for labor, and was a main reason there was always full employment in the Soviet Union.

Full employment didn't mean efficient use of labor, of course. Often, enterprises would employ workers who didn't do anything at all. But they were around in case production needed to be increased quickly to meet the target, as the month came to a close. This practice of feverishly rushing to meet the target at the end of each month was called "storming." My students understand this phenomenon perfectly. They call it "cramming" right before a big test. Storming and cramming are both pretty inefficient ways to get the job done.

Storming leads to shoddy quality of products, and exhaustion of the workers. Afterward, the workers might need to rest a bit at the beginning of the next month. And, of course, if they rest too long, they will need to storm again. In the same way, cramming leads to superficial retention which quickly goes away, and you need to cram again for the next test.

As the Soviet economy developed throughout the 20th century, this situation of shoddy and old-fashioned products got worse and worse. Everyone in the West heard stories of Soviet citizens hounding visiting tourists for jeans, portable radios, and makeup. Makeup for Soviet women was always in short supply. It was a product that was hard to make, and also was something that enhanced one's individuality.

One of my Soviet students in Ekaterinburg—her name was Alyona—was fortunate enough to have a father who was a rather prominent physicist. As such, he was allowed to travel to France to attend a scientific conference. One of the prize presents he brought back to Alyona and her mother was an eyelash curler with a dark color. Alyona and her mother made that eyelash makeup last for more than a year by refilling it occasionally with drops of alcohol.

Raisa Gorbachev, the secretary general's wife, was interested not only in philosophy and sociology, but also in fashion, and in helping Soviet women look and feel good about themselves. She was the first spouse of a Soviet leader to have a public persona of her own, and to dress stylishly in a modern style. Previously, all wives of the general secretary were either completely unknown, or photographed just once—in old-fashioned clothes.

As bad as Soviet consumer goods were, the problem was surpassed by the problem of consumer services. In part, that's because in the Soviet planning system, if you couldn't weigh or measure something, it wasn't counted in the total production figures. So, services didn't get counted as something valuable. In the words of many economic statisticians, "If you don't measure it, it's not important." Repair services, communication, personal care, restaurants, and retail sales were almost non-existent in the Soviet economy.

One Soviet joke relates the story of a man who had finally saved up enough money to put his order in for a car. Once you got on the list, you usually had to wait about six months to take ownership of your vehicle. The man put his money down on January 10 and was told that he could come pick up his car on July 3. "Oh no," the man says, "I can't pick it up on that day." The dealer asks why. The man says, "July 3 is when the plumber is coming!"

Many of my students in Ekaterinburg had never been to a restaurant in their entire lives. Of course, Soviet restaurants were famous for having huge menus with many pages listing all kinds of dishes. The only problem is that almost none of the dishes were available. If you pointed to something on the menu, the waiter or waitress would shake their heads and say *nyet*, or *defizit*. Defizit meant shortage and not available. After a few times dealing with this, the experienced diner would not even look at the menu. Instead, you were better off asking the waitress what they had to serve. Once I got the answer "meat." When I asked what kind, I got a shrug of the shoulders. You couldn't be sure. And the restaurants that did exist were no picnic anyway. Because restaurant workers were guaranteed employment—and tips were forbidden—customers weren't all that welcome.

Gorbachev set out to reform the Soviet system. And that meant giving enterprise managers more freedom to decide output and prices. But because the managers had little or no experience in this kind of decision making, the system became even less efficient and more chaotic. The freedom to set prices touched off rapid inflation. Goods became available but only at prices that most Soviets couldn't afford. And the ruble itself became worth less and less. Some enterprises even paid their workers in whatever they produced. A car parts enterprise began paying its workers in fenders. The entire system of enterprise supply and production broke down, and the scarcity of many goods became chronic.

Amid such difficulties, Gorbachev began to allow other Soviet republics—especially the Baltic republics of Estonia, Latvia, and Lithuania—greater latitude. Soon, these republics and the Ukraine and Belarus began to demand complete independence. Finally, on Christmas Day 1991, Mikhail Gorbachev signed the documents that officially ended the Union of Soviet Socialist Republics. Six years after Mikhail Sergeyevich Gorbachev had been appointed the last general secretary, the Soviet Union disappeared off the map of the world. The historian Martin Malia says, "It was an absolute system, and it collapsed absolutely."

Lecture 19

"Blinkered and Bankrupt" in Eastern Europe

B Y THE END OF 1989, ALL COMMUNIST GOVERNMENTS in eastern Europe were gone, replaced by semblances of democracy and market economies. In greater and smaller ways, each Eastern European regime had been different and collapsed in different ways. What came after was also different. These differences can best be understood by studying the kind of communist system each at first embraced and then abandoned. ◆

Eastern European Economies

◀ All communist economies of eastern Europe were modeled on the Soviet Union's. Each one nationalized important industries and economic sectors, including agriculture. All adopted five-year economic planning models that emphasized heavy industry and neglected the production of consumer goods and services.

◀ This neglect of consumer goods and services was to play a key role in their eventual demise. The lack of attention to, or even regard for, consumer needs and wants became more noticeable, and increasingly aggravating, as the neighboring economies of western Europe took off after World War II.

◀ Even in battered Germany—and maybe especially there—the West began to produce prodigious amounts of modern and stylish consumer goods while providing citizens with valuable services, such as housing, entertainment, communications, and retail shopping. What made this disparity so obvious was the availability of Western television and movies to most of the population on the eastern side of the Iron Curtain.

◀ Soviet-style economic planners made a conscious choice to limit the production of desirable consumer goods. Instead, the central planners ordered economic enterprises to produce industrial goods and supplies. So, Soviet bloc factories turned out vast quantities of steel, coal, industrial chemicals, cement, electrical equipment, and other industrial goods.

◀ Soviet ideology held that industrial growth was the measure of success of a planned economy. So, enterprise managers were rewarded for meeting their production goals. And because the primary objective was maximum production, less attention was paid to efficiency and cost controls.

Not only did the Soviet-style economies typically not incorporate computers into industrial production, but computers were ideologically suspect. Soviet ideologues suspected that computer technology was a capitalist plot to subvert socialist planning and information.

◀ Communist bureaucrats—whether political functionaries or economic managers—were frequently promoted primarily on loyalty and obedience to authority. There was no tolerance for risk taking or independent thinking. Conformity was a function of the political system and of the ideological control exercised by the ruling Communist Party.

The Communist System

◀ All eastern European societies were one-party, nondemocratic states. The power of the Communist Party—and its leaders in state office—was absolute and not to be questioned. And the top priority of the leadership of the ruling party was staying in power.

◀ The system rewarded loyalty, conformity, and group thinking. That's a pretty good recipe for a system that will be stagnant and rigid, without the ability to change or adapt. Large organizations that operate along such lines almost always die out or collapse.

◀ The communist embrace of central planning also contained some benefits for ordinary workers. But these benefits were double-edged.

◀ Because each manager of an industrial enterprise was rewarded for maximum production, he tried to accumulate the greatest amount of resources he could. This included trying to maximize the size of the labor force that would work at his enterprise. The more workers he had to put on the production line, the easier it would be for him to achieve his production targets. This meant that the entire system incentivized excess demand for labor inputs.

◀ Unlike a capitalist enterprise that tries to maximize profits, a communist enterprise had little concern for profits or costs of production. Most communist enterprise managers had no clear idea—and didn't care—what their production expenses were. It didn't affect their success.

- One of the cruel things about capitalist enterprises is they're always trying to minimize costs. Often, this means laying off workers who it's thought are no longer needed or who cost too much. But a benefit of occasionally pruning your labor base is that production per worker might increase, and the economy as a whole may be more efficient.

- Greater output per labor input is the basic driving force for higher standards of living. What a capitalist economy may have to do to avoid mass unemployment is use fiscal and monetary policy to promote economic growth. This growth should provide jobs for workers laid off from other capitalist enterprises.

- Because a communist enterprise had no need to minimize labor use, or costs, workers were always in demand—and rarely laid off. Jobs were more or less guaranteed.

- For workers, this has some benefits. Job security is pretty ironclad, so there is no need to stress about unemployment. But self-satisfaction also comes with a cost. Motivation and productive effort might be harder to achieve with workers who have no reason to fear dismissal or transfer.

- Communist workers were paid a fairly standard wage. This was part of the ideology's promise of equality.

- Because most communist societies had comparatively undeveloped financial systems relative to those in the West— typically, there were no credit cards, mortgage banks, or consumer loans—a communist country was predominantly a cash society. So, its workers would be paid cash, which they could use to buy whatever consumer goods and services were available.

> If goods were scarce in communist societies, then you might need to stand in line to wait until something became available. This condition inspired the well-worn phrase of workers in a communist economy: "We pretend to work, and they pretend to pay us."

◀ And here's the problem: With a low priority on consumer goods and services, there was rarely enough to buy—even if you had money to pay for goods or services. There was a continuous and general shortage. It also meant that what was available to the typical consumer in eastern Europe were goods and services behind the current styles and fashions of the West.

◀ Citizens who received approval to buy big-ticket items, such as cars or appliances, would first need to save the money required to pay the full price. In other words, because there were no consumer credit facilities or credit cards, cash was necessary to make the entire payment.

◀ But just having enough cash to buy a car didn't mean that you could buy one. You had to be approved. The approval might come from your enterprise manager. This was one of the few tools the boss had available to motivate and reward better workers in a communist economy.

◀ Perhaps surprisingly, most families in Soviet bloc communist states had large amounts of cash. Economists often refer to this phenomenon as forced savings. Workers would accumulate cash as they were paid weekly. And if there wasn't enough to buy, then they would just hold onto the cash. Sometime in the future, maybe there'd be something to buy.

◀ The problem of larger and larger amounts of cash in the hands of the population is known as monetary overhang. In market economies, an excess of cash usually leads to inflation. But one promise of the communist economic system was stable prices and no inflation. This promise was kept: Goods were cheap—at the cost of being unavailable.

◀ One problem that occurred in all former communist economies—right after the collapse of central planning economies and fixed prices—was an explosion in inflation and some periods of hyperinflation. It can be said that monetary overhang created conditions of repressed inflation.

> Economists typically define hyperinflation as anything above 50 percent a year. In eastern Europe, most postcommunist inflation rates were initially in the thousands of percent.

◀ What was required to get rid of the inflation that came now was a complete monetary overhaul (and replacement) of the old money—with a new monetary standard and new money supply. This is what the immediate postwar West German government did by replacing the old reichsmark with the new deutsche mark. But many people lose most of their savings—and wealth—in such monetary transformations.

Living Standards in Eastern Europe

◀ Aside from what eastern Europeans got to see on television and at the movies, the appearance of tourists from western Europe and the United States was another sign of the relative backwardness of living standards in eastern Europe. Ordinary citizens in East Berlin, Prague, Warsaw, and Budapest could see that their clothes, electronics, sporting goods, and luggage were all quite shabby compared to the possessions of ordinary tourists from the West.

◀ Although most leaders of eastern European communist parties, state offices, and big enterprises were all true believers in the promise of communism—and in the superiority of their system— to be confronted each day with their relative backwardness and second-class status compared with western Europe and the capitalist United States was extremely demoralizing.

◀ So, the only hold on power that the leaders of eastern Europe could count on was the presence of Soviet troops who enforced the Brezhnev Doctrine. And that started to change in 1985.

◀ The Brezhnev Doctrine was named for Leonid Brezhnev, the Soviet leader from 1964 to 1982. It stated that the Soviet Union and its allies had the right to intervene militarily in any eastern European communist country that was suspected of deviating from the Soviet model.

◀ The coming to power of Mikhail Gorbachev a few years later, in 1985, changed everything. Gorbachev needed to reform the Soviet economy to save it from collapsing. To do this, he needed to reduce the number of Soviet troops deployed in eastern

Europe and reduce the subsidies the Soviet Union was paying to its eastern European satellites. And he had to make them pay more for the Soviet oil sent to power their industries and electric grids.

◀ Oil prices crashed in the mid-1980s. In the Soviet Union, the bust in oil prices meant that right about when Gorbachev was coming to power, the state budget of the Soviet government had to be reduced, leaving less money to spend propping up the country and much less supporting eastern European satellite economies.

◀ Gorbachev began to tell his eastern European comrades that they were going to have to sink or swim on their own. They would need to reform their backward and stagnant economies themselves if they were to maintain their positions of power and authority.

◀ Unfortunately, the oligarchs were used to following Soviet orders, and the men in charge of eastern European countries in the mid- to late 1980s were creatures of the old system. Stephen Kotkin, a professor at Princeton University, described these men as "incompetent, blinkered, and ultimately bankrupt." In other words, it wasn't going to take much to topple them.

◀ The oligarchs' minimal attempts at reform came to nothing. They tried to produce clothing and electronics for export to western Europe and North America, but these attempts essentially failed.

◀ Other economies in the world market were already making much cheaper and higher-quality goods. Notable among them were the rising economies of Asia, and new waves of consumer goods from Asia destroyed any hope that the market-ignorant oligarchs and enterprises in eastern Europe might have had.

◀ A final attempt to raise living standards by communist leaders in eastern Europe involved massive borrowings from the capitalist West. Eastern European leaders took out sovereign loans to buy Western consumer goods and technology for their economies.

◀ But they couldn't produce anything marketable to earn the hard currency needed to repay their loans, so they simply borrowed more. Eventually, they would default. Kotkin refers to this process as a Ponzi scheme.

Communist Collapse

◀ On November 9, 1989, an East German Communist Party official named Gunther Schabowski made the mistake of stating during a press conference that East Berlin's border with West Berlin—the Berlin Wall—was now open, and citizens were free to travel to West Berlin and West Germany. The decision hadn't been taken formally by the communist leadership, but Berliners took matters into their own hands and headed for the wall.

◀ Soon after, the East German government collapsed, and citizens demanded unification and the freedoms of the West. In December 1989 and January 1990, in demonstrations throughout East Germany, protesters' signs and chants proclaimed, *"Wir sind ein Volk"* ("We are one people").

◀ The collapse of eastern Europe happened quickly and unexpectedly. But in hindsight, once Gorbachev pulled the plug, the leadership had nothing to support it. Most leaders decided that stepping down and saving their own skins was probably the wisest survival strategy.

◀ A key factor in the collapse of the former communist states with remarkably little violence or bloodshed was the restraint of Soviet troops under the direct control of Soviet General Secretary Mikhail Gorbachev. The outcome might have been much deadlier, as substantial numbers of Soviet troops remained deployed in East Germany, Poland, Hungary, and Czechoslovakia. The last of them would not leave until years later. But in the closing days of 1989, most Soviet soldiers deployed in Eastern Europe were under strict orders to stay in their barracks and not interfere in the domestic upheavals taking place in the streets.

Readings

GEDMIN, *The Hidden Hand.*
KOTKIN, *Uncivil Society.*
SCHNEIDER, *The German Comedy.*

Questions

1 Why were the chronic shortages of consumer goods and the complete absence of any inflation two sides of the same economic system coin?

2 Why was the presence of Mikhail Gorbachev as the leader of the Soviet Union and the ultimate commander of all Soviet troops the key factor in the peaceful revolutions in eastern Europe in 1989?

"Blinkered and Bankrupt" in Eastern Europe

D uring the height of the Cold War, it was widely feared that if communism weren't stopped it would spread. This "Domino Theory" helped motivate wars in Vietnam and Nicaragua; the blockade of Cuba; and support for anti-communist governments around the world. Instead, communist dominoes ended up falling all across Eastern Europe. It was a reversal hardly anyone had expected or predicted. And what do I mean by that? I mean the decline of communism caught most intelligence agencies and government analysts by surprise. Who expected the dominoes to fall? Not the CIA, not the State Department, not NATO, and none of the academic specialists I can think of who'd focused on the Soviet Union and East Europe.

By the end of 1989—a year when the physicist Stephen Hawking published *A Brief History of Time*, and you could buy ribeye steak for about $3.79 a pound—all communist governments in Eastern Europe were gone, replaced by semblances of democracy, and market economies. In greater and smaller ways, each east European regime had been different, and collapsed in different ways. What came after was also different. These differences can best be understood by studying the kind of communist system each at first embraced, and then abandoned.

First, let me stipulate that all communist economies of Eastern Europe were modeled on the Soviet Union's. Each one nationalized important industries and economic sectors, including agriculture. All adopted five-year economic planning models that emphasized heavy industry, and neglected the production of consumer goods and services. Of course, this neglect of consumer goods and services was to play a key role in their eventual demise.

The lack of attention, or even regard, for consumer needs and wants became more noticeable—and increasingly aggravating—as the neighboring economies of Western Europe took off after World War II. Even in battered Germany—and maybe especially there—the West began to produce prodigious amounts of modern and stylish consumer goods while providing citizens with valuable services such as housing, entertainment, communications, and retail shopping. What made this disparity so obvious was the availability of western television and movies to most of the population on the eastern side of the Iron Curtain.

Soviet-style economic planners made a conscious choice to limit the production of desirable consumer goods. Instead, the central planners ordered economic enterprises to produce industrial goods and supplies. So, Soviet bloc factories turned out vast quantities of steel, coal, industrial chemicals, cement, electrical equipment, and other industrial goods. Soviet ideology held that industrial growth was the measure of success of a planned economy.

So, enterprise managers were rewarded for meeting their production goals. And since the primary objective was maximum production, less attention was paid to efficiency and cost controls. Planning methodology was rather simple. It had to be. This was mostly before the age of the computer. So, numbers were worked out with paper and pencils. Not only did the Soviet-style economies typically not incorporate computers into industrial production, but computers were ideologically suspect. Soviet ideologues suspected that computer technology was a capitalist plot to subvert socialist planning and information. Just imagine—in a country of 10 or 20 million people—trying to put together realistic numbers for all production decisions over the next five years with pencils and paper!

Communist bureaucrats—whether political functionaries or economic managers—were frequently promoted primarily on loyalty and obedience to authority. There was no tolerance for risk-taking, or independent thinking. Conformity was a function of the political system, and of the ideological control exercised by the ruling communist party. All eastern European societies were one-party, non-democratic states. The power of the communist party—and its leaders in state office—was absolute and not to be questioned. And the number one priority of the leadership of the ruling party was staying in power. The system rewarded loyalty, conformity, and group thinking. That's a pretty good recipe for a system that will be stagnant and rigid, without the ability to change or adapt. Large organizations that operate along such lines almost always die out, or collapse.

The communist embrace of central planning also contained some benefits for ordinary workers. But as we will see, these benefits were double-edged. Because each manager of an industrial enterprise was rewarded for maximum production, he tried to accumulate the greatest amount of resources he could. This included trying to maximize the size of the labor force that would work at his enterprise. The more workers he had to put on the production line, the easier it would be for him to achieve his production targets.

Stated otherwise, this meant the entire system incentivized excess demand for labor inputs. Unlike a capitalist enterprise that tries to maximize profits, a communist enterprise had little concern for profits or costs of production.

Most communist enterprise managers had no clear idea—and didn't care—what their production expenses were. It didn't affect their success.

One of the cruel things about capitalist enterprises is they're always trying to minimize costs. Oftentimes, this means laying off workers who it's thought are no longer needed, or who cost too much. But a benefit of occasionally pruning your labor base is that production per worker might increase, and the economy as a whole may be more efficient. Greater output per labor input is the basic driving force for higher standards of living. What a capitalist economy may have to do to avoid mass unemployment is use fiscal and monetary policy to promote economic growth. This growth should provide jobs for workers laid off from other capitalist enterprises.

Because a communist enterprise had no need to minimize labor use, or costs, workers were always in demand—and rarely laid off. Jobs were more or less guaranteed. For workers, this has some benefits. Job security is pretty iron-clad, so no need to stress about unemployment. But, of course, self-satisfaction also comes with a cost. Motivation and productive effort might be harder to achieve with workers who have no reason to fear dismissal or transfer.

Communist workers were paid a fairly standard wage. This was part of the ideology's promise of equality. Because most communist societies had comparatively undeveloped financial systems relative to in the West— typically, there were a few credit cards; few checking accounts; and no credit unions, mortgage banks, or consumer banks—and what banks did exist were mainly cash distribution centers—a communist country was, therefore, predominantly a cash society.

So, its workers would be paid cash, which they could use to buy whatever consumer goods and services were available. And here's the problem. With a low priority on consumer goods and services, there was rarely enough to buy—even if you had money to pay for goods or services. There was a continuous and general shortage. It also meant that what was available to the typical consumer in eastern European economies were goods and services behind the current styles and fashions of the West: clothes made of older materials, and sporting equipment that was heavy and ugly.

Several times in my travels in Eastern Europe, I'd be approached by people interested in my Nike Tailwind running shoes. Although they were nothing special back home in Chicago, they were made of relatively new materials, like polyurethane soles instead of heavy rubber. The materials were also colorful—high-tech. I ran pretty slow, but I looked fast! Once, when I was touring Eastern Europe, I was carrying an Arthur Ashe PDP Open tennis racket.

It was bright orange and white, and made with a new graphite material at the time that was stronger and lighter than the old-fashioned wooden tennis rackets. Once again, I couldn't hit very good shots but I looked like a pro! The tennis rackets used by ordinary eastern Europeans were old fashioned, heavy wooden beaters that looked like something my mom might have wielded when she was an undergraduate at the University of Texas in the late 1940s.

So, having money didn't necessarily mean you had the possibility of making purchases. If goods were scarce, then you might need to stand in line to wait until something became available. This condition inspired the well-worn phrase of workers in a communist economy: "We pretend to work and they pretend to pay us." It was funny—but it reflected the reality of the situation.

Now, citizens who received approval to buy big-ticket items like a car or appliances would first need to save the money required to pay the full price. In other words, because there were no consumer credit facilities or credit cards, cash was necessary to make the entire payment. But just having enough cash to buy a car didn't mean you could buy one. You had to be approved. This approval might come from your enterprise manager. This was one of the few tools the boss had available to motivate, and reward, better workers in a communist economy. Cars might also be made available to successful national athletes or cultural stars. This was a reward for performance, of course. But it also recognized that you worked in approved cultural events and creations: pro-regime movies, television shows, concerts, and plays.

Now, it might surprise you, but most families in Soviet-bloc communist states had large amounts of cash. Economists often refer to this phenomenon as "forced savings." Workers would accumulate cash as they were paid weekly. And if there wasn't enough to buy, then they would just hold onto the cash. Sometime in the future, maybe there'd be something to buy. The problem of larger and larger amounts of cash in the hands of the population is known as the problem of "monetary overhang." In market economies, an excess of cash usually leads to inflation. But one promise of the communist economic system was stable prices, and no inflation. This promise was kept—goods were cheap—at the cost of being unavailable.

On one of my favorite evenings during a stay in Ekaterinburg, Russia—which is just over a two-hour flight from Moscow, or a little more than a day by express train—a dinner was given for me at the apartment of a faculty host. I was teaching at his university that semester. Sergei was a professor of mathematics, and spoke good English. So, he'd been assigned to be one of my interpreters. One day, he informed me he'd like to invite me home to meet his wife, son, and his father. Multiple generations living in a single apartment was a legacy of the Soviets' general neglect of building enough housing. Still, Russian hospitality can be among the most generous and friendly in the world. And Sergei's wife prepared a magnificent multi-course meal of typical Russian dishes such as fish soup, beet salad, blinis with sour cream, pelmenis stuffed with meat and cheese, and cabbage salad.

At dinner, I discussed economics and education and travels with Sergei, while his son and father—both also named Sergei—listened. We discussed the problem of high inflation, which was afflicting the Russian economy at that time, and the hardships that escalating prices imposed on teachers who received fixed salaries, and older people living on fixed pensions. After some time, the elder Sergei made it known that he wanted to say something about life in the Soviet Union. I thought he might state a criticism of contemporary economics along with favorable views of the good old days in the Soviet Union. But what he said was actually quite brilliant. And I could understand his Russian, because he spoke very plainly and directly. He said that in the Soviet Union, *"Ne inflatsia"*—meaning no inflation. Then he said, *"Ne produkti!"* We had no inflation but we didn't have anything to buy! That about sums up the nature of price control in a Soviet-type economy.

One problem that occurred in all former communist economies—right after the collapse of central planning economy and fixed prices—was an explosion in inflation, and some periods of hyperinflation. Economists typically define hyperinflation as anything above 50 percent a year. In Eastern Europe, most post-communist inflation rates were initially in the thousands of percent. Realizing this, it can be said that monetary overhang created conditions of repressed inflation.

What was required to get rid of the inflation that came now was a complete monetary overhaul (and replacement) of the old money: with a new monetary standard, and new money supply. This is what the immediate post-war West German government did by replacing the old reichsmark with the new deutsche mark. But many people lose most of their savings—and wealth—in such monetary transformations.

Aside from what eastern Europeans got to see on television and at the movies, the appearance of tourists from Western Europe and the United States was another sign of the relative backwardness of living standards in Eastern Europe. Ordinary citizens in East Berlin, Prague, Warsaw, and Budapest could see that their clothes, electronics, sporting goods, and luggage were all quite shabby compared to the possessions of ordinary tourists from the West.

And not only the ordinary citizens and workers were ashamed of their backward conditions.

Although most leaders of eastern European communist parties, state offices, and big enterprises were all true believers in the promise of communism—and in the superiority of their system—even so, to be confronted each day with their relative backwardness and second-class status compared with Western Europe and the capitalist United States was extremely demoralizing. So, the only hold on power that the leaders of Eastern Europe could count on was the presence of Soviet troops who enforced something called the Brezhnev Doctrine. And that started to change in 1985.

The Brezhnev Doctrine was named for Leonid Brezhnev, the Soviet leader from 1964 to 1982. It stated that the Soviet Union and its allies had the right to intervene militarily in any eastern European communist country that was suspected of deviating from the Soviet model. This doctrine was used to justify the Soviet invasion of Czechoslovakia in August 1989—to crush the Prague Spring. As you'll recall, the Prague Spring was an attempt by reform-minded communists to open Czech society to public criticism and possible reform. The Brezhnev Doctrine was also used to threaten the Polish government, and force it to institute martial law in 1981 to crush a union-led opposition movement.

And then, the coming to power of Mikhail Gorbachev a few years later—in 1985—changed everything. Gorbachev needed to reform the Soviet economy, to save it from collapsing. To do this, he needed to reduce the number of Soviet troops deployed in Eastern Europe; and reduce the subsidies the Soviet Union was paying to its eastern European satellites. And he had to make them pay more for the Soviet oil sent to power their industries and electric grids.

As a native Texan, I'm always conscious of the essential role that oil plays in people's lives. I also recognize that—like most things in economics and life—what goes up must come down. Oil prices crashed in the mid-1980s. When I traveled home to Houston during this time, the good ole boys would be standing by freeway entrances with Rolex watches and Cadillacs for sale.

In the Soviet Union, the bust in oil prices meant that right about when Gorbachev was coming to power, the state budget of the Soviet government had to be reduced, leaving less money to spend propping up the country, much less supporting eastern European satellite economies. So, Gorbachev began to tell his eastern European comrades that they were going to have to sink or swim on their own. They would need to reform their backward and stagnant economies themselves, if they were to maintain their positions of power and authority. Unfortunately, the oligarchs were used to following Soviet orders; and the men in charge of eastern European countries in the mid to late 1980s were creatures of the old system.

Stephen Kotkin, a professor of history and international affairs at Princeton University—and a research scholar at Stanford University's Hoover Institution—says these men were "incompetent, blinkered, and bankrupt." In other words, it wasn't going to take much to topple them.

In any event, the oligarchs' minimal attempts at reform came to nothing. They tried to produce clothing and electronics for export to Western Europe and North America. Polish communist leaders, for example, targeted a market niche in golf carts. East Germany tried to produce small computers. Hungary tried to export its buses. All these attempts essentially failed.

Other economies in the world market were already ahead making much cheaper and higher quality goods. Notable among them were the rising economies of Asia: South Korea, Taiwan, Hong Kong, and Singapore. So, new waves of consumer goods from Asia destroyed any hope that market-ignorant oligarchs and enterprises in Eastern Europe might have had.

A final attempt to raise living standards by communist leaders in Eastern Europe involved massive borrowings from the capitalist West. Eastern European leaders took out sovereign loans to buy Western consumer goods and technology for their economies. But they couldn't produce anything marketable to earn the hard currency necessary to repay their loans, so they'd simply borrowed more. Eventually, they would default. Stephen Kotkin refers to this process as a "Ponzi scheme."

In one potent example, the cash-strapped Hungarian government—as a condition to obtain much-needed additional loans from West Germany— agreed to permit free passage for its citizens across the Iron Curtain to Austria. As of August 1989, this meant Hungarian citizens could travel freely to the West. It also meant that other eastern Europeans could cross the Iron Curtain if they could just get to Hungary. Soon, thousands of East Germans were imbued with a taste for Hungarian goulash and a desire to travel to Budapest. And once in Budapest, they were able to cross into Austria. As East German citizens, they were also entitled automatically to West German citizenship, and also to all social-welfare benefits of West German citizens. Freedom—and an instantly higher standard of living—were magnets that drew thousands of East Germans to Hungary.

In Leipzig, the second-largest city in the German Democratic Republic—that is, the second-largest city in East Germany—demonstrations began each Monday evening in the main Lutheran church. Soon, these demonstrations spread to Dresden, Berlin, and other cities of the GDR.

Meanwhile, in Poland, the union-led Solidarity movement personified by Lech Walesa—a former shipyard electrician and labor organizer—had proposed limited free elections in which Solidarity would oppose the official Polish United Workers Party. The Polish Workers Party agreed to let Solidarity contest some parliamentary seats in June 1989. The union movement ended up winning every campaign it ran. In August, a Solidarity leader took over as prime minister of Poland, the first noncommunist premier of an eastern European country since the late 1940s.

Then, on November 9, 1989—three months after Hungarians had gained the opportunity to travel freely to the West—an East German Communist Party official named Gunther Schabowski made the mistake of stating during a press conference that East Berlin's border with West Berlin—the Berlin Wall—was now open, and citizens were free to travel to West Berlin and West Germany. The decision hadn't been taken formally by the communist leadership. But Berliners took matters into their own hands, and headed for the wall.

Soon after, the East German government collapsed, and citizens demanded unification, and the freedoms of the West. In December 1989 and January 1990—in demonstrations throughout East Germany—protesters' signs and chants proclaimed, "*Wir sind ein Volk.*" We are one people.

Hundreds of thousands of Czech workers now initiated a general strike, and demanded the end of the communist rule. Vaclav Havel—a leading Czech dissident and leader of a small opposition movement—addressed student protestors and striking workers gathered on Prague's Wenceslas Square. Havel had been jailed for dissident activity only months before, in February 1989. But the communist government was about to collapse. And in December 1989, he was on his way to the president's office in the castle on Hradcany Hill, overlooking the Vltava River.

The only eastern European country to suffer extensive violence was Romania, which for years had not directly participated in the Warsaw Pact military relationship with the Soviet Union and its other eastern European neighbors. The popular opposition to Nicolae Ceausescu—and his iconoclastic but essentially dictatorial communist government—began in the western Romanian town of Timisoara. The Romanian government sought to evict a Lutheran pastor from his church there because he was allowing students to recite poetry, and sing anti-government songs. But when government security police came to evict him, parishioners formed a human chain around the church. Others came to their assistance. The first to arrive were members of other religious denominations: Baptists, Pentecostals, Catholics. But soon, other citizens also joined in. The protest spread throughout Timisoara and then to other Romanian cities, finally leading to the capital city of Bucharest. And now, when Ceausescu appeared on the balcony of the main government building—in an effort to quiet the crowd—he was loudly booed.

I remember watching television footage of the event. As the first boos erupted, you could tell Ceausescu was completely flabbergasted. No-one had ever publicly shown the slightest opposition to him before. This was completely new, and inexplicable. This was on December 22, 1989. Ceausescu and his wife immediately boarded a helicopter and fled Bucharest. Three days later, on Christmas, I was passing though the Munich train station when I checked a newsstand to see if I wanted to buy a paper to read on my trip back to Salzburg. Almost every German paper had a huge headline: "*Ceausescu Tod!*" Ceausescu is dead. He and his wife had been machine-gunned by military officers staging a coup. The new Romanian regime would be a military government of uncertain character, but the Ceausescu dictatorship was over.

So, the collapse of Eastern Europe happened quickly and unexpectedly. But in hindsight, once Gorbachev pulled the plug, the leadership had nothing to support it. Most leaders decided that stepping down and saving their own skins was probably the wisest survival strategy.

A key factor in the collapse of the former communist states with remarkably little violence or bloodshed was the restraint of Soviet troops under the direct control of Soviet General Secretary Mikhail Gorbachev. The outcome might have been much deadlier, as substantial numbers of Soviet troops remained deployed in East Germany, Poland, Hungary and Czechoslovakia. The last of them would not leave until years later.

But in the closing days of 1989, most Soviet soldiers deployed in East Europe were under strict orders to stay in their barracks, and not interfere in the domestic upheavals taking place in the streets. What might have been going on in the head of a young Vladimir Putin, at the time, one can only guess. The young Russian KGB officer was stationed in Dresden, East Germany. He occupied himself by destroying documents linking the Soviet Union to the former Stasi state.

Lecture 20

From Chairman Mao to the Capitalist Roaders

B Y THE END OF THE FIRST MILLENNIUM, CHINA WAS the most economically developed area of the world. Yet by the middle of the second millennium, Europe surpassed China, which went into a centuries-long period of isolation and decline, followed by foreign conquest, occupation, and humiliation. This history of oppression by foreign powers plays a large part in contemporary Chinese economic, political, and military policy. Today, China is again a major economic power, but its reemergence took almost 1,000 years to accomplish. ◆

Premodern Chinese History

◀ Historically, Chinese emperors based their power and wealth on agriculture. China was a vast area populated by millions of peasants toiling on the lands of distant landlords. The income that these plantations produced fed the treasuries of the Chinese imperial class and their bureaucrats and servants.

◀ Because the peasants were so numerous—and the ruling class was so small—there was little pressure to increase agricultural output or think about technological improvements. Even illiterate peasants working with simple tools could produce more than enough food.

◀ The technical marvels of Chinese civilization—the water clocks and gunpowder—were considered interesting and entertaining toys. They were not considered marketable commodities capable of generating profits for further investments. The ruling class of China was bureaucratic and governmental, without the vision to create or expand markets.

◀ There was also little interest in the outside world and little or no desire to trade or exchange goods with foreigners. The Chinese rulers considered themselves a superior culture with nothing to gain from interacting with barbaric foreigners.

◀ The dominant religious or philosophical belief in imperial China was Confucianism, which taught deference to superiors and the maintenance of established social relations. It was hardly a philosophy to encourage innovation and entrepreneurship.

◀ For most of premodern Chinese history, there was an excess supply of labor and a shortage of arable land. This leads to low wages and high rents. Peasant laborers will stay poor, and landlords will get rich. This is not a situation that fosters market demand for consumer goods or leads owners to search for labor-saving technology.

◀ By the middle of the 19th century, many Chinese got hooked on imported opium from British-ruled India. The so-called opium wars—resulting in new commercial privileges and legal and territorial concessions for Britain—became a further source of humiliation for the Chinese. Over time, the Chinese became less able to protect their citizens from the pushers of debilitating drugs, namely the British Empire.

◀ Further humiliation came in 1894, when the Japanese attacked China and seized the island of Formosa. This island was not returned to China until after World War II and then separated again after the communist revolution in 1949. It's known today as Taiwan, or the Republic of China.

Chinese Leaders

◀ Two Chinese leaders emerged in the early 20th century who would attempt to drive out foreigners and modernize China. The first was Sun Yat-sen, leader of the Chinese Nationalist Party, who succeeded at establishing a new government in 1911 that drove out the last imperial rulers of the Qing dynasty, who had reigned since 1644. But Sun's government was not powerful enough to seize lasting power from the nation's landlord class, so political instability prevailed.

Sun Yat-sen

◀ Then came Mao Zedong, who helped found the Chinese Communist Party in 1921. Impressed with Marxist theory and the Russian Revolution, Mao saw the same revolutionary potential in China's peasant class. He was invited to Moscow by the new Soviet government and given education and training in communist theory and tactics.

◀ Sun Yat-sen died in 1925 and was succeeded by the anti-communist soldier and nationalist Chiang Kai-shek. A civil war broke out between the forces of Mao and those of Chiang Kai-shek. The Nationalists scored several victories over the communists, who were forced to retreat to a mountain stronghold in northwest China. This "Long March" by Mao's forces was turned into one of the foundation myths of the Chinese Communist Party.

◀ The Japanese invaded again in 1931, seizing the province of Manchuria and occupying several coastal cities of China. Japanese soldiers engaged in mass executions and rape that are today considered one of the more horrific crimes against humanity during the 20th century.

◀ After the Japanese invaded Manchuria, Mao and Chiang Kai-shek agreed to a temporary truce while they fought to drive out the Japanese. During this period, about 20 million Chinese lost their lives in the fight against the Japanese.

◀ Later, when World War II ended and the Japanese were defeated, hostilities broke out again between Mao's communist forces and the Nationalist army led by Chiang Kai-shek. By this time, Mao had secured the backing of most of the Chinese peasantry. He did so by promising land redistribution from the landlords to the peasants. And because the peasantry was the dominant class in Chinese society, Mao had the majority of the population on his side.

◀ Mao defeated the forces of Chiang Kai-shek in 1949, and Chiang fled with the Nationalist forces to the island of Formosa. After the People's Republic of China was founded in October 1949, Mao initially kept his promise and redistributed land to more than 300 million peasants. While this was politically popular, it was economically damaging. The peasants' plots were very small—suitable only for small-scale production with simple tools and unskilled labor.

◀ One key concept in economics is the idea of economies of scale. To achieve efficiencies and lower costs of production, output should be above a certain level. If output is too small, then labor-saving machinery and efficiencies of large-scale production are not possible.

◀ Peasants have little interest in improving productivity because they're mainly interested in feeding themselves and their families. The Chinese communists were not big on markets and producing for profits. And the peasants didn't have much of an incentive to expand production beyond their own needs.

From Agriculture to Industry

◀ One key force in any country's transition from an agricultural to an industrial economy is an increase in agricultural productivity. Increases in agricultural output make industrialization possible in several ways:

1 Agricultural output is the input for industry. For example, for a food industry to develop, farmers need to produce wheat for bakeries.

2 As farms become more productive and need less labor, the excess labor can move to the cities to become workers in industry. Societies modernize by moving people off the farm and into the cities.

3 Farmers must produce enough food not only to feed themselves but also a growing urban and industrial labor force.

◀ The small plots created by Mao's land-redistribution program for China's peasants did not permit or create the incentives for increased output. And without increased output, the country would find it next to impossible to industrialize.

◀ But industrialization is what Mao wanted for his country. Mao's initial ideas about industrialization came from the leadership of the Soviet Union. In 1953, Mao introduced the first five-year plan for China. It was a faithful copy of the Soviet approach to economic development and contained all the basic components of the initial Soviet five-year plans, including the nationalization of all large enterprises and elimination of most private property.

◀ The process of constructing a national, comprehensive economic plan for a country as large as China was extremely difficult. The key problem that Mao and the economic planners faced was low productivity in Chinese agriculture. China during the 1950s was almost entirely rural and agricultural, so it was incumbent on the Chinese planners to raise agricultural productivity.

◀ But most Chinese farms were too small. Land redistribution had created hundreds of millions of very small farms. These plots were too small to use even basic farm machinery. They were also unsuited to take advantage of fertilizers, as peasant farmers were used to using the manure produced by farm animals as their primary fertilizer.

◀ Again following the Soviets, Mao initiated a process of collectivization to force farmers into large cooperative or state-owned farms. These collectives were required to sell most of their output to state agencies at very low prices. The state agencies, mostly under the direction of the ministry of agriculture, would then sell the farm products at considerably higher retail prices. This price differential was one of the key sources of finance that the state could use to purchase machinery and begin the process of industrialization.

◀ The collective farms were theoretically owned by all of the farm workers. They would share whatever income was earned by the sale of their products to the state procurement agencies. Their share of the income would be determined by their hours of work and level of skill of the work they did. In theory, this would be determined by the votes of the collective farmers. But in fact, all key decisions of the collective farm were determined by the farm manager, who was appointed by the central ministry of agriculture.

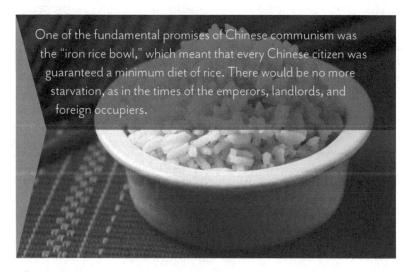

One of the fundamental promises of Chinese communism was the "iron rice bowl," which meant that every Chinese citizen was guaranteed a minimum diet of rice. There would be no more starvation, as in the times of the emperors, landlords, and foreign occupiers.

◀ State farms were somewhat different in that they were organized to resemble factories in cities. Farmers were treated as laborers and paid an hourly wage. Typically, state farms tended to be much larger than collective farms and produced more important products for the planned economy.

◀ Even so, the farm workers on the collectives and state farms earned meager incomes and would have had a hard time feeding themselves and their families if it wasn't for the tiny plots of land where they were allowed to grow their own food.

◀ For most Chinese farmers, the family plot was their chief source of food. They were also able, at times, to sell a small amount of their surplus produce in local markets. This gave them money to buy clothes or simple household items, if those items were available.

Mao's Decline

◀ At the end of the first five-year plan in 1958, Mao was disillusioned with the results. The growth of Chinese industry was slow and did not replicate the rapid industrial development that the Soviet Union had achieved in the 1930s. So, Mao decided to break with the Soviet Union model.

◀ Instead, he launched what became known as the Great Leap Forward. As part of this, all Chinese, including farmers and rural inhabitants, would participate in the drive to rapidly industrialize the Chinese economy. Mao ordered the creation of much larger collective farms that would each consist of at least 5,000 households. These large collective enterprises would also build "backyard factories" that would produce iron, steel, and cement in the countryside.

- The Great Leap Forward caused agricultural production to decline, and much of the output of the backyard factories was unusable. The decline in agricultural production lead to widespread famine. The death estimates caused by such privation range as high as 20 million Chinese.

- The catastrophic failure of Mao's Great Leap Forward caused him a great loss of prestige and criticism inside the leadership of the Chinese Communist Party. To protect his leadership position—and to fight his enemies within the Chinese Communist Party—Mao launched the Great Proletarian Cultural Revolution of 1966.

During the Great Proletarian Cultural Revolution of 1966, elite knowledge, science, philosophy, and literature were all denigrated in China. All that was needed was a knowledge of Mao Zedong's thought, found in a little red book that contained Mao's most important sayings.

◀ Many Chinese people suffered from the Cultural Revolution. Writers, scientists, intellectuals, teachers—anyone who used their brains in their work—were likely to suffer persecution and worse. The effect of the Cultural Revolution on the Chinese economy was disastrous. Economic output fell steadily from 1966 to 1970. Significant Chinese resources of human capital and brainpower were wasted and destroyed.

◀ From Mao's perspective, the Cultural Revolution was a success. It sidelined—or eliminated—most of his opposition within the leadership of the Chinese Communist Party. He was able to maintain his position with no more significant challenges until his death in 1976. But the cost to the Chinese of Mao's bureaucratic victory was a decade of lost potential and reduced standards of living.

At the time of Mao's death, most Chinese did not live significantly better than they had at the time of the revolution in 1949.

◀ Immediately after Mao's passing, a new leadership struggle broke out in the top ranks of the Chinese Communist Party. There were two basic factions. One side contained those who wanted to continue Mao's policies. This faction included Mao's widow, Jian Qing—the Madame—and was labeled the Gang of Four.

◀ However, the victorious faction, led by Deng Xiaoping, advocated significant reforms in the Chinese economy. These reforms included using material incentives to encourage productive work, permitting some private ownership and decision making, an openness to foreign trade and investment, and a decentralization of decision making with much less emphasis on central planning.

◀ Madame Mao's faction labeled Deng's movement the capitalist roaders, combining the notion of going down the wrong road with the idea that capitalism is evil. But the reforms that Deng introduced, starting in 1979, would have profound consequences for China, the United States, and the rest of the world.

Readings

SNOW, *Red Star over China.*
WALDER, *China under Mao.*

Questions

1 What historical and economic forces led a large part of the Chinese population to support the revolution led by Mao Zedong in 1949?

2 Why did Mao abandon the Soviet model of an economic system? What did he put in its place, and what were the consequences of his change?

Lecture 20 Transcript

From Chairman Mao to the Capitalist Roaders

By the end of the first millennium, China was the richest civilization on earth. It was the leader in technological developments and living standards. And it was the inventor of paper, silk, gunpowder, porcelain, and mechanical clocks. When the Venetian explorer Marco Polo visited China some 300 years later, in about 1300, he was astounded by the riches and lavish living of the Chinese monarchs and their administrators. He'd come from a Europe that was backward, poor, rural, agrarian, and illiterate. Yet by the middle of the second millennium, Europe had surpassed China as the most economically developed area of the world. China went into a centuries-long period of isolation and decline. This was followed by foreign conquest, occupation and humiliation. This history of oppression by foreign powers plays a large part in contemporary Chinese economic, political, and military policy. Today, China is again a major economic power. But its reemergence took almost 1,000 years to accomplish.

Historically, Chinese emperors based their power and wealth on agriculture. China was a vast area populated by millions of peasants toiling on the lands of distant landlords. The income these plantations produced fed the treasuries of the Chinese imperial class, and their bureaucrats and servants. Because the peasants were so numerous—and the ruling class was so small—there was little pressure to increase agricultural output, or think about technological improvements. Even illiterate peasants working with simple tools could produce more than enough food.

This situation was not that different from prerevolutionary society in Russia. There, a large peasant class worked in the fields of the imperial and religious landlords, and had no meaningful incentive to work harder or smarter. The technical marvels of Chinese civilization—the water clocks and gunpowder—were considered interesting and entertaining toys. They were not considered marketable commodities capable of generating profits for further investments. The ruling class of China was bureaucratic and governmental, without the vision to create or expand markets. There was also little interest in the outside world, and little or no desire to trade or exchange goods with foreigners. The Chinese rulers considered themselves a superior culture with nothing to gain from interacting with barbaric foreigners.

It seems to me that one of the chief economic lessons of history is that isolation leads to stagnation and declining standards of living: think of ancient China, the Soviet Union, and North Korea. The dominant religious or philosophical belief in imperial China was Confucianism. This taught deference to superiors, and the maintenance of established social relations. It was hardly a philosophy to encourage innovation and entrepreneurship. Learning under a Confucian code meant memorization of approved texts, and disapproval of critical thinking.

For most of premodern Chinese history, there was an excess supply of labor, and a shortage of arable land. The basic laws of demand and supply will tell you that this situation leads to low wages and high rents. Peasant laborers will stay poor, and landlords will get rich. This is not a situation that fosters market demand for consumer goods, or leads owners to search for labor-saving technology. If labor is cheap, there's no need to try to economize.

Paradoxically, one of the main drivers of labor-saving technology in medieval Europe was the coming of the Black Death in the mid-14th century. The plague wiped out hundreds of thousands of workers. This made labor relatively scarce—and expensive. Business owners and landlords now had incentives to find ways to economize on labor. And this gave strong emphasis to technological development. So, things were not so good for workers who got sick and died from the plague. But for those who survived—and their descendants—life got better.

By the middle of the 19th century, the British had developed a taste for Chinese tea and silk. Unfortunately, the Chinese didn't really want anything from the British. The Chinese considered their fabrics and clothing superior to anything that was coming out of the British textile mills. However—and unfortunately for the Chinese—many Chinese got hooked on imported opium from British-ruled India. And the so-called Opium Wars of the mid-19th century—resulting in new commercial privileges and legal and territorial concessions for Britain—became a further source of humiliation for the Chinese. Over time, the Chinese became less able to protect their citizens from the pushers of debilitating drugs, namely the British empire.

Can you get some idea of why the Chinese today are driven to make their country strong and independent and proud? Further humiliation came in 1894, when the Japanese attacked China, and seized the island of Formosa. This island was not returned to China until after World War II, and then separated again after the Communist Revolution in 1949. It's known today as Taiwan, or the Republic of China,

Two Chinese leaders emerged in the early 20th century who would attempt to drive out foreigners, and modernize China. The first was Sun Yat-sen, a medical student and founder of China's Nationalist Movement. He succeeded at establishing a new government in 1911 that drove out the last imperial rulers of the Qing dynasty, which had reigned since 1644. But Sun's government was not powerful enough to seize lasting power from the nation's landlord class, and so political instability prevailed.

And then came Mao Zedong, the son of a peasant who had prospered as a farmer and grain dealer. Mao was a student activist and educator who helped to found the Chinese Communist Party in 1921. Impressed with Marxist theory and the Russian Revolution, Mao saw the same revolutionary potential in China's peasant class. He was invited to Moscow by the new Soviet government, and given education and training in communist theory and tactics.

Sun Yat-sen died in 1925, and was succeeded by the anti-communist soldier and nationalist Chiang Kai-shek. Now, a civil war broke out between the forces of Mao and those of Chiang Kai-shek. In the early going, the Nationalists scored several victories over the communists, who were forced to retreat to a mountain stronghold in northwest China. This "Long March" by Mao's forces was turned into one of the foundation myths of the Chinese Communist Party.

The Japanese invaded again in 1931, seizing the province of Manchuria and occupying several coastal cities of China. Japanese soldiers engaged in mass executions and rape that are today considered one of the more horrific crimes against humanity during the 20th century.

I've had three different tours as a guest professor at the Chinese University of Petroleum's Academy of Chinese Energy Strategy in Beijing. My accommodations have always included a nice television. The only problem is that my Chinese language skills are non-existent. So, I end up watching basketball games, and badminton matches—my parents were both champion badminton players—and action movies. Many of the action movies are war stories about Chinese soldiers and civilians fighting Japanese soldiers. Even with no knowledge of Chinese, it's very easy for me to identify the good guys and the bad guys.

After the Japanese invaded Manchuria, Mao and Chiang Kai-shek agreed to a temporary truce while they fought to drive out the Japanese. During this period, about 20 million Chinese lost their lives in the fight against the Japanese.

Later, when World War II ended and the Japanese were defeated, hostilities broke out again between Mao's communist forces and the Nationalist army led by Chiang Kai-shek. By this time, Mao had secured the backing of most of the Chinese peasantry. He did so by promising land redistribution from the landlords to the peasants. And since the peasantry was the dominant class in Chinese society, Mao had the majority of the population on his side.

This reminds me of something the behavioral economist and U.S. military analyst Daniel Ellsberg said about American involvement in the Vietnam War. Ellsberg was one of the chief authors of a government study of U.S. decision-making in Vietnam, later known as the Pentagon Papers. Ellsberg said, "It's hard to win a peasant war when you are fighting on the side of the landlords." There are always a lot more peasants than landlords. And throughout their history, peasants have always wanted one thing: their own land. Whoever promises that will have their support.

Vladimir Lenin understood this as he was advancing the cause of the Bolsheviks during the Russian Revolution. The Bolshevik slogan was "Land, Peace, and Bread." That is, land for the Russian peasant, peace for the peasants conscripted into the Tsar's army to fight during World War I, and bread for the urban workers. There were very few urban workers in post-World War II China, so Mao needed only to appeal to the peasantry. He defeated the forces of Chiang Kai-shek in 1949, and Chiang fled with the Nationalist forces to the island of Formosa.

After the People's Republic of China was founded in October 1949, Mao initially kept his promise, and redistributed land to more than 300 million peasants. While this was politically popular, it was economically damaging. The peasants' plots were very small—suitable only for small-scale production with simple tools and unskilled labor.

One key concept in economics is the idea of "economies of scale." To achieve efficiencies, and lower costs of production, output should be above a certain level. If output is too small, then labor-saving machinery and efficiencies of large scale production are not possible. Peasants have little interest in improving productivity because they're mainly interested in feeding themselves and their families. The Chinese communists were not big on markets and producing for profits. And the peasants didn't have much of an incentive to expand production beyond their own needs.

One key force in any country's transition from an agricultural to an industrial economy is an increase in agricultural productivity. Increases in agricultural output make industrialization possible in several ways. First, agricultural output is the input for industry. For instance, for a textile industry to develop, farmers need to produce cotton or wool. For a furniture industry to develop, farmers and foresters need to produce timber. For a food industry to develop, farmers need to produce wheat for bakeries.

Second, as farms become more productive and need less labor, the excess labor can move to the cities to become workers in industry. Societies modernize by moving people off the farm, and into the cities. Before the Second World War, more than 20 percent of the American labor force was on the farm. Today, it's is less than 2 percent. And American farmers produce more output with 2 percent of the labor force than they did with 20 percent of the labor force a 100 years ago.

Because I've always taught at big-city universities, I've emphasized to my students that modern American agriculture is possibly the most high-tech sector in the U.S. economy. The typical American farmer today has a bachelor's degree in plant biology or animal genetics, and an MBA in agricultural economics. American farmers use genetically created seeds, satellite moisture calculation, and sophisticated computer-trading software. And finally, farmers must produce enough food not only to feed themselves but also a growing urban and industrial labor force.

The small plots created by Mao's land-redistribution program for the China's peasants did not permit or create the incentives for increased output. And, without increased output, the country would find it next to impossible to industrialize. But industrialization is what Mao wanted for his country. Mao's initial ideas about industrialization came from the leadership of the Soviet Union. Because he had been trained in the Soviet Union, and seen some of the initial Soviet successes in building the foundations of an industrial economy, he wanted to adopt the same concepts for China.

In 1953, Mao introduced the first five-year plan for China. It was a faithful copy of the Soviet approach to economic development, and contained all the basic components of the initial Soviet five-year plans. These components included the nationalization off all large enterprises, and elimination of most private property. Chinese communism would not have an initial phase of some private property like the Soviet Union did during its New Economic Policy (NEP) period, from 1921 to 1928. Instead, China's state-owned enterprises would be directed by a central plan devised in the capital city of Peking. The basic plan would set output targets for a five-year period. The plan would be broken down into monthly increments, with output targets set in physical terms. As the Soviets had, enterprise managers would be rewarded for meeting the targets, and punished for failure. But the process of constructing a national, comprehensive economic plan for a country as large as China was extremely difficult.

The key problem that Mao and the economic planners faced was low productivity in Chinese agriculture. China during the 1950s was almost entirely rural and agricultural. So, it was incumbent on the Chinese planners to raise agricultural productivity. But most Chinese farms were too small. Land redistribution had created hundreds of millions of very small farms. These plots were too small to use even basic farm machinery, such as simple tractors. They were also unsuited to take advantage of fertilizers, as peasant farmers were used to using the manure produced by farm animals as their primary fertilizer.

Again, following the Soviets, Mao initiated a process of collectivization to force farmers into large cooperative or state-owned farms. These collectives were required to sell most of their output to state agencies at very low prices.

The state agencies, mostly under the direction of the ministry of agriculture, would then sell the farm products at considerably higher retail prices. This price differential was one of the key sources of finance that the state could use to purchase machinery, and begin the process of industrialization.

The collective farms were theoretically owned by all of the farm workers. They would share whatever income was earned by the sale of their products to the state procurement agencies. Their share of the income would be determined by their hours of work, and level of skill of the work they did. In theory, this would be determined by the votes of the collective farmers. But in fact, all key decisions of the collective farm were determined by the farm manager, who was appointed by the central ministry of agriculture.

State farms were somewhat different in that they were organized to resemble factories in cities. Farmers were treated as laborers, and paid an hourly wage. Typically, state farms tended to be much larger than collective farms, and produced more important products for the planned economy. Rice production was usually a crop of state farms. Rice was important both economically and symbolically. Rice was important as a primary source of calories and energy for urban factory workers.

One of the fundamental promises of Chinese communism was called "the iron rice bowl." What this meant was that every Chinese citizen was guaranteed a minimum diet of rice. No more starvation, as in the times of the emperors, landlords, and foreign occupiers. Even so, the farm workers on the collectives and state farms earned meager incomes, and would have had a hard time feeding themselves and their families if it wasn't for the tiny plots of land where they were allowed to grow their own food.

The Soviet Union's agricultural system also relied on private plots to supplement the income of the collective and state farm workers. For most Chinese farmers, the family plot was their chief source of food. They were also able, at times, to sell a small amount of their surplus produce in local markets. This gave them some money with which to buy clothes or simple household items, if those items were available.

At the end of the first five-year plan in 1958, Mao was disillusioned with the results. The growth of Chinese industry was slow, and did not replicate the rapid industrial development that the Soviet Union had achieved in the 1930s. So, Mao decided to break with the Soviet Union model. Instead, he decided to launch what became known as "The Great Leap Forward." Fond of grandiose slogans and dramatic gestures, Mao thought that such exhortations could drive the Chinese farmer and worker to new heights of economic achievement.

Mao thought that relying on material incentives and gradual economic progress should be replaced with an attempt to create a New Socialist Man. This new socialist man would be infused with a spirit of altruism, patriotism, and social consciousness. The new man would work for the glory of China, and the greater good of the entire country.

Selflessness would replace a desire for individual gain, and good intentions would provide the main motivation for economic progress.

As part of this Great Leap Forward, all Chinese, including farmers and rural inhabitants, would participate in the drive to rapidly industrialize the Chinese economy. So now, Mao ordered the creation of much larger collective farms that would each consist of at least 5,000 households. These large collective enterprises would also build "backyard factories" that would produce iron and steel and cement in the countryside.

To put it bluntly, the policy was a disaster. And disaster might be too mild a word. The Great Leap Forward caused agricultural production to decline, and much of the output of the backyard factories was unusable. The decline in agricultural production lead to widespread famine. The death estimates caused by such privation ranges as high as 20 million

Chinese. The catastrophic failure of Mao's Great Leap Forward caused him a great loss of prestige and criticism inside the leadership of the Chinese Communist Party.

As in the Soviet Union, there was no democratic process to remove leaders whose policies were failures. The leadership conflicts and struggles were carried out by bureaucratic intrigues, and jockeying for key positions in the party hierarchy. But now, Mao was now in danger of being forced out of his leading position. And losers in bureaucratic struggles in a one-party communist state lose might almost everything.

In a communist system, every part of a leader's standard of living is tied to his or her position. If forced out, the leader loses influence, and access to privileged housing, medical care, food, travel, and education for their children. This is why leadership fights in one-party communist systems are so serious and hard-fought. Losing really means losing. A lot!

Mao, to protect his leadership position—and to fight his enemies within the Chinese Communist Party—now launched the Great Proletarian Cultural Revolution of 1966. And the cultural revolution that Mao launched was not just an attack on leading cadres within the Chinese Communist Party, but also an attack on all elites. Mao encouraged Chinese youths to attack their professors; he urged urban workers to attack their bosses; and ordinary citizens to attack intellectuals, artists, writers, and other leading cultural icons. Elite knowledge, science, philosophy, and literature were all denigrated. All that was needed was a knowledge of Mao Zedong's thought. And this could be found in a little red book that contained Mao's most important sayings.

This little red book of Mao's quotations was not only idolized by Chinese youth but even by some young students in the West. Campuses from Berkeley to Oxford to Paris would see crowds of bourgeois, middle-class students waving their little red books of Maoist revolution. I was a student during those times, and even though there was a certain romantic attraction in following a third-world revolutionary, Mao's quotations seemed simple-minded to me. Much later, as a professor, I understand even better the attraction of the little red book for some students. How much easier to do away with studying all kinds of books and literature and science, and instead, just memorize one book of sayings as the sum of all necessary knowledge.

One of the more understandable attractions of Chairman Mao and his little red book during the late 1960s was realized in the support that the Peoples Republic of China was giving to the Vietnamese resistance to the American war in Indochina. Broadly, there was massive opposition to the American war in Vietnam, not only in the United States but also in Europe. And since Mao was providing some aid to the Northern Vietnamese campaign in the south, he enjoyed something of a "halo effect" among all those opposed to the American military presence in Vietnam.

Yet many Chinese people suffered from the Cultural Revolution. Writers, scientists, intellectuals, teachers—anyone who used their brains in their work—were likely to suffer persecution and worse. Intellectuals and the educated were often sent into the countryside for "reeducation" at the hands of the rural peasants. This reeducation often took the form of physical torture, starvation, and even death. And the effect of the Cultural Revolution on the Chinese economy was disastrous. Economic output fell steadily from 1966 to 1970. Significant Chinese resources of human capital and brain power were wasted, and destroyed.

From Mao's personal perspective, the Cultural Revolution was a success. It sidelined—or eliminated—most of his opposition within the leadership of the Chinese Communist Party. He was able to maintain his position with no more significant challenges until his death in 1976. But the cost to the Chinese of Mao's bureaucratic victory was a decade of lost potential, and reduced standards of living. At the time of Mao's death, most Chinese did not live significantly better than they had at the time of the revolution in 1949.

Immediately after Mao's passing, a new leadership struggle broke out in the top ranks of the Chinese Communist Party. There were two basic factions. One side contained those who wanted to continue Mao's policies. This faction included Mao's widow, Jian Qing—the Madame—who wanted to retain the perks of leadership that she had enjoyed as Mao's wife. This faction was labeled The Gang of Four.

However, the victorious faction led by Deng Xiaoping advocated significant reforms in the Chinese economy. These reforms included using material incentives to encourage productive work; permitting some private ownership and decision making, especially in agriculture; an openness to foreign trade and investment; and a decentralization of decision making with much less emphasis on central planning.

Madame Mao's faction labelled Deng's movement "the capitalist roaders." Calling someone a roader was not a compliment, as it implied that you were trying to lead the people down the wrong road. And a capitalist roader was doubly bad because every good communist knew that capitalism was evil. But the reforms that Deng introduced, starting in 1979, would have profound consequences for China, the United States, and the rest of the world.

Lecture 21

After Deng, China Privatizes and Globalizes

C HINA HAS MADE ONE OF THE MOST DRAMATIC transitions in history—from a poor, rural society to a modern global economy with a predominantly urban population and a large middle class. How did China make such a miraculous transformation in only a few decades? And how has this transformation affected the rest of the world, especially the United States? The answers can be found by going back to the time right after the death of Mao Zedong in 1976, when the leadership of China's Communist Party made major changes. Deng Xiaoping marginalized and then ousted Mao's designated successor, Hua Guofeng, from party leadership. Now, the country would privatize, decentralize, and globalize. ◆

Transition Reforms: China versus Russia

◀ From such modest beginnings, China's economic reforms under Deng Xiaoping have turned out much more successful and beneficial to his country than the transition reforms that Mikhail Gorbachev introduced to the former Soviet Union, beginning in the mid-1980s.

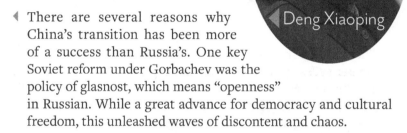

Deng Xiaoping

◀ There are several reasons why China's transition has been more of a success than Russia's. One key Soviet reform under Gorbachev was the policy of glasnost, which means "openness" in Russian. While a great advance for democracy and cultural freedom, this unleashed waves of discontent and chaos.

◀ Soon after Gorbachev's opening of political dissent, the Soviet Union plunged into a period of no control or direction. All sectors of society began to connive and steal for their own benefit, with the strongest and best-connected individuals coming out on top.

◀ In contrast, the Chinese Communist Party has never allowed completely free political or cultural freedom and dissent. They have been much more authoritarian and dictatorial than Gorbachev was. In fact, the former Soviet Union's example of chaos and ultimate collapse was an object lesson for the leadership of the Chinese Communist Party. Their major fear became experiencing a Soviet-style collapse and the loss of power.

◀ What makes this study in contrasts all the more remarkable is that China was a much poorer economy in 1978 than the Soviet Union's was in 1985, when Gorbachev began his reforms. The Chinese were much more rural and agricultural. There was not a large industrial sector created and organized on the Soviet model. So, the Chinese didn't have to dismantle and reorganize a large industrial economic system, as the Russians had to do.

◀ Also, China had been a communist economic system for fewer than 30 years when Deng began his reforms. In comparison, Russia had been a communist economy for 68 years when Gorbachev came to power. So, in China, there was less to undo and unlearn.

◀ Then, in undertaking reform, China was blessed with much greater access to foreign financial capital and human capital. The former crown colony of Hong Kong is among the world's leading financial centers, and the Chinese diaspora in Hong Kong, Taiwan, and the rest of Asia was available—and usually willing—to provide expertise, advice, and management. There's also a large, interconnected Chinese population in Canada and the United States.

◀ The availability of such invaluable knowledge and human capital, even abroad, has been a tremendous boost to the economic transformation of mainland China. Russia had no equivalent diaspora. It was never a capitalist country. And few Russian expatriates were successful enough, on an international level, to effectively advise Gorbachev or the post-Soviet governments.

◀ China—directed by its authoritarian leadership, funded by deep wells of financial capital, and guided by a network of entrepreneurs, both onshore and off—has also understood the benefits of gradual change. Its planners introduced reform measures one at a time.

◀ Often, such reforms were instituted locally and regionally first, rather than throughout the entire country. This way, if the reforms were unsuccessful, they didn't damage the national economy. The gradualist approach was different than advocated by Western "experts" advising the post-Soviet government of President Boris Yeltsin.

◀ These experts were mostly from the United States, and they advocated rapid privatization, the complete freeing of prices, and the dismantling of all economic planning. This neoliberal advice was based on the Washington Consensus, which maintained that what countries needed to grow their economies was to free prices, privatize as much as possible, and reduce the government's role in the economy.

◀ The fact that this consensus had not been followed by the rich countries of the world and that there was little evidence that the policies had actually worked anywhere didn't deter legions of economists flocking to Moscow from Washington and many prominent American universities and think tanks. They proclaimed their unproven formulas with almost religious zeal.

Deng-Era Reforms

◀ Chinese reforms began with the comprehensive overhaul of the country's agricultural system and the encouragement of individual Chinese farmers to become economically successful. This was carried out by reducing the number of collective farms and giving individual growers the opportunity to lease land for their own use.

◀ Such leases included an obligation that the farmers sell half of their crop to the state at fixed prices. But they could sell the remainder on private markets at higher prices and keep the income from both types of sales. In this manner, the state created incentives for greater production while also maintaining some control of farm output, including food for urban residents and inputs for manufacturing.

◀ The terms of such farm leases could be as long as 30 years. This gave the farmers a stake in maintaining the quality of the land and an incentive to improve productivity through better seeds, fertilizer, and mechanization. Furthermore, the farmers could

Today, only about 20 percent of China's farm output is sold to the state and 80 percent is sold on private markets. But the state remains actively engaged in the agricultural sector, in part by providing equipment leases to its farmers and subsidies for their infrastructure.

CAPITALISM VS. SOCIALISM

sell the lease rights to other farmers. Although the state still owned the land, this went about as far toward a private-property system in agriculture that any socialist economy has gone to date.

◀ In China, a mixture of private incentives and government support has led to significant increases in farm productivity and has allowed many rural residents to move from countryside to city. This movement was necessary to support the leadership's industrialization and trade policies.

◀ In turn, reform in the manufacturing sector started with local authorities being given the power to start up small enterprises and retain the income to support local needs. If these local manufacturing enterprises were successful, then the local authorities would have more income to support their schools, hospitals, roads, and other municipal needs.

◀ At the beginning of the Deng Xiaoping–era reforms, most private enterprises were either restaurants or small retail stores. Eventually, Deng's reforms allowed centrally planned large enterprises to become independently run. They were still owned by the state, but the state-owned enterprises (SOEs) were expected to perform like market-driven corporations, albeit frequently in state-protected economic sectors and with some big consequences for American businesses and markets.

◀ China's SOEs became prominent in large-scale manufacturing, transportation, and natural resources as well as in steel production, mining, and petroleum refining.

◀ Although Chinese SOEs share some characteristics of large capitalist corporations, there are also some very big differences. For example, because the Chinese government is the principal owner, the government can decide on the SOE's operating objectives.

- Like other enterprises in a planned economy, the SOEs might be given output targets, delivered to state bureaucracies or other SOEs. And because the primary objective of the SOE is output, management has an inherent incentive to understate its productive capacity and to overstate its demand for resources.

- This was also typical behavior for an enterprise in the Soviet Union. By having output as the main objective, one by-product is maximizing employment. Maximizing output and employment are two sides of the same coin.

- SOEs enjoyed what the Hungarian economist János Kornai calls a soft budget constraint. This is different than the hard budget constraint faced by a typical capitalist corporation.

- If a capitalist corporation doesn't make profits, sooner or later its bankers or stockholders will force changes, or the enterprise will go bankrupt. If the corporation gets most of its operating funds from a bank, the bank will cut off credit. If the corporation gets most of its financial capital from investors, they will balk, and management will be forced to cut expenses, often by laying off employees or selling parts of the business. If this doesn't stem losses, the company will fail.

- An SOE might not face any hard budget constraint from its state sponsor. Often, the SOE is the major employer in a particular town or region. Shutting down the SOE would mean that the town will suffer both in terms of unemployment and reduction in tax revenues. But government subsidies can make up for temporary losses. The management of the SOE knows this and therefore might be tempted to expand production and employment beyond purely economic limits.

◀ Compared to purely private enterprises, SOEs are less efficient and a drain on the central government's budget. However, employment in a communist system is very much a political issue that is central to the state's stability and survival. That's why they are a continual problem for sponsoring governments. In a capitalist system, by comparison, if a company goes bankrupt— and employees lose their jobs—this is often understood as a consequence of market competition.

◀ The U.S. government sometimes does bail out money-losing firms because they are too big and too important. But in China, when an SOE shuts down or lays off workers, this is understood as a government decision. The people believe that the government is responsible. And the Chinese government, led by the Communist Party, relies on the support of the population for its hold on power.

◀ Another key example of the Deng Xiaoping–era reforms was the introduction of special economic zones (SEZs), which allowed foreign businesses to operate joint ventures with Chinese enterprises. The objective was to get the benefits of foreign financial investment, foreign technology, and access to foreign markets. The SEZs offered foreign investors low taxes, low utility rates, low rents, and the ability to export. Soon, their output began showing up in American retail stores.

China's first special economic zones were located mostly in the south and along the east coast of the country so that they would be close to financial centers and international ports of Hong Kong and Shanghai and to the Chinese diaspora working in Indonesia, Singapore, and Taiwan, as well as in Hong Kong.

◀ Even though China's SEZs were limited and controlled by the Chinese government, the benefits to China of allowing foreigners to produce and do business in the country were quite large. Economists talk about "external economies" arising from the operations of businesses in a particular area. These external economies include knowledge spillover effects, where local businesspeople and workers learn new ways of organizing work as well as the existence of foreign markets and gain access to new technology.

Chinese Exports to the United States

◀ The Chinese pattern of exports and imports followed the classic principles of comparative advantage laid out by the British political economist David Ricardo during the 1800s.

The first wave of Chinese exports to America was clothes and shoes. Nearly every industrializing country starts their path toward industrialization with textiles.

◀ In the beginning, China had a large supply of unskilled labor and, therefore, a comparative advantage in products that would employ unskilled workers, such as T-shirts and flip-flops. China did not have a comparative advantage in complex products requiring highly skilled workers, so they imported Boeing 747s, for example.

◀ Still, the growth of Chinese exports to the United States was spectacular. From 1991 to 2007, Chinese exports to America rose nearly 13-fold, from 26 billion dollars to 330 billion dollars.

◀ The effects of Chinese exports to the United States are controversial, and much debated by economists. The benefits are pretty clear: Americans gain access to much less expensive goods, and this raises their standard of living, especially among low-income Americans who can afford only cheaper goods.

◀ The costs are not so clear, but there have been serious attempts to measure them. MIT economist David Autor has written several articles and papers on the effects of Chinese imports on American workers and regions. He estimates that about half of the decline in American manufacturing employment is due to Chinese imports.

◀ Imports from China are produced by unskilled labor, and this reduces the demand for American products produced by competing labor. Furthermore, declines in employment increase the need for unemployment benefits, disability, and other government transfer payments. This leads to pressure on public-sector budgets and increases the likelihood of government budget deficits.

◀ Autor attributes the Deng-inspired rise in Chinese exports to the United States to its investments in labor-intensive industries and rising productivity, as well as developments in transportation.

◀ Unfortunately, there's no simple answer that the United States can apply to the resulting problems in its own economy. The simple solution might be to block all imports from China. But if we stopped all imports from China, production of most goods that come from there would unlikely come back to the United States; instead, they would likely move to Indonesia, Vietnam, or some other developing country.

Readings

AUTOR, DORN, AND HANSON, "The China Syndrome."
CHOW, *China's Economic Transformation.*

Questions

1 The reforms of Deng Xiaoping were a dramatic break from the standard communist economic system. What was the first key change that Deng instituted in the Chinese economy, and why was this so important?

2 How did China go from a completely isolated economy to a major player in the global economy? What were the consequences of this change for the U.S. economy?

After Deng, China Privatizes and Globalizes

C hina has made one of the most dramatic transitions in history from a poor, rural society to a modern global economy with a predominantly urban population, and a large middle class. I remember watching President Nixon's historic visit to Beijing in 1972 on television. China's capital city was filled with bicycles, and monotonously dressed residents. There were no tall or modern buildings. Most of the people were thin and short. What a contrast today!

I made my first visit to China as a guest professor in 2014. I arrived at Beijing Capital Airport's Terminal 3, which had been completed at a cost of $3.5 billion a few years earlier—in time for the 2008 Olympic Games. Terminal 3 was designed by the British architect Sir Norman Foster, as the single-largest airport terminal project in the world. It was an ultramodern facility, representing a globally important country. Today's Beijing is lined with skyscrapers, modern luxury shops, hotels, restaurants and apartments. It seems to me that all 20-plus million inhabitants have a car, and are on the roads and freeways all the time. The traffic jams are legendary, and monstrous.

The university there where I taught—the China University of Petroleum—has a modern campus in the northwest part of the city. Its students are bright and energetic. And they seem to be interested in my economics courses, although many of them might be even more interested in the NBA basketball prospects of the Chicago Bulls. I gain some status by telling them I was born in Texas, and am still a fan of the Houston Rockets. China's most-famous basketball player, Yao Ming, is a 7-feet 6-inches former star center for the Rockets. He's since returned to China, and gotten a degree in economics. He's also the owner of the Shanghai Sharks, a pro team in the China Basketball Association.

How did China make this miraculous transformation in only a couple of decades? And how has this transformation affected the rest of the world—especially, the United States? To find answers, we need to go back to the time right after the death of Mao Zedong in 1976, and the end of his disastrous Cultural Revolution, during which he temporarily shut down schools, deposed party leaders, and forced millions of urban dwellers into the countryside.

The leadership of China's Communist Party decided on some major changes. Deng Xiaoping—a communist revolutionary who had participated in the Long March of communist forces under Chairman Mao, and later became estranged from him as a pragmatist and policymaker, marginalized, and then ousted, Mao's designated successor, Hua Guofeng, from party leadership. Now, the country would privatize, decentralize, and globalize.

Immediately, Deng began to lead China in a much different direction, starting with a visit to Singapore where he held serious discussions with Prime Minister Lee Kuan Yew, who had transformed the city-state with his authoritarian leadership and unstinting belief in free trade. That same year, China announced the purchase of several Boeing 747s for its state-owned airlines. And Coca-Cola announced plans to build a bottling plant in Shanghai, the country's most populated city.

In 1979, Deng visited the United States. In addition to meeting President Jimmy Carter in Washington, Deng also visited Coca-Cola's headquarters in Atlanta, and Boeing's headquarters in Seattle. Today, Boeing's headquarters are in Chicago, where I live. And on a few of my flights between Beijing and Chicago, I've winged it on Air China Boeing 747s. Air China is part of the Star Alliance global airline network, which also includes Chicago-based United Airlines.

From such modest beginnings, China's economic reforms under Deng Xiaoping have turned out much more successful—and beneficial—to his country than the transition reforms that Mikhail Gorbachev introduced to the former Soviet Union, beginning in the mid-1980s. There are several reasons why China's transition has been more of a success than Russia's.

One key Soviet reform under Gorbachev was the policy of *Glasnost*, or openness. While a great advance for democracy and cultural freedom, this unleashed waves of discontent and chaos. Soon after Gorbachev's opening of political dissent, the Soviet Union plunged into a period of no control, or direction. All sectors of society began to connive and steal for their own benefit, with the strongest and best-connected individuals coming out on top.

In contrast, the Chinese Communist Party has never allowed completely free political, or cultural, freedom and dissent. They've been much more authoritarian and dictatorial than Gorbachev was. In fact, the former Soviet Union's example of chaos and ultimate collapse was an object lesson for the leadership of the Chinese Communist Party. Their major fear became experiencing a Soviet-style collapse, and the loss of power.

What makes this study in contrasts all the more remarkable is that China was a much poorer economy in 1978 than the Soviet Union's was in 1985—when Gorbachev began his reforms. The Chinese were much more rural and agricultural. There was not a large industrial sector created, and organized, on the Soviet model. So, the Chinese didn't have to dismantle, and reorganize, a large industrial economic system, as the Russians had to do.

Also, China had been a communist economic system for fewer than 30 years when Deng began his reforms. In comparison, Russia had been a communist economy for 68 years when Gorbachev came to power. So, in China, there was less to undo and unlearn. Then, in undertaking reform, China was blessed with much greater access to foreign financial capital and human capital. The former crown colony of Hong Kong is among the world's leading financial centers. And the Chinese diaspora in Hong Kong, Taiwan and the rest of Asia was available—and usually willing—to provide expertise, advice, and management.

There's a large, interconnected Chinese population in Canada and the United States. My favorite Chinese ex-patriot was my dissertation supervisor at the University of Oklahoma, Professor Siu-Hung Yu. A brilliant international economist, and a wise and humane scholar, he's now back in Hong Kong as the chair of the economics department of Hong Kong University. It was Professor Yu who pointed out to me the large number of Chinese entrepreneurs and businessmen across Asia. In countries from Indonesia to Singapore to Malaysia, the Chinese were disproportionately the leading businessmen and financial executives.

The availability of such invaluable knowledge and human capital, even abroad, has been a tremendous boost to the economic transformation of mainland China. Russia had no equivalent diaspora. It was never a capitalist country. And few Russian ex-pats were successful enough, on an international level, to effective advice Gorbachev or the post-Soviet governments. The world has benefited from all kinds of Russian ex-pats but these were artists such as the novelist Vladimir Nabokov, and the ballet artists Mikhail Baryshnikov and Sergei Diaghilev.

China, directed by its authoritarian leadership, and funded by deep wells of financial capital, and guided by a network of entrepreneurs—both off-shore and on—has also understood the benefits of gradual change. Its planners introduced reform measures one at a time. Often, such reforms were instituted locally and regionally first, rather than throughout the entire economy. This way, if the reforms were unsuccessful, they didn't damage the entire national economy.

The gradualist approach was different than advocated by Western "experts" advising the post-Soviet government of President Boris Yeltsin. These experts were mostly from the United States, and they advocated rapid privatization, complete freeing of prices, and the dismantling off all economic planning. This neo-liberal advice was based on something called the Washington Consensus. It maintained that what countries needed to grow their economies was to free prices, privatize as much as possible, and reduce the government's role in the economy.

The fact that this consensus had not been followed by the rich countries of the world, and that there was little evidence that the policies had actually worked anywhere, didn't deter legions of economists flocking to Moscow from Washington and many prominent American universities and think tanks. They proclaimed their unproven formulas with almost religious zeal.

One of the real costs of Soviet communism was how Marxist theory succeeded at instituting societal prejudice against economic success. In Russian society, if someone is getting rich this must be because he is cheating someone, and getting the good end of a bargain. Having had the opportunity to teach in Russia as well as China, I found it interesting when my Russian students instructed me on the differences between what they called "white envy" and "black envy." White envy is discomfort with someone else's success, and the desire to achieve comparable success. Black envy is the same discomfort, but also the desire to destroy the other person's success. Black envy was abundant in Russia, especially in rural areas. And this made it hard to create economic incentives for agricultural success, or any other kind.

There wasn't much black envy in China, possible another benefit of only 30 years of communism before the reform process began. Chinese reforms began with the comprehensive overhaul of the country's agricultural system, and the encouragement of individual Chinese farmers to become economically successful. This was carried out by reducing the number of collective farms, and giving individual growers the opportunity to lease land for their own use. Such leases included an obligation that the farmers sell half of their crop to the state at fixed prices. But they could sell the remainder on private markets at higher prices, and keep the income from both types of sales.

In this manner, the state created incentives for greater production while also maintaining some control of farm output, including food for urban residents, and inputs for manufacturing. The terms of such farm leases could be as long as 30 years. This gave the farmers a stake in maintaining the quality of the land, and an incentive to improve productivity through better seeds, fertilizer, and mechanization. Furthermore, the farmers could sell the lease rights to other farmers. Although the state still owned the land, this went about as far towards a private-property system in agriculture that any socialist economy has gone, to date.

Today, only about 20 percent of China's farm output is sold to the state, and 80 percent is sold on private markets. But the state remains actively engaged in the agricultural sector, in part by providing equipment leases to its farmers and subsidies for their infrastructure. This includes irrigation systems, transportation links, and food processing and storage facilities.

Speaking broadly, there is no such thing as free-market agriculture, in China or anywhere else; at least not that I'm aware of. In the spectacularly successful example of American agriculture, the federal government continues to play a crucial role. The U.S. Department of Agriculture guarantees some prices; it's taken land out of production to stabilize prices; provided crop loans to guarantee income; and subsidized rural electricity and communication systems. The late American economist John Kenneth Galbraith maintained that guaranteed price supports were the most important assistance the U.S. government had provided to American farmers. Federal supports encouraged increased output, because farmers knew they could sell whatever they produced for at least the government's minimum price. This floor on prices also encouraged capital investments, and technological development.

In China, a mixture of private incentives and government support has led to significant increases in farm productivity, and allowed many rural residents to move from the countryside to the city. This movement was necessary to support the leadership's industrialization and trade policies. In turn, reform in the manufacturing sector started with local authorities being given the power to start up small enterprises, and retain the income to support local needs. If these local manufacturing enterprises were successful, then the local authorities would have more income to support their schools, hospitals, roads, and other municipal needs.

An excellent example of small-scale production in China is the town of Qiaotou in Zhejiang province, on the east coast. One small button manufacturer began there in the early 1980s. Today, the town produces 80 percent of the world's buttons and 60 percent of its zippers. Buttons and zippers might seem like small things but if you dominate a global market, you've probably got something. Imagine life without buttons and zippers!

The Qiaotou phenomenon has since fostered concentrations of small-scale enterprises known as Town and Village Enterprises, or TVEs, throughout Zhejiang province. For example, a place known as Datang Township has been reported as producing one-third of the world's socks. An estimated 40 percent of the world's neckties are said to be made in Shengzhou Township. TVEs receive no government subsidies, and must rely on private market sales for their incomes. This focus on market success forces them to be efficient, and attuned to market needs.

At the beginning of the Deng Xiaoping-era reforms, most private enterprises were either restaurants or small retail stores. This was somewhat like the reforms allowed in Hungary in 1968, when families were allowed to open private restaurants and stores. The restaurants in Hungary were among the best in Eastern Europe until the end of communism in 1989. Today, the restaurants in Budapest are still very good. But now there are also excellent restaurants in Prague, Warsaw, and Zagreb, among other places.

But whereas Hungary took no further steps at the time, this was just a first step in China. In 1979, Deng Xiaoping supposedly made his famous declaration—"To get rich is glorious"—in part to encourage small enterprises and farmers. This blessing from a top leader in the communist party signaled a radical change from Chairman Mao's previous attempts to create a new socialist man.

Eventually, Deng's reforms allowed centrally planned large enterprises to become independently run. They were still state-owned. But the SOEs—state-owned enterprises—were expected to perform like market-driven corporations, albeit frequently in state-protected economic sectors; and with some big consequences for American businesses and markets.

China's SOEs became prominent in large-scale manufacturing, transportation, and natural resources, as well as in steel production, mining, and petroleum refining. Some examples include Air China and COSCO (not Costco). It stands for China Ocean Shipping Group. You might have seen their containers on freight trains and semi-trailers across the United States. These containers are frequently hauling consumer goods from televisions to running shoes.

Although Chinese SOEs share some characteristics of large capitalist corporations, there are also some very big differences. For instance, because the Chinese government is the principal owner, the government can decide on the SOE's operating objectives. Like other enterprises in a planned economy, the SOEs might be given output targets, delivered to state bureaucracies or other SOEs. And because the primary objective of the SOE is output, management has an inherent incentive to understate its productive capacity, and to overstate its demand for resources. This was also typical behavior for an enterprise in the Soviet Union. By having output as the main objective, one byproduct is maximizing employment. Maximizing output and employment are two sides of the same coin.

SOEs enjoyed what the Hungarian economist Janos Kornai calls a "soft budget constraint." This is different than the hard budget constraint faced by a typical capitalist corporation. If a capitalist corporation doesn't make profits, sooner or later its bankers or stockholders will force changes; or the enterprise will go bankrupt. If the corporation gets most of its operating funds from a bank, the bank will cut off credit. If the corporation gets most of its financial capital from investors, they will balk, and management will be forced to cut expenses, often by laying off employees—or selling parts of the business. If this doesn't stem losses, the company will fail.

An SOE might not face any "hard budget constraint" from its state sponsor. Often, the SOE is the major employer in a particular town or region. Shutting down the SOE would mean the town will suffer both in terms of unemployment and reduction in tax revenues. But government subsidies can make up for temporary losses. The management of the SOE knows this, and so it might be tempted to expand production and employment beyond purely economic limits.

Compared to purely private enterprises, SOEs are less efficient and a drain on the central government's budget. However, employment in a communist system is very much a political issue, central to the state's stability and survival. That's why they are a continuing problem for sponsoring governments. In a capitalist system, by comparison, if a company goes bankrupt—and employees lose their jobs—this is often understood as a consequence of market competition.

When the Chicago-based retailer Montgomery Ward went bankrupt years ago, most employees understood this was a consequence of competition from the likes of Home Depot, Walmart, and Target. The U.S. government sometimes does bail out money-losing firms because they are too big and too important. General Motors is an example. But in China, when a SOE shuts down, or lays off workers, this is understood as a government decision. The people believe the government is responsible. And the Chinese government, led by the Communist Party, relies on the support of the population for its hold on power.

Another key example of the Deng Xiaoping-era reforms was the introduction of Special Economic Zones, or SEZs. These allowed foreign businesses to operate joint-ventures with Chinese enterprises. The objective was to get the benefits of foreign financial investment, foreign technology—and access to foreign markets. The first four SEZs were established in the southern and coastal regions of China: Shenzhen, Zhuhai, and Shantou in Guangdong Province, and Xiamen in Fujian Province. These regions have been spectacular growth areas, ever since. Shenzhen went from a town of 30,000 inhabitants to more than a million. The SEZs offered foreign investors low taxes, low utility rates, low rents, and the ability to export. Soon, their output began showing up in American retail stores.

The first wave of Chinese exports to America was clothes and shoes. Nearly every industrializing country starts their path towards industrialization with textiles. This was true of the first Industrial Revolution in Britain, with the textile mills of Manchester and Birmingham. It was also true of American industrialization, with the first factories in New England. But China's SEZs were limited and controlled by the Chinese government. Memories of previous foreign domination and control kept the Chinese authorities fearful and watchful. Still, the benefits to China of allowing foreigners to produce and do business in the country were quite large. Economists talk about "external economies" arising from the operations of businesses in a particular area. These external economies include knowledge spillover effects, where local businesspeople and workers learn new ways of organizing work, as well as the existence of foreign markets, and gain access to new technology.

China's first SEZs were located mostly in the south and along the east coast of the country, and for several reasons. They would be close to financial centers and international ports of Hong Kong and Shanghai. And they would be closer to the Chinese diaspora working in Indonesia, Singapore, and Taiwan, as well as in Hong Kong. The Chinese pattern of exports and imports followed the classic principles of comparative advantage laid out by the British political economist David Ricardo during the 1800s.

In the beginning, China had a large supply of unskilled labor, and, therefore, a comparative advantage in products that would employ unskilled workers: products like T-shirts, flip flops, and basic housewares. China did not have a comparative advantage in complex products requiring highly skilled workers. So, they imported Boeing 747s. Still, the growth of Chinese exports to the United States was spectacular. From 1991 to 2007, Chinese exports to America rose nearly 13-fold, from $26 billion to $330 billion. At the same time, exports from Mexico to America rose only about five-fold, from $38 billion to $183 billion. And Mexico had the benefit of being part of the North American Free Trade Agreement.

The effects of Chinese exports to the United States are controversial, and much debated by economists. The benefits are pretty clear. Americans gain access to much less expensive goods. And this raises their standard of living, especially among low-income Americans who can afford only cheaper goods. The costs are not so clear, but there have been serious attempts to measure them. MIT economist David Autor has written several articles and papers on the effects of Chinese imports on American workers and regions. Professor Autor estimates that about half of the decline in American manufacturing employment is due to Chinese imports. This deterioration in manufacturing employment is concentrated in specific parts of the country, including San Jose, California; Providence, Rhode Island; and Buffalo, New York. Autor documents this decline in manufacturing employment, and an increase in service-sector unemployment, as well. The effects are especially hard on non-college educated workers, just as standard international trade theory would predict.

Imports from China are produced by unskilled labor, and this reduces the demand for American products produced by competing labor. Furthermore, declines in employment in the affected areas increase the need for unemployment benefits, disability, and other government transfer payments. This leads to pressure on public-sector budgets, and increases the likelihood of government budget deficits. Autor attributes the Deng-inspired rise in Chinese exports to the United States to its investments in labor-intensive industries, and rising productivity, as well as developments in transportation.

Unfortunately, there's no simple answer the United States can apply to the resulting problems in its own economy. The simple solution might be to block all imports from China. If it were only that easy. But if we stopped imports from China, flip flop production would be unlikely to come back to the United States. It would go to another country, instead, with lots of cheap labor.

I looked in a closet at home to see where my running shoes came from. They used to be made in China. Not anymore; at least not for the most part. My Adidas Supernova Cushions come from Indonesia. My Nike Air Jordans come from Vietnam. However, I do have a pair of retro Converse All Star white low tops. These still come from China. So, if we stop all imports from China, production of most goods that come from there would likely move to Indonesia, Vietnam, or some other developing country. Economics is a dynamic science. The world is changing all the time. China today is not primarily a producer of T-shirts and flip flops any more. It now produces 30 percent of the world's automobiles. There's a growing service sector in China, too.

One great success story to come out of China is the Internet retailer Qiangdong Liu, who is also known as Richard Liu. He came from a family of affluent business people and entrepreneurs. But his parents and grandparents were persecuted during Mao's Cultural Revolution, and lost everything. Mr. Liu started out with $2,000 in personal savings to capitalize a little market stall in Beijing, selling audio equipment. Eventually he decided that online retail was a better market. Today, his company—JD.com—is one of the world's largest online retailers.

Here's an excellent example of how the short history of communism in China did not entirely extinguish entrepreneurial traditions or knowledge. In stark contrast, there was no such tradition in Russia, nor the requisite knowledge to draw on after the collapse of the Soviet Union. By the way, Mr. Liu is worth about $10 billion, these days—give or take a billion. It's not Mao's China any more.

Lecture 22

Asian Tigers: Wealth and State Control

S OUTH KOREA, TAIWAN, AND SINGAPORE MADE
remarkable transformations from poor countries
to high-income economies between 1950 and
2000. Their economic progress is unprecedented
in history. At first, they were referred to as newly
industrialized countries, and then—along with
Hong Kong—as the Asian Tigers. What were the
secrets of their miraculous growth? And can other
countries copy them? This lecture will uncover
some of their secrets and critique their strategies. ◆

Common Approaches to Economic Growth

◀ The approaches to economic growth of South Korea, Taiwan, and Singapore have many similarities. The island of Formosa, or Taiwan, became dominated by the former Kuomintang government of mainland China in about 1947 and has operated autonomously ever since, though the United Nations has recognized communist China as its rightful government since 1971.

◀ South Korea gained its independence from Japan after colonial rule ended there in 1945. And Singapore gained its independence from Great Britain in 1959. All three were led by authoritarian, one-party governments. Korea and Taiwan were under martial law for almost 20 years. So, the question can be asked as to whether a developing country needs to be led by a forceful hand through the difficult process of building an economy.

◀ At first blush, the example of the three Asian Tigers suggests that autocratic rule can be a successful approach—if the authoritarian leader is truly focused on developing the country and making wise decisions that benefit its citizens in the long run.

◀ But authoritarian rule by a single strongman does not guarantee economic success. So, it might be that South Korea, Singapore, and Taiwan were fortunate in their choice of dictators: Park Chung Hee, Lee Kuan Yew, and Chiang Kai-shek, respectively. Whether or not they would be as successful in more democratic societies is open to question.

◀ One key aspect of the development strategies in all three countries was an emphasis on education and the formation of human capital. Economists use the concept of human capital to cover all aspects of education and training. A significant part of human capital is primary and secondary education.

Singapore is so successful at promoting primary and secondary education that it ranked first in the world in a recent ranking of 15-year-old students by the Organization for Economic Cooperation and Development. South Korea and Taiwan also typically score very well—higher than the United States, for example—though the triennial rankings do shift a bit.

◀ Another part is the development of skills and experience necessary for rapid industrialization. In practice, skills and experience means an emphasis on math and science in primary and secondary schools and engineering in higher education.

◀ Along with a heavy emphasis on education, all three Tigers also employed some type of formal state-level economic planning and emphasis to identify priority sectors of economic development. The planning was not dictatorial, Soviet style, but more like France's system of indicative planning, which relies on incentives and economic support rather than fiat.

◀ The Tigers also all relied on some form of state ownership for key enterprises and other enterprises that might not be profitable if operated as strictly private capitalist firms. All three Tiger countries used tariffs (taxes on imported goods that make foreign products more expensive than domestic ones) and quotas (a numerical limit on the quantity of imports that can be brought into a country) to protect favored infant industries—that is, economic sectors and enterprises in the early stage of development.

◀ South Korea, Singapore, and Taiwan placed tariffs and quotas alike on imports of manufactured goods that might compete with favored domestic manufacturers. Because the favored domestic manufacturers of Korea, Taiwan, and Singapore were relatively new at the time, they were infant industries in the world trade in manufactured goods.

◀ There are significant problems with the infant-industry argument for high tariff and quota protection. One of them is identifying which industries are truly infant and deserving of protection. Every business wants protection from foreign competition. And once infant industry protection is introduced, it might be very difficult to remove.

◀ The Asian Tigers had to be judicious in picking the particular sectors to be protected from foreign competition. The Tigers' protections were geared to developing export industries—and participating in the global economic system—rather than to help their domestic consumers. Although the governments specifically protected some industries, they were also willing to develop all domestic industries that they believed could compete in world markets.

◀ The Tigers also were keen on taking advantage of foreign investment to finance national development. Foreign investment would bring in needed capital, but most importantly, it would bring in know-how and advanced technology.

◀ Newly industrializing countries—by observing and learning the methods of more advanced foreign enterprises—could reap the spillover effects of knowledge. Workers in a foreign enterprise would develop skills and experience that they could transfer to their domestic enterprises.

◀ Some production in the Tiger countries was state-owned, but most was in private hands. And these businesses were not *commanded* to produce certain products, as would have been the case in the former Soviet Union or the communist economies of eastern Europe. But they were *encouraged* to follow central government preferences, through a variety of means.

◀ These means included concessionary loans and interest rates to support the state's high-priority industrial investments. And because the governments of the Tigers owned or controlled the banking system, the direction and terms of business loans was an instrument of state control.

◀ Business firms that did not produce products explicitly favored by the government might face higher interest rates, if they could borrow money—and they might not have access to credit at all. Being denied access to loans for financing current operations or for expansion plans is not necessarily a dictatorial command, but it comes pretty close to government directive.

◀ Tax policy is another avenue of indicative planning, and it is used in all market economies, including in the United States. For a country focused on rapid economic

No high-income country has ever developed its own advanced technology at the beginning of its industrialization process. For example, the United States adopted British railroad technology.

development, tax policy is directed at enterprises that the state considers key to the industrialization process. Tax policy might consist of lower tax rates on profits or higher deductions on capital expenditures.

◀ Lower tax rates provide favored enterprises with more retained earnings and, hence, more funds for expansion. Higher deductions for capital or equipment expenditures accomplish the same thing, in a different way. Expenses authorized to be treated as deductions can be more directly targeted by government planners than rates themselves. Either way, greater retained earnings leave more funds for the enterprise to spend on investment.

◀ Governments in the Tiger countries usually owned the power and water utilities. The state could, therefore, charge high-priority enterprises advantageous prices for power and water. Additionally, if the state owned key input enterprises—a steel producer, for example—the state could supply these key inputs to favored enterprises, again at lower prices.

◀ Finally, all three governments maintained controls on foreign-exchange transactions during their development. Domestic access to foreign exchange was usually limited to purchases of needed foreign technology or other inputs not available locally. Foreign exchange earned from exporting domestic products was used wisely to purchase foreign machinery and key inputs in the industrialization process.

◀ One advantage that the three Tigers had was what the late-19th-century and early-20th-century Norwegian American economist Thorstein Veblen called the advantage of backwardness. When you are behind in technology and industrial development, you don't have to discover or innovate. You just have to be sure to adopt the best practices. You can take advantage of someone else's genius and leap forward in the development process.

South Korea

◀ At the end of the Korean War in July 1953, the Republic of Korea—South Korea—was a backward country, even compared to North Korea, or the Democratic People's Republic of Korea. It had a lower gross domestic product and a less industrial economy than the north did, mainly as a legacy of Japanese colonialism.

◀ Imperial Japan had envisioned the northern part of the peninsular protectorate as an industrial supplier to another Japanese colony in Manchuria, in northeastern China. The northern part of Korea was relatively closer to Manchuria, and for this reason it was more industrially developed than the agricultural south.

◀ The partition of the Korean peninsula into the communist north and the market-oriented south was formalized as part of an armistice agreement ending the war in July 1953. A few years after the formal partition, an enterprising South Korean general named Park Chung Hee staged a coup that overthrew the unstable and short-lived parliamentary Second Republic.

◀ In 1961, he took over control of a country with a per capita gross domestic product of about 82 dollars. About 50 years later, South Korea's per capita gross domestic product had grown more than 400-fold to in excess of 34,000 dollars. By comparison, it took the United States 150 years to industrialize to a similar level. Some of the rapidity of the South Korean advance can be attributed to the "catching-up" effect of a backward country emulating the best practices of technological leaders.

◀ How did the South Korean economy accomplish this miracle? The answer lies in a focused and rigorous economic effort. This effort was channeled by a wise government into forcing an agrarian, underdeveloped economy to save and invest for future growth.

◀ Resources were to be channeled into specific industries: steel, shipbuilding, electronics, chemicals, and automobiles. Most production in these priority industries was carried out by privately owned enterprises rather than by the state directly. In turn, these domestic enterprises were grouped into industrial conglomerates called chaebols, typically by a founding family. These chaebols are still the backbone of the Korean economy. Among the most important chaebols are Samsung and Hyundai.

◀ South Korea also had a somewhat laissez-faire attitude toward other people's intellectual property at the beginning. Knock-off shoes and purses, bootleg tapes and movies, and noncopyrighted books were all permitted—chiefly as a way to minimize the use of foreign exchange for import goods.

Taiwan

◀ After the communist Chinese revolutionary Mao Zedong achieved victory against Chiang Kai-shek's Nationalists in a long-running civil war that culminated in 1949, Chiang and his Kuomintang party fled across the Formosa Strait to the island of Taiwan, where they established what Chiang called the Republic of China.

◀ One of Chiang's first economic policies in the new island state was massive land reform: taking property away from holders and redistributing it to individual farmers. The Kuomintangs' intent was to redistribute the holdings of former Japanese landlords who had occupied Taiwan until the end of World War II.

◀ Taking land from oppressive Japanese created little or no domestic opposition and created much good will. Also, because Chiang Kai-shek and the Kuomintang were predominantly mainland Chinese, they were not expropriating property from any of the new government's immediate supporters and allies.

◀ Taiwan's land-reform program accomplished many things crucial to economic development. It increased agricultural production. In turn, this provided more food for urban workers and raw materials for new factories. And by making agriculture more productive, fewer workers were needed on Taiwan's farms. Some could move to the cities to be urban factory workers.

Chiang Kai-shek

◀ To support and facilitate the new farmers getting money for needed equipment, seeds, and fertilizer, the Chiang government created the Land Bank of Taiwan, a state-owned entity that provided low-cost loans to farmers. Because it was state-owned, the land bank did not need to worry about making immediate profits and could take a much longer view. Loans from the United States government were another key element in Taiwan's early development.

> Chiang's land-reform efforts were so successful— and such an important element of Taiwan's development—that the national government created a Land Reform Museum in Taipei in 1967.

◀ In Taiwan, the Chiang government chose to prioritize a domestic electronics industry. To jump-start the sector, it created a state-owned enterprise known as the Taiwan Semiconductor Manufacturing Company, which developed technology and components for some of Taiwan's newly emerging private companies.

◀ Taiwan also established and funded science and industrial parks in several of its larger cities. Most business activity in these parks is devoted to research related to information technology and biotechnology—leading sectors in contemporary high-income economies.

Singapore

◀ Lee Kuan Yew, Singapore's leader after independence, was adamant in his drive to educate fellow citizens. Early in his administration, Lee Kuan Yew invited select Western technology companies to Singapore to instruct his countrymen on the organizations' best practices. Among the companies who came—and became eligible for special treatment on taxes, profits, and property—were Texas Instruments, General Electric, and Hewlett-Packard.

◀ Singapore also developed expertise in shipping and logistics. The former British Royal Naval base there provided basic infrastructure for what was about to become the age of container shipping. In addition, foreign bankers were invited to set up subsidiaries in Singapore; these arrivals formed the nucleus of one of the major banking and financial centers of Asia. And the British colonial legacy of the English language—the language of international finance—was invaluable.

◀ Lee Kuan Yew was obsessed with creating a strong and independent Singapore so that it would never again suffer the humiliations of colonialism.

Today, Singapore is an interesting mix of private and public property. Most of its banks, shipping companies, and electronics firms are privately owned. However, there's extensive state ownership of property and other assets.

CHANG, *Bad Samaritans.*
CHANG AND GRABEL, *Reclaiming Development.*

Questions

1 What were the advantages to the Asian Tiger economies of having a strongman in charge of development? What were the goals of these strongmen?

2 Are the stories about the economic miracles in South Korea, Singapore, and Taiwan stories about the wonders of the free enterprise system?

Asian Tigers: Wealth and State Control

S outh Korea, Taiwan, and Singapore made remarkable transformations from poor countries to high-income economies, in the half-century between 1950 and 2000. Their economic progress is unprecedented in history. At first, they were referred to as New Industrialized Countries, or NICs; and then—along with Hong Kong—as the Asian Tigers. Their growth has been ferocious! So, what were the secrets of their miraculous growth? And can other countries copy them? In this lecture, I'm going to uncover some of their secrets—and critique their strategies.

Let's start with a general overview of some common components in their approaches to economic growth. The three countries' strategies have many similarities. I'm not including a discussion of Hong Kong in this account because of its unusual status, first as a crown colony of Britain, and then as a special administrative region of China.

The island of Formosa—or Taiwan—became dominated by the former Kuomintang government of mainland China in about 1947, and has operated autonomously ever since, though the United Nations has recognized communist China as its rightful government since 1971. South Korea gained its independence from Japan after colonial rule ended there in 1945. And Singapore gained its independence from Great Britain in 1959. All three were led by authoritarian, one-party governments.

At first blush, the example of our three Asian Tigers suggests autocratic rule can be a successful approach—if the authoritarian leader is truly focused on developing the country, and making wise decisions that benefit its citizens in the long run. But authoritarian rule by a single "strong man" does not guarantee economic success. If that were true, then Haiti under the Duvaliers, and the Philippines under Ferdinand Marcos would also be rich countries. So, it might be that South Korea, Singapore, and Taiwan were fortunate in their choice of dictators: Park Chung-Hee, Lee Kuan Yew, and Chiang Kai-shek. Whether or not they would be as successful in more democratic societies is open to question.

One key aspect of the development strategies in all three countries was an emphasis on education, and the formation of human capital. Economists use the concept of human capital to cover all aspects of education and training. A significant part of human capital is primary and secondary education. Another part is the development of skills and experience necessary for rapid industrialization. In practice, skills and experience means an emphasis on math and science in primary and secondary schools, and engineering in higher education.

Singapore is so successful at promoting primary and secondary education that it ranked first in the world, in a recent ranking of 15-year-old students by the OECD, or the Organization for Economic Co-operation and Development. The OECD is based in Paris, and an excellent source of data and analysis. South Korea and Taiwan also typically score very well—higher than the United States, for example—though the triennial rankings do shift a bit.

Along with a heavy emphasis on education, all three Tigers also employed some type of formal state-level economic planning and emphasis to identify priority sectors of economic development. The planning was not dictatorial, Soviet style, but more like France's system of indicative planning, which relies on incentives and economic support rather than fiat. The Tigers also all relied on some form of state ownership for key enterprises and other enterprises that might not be profitable if operated as strictly private capitalist firms.

Following an approach advocated nearly two and a half centuries ago by the American federalist Alexander Hamilton, all three Tiger countries used tariffs and quotas to protect favored "infant industries"—that is, economic sectors and enterprises in the early stage of development. Tariffs are taxes on imported goods that make foreign products more expensive than domestic ones. Quotas are a numerical limit on the quantity of imports that can be brought into a country. In some cases, the quota is set at zero—to prohibit any imports. South Korea, Singapore, and Taiwan— all three—placed tariffs and quotas alike on imports of manufactured goods that might compete with favored domestic manufacturers. Since the favored domestic manufacturers of Korea, Taiwan, and Singapore were relatively new at the time, they were infant industries in the world trade in manufactured goods.

Alexander Hamilton created the term infant industries when he was advocating relatively high tariffs for the new American government to impose on imports. Hamilton was a pretty impressive guy. He had time to advise and write about economic policy for the new American republic at the same time he was writing a contemporary hit musical!

Even so, there are significant problems with the infant-industry argument for high tariff and quota protection. One of them is identifying which industries are truly infant, and deserving of protection. Every business wants protection from foreign competition—just try asking. And once infant industry protection is introduced, it might be very hard to remove. As most of us have heard by now, the United States government has been protecting the American sugar industry for decades. Sugar prices in the U.S. are much higher than world sugar prices. But the cane sugar producers in Florida—and beet sugar producers in North Dakota—are very active politically to preserve their protections. Other barriers come and go, reflecting the rise and fall of perceived threats around the world, and as trade alliances form or are disbanded.

Asia's Tigers had to be very judicious in picking the particular sectors to be protected from foreign competition. We'll discuss which industries in each country were favored in just a bit. First, I should point out that the Tigers' protections were geared to developing export industries—and participating in the global economic system—rather than to help their domestic consumers. And although the governments specifically protected some industries, they were also willing to develop all domestic industries they believed could compete in world markets.

The Tigers also were keen on taking advantage of foreign investment to finance national development. Foreign investment would bring in needed capital. Most importantly, foreign investment would bring in know-how and advanced technology. This is a much faster way to ramp up industrial technology than to try to develop it all by yourself.

In fact, no high-income country has ever developed its own advanced technology at the beginning of its industrialization process. The United States adopted British railroad technology; the British adopted Dutch financial innovations; the Dutch adopted Italian monetary creations. Newly industrializing countries—by observing and learning the methods of more advanced foreign enterprises—could reap the "spillover" effects of knowledge. Workers in a foreign enterprise would develop skills and experience they could transfer to their domestic enterprises.

Some production in the Tiger countries was state-owned, but most was in private hands. And these businesses were not commanded to produce certain products, as would have been the case in the former Soviet Union or the communist economies of Eastern Europe. But they were encouraged to follow central government preferences, through a variety of means. These means included concessionary loans and interest rates to support the state's high-priority industrial investments. And since the governments of the Tigers owned or controlled the banking system, the direction and terms of business loans was an instrument of state control.

Business firms that did not produce products explicitly favored by the government might face higher interest rates, if they could borrow money, or they might not have access to credit at all. Being denied access to loans for financing current operations or for expansion plans is not necessarily a dictatorial command, but it comes pretty close to government directive.

Tax policy is another avenue of indicative planning, and is used in all market economies, including in the United States. For a country focused on rapid economic development, tax policy is directed at enterprises the state considers key to the industrialization process. Tax policy might consist of lower tax rates on profits, or higher deductions on capital expenditures. Lower tax rates provide favored enterprises with more retained earnings and, hence, more funds for expansion. Higher deductions for capital or equipment expenditures accomplish the same thing, in a different way. Expenses authorized to be treated as deductions can be more directly targeted by government planners than rates themselves. Either way, greater retained earnings leave more funds for the enterprise to spend on investment.

Governments in the Tiger countries usually owned the power and water utilities. The state could, therefore, charge high-priority enterprises advantageous prices for power and water. Additionally, if the state owned key input enterprises—a steel producer, for example—the state could supply these key inputs to favored enterprises, again at lower prices. Finally, all three governments maintained controls on foreign-exchange transactions during their development. Domestic access to foreign exchange was usually limited to purchases of needed foreign technology, or other inputs not available locally.

In Asia's Tigers, foreign exchange earned from exporting domestic products was used wisely to purchase foreign machinery, and key inputs in the industrialization process. But in the hands of a less-responsible dictator, foreign exchange might be used to purchase villas on the French Riviera, as was the case with the Duvalier dictators in Haiti. I don't know for sure, but I'd be willing to bet dollars to donuts—as we'd say in Texas—that more dictators use scarce foreign exchange for villas than for metal-forming machinery.

One advantage the three Tigers had was what the late 19th century and early 20th century Norwegian-American economist, Thorstein Veblen, called "the advantage of backwardness." When you are behind in technology and industrial development, you don't have to discover or innovate. You just have to be sure to adopt the best practices. You can take advantage of someone else's genius, and leap forward in the development process. This is not necessarily simple to accomplish, but it's easier than trying to innovate when you are the technological leader.

At the end of the Korean War in July, 1953, the Republic of Korea—South Korea—was a backward country; backward even compared to North Korea, the Democratic People's Republic of Korea, or DPRK. It had a lower gross domestic product, and a less-industrial economy than the north did, mainly as a legacy of Japanese colonialism. That's because imperial Japan had envisioned the northern part of peninsular as an industrial supplier to another Japanese colony in Manchuria, in northeastern China. The northern part of Korea was relatively closer to Manchuria, and for this reason it was more industrially developed than the agricultural south.

The partition of the Korean peninsula into the communist north and the market-oriented south—formalized as part of an armistice agreement ending the war in July 1953—was a comparative systems economist's dream. It's as close as you can get in economics to a controlled laboratory experiment. Here you had two countries—with two contrasting economic systems—but everything else was almost identical. Same people, same language, same history, same cultural values, and—even better—the north started ahead of the south.

For comparison purposes, this was even better than the division of Germany into the communist German Democratic Republic in the east and the market economy of the Federal Republic in the west. In turn, the ultimate collapse of the East Germany—symbolized by the demolition of the Berlin Wall in November 1989—can be seen as something of a dress rehearsal for some of the issues that North Korea will face just as soon as its economy collapses. And I'm pretty sure that will happen—just don't ask me when.

A few years after the formal partition of the two Koreas at the 38th parallel, an enterprising South Korean general named Park Chung-Hee staged a military coup that overthrew the unstable and short-lived parliamentary Second Republic. In 1961, he took over control of a country with per capita GDP of about $82 per year. How little is that?

Some 50 years later, South Korea's per capita GDP had grown more than 400-fold to an excess of $34,000 a head, according to OECD statistics. A comparable leap took industrializing Great Britain 200 years to achieve, and the United States 150 years. Some of the rapidity of the South Korean advance can be attributed to the "catching-up" effect of a backward country emulating the best practices of technological leaders. Life expectancy itself has risen half again, from 53 years to 81.4 years. By comparison, the life expectancy of a child born in the United States is about 78.7 years.

How did the South Korean economy accomplish this miracle? The answer lies in a very focused and rigorous economic effort. This effort was channeled by a rather wise government into forcing an agrarian, underdeveloped economy to save and invest for future growth. The planning document and strategy of the Park government was something known as the Heavy and Chemical Industrial Program, or HCIP. Under this framework, resources were to be channeled into specific industries: steel, shipbuilding, electronics, chemicals, and automobiles.

As I mentioned a moment ago, most production in these priority industries was carried out by privately owned enterprises rather than by the state directly. In turn, these domestic enterprises were grouped into industrial conglomerates called chaebols, typically by a founding family—some up to present day. These chaebols are still the backbone of the Korean economy.

You've probably owned many products made by the largest of these industrial conglomerates—or seen them driving down the street, or through a showroom window. Among the most important chaebols are: Samsung; Hyundai; LG—reflecting a merger of two previously separate chaebols, Lucky and Goldstar; Lotte—a food, tourism, petrochemicals, construction, and finance conglomerate; and SK Group, which specializes in chemicals, telecom, and semi-conductors. The last time I looked, these five chaebols accounted for more than 50 percent of the South Korean stock index—the Kospi.

Samsung is the largest of these, and its story is illustrative of the development strategy of the South Korean government under former strongman Park Chung-Hee. Samsung was founded in 1938 as a producer and exporter of fresh vegetables and fruit. The South Korean economist Ha-Joon Chang relates Samsung's evolution within the rising Tiger in his lucid and fascinating book, *Bad Samaritans: The Myth of Free Trade and the Secret History of Capitalism.* By the way, the provocative title comes from Professor Chang's assertion that today's high-income countries, like the United States, tend to give advice to less developed countries that they didn't follow themselves.

For example, the United States and other member countries of the International Monetary Fund and World Bank have frequently advised less-developed countries to follow neo-liberal economics, sometimes referred to as the "Washington consensus." This consensus counsels privatizing all important economic activity; opening developing economies to free trade; focusing on inflation; and minimizing regulation. Professor Chang calls it hypocrisy since the high-income countries executed few if any of these policies during their own initial growth periods. I've already mentioned Alexander Hamilton's vision of high tariffs to protect infant industries. For that matter, many of the United States' key technological developments evolve out of the Department of Defense, not private enterprise.

So, in South Korea, Park Chung-Hee ordered Samsung to begin developing an electronics sector for the country. The South Korean government would protect it by restricting the imports of competing electronics products. In addition, South Korean universities would produce large numbers of electrical engineers. And Samsung would get cheap loans and tax breaks. Not so many years ago, South Korea produced cheap electronics goods: cheap transistor radios and simple mobile phones. Today, my younger undergraduates assume that the name Samsung means high-quality mobile phones, fine HDTV's, and groovy laptops. My undergraduates don't really say groovy, but I do. And usually my students laugh at me when I use the word.

Something similar to the Samsung example occurred with Hyundai Motors. Hyundai was originally a construction firm in the post-war era that was given a protected domestic market for automobiles, beginning in 1967. Initially, most Hyundai cars were built with imported parts, and assembled only in South Korea. But assembling and reverse-engineering automobile parts taught the South Koreans a lot about car-production technology.

In turn, because steel production is an expensive proposition—and, quite often, unprofitable for a private enterprise, at least in the short run—the South Korean government created a state-owned steelmaker called POSCO, or the Pohang Iron and Steel Company. POSCO produced the steel necessary for a domestic automobile industry. Today, Hyundai sells more than four million vehicles a year all around the world, and it employs more than 80,000 people.

This cooperative approach has since become common in developing countries. Sometimes private enterprise is the best way to create products. But often, some kind of government activity is necessary, especially in the beginning when private enterprises are mostly small. South Korea also had a somewhat laissez-faire attitude toward other people's intellectual property at the beginning. Knock-off shoes and purses, bootleg tapes and movies, and non-copyrighted books were all permitted—chiefly as a way to minimize the use of foreign exchange for import goods.

If Korean consumers weren't buying genuine Nike shoes but domestic knock-offs instead, then any surplus foreign exchange could be used for automobile parts.

The intellectual property climate in South Korea has since changed. Today, the country is a successful exporter of cultural goods. In most of Asia—and even America—South Korean popular music known as K-pop is hugely popular. And South Korean-produced soap operas are distributed to many Asian broadcast networks. With this cultural popularity came the South Korean government's belated appreciation of intellectual property copyrights and royalties.

A similar story of an autocratic government forcing radical economic change is found in Taiwan. After the communist revolutionary Mao Zedong achieved victory against Chiang Kai-shek's Nationalists in a long-running civil war that culminated in 1949, Chiang Kai-shek and his Kuomintang Party fled across the Formosa Strait to the island of Taiwan. There, they established what Chiang called the Republic of China. It sounds a lot like what Mao Zedong called his own country, the People's Republic of China. But they were more different than alike.

One of Chiang Kai-shek's first economic policies in the new island state was massive land reform: taking property away from holders and redistributing it to individual farmers. A "land-to-the-tiller" campaign might seem strange for an anti-communist government. Land wrested from rich landlords and given to peasants is something that Lenin himself would advocate. But the Kuomintangs' intent was to redistribute the holdings of former Japanese landlords who'd occupied Taiwan until the end of World War II. Taking land from oppressive Japanese created little or no domestic opposition, and created much good will. Also, since Chiang Kai-shek and the Kuomintang were themselves predominantly mainland Chinese, they were not expropriating property from any of the new government's immediate supporters and its allies.

Taiwan's land-reform program accomplished many things crucial to economic development. It increased agricultural production. In turn, this provided more food for urban workers, and raw materials for new factories. And by making agriculture more productive, fewer workers were needed on Taiwan's farms. Some could move to the cities and be urban factory workers. To support and facilitate the new farmers getting money for needed equipment, seeds, and fertilizer, the Chiang government created the Land Bank of Taiwan. This was a state-owned entity that provided low-cost loans to farmers. Because it was state-owned, the land bank did not need to worry about making immediate profits. It could take a much longer view. Chiang's land-reform efforts were so successful—and such an important element of Taiwan's development—that the national government created a Land Reform Museum in Taipei in 1967.Maybe only economists get a thrill out of knowing about this!

Loans from the United States government were another key element in Taiwan's early development. This aid was partially motivated by Washington's anti-communist sympathies, as well as by the feeling that "free" China deserved support in the Cold War contest with communism. Foreign aid almost always gets a bad rap in the United States. It's an easy target for politicians who complain about the federal government giving money away to foreigners. A defense of foreign-aid programs is that a relatively small amount of money often doing remarkably good things, and is, in fact, a miniscule percentage of the federal budget.

In Taiwan, the Chiang government chose to prioritize a domestic electronics industry. To jump-start the sector, it created a state-owned enterprise known as the Taiwan Semiconductor Manufacturing Company. This basic-research enterprise developed technology and components for some of Taiwan's newly emerging private companies. Some private companies that benefitted from this government initiative, and would produce electronic products for the world market, were Acer, Asus, and Foxconn. Foxconn is a primary manufacturer of Apples' iPhones.

Basic research might not be immediately profitable, but, as in this example, often it will produce new technologies that can be turned into profitable goods and services. Today, the funding of basic research is a key function of governments in the information-technology age. Taiwan also established—and funded—science and industrial parks in several of its larger cities. Most business activity in these parks is devoted to research related to information technology, and biotechnology—leading sectors in contemporary high-income economies.

Our third Tiger economy is Singapore, where the role of government was again crucial; albeit authoritarian one-party government. Lee Kuan Yew, Singapore's leader after independence, was educated at the London School of Economics and Cambridge University—and adamant in his drive to educate fellow citizens. Early in his administration, Lee Kuan Yew invited select Western technology companies to Singapore to instruct his countrymen on the organizations' best practices. Among the companies who came, and became eligible for special treatment on taxes, profits, and property, were Texas Instruments, General Electric, and Hewlett-Packard.

Singapore also developed expertise in shipping and logistics. The former British Royal Naval base there provided basic infrastructure for what was about to become the age of container shipping. In addition, foreign bankers were invited to set up subsidiaries in Singapore. These arrivals formed the nucleus of one of the major banking and financial centers of Asia. And the British colonial legacy of the English language was invaluable. English is the language of international finance, and has been since the City of London began bankrolling British imperialism in the 18th century.

A strongman himself, Lee Kuan Yew was obsessed with creating a strong and independent Singapore so that it would never again suffer the humiliations of colonialism. Today, Singapore is an interesting mix of private and public property. Most of its banks, shipping companies, and electronics firms are privately owned. You can buy shares in them on the Singapore Stock Exchange.

However, there's extensive state ownership of property and other assets, too. Almost all of Singapore's residential land and housing is publicly owned and controlled. Neighborhoods are developed to house both rich and poor together. Being a rather small city-state with more five million people, high-rise apartments abound. Neighborhoods are planned with adequate gardens and parks. Public transportation is virtually spotless and efficient. Automobile traffic is strictly controlled, and so-called congestion fees limit auto trips.

Harvard economist, Edward Glaeser describes the Singapore model as "close to an ideal" form of urban development, although some of its own citizens refer to it as the "City of Complaints." And I must say reiterate that all three Tiger countries have been less than democratically governed. In each, democracy is a relatively recent and not fully established movement.

So, was the trade-off worth it? Was it an equitable exchange, giving up democracy for rapid economic development?

My impression is that most citizens of South Korea, Taiwan, and Singapore would say yes. And even if they wouldn't, as beneficiaries of this sacrifice, their parents, and grandparents very likely would. Yet now that the Tigers have achieved higher standards of living, it's human nature to want more control over your lives—and countries.

Lecture 23

European Union: Success or Failure?

T HE EUROPEAN UNION (EU) HAS BEEN BOTH A GREAT
success and a disappointing failure. Established
by a succession of treaties beginning in 1951,
the EU has been spectacularly successful in its
primary mission: the prevention of war among
the major European powers. Yet another
success of the EU has been the peaceful and
largely successful transformation of former
dictatorships and former communist states
to modern democracies. The failures of the
EU include its inability to sustain increasing
incomes and opportunity for everyone. Several
regions and pockets of Europe have suffered
disproportionately from the forces of globalization
and from increased international competition. ◆

The Creation of the European Union

◀ The European Union owes much of its foundation to the United States, and especially the post–World War II economic policies of the Truman administration. But some of the solutions Europe introduced during and after World War II are a direct result of earlier, failed policy prescriptions.

◀ Specifically, after World War I, the victorious French and British governments insisted that the Allied powers should impose heavy reparation burdens on the defeated Axis economies—especially Germany. The French and British also imposed high tariffs on the imports from other countries, and they set the values of their currencies too high relative to the price of gold and thus made their exports too expensive.

Since World War II, there has been peace among the European powers, and sustained growth and prosperity have brought most Europeans unprecedented levels of well-being. The European Union can be thanked for this.

◀ After World War II, the U.S. government took a much more active and enlightened approach to postwar policy in Europe than its European allies had previously. Congress and the administration created a project called the European Recovery Program, or Marshall Plan, which offered U.S. taxpayer funds to all combatant countries in Europe, winners and losers alike. And the recipient countries were required to create a common organization to administer these funds. This umbrella body became the Organisation of European Economic Co-operation.

◀ With the help mainly of the British, especially the economist John Maynard Keynes—a key advisor to Winston Churchill—the United States also led the way in establishing the International Monetary Fund (IMF), which became a vehicle for establishing a system of fixed exchange rates among all the major currencies of western Europe, North America, and Japan.

◀ In turn, this cooperative currency arrangement was a precursor of EU monetary unification years later, in 1999. Among other early advantages, the postwar system of fixed exchange rates prevented countries from practicing competitive devaluations of their currencies.

◀ Competitive devaluations were an especially harmful practice during the Great Depression years of the 1930s. Countries would drive down the value of their own currency in a bid to increase exports and decrease imports. But this practice works only if just one country is devaluing.

◀ In practice, if one country tries to gain an advantage by depreciating its currency, then other countries might do the same out of self-defense. This results in chaos and the breakdown of international trade and finance. It illustrates a principle known as the fallacy of composition—the false belief that if something is good for one actor, it will be beneficial for all actors.

◀ Another postwar economic accord with significant lasting effects was the 1947 General Agreement on Tariffs and Trade (GATT), which fostered lower trade barriers and the freer flow of goods among participating countries. It was yet another proposed solution to failed policy prescriptions of the past—specifically, the imposition of high tariffs by one country to decrease imports from other countries, supposedly to protect domestic businesses and workers. Again, this works only if just one country takes the peremptory action. But other countries almost always follow. If they didn't, their own businesses and workers would be at risk.

◀ For better or worse, each of the postwar policy prescriptions and institutions, including the IMF and GATT, were designed to make market-based economies work better. While social democratic politicians—that is, those who seek to promote social justice within a capitalist framework—were involved in the creation of the EU, it was nevertheless intentionally designed to make private businesses more stable, efficient, and dynamic.

◀ The EU was erected through a series of treaties that led to greater and greater degrees of economic integration. As economies become closer, their populations trade more with one another and they invest in each other's economy, allow (or insist on) businesses and workers moving between the countries, and tend to reduce trade barriers.

Stages of Economic Integration

◀ The process of economic integration can be modeled in four stages, as was first described by the Canadian economist Jacob Viner, who viewed these four stages through increasing levels of economic integration: a free-trade area, a customs union, a formal common market, and an economic and monetary union.

1   The first stage is a free-trade area. This reflects an agreement between two or more countries to remove trade barriers between their economies. That limited framework of cooperation notwithstanding, no common tariffs or quotas apply to countries outside of the free-trade agreement.

2   The second stage is a customs union. It adds a common external tariff and quota policy. In Europe, the 1958 Treaty of Rome established a customs union among the original six-member states of the European Economic Community (EEC): West Germany, France, Italy, Belgium, the Netherlands, and Luxembourg. In 1973, the EEC added the United Kingdom, the Republic of Ireland, and Denmark. Greece was admitted to the EEC in 1981, and Portugal and Spain were admitted in 1986.

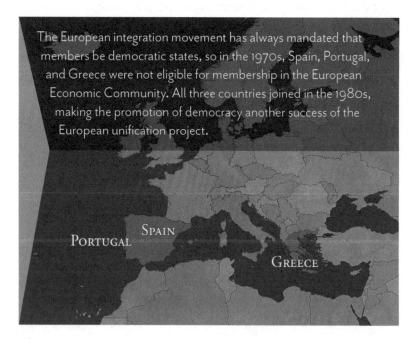

The European integration movement has always mandated that members be democratic states, so in the 1970s, Spain, Portugal, and Greece were not eligible for membership in the European Economic Community. All three countries joined in the 1980s, making the promotion of democracy another success of the European unification project.

3 The third stage is a formal common market, which includes not only the free movement of goods among member states but also the free movement of labor, capital, and services. In Europe, this stage was created in 1986 by the Single European Act, which was designed to increase competition, promote efficiency, and establish a bigger market. Under this act, new sources of workers within the EU could seek employment in the United Kingdom from Poland, Romania, Bulgaria, and elsewhere.

4 The fourth stage—which the EU was ready to begin in the early 1990s—is an economic and monetary union. This phase was established by the Maastricht Treaty, or the Treaty on European Union, whose main purpose was to create a single currency and a central bank. It also changed the name of the European Economic Community to the European Union.

> The perception that the European Union is some kind of socialist organization is not true. In fact, member states often argue among themselves that the EU is much too focused on the interests of corporations and not sufficiently concerned with the interests of workers.

A Single European Currency

◀ The desire for a single European currency began in August 1971, when the United States, under President Richard Nixon, abandoned the World War II–era Bretton Woods system of fixed exchange rates. Under floating rates, flows of goods, services, capital, and people among closely integrated EU member states could be highly disruptive.

- Under a floating-rate regime, the Sofitel hotel in Berlin would earn German marks and then have to convert its receipts to French francs either before or after the funds were sent back to corporate headquarters in Paris. If the exchange values of the German mark and French franc were constantly changing, this would create havoc with bookkeeping, taxes, and planning.

- The process to create the single currency and the European Central Bank was methodically laid out and minutely planned. The Maastricht Treaty is 253 pages long, and one of its most important and controversial components is the criteria imposed on each member state for entry and conduct. There are budget criteria, inflation criteria, and interest rate criteria.

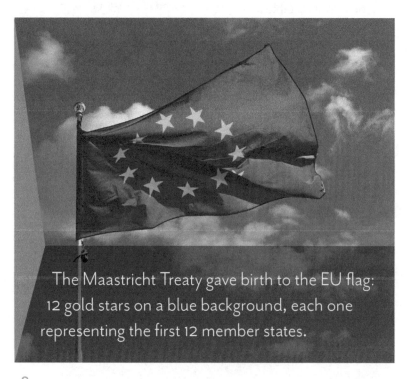

The Maastricht Treaty gave birth to the EU flag: 12 gold stars on a blue background, each one representing the first 12 member states.

◀ Member states had to meet stringent budget requirements to participate in what became known as the Eurosystem. Public budget deficits—the national fiscal deficit—could not exceed three percent of gross domestic product. Total public debt—the aggregate of all stage borrowing—was not to exceed 60 percent of gross domestic product. Inflation was not to be higher than 1.5 percent of the average inflation rate of the three lowest-inflation member states.

◀ These very specific percentages were put in to placate the nervous Germans. The German government and monetary authorities were extremely reluctant to give up their valuable Deutschmark. They feared that a monetary system partially controlled by the Italians, Spaniards, and Greeks would be unstable and prone to inflation.

◀ Of the 12 countries who signed the Maastricht Treaty, only one— the United Kingdom—chose not to join the single currency. That now seems like a harbinger of the Brexit vote. All other member states gave up national control of domestic money supply, interest rates, and exchange rates.

◀ They also gave up some room to maneuver with regard to fiscal policy. In cases of severe recession, such as the financial markets crisis of 2007 to 2009, they were hamstrung in their ability to promote spending to counteract the slump in economic activity.

◀ This was particularly onerous for Greece and Spain, both of which suffered severe levels of unemployment, reaching upward of 25 percent of the labor force. Pensions, unemployment benefits, student stipends, and family benefits had to be cut. This was due to the mandate that budget deficits could not be increased above three percent of gross domestic product. Severe human suffering resulted from some quite arbitrary rules that had very little logical or economic basis.

- The Canadian American economist Robert Mundell predicted this disastrous result arising from his Nobel Prize–winning research on the subject of optimal currency areas. Mundell concluded that Europe, unlike the United States, was not an area well suited for a single currency.

- Mundell believes that America is better suited for a single currency for two basic reasons. First, labor and capital are pretty mobile in the United States; if unemployment increases in Michigan, it's not difficult for workers to move to Texas. Second, if one state in the United States is suffering from declining income and tax revenues, the pensions and unemployment benefits for its residents don't have to be cut.

- The economist Paul Krugman, in one of his *New York Times* columns, compared Florida to Greece. During the financial markets crisis, the U.S. government transferred billions of dollars to Florida residents in the form of Social Security benefits. The state of Florida does not have to fund the Social Security payments to its residents. Therefore, although the state of Florida does have to cut some spending due to the recession, the older residents of Florida do not have their federal pensions cut.

- The Greek government was the source of pension payments to its older citizens. Due to the effects of the Great Recession and the EU mandate to limit budget deficits, the Greek government had to cut the pension payments to its older citizens. There were no funds from the EU budget to provide money for Greek pensions.

- Europe's single currency does have enormous benefits, as well as some drawbacks. For multinational U.S. businesses who do business throughout the eurozone, it is much easier to manage exchange costs—and do accounting and planning—in one currency instead of several.

◀ Whether all of Europe will eventually adopt a single currency and complete the process of economic integration is a political choice as well as an economic one. The EU operates on democratic principles and cannot force its member states to adopt the euro or proceed along the path to further economic and political integration. The citizens of the member states have the power to decide the future of the EU.

Readings

DE GRAUWE, *Economics of Monetary Union.*
REID, *The United States of Europe.*

Questions

1 What are the real successes of the European Union, and why do these successes owe quite a lot to U.S. policy in the aftermath of World War II?

2 How do the particular requirements for joining the Eurosystem create real problems for member states who are suffering during recessions and depressions?

European Union: Success or Failure?

T he European Union has been both a great success and disappointing failure. Established by a succession of treaties beginning in 1951, the EU has been—I'm willing to say—spectacularly successful in its primary mission: the prevention of war among the major European powers. So, when I refer to the EU as spectacularly successful—in almost the same breath as stating that a unified Europe has been a disappointing failure—I'm underscoring the fact that since World War II, there has been peace among the European powers; and that sustained growth and prosperity have brought most Europeans unprecedented levels of well-being.

Yet another success of the European Union has been the peaceful—and largely successful—transformation of former dictatorships, and former communist states, to modern democracies. In western Europe, the military dictatorship of Greece, Spain, and Portugal have long since been transformed into functioning democracies. In eastern Europe, the communist nations locked behind the Iron Curtain before 1989 have become more prosperous parliamentary states. And this transition has been immensely aided by European Union money and expertise.

But that's the good news. Now for the bad news. The failures of the European Union include its inability to sustain increasing incomes and opportunity for everyone. Several regions—and pockets—of Europe have suffered disproportionately from the forces of globalization; and from increased international competition. I'll return to discuss the structural basis of these failures in just a bit.

The European Union owes much of its foundation to the United States, and especially the post-World War II economic policies of the Truman administration. But some of the solutions Europe introduced during and after World War II are a direct result of earlier, failed policy prescriptions. Specifically, after World War I, the victorious French and British governments insisted that the Allied powers should impose heavy reparation burdens on the defeated Axis economies—especially Germany.

The French and British also imposed high tariffs on the imports from other countries. And they set the values of their currencies too high, relative to the price of gold, and thus made their exports too expensive.

John Locke, the 17th-century English philosopher, once said, "No man's knowledge...can go beyond his experience." And perhaps this is as true of the post-World War II environment as it was of the post-World War I political equation. After World War II, the United States government took a much more active and enlightened approach to post-war policy in Europe than its European allies had done previously.

Congress and the administration created a project called the European Recovery Program—or Marshall Plan—which offered U.S. taxpayer funds to all combatant countries in Europe, winners and losers alike. And, in a stroke of real genius, the recipient countries were required to create a common organization to administer these funds. This umbrella body became the Organization for European Economic Cooperation, or OEEC.

With the help mainly of the British, especially the economist John Maynard Keynes—a key advisor to Winston Churchill—the United States also led the way in establishing the International Monetary Fund. The IMF became a vehicle for establishing a system of fixed exchange rates among all the major currencies of western Europe, North America, and Japan. In turn, this cooperative currency arrangement was a precursor of EU monetary unification years later, in 1999. Among other early advantages, the post-war system of fixed exchange rates prevented countries from practicing competitive devaluations of their currencies.

Competitive devaluations were an especially harmful practice during the Depression years of the 1930s. Countries would drive down the value of their own currency in a bid to increase exports and decrease imports. But this practice works only if just one country is devaluing. In practice, if one country tries to gain an advantage by depreciating its currency, then other countries might do the same out of self-defense. This results in chaos, and the breakdown of international trade and finance. It illustrates a principle known as the "fallacy of composition"—the false belief that if something is good for one actor, it will be beneficial for all actors.

Another post-war economic accord—with significant lasting effects—was the General Agreement on Tariffs and Trade, in October 1947. GATT fostered lower trade barriers and the freer flow of goods among participating countries. It was yet another proposed solution to failed policy prescriptions of the past; specifically, the imposition of high tariffs by one country to decrease imports from other countries, supposedly to protect domestic businesses and workers. Again, this works only if just one country takes the peremptory action. But other countries almost always follow. If they didn't, their own businesses and workers would be at risk.

For better or worse, each of the post-war policy prescriptions and institutions—the IMF and World Bank, GATT, and the cans of alphabet soup that came with them—were designed to make market-based economies work better.

What you think about these initiatives may reflect your own philosophic viewpoint, across the spectrum. But it's worth pointing out that while social democratic politicians were involved in the creation of the European Union—that is, those who seek to promote social justice within a capitalist framework—the EU was nevertheless intentionally designed to make private businesses more stable, efficient, and dynamic. And if the EU truly were a socialist organization—as is sometimes argued—then Porsche, Louis Vuitton, Danone, and Accor hotels, among others, probably wouldn't be world class corporations they are.

The European Union was erected through a series of treaties that led to greater and greater degrees of economic integration. As economies become closer, their populations trade more with one another; they invest in each other's economy; they allow—or insist upon—businesses and workers moving between the countries; and they tend to reduce trade barriers.

The process of economic integration can be modeled in four stages, as was first described by the late Canadian economist Jacob Viner, who taught at the University of Chicago and Princeton. Viner viewed these four stages through increasing levels of economic integration: The first stage is a free-trade area. This reflects an agreement between two or more countries to remove trade barriers between their economies. That limited framework of cooperation notwithstanding, no common tariffs or quotas apply to countries outside of the free trade agreement. The North American Free

Trade Agreement between the United States, Canada, and Mexico is one example of a free-trade area. While most trade barriers between the three NAFTA economies were reduced, or eliminated, these countries' trade policies toward non-NAFTA countries remained completely independent.

The second stage of cross-border economic integration is a customs union. It adds a common external tariff and quota policy. In Europe, the 1958 Treaty of Rome established a customs union among the original six-member states of the European Economic Community: West Germany, France, Italy, Belgium, the Netherlands, and Luxembourg.

Notice that these consisted of three large economies and three smaller ones; and three republics and three constitutional monarchies. I point out the foregoing because this is always a bonus trivia question on my exams. Be prepared.

You might also have noticed that the United Kingdom was not an original member state. This was primarily due to the determination of the French president, Charles de Gaulle, to keep the British out. He feared that Great Britain's close relationship with the United States would give the U.S. too much influence in the fledgling European-integration process. The U.K. eventually was invited to join the EEC, and so in 1973—after de Gaulle's death.

British entry into the EEC was led by the Conservative Prime Minister Edward Heath. Heath represented the international business faction within Britain's Conservative Party. These were outward-looking British capitalists who saw the European market as a promising area of sales and investment. British Petroleum, Rolls Royce aircraft engines, Unilever, Shell Oil, and HSBC were all large U.K. corporations that expected to benefit from a larger European market.

Even though the EEC was labeled a customs union by economists—reflecting the second stage of cross-border integration—it was usually referred to (incorrectly) as a common market. I'll explain more in a minute. One real challenge in teaching European Union economics is keeping all the labels and abbreviations straight. So, please bear with me.

As EEC integration was progressing, the organization also kept expanding membership. In 1973, the EEC added not only the United Kingdom but also the Republic of Ireland, and Denmark. So, in 1973 EEC membership stood at nine member-states. The European integration movement has always mandated that members be democratic states. So, in the 1970's, Spain, Portugal, and Greece were not eligible for membership.

At the time, Spain was ruled by Generalissimo Francisco Franco and Portugal by Antonio de Oliveira Salazar—both of whom came to power through army overthrows of democratically elected governments. Greece was led by a group of army colonels. Now, Salazar was overthrown in 1974. Franco died in 1975, and the Spanish king, Juan Carlos prevented a coup to maintain military dictatorship. Greece was admitted to the EEC in 1981. Portugal and Spain in 1986. So, another success of the European unification project has been its promotion of democracy.

The third stage of economic integration that Jacob Viner identified is a formal common market, which includes not only the free movement of goods among member states but also the free movement of labor, capital, and services. The old EEC had established a customs union, but it was not so comprehensive as a fully developed common market.

In Europe, this third—more comprehensive—stage was created in 1986 by something known as the Single European Act. Most of its provisions were fulfilled by 1992. This step meant not only that French goods could be sold freely in Germany but also that French workers could work in Germany; French companies could locate subsidiaries in Germany; and French companies could sell services in Germany. The French hotelier Sofitel could own accommodations in Munich; the French telephone company Orange could sell services in Frankfurt; and the French bank Societe General could make loans to German businesses and German consumers. You can see some obvious advantages to businesses and consumers from this market widening. German borrowers would now have more banks competing for their business. Better service and lower interest rates should be the result. For French businesses, this meant more customers—and more profit potential. Obviously, there are costs as well. Some businesses would lose, and possibly go out of business.

The Single European Act was designed to increase competition, promote efficiency, and establish a bigger market. This larger market was believed necessary for European businesses to achieve what micro economists call "economies of scale." Economies of scale refers to the process of reducing per-unit costs as production levels increase. In my classes, I call it the "Henry Ford" effect. First, I have to explain who Henry Ford was. But, after that, students get it. You make more cars and the cost per unit goes down.

One example of European economies of scale is the creation of Airbus, a consortium of German, British, Spanish, and French aerospace companies. Back in the beginning, the individual national markets of Germany, France, and Britain were thought not large enough to support the production of large commercial aircraft, or to compete with a U.S. manufacturer like Boeing. Today, Airbus headquarters are in Toulouse, France, and production occurs in all four countries. And at the risk of sounding ungrateful to my hometown airplane manufacturer Boeing, now based in Chicago, my favorite plane to fly in is the Airbus A-340. I get in huge arguments with my friend Jack, a pilot for United Airlines, whose slogan is: "If it ain't Boeing, I ain't going."

The banana wars of the 1990s illustrates another colorful example of trade competition—even combat—between the United States and Europe. Some years ago, the French persuaded the rest of the EU to give preferential treatment to the imports from its former colonies and current overseas departments. These countries were known as the ACAP group—Africa, Caribbean, and Pacific economies—and one of their chief exports to the European Union nations is bananas. The U.S.-based Chiquita Brands International—formerly known as the United Fruit Company, and among the most important companies in Central American during an age when they were known as banana republics—was put at a competitive disadvantage by the EU trade preference. Chiquita convinced the Clinton administration to act. And it did so, slapping tariffs on French cognac and Scottish cashmere in retaliation.

The Clinton administration then brought the dispute before the World Trade Organization in Geneva, Switzerland. The WTO is the successor to the General Agreement on Tariffs and Trade (one of those World War II-era institutions I mentioned earlier). It was a slippery case—banana peel and all—but eventually the World Trade Organization ruled in the United States' favor, and Chiquita bananas were once more prominent in European supermarkets.

But the dispute arises from yet another example of the European Union, and its member states, promoting the interests of European capitalist businesses. I keep harping on this because I constantly hear the EU referred to as some kind of socialist organization. It's most definitely not that. Instead, member states often argue among themselves that the EU is much too focused on the interests of corporations, and not sufficiently concerned with the interests of workers.

This perception—that the EU is mostly about big business—is an important reason that the organization, and membership in it, eventually lost the support of much of the British Labour Party. When former British Prime Minister Tony Blair was in power from 1997 to 2007, his Labour Party largely supported the EU. Many of Blair's constituents were young, urban, well-educated Brits who worked in banking, advertising, management consulting, and design in the City of London. These 30-somethings would pop over to Brussels and Paris on the Chunnel train for a business meeting and a croque-monsieur sandwich.

More traditional Labour Party stalwarts consisted of steel workers, coal miners, and ship builders who were much less enthusiastic about European integration. Their industries were decimated by globalization. And not all this harm came from the EU. Some came from Asia. But these guys were nevertheless upset as they groused into pints of bitters at their local pubs. And they were among the core voters in the June 2016 Brexit vote to end British membership in the European Union. Of course, some of the pro-Brexit vote was also motivated by racism and xenophobia against new immigrants to the European Union, and to Britain itself.

Under the Single European Act—bringing the free movement of workers—new sources of workers within the EU could seek employment in the U.K. from Poland, Romania, Bulgaria, and elsewhere. The issue of internal immigration within the European Union became known euphemistically as the "Polish plumber" problem: skilled, motivated Polish plumbers taking working class jobs.

We had something like this Texas after the Vietnam War. Vietnamese immigrant fishermen arrived in the Gulf Coast, and worked hard catching shrimp and crawfish. Their incomes in Texas were fabulously higher than they had been in Vietnam. And many of these fishermen worked hard to enjoy the benefits of their work. Needless to say, the good ol' boys who had been fishing a long time by then were upset by the new competition.

My favorite EU program promoting the free movement of peoples is known as the Erasmus Student Network. Under this initiative, the EU subsidizes students who seek to study at universities outside their home country in Europe. At my own university in the Chicago area, we have some Polish exchange students, for example; and many of them have been Erasmus students.

Malgorzata, a student at the Warsaw School of Economics—and, for one semester, an exchange student at my university in Chicago—studied for a year at the University of Brussels. She now works for the European Commission in Brussels. Kamil, a student at the University of Warsaw, and also a former exchange student of mine, also studied at the Charles University in Prague. He is now a public relations specialist back home in Warsaw. The Erasmus program seeks to promote a European identity among young people while also giving these future professionals valuable exposure to other cultures and economic systems.

There is an excellent French movie that gently pokes fun at the Erasmus experience. The movie is *L'Auberge Espagnole*, known in English as *The Spanish Apartment*. It features a combination of stereotypical Germans, very serious philosophical French, romantic Spaniards, and drunken Englishmen. The most unlikeable of them all is a visiting American student.

Returning to my principal storyline, the European Union—after adding Greece, Portugal, and Spain—the EU was ready to begin the fourth stage of economic integration, beginning in the early 1990s. The fourth stage of economic integration is an economic and monetary union. This phase was established by the Maastricht Treaty—its more formal title is the Treaty on European Union—signed in the lovely little Dutch town of Maastricht on 7 February 1992. For the Maastricht Treaty to be valid, it had to be approved and signed by all 12 member states at the time. Some of these countries chose general elections to ratify it. The votes were often very close. The French approved the Maastricht Treaty by a narrow margin of 52 percent to 48 percent.

The treaty's main purpose was to create a single currency, and a European central bank. But it also changed the name of the European Economic Community, or EEC, to the European Union. And it gave birth to the EU flag: 12 gold stars on a blue background, each one representing the first 12 member states. There's also an official European Union anthem. It's the third movement of Beethoven's Ninth Symphony—the "Ode to Joy"—based upon the poem by Friedrich Schiller. I would sing a little but that would crack whatever device you are watching this on.

The desire for a single European currency began about in August 1971when the United States—under President Richard Nixon—abandoned the World War II-era Bretton Woods system of fixed exchange rates. Under floating rates, flows of goods, services, capital, and people among closely integrated EU member states could be highly disruptive. Under a floating-rate regime, the Sofitel Hotel in Berlin would earn German marks, and then have to convert its receipts to French francs either before, or after, the funds were sent back to corporate headquarters in Paris. If the exchange values of the German mark and French franc were constantly changing, this would create havoc with bookkeeping, taxes, and planning.

The process to create the single currency and the European Central bank was methodically laid out, and minutely planned. The Maastricht Treaty itself is 253 pages long. One of its most important and controversial components is the criteria imposed on each member state for entry and conduct. There are budget criteria, inflation criteria, and interest-rate criteria. Member states had to meet stringent budget requirements to participate in what became known as the Eurosystem. Public budget deficits—the national fiscal deficit—could not exceed 3 percent of gross domestic product. Total public debt—that is the aggregate of all stage borrowing—was not to exceed 60 percent of gross domestic product. Inflation was not to be higher than 1.5 percent of the average inflation rate of the three lowest-inflation member states.

You might be asking how were these very specific percentages decided? The answer is that they were more or less picked out of the air, and put in to placate the nervous Germans. The German government and monetary authorities were extremely reluctant to give up their valuable deutschmark. They feared that a monetary system partially controlled by the Italians, Spaniards, and Greeks would be unstable, and prone to inflation. Of the 12 countries who signed the Maastricht Treaty, only one—the United Kingdom—chose not to join the single currency. That now seems to be a harbinger of the Brexit vote.

All other member states gave up national control of domestic money supply, interest rates, and exchange rates. They also gave up some room to maneuver with regard to fiscal policy. In cases of severe recession, like the financial markets crisis of 2007-2009, they were hamstrung in their ability to promote spending to counteract the slump in economic activity.

This was particularly onerous for the Greeks and Spaniards. Greece and Spain both suffered severe levels of unemployment, reaching upwards of 25 percent of the labor force. Pensions, unemployment benefits, student stipends, and family benefits had to be cut. This was due to the mandate that budget deficits could not be increased above 3 percent of GDP. Severe human suffering resulted from some quite arbitrary rules that had very little logical or economic basis.

The Canadian-American economist Robert Mundell predicted this disastrous result from his Nobel Prize winning research on the subject of optimal currency areas. Mundell concluded that Europe, unlike the United States, was not an area well-suited for a one single currency. Mundell believes that America is better suited for a single currency for two basic reasons. First, labor and capital are pretty mobile in the United States. If unemployment increases in Michigan, it's not so hard for workers to move to Texas. Second, if one state in the United States is suffering from declining income and tax revenues, the pensions and unemployment benefits for its residents don't have to be cut.

The economist Paul Krugman, in one of his *New York Times* columns, has compared Florida to Greece. Here's why: during the financial markets crisis, the U.S. government transferred billions of dollars to Florida residents in the form of Social Security benefits. The state of Florida does not have to fund the Social Security payments to its residents. Therefore, although the state of Florida does have to cut some spending due to the recession, the older residents of Florida do not have their federal pensions cut.

The Greek government was the source of pension payments to its older citizens. Due to the effects of the Great Recession and the EU mandate to limit budget deficits, the Greek government had to cut the pension payments to its older citizens. There were no funds from the EU budget to provide money for Greek pensions. Of course, Europe's single currency does have some enormous benefits, as well as some drawbacks.

I sometimes joke to the students I take on foreign study trips to Europe that the euro was created just for them. In January of 2002 just after the euro came into circulation, I took students to Amsterdam, Brussels, and Paris. We only had to change money once. Before 2002, we would have needed Dutch guilders, Belgian francs, and French francs.

We saved money on exchange fees, and we saved a lot of time. We didn't have to stand in line at currency exchanges or ATM machines waiting for each student to change their Dutch guilders to Belgian francs. Imagine the benefit to multinational U.S. businesses who do business throughout the Eurozone. Think of how much easier it is for them to manage exchange costs—and how much simpler it is to do accounting and planning—in one currency instead of several of them.

Will all of Europe eventually adopt a single currency and complete the process of economic integration? This is a political choice as well as an economic one. The European Union operates on democratic principles, and cannot force its member states to adopt the euro or proceed along the path to further economic and political integration.

The citizens of the member states have the power to decide the future of the European Union. And this is how it should be!

Lecture 24

Both Sides Now: Experiment in Slovenia

COMPARATIVE ECONOMICS IS THE STUDY OF different systems of economic organization—notably capitalism, socialism, communism, and mixed economies. Today, debates about the nature of capitalism, socialism, and communism—and whether any or all of them can be reformed to function better in the interests of the general population—are common. What is the best path forward? In this lecture, a small central European country provides us with some clues about the future. ◆

A Brief History of Slovenia

◀ Slovenia was a sliver of the Habsburg Empire for nearly 1,000 years, right up until World War I. After the war—torn between the forces of assimilation and independence—these south Slavic people (along with ethnic Croats and Serbs) hitched their star to what became the Kingdom of Yugoslavia, beginning in 1918. Later, during World War II, much of Yugoslavia was occupied by Nazi Germany and temporarily broke up as the Croats formed a Nazi-allied independent state.

◀ Under the communist partisan forces of Josip Broz Tito, Yugoslavia then reunited and broke away from Soviet influence in 1948. In 1961, Tito's Yugoslavia became a founder of the Non-Aligned Movement, which pursued a less orthodox path to communism than in the Soviet Union and east bloc.

◀ In June 1991, six months before the Soviets' ultimate collapse, Slovenia declared its independence from the disintegrating Yugoslav federation. A little more than a decade later, in May 2004, it completed its reorientation by joining the European Union (EU) and adopting the euro.

◀ Today, in many ways, Slovenia is attempting to be a modern, mixed economy with significant roles for private initiative, private property, and market incentives. But even as some Slovene citizens embrace participation in a European social market economy, others prefer to look backward to what they perceive as a more secure, and less stressful, socialist economy.

Slovenia's Rapid Transition

◀ Slovenia made a rapid transition in recent decades from a socialist economy to a modern, middle-income market economy. It started on this path with many advantages, including both geography and history.

◀ As part of the former Austro-Hungarian Empire, Slovenia had always been linked to the important economies of central Europe. It borders Austria to the north and Italy to the west, and as the richest of the six constituent republics of the former Yugoslavia, and the one most involved in foreign trade, this strategic location helps us understand why.

◀ At one time, Slovenia accounted for less than 10 percent of Yugoslavia's population yet produced more than 20 percent of the country's gross domestic product and accounted for 40 percent of its exports.

◀ Another advantage the Slovenes enjoyed over many of their Slav neighbors is a language that employs the Latin alphabet, unlike Serbo-Croatian, which uses the Cyrillic alphabet. This gave it a linguistic advantage over the rest of Yugoslavia in adapting to the global language of English.

◀ The Yugoslav leader Josip Broz adopted the nickname "Tito" in the 1930s, when he rose to prominence as one of the leaders of the Communist Party of Yugoslavia. Because the party was illegal, it had to operate underground—and anonymously.

> Throughout Europe in the 1930s, communist leaders often used nicknames to conceal their identities: Vladimir Illyich Ulyanov became Lenin, Lev Davidovich Bronshtein became Trotsky, and Ioseb Dzhugashvili became Stalin.

◀ During World War II, Tito led his army of Yugoslav partisans in the fight against Germany and Italy as well as against domestic fascists and royalists. The partisans were victorious, and Tito would end up leading Yugoslavia from 1945 until his death in 1980.

◀ He was able to break with the Soviet Union in part because he had his own army and had not been put in power by the Soviet Red Army. He also succeeded at creating his own version of communism, which was not as inefficient or stagnant as elsewhere in the eastern bloc.

◀ Still, Tito did adopt many components of the classic communist system. He led a one-party dictatorship that tolerated little dissent. And while communism promises equality, Tito was a bit more equal than all the rest of his fellow Yugoslavs, owning villas, a yacht, and an airplane.

◀ In contrast to Tito's strict dictatorial political control, he allowed some economic freedom, including a unique system of worker self-management. Each enterprise had some discretion about where to buy its inputs and where to sell its products. These decisions were made based on price and profit. This created—in workers and managers alike—some familiarity with market-oriented decision making that was almost completely absent elsewhere in eastern Europe (where virtually all important economic decisions were governed by central planners).

◀ Yugoslav enterprise managers had some knowledge of how markets determine prices and profits, and the Slovenes, in particular, had more of this knowledge than other Yugoslavs because they had constant exposure to the prices of the goods, services, and resources in their trade with Austria, Italy, and West Germany.

◀ That said, Yugoslavia's system of worker self-management was not without its idiosyncrasies. When workers have a say in how wages should be set and profit goals are determined, wages are pretty high—and profits are rather low.

◀ On the other hand, one of the real drawbacks of Soviet-style central planning was its emphasis on production, without equal consideration of input costs and markets. Soviet enterprises were evaluated on output. Whether the products actually sold, or were useful, was a secondary question.

◀ In the Soviet system, there was almost no incentive to limit resource use. In fact, the incentive was to accumulate—and use—as many resources as possible. More labor resources and stockpiled supplies, for example, meant greater ability to meet production targets.

◀ In the Yugoslav system, by comparison, enterprises could keep a large part of the profits they generated. This incentivized managers and workers to economize on their resources. Resource conservation, in terms of power and raw materials, meant lower costs and higher earnings, whereas hiring more workers meant a smaller slice of the profit share.

◀ Another lasting value of worker self-management is the shared sense of equality and solidarity. Modern production processes tend to turn on team efforts. You need many skills and individuals to produce most goods and services. Workers know this. Everybody working with the team is valuable. They are also human beings, with individual dignity.

◀ Tito emphasized his independence by leading the Non-Aligned Movement of countries, along with Egypt under Gamar Abdel Nasser and Indonesia under Sukarno. By playing both sides in the Cold War against each other, the Non-Aligned countries gained benefits from both sides.

Slovenia's Economy

◀ The Slovenian economy's many differences uniquely poised it to take advantage of the eventual fall of the Yugoslav federation.

◀ At the time of independence, Slovenia had three times the per capita gross domestic product of fellow ex-communist states Poland, Hungary, and Czechoslovakia and was at a level of income and development not far behind Portugal. But do all the factors contributing to Slovenia's economic and social success have to do with adopting a free market, capitalist system? Or have the Slovenes continued some of their own unique values? The answers to these questions—to the extent we have them—are complicated.

◀ Slovenia adopted a market economy with private property and monetary incentives, and it also became even more oriented to international trade. But it also retained some of the solidarity and cohesion of a more socially oriented system.

◀ To be admitted to the EU, a country must meet three basic criteria, known as the Copenhagen criteria, adopted by the EU before the accession of some of the former communist countries of eastern Europe in 2004. The three Copenhagen criteria were parliamentary democracy, human rights, and a market-based economy.

1 Parliamentary democracy means freedom for political parties and voting based on nondiscriminatory eligibility of citizens. Russia would fail to meet these criteria today.

2 Human rights mean equality for women and religious, ethnic, and national minorities. It also means the abolition of capital punishment. The United States fails to meet these criteria.

3 A market-based economy means support for private enterprise and private property. It does not mean the abolition of all state property or the elimination of government regulation. It means that the majority of production and consumption decisions are made on the basis of enterprise profit and consumer choice. Slovenia met these criteria.

◀ But even after joining the EU, Slovenia and the other former east bloc states had to meet a second set of requirements to adopt the euro in 2007. This was an additional step for Slovenia in its progress to becoming a full member of the European economic integration process.

◀ These additional criteria were established by the 1992 Maastricht Treaty to integrate the European economies. They include guidelines on domestic inflation, interest rates, fiscal deficits, and public debt levels. Slovenia was the first of its eastern peers to meet all these criteria.

◀ In the years since, Slovenia has been a fast globalizer and international trader. Consistent with its history in trade, Slovenia exports a sizeable portion of its gross domestic product—about three-quarters of gross domestic product, according to the Organization for Economic Cooperation and Development (OECD). The OECD average is 28.9 percent. At the same time, as an export engine, Slovenia is heavily dependent on the rest of the world's economies. And that means it gets hit hard when there is a global recession.

Most of the U.S. economy is domestic while most of the Slovenian economy is globalized.

◀ Slovenia has also maintained a strong social safety net—and a high level of economic security—while achieving impressive growth and exports. The Slovenian constitution states that it is a social state, which means that the government takes significant responsibility for the health, welfare, and economic security of the population.

◀ The results of Slovenia's social welfare approach to caring for its population have been impressive. Not only has the life expectancy of Slovenians increased substantially, but measures of social solidarity have also been impressive. For example, the poverty rate is relatively low in Slovenia, even compared to the United States.

◀ Across the world, incomes have been becoming more and more unequal in recent decades. An economist's most commonly used measure of inequality is the Gini coefficient, which can range in value from 0 (meaning complete equality) to 100 (meaning that one person has all the money).

◀ For the OECD countries as a whole, the Gini coefficient is 32, and for the European Union more narrowly, it is 29. In the United States, by comparison, the Gini coefficient is 39 and has been increasing since the early 1980s. In Slovenia, the Gini coefficient is 25—the lowest of all OECD countries.

◀ But you get what you pay for. And the Slovenes pay a lot. As a percentage of total income, the Slovenes pay 44.9 percent of their incomes in taxes. The OECD average is about 40 percent. And of all the OECD countries, the Norwegians pay the most, at 54.8 percent. The United States is one of the lowest-tax countries in the OECD, with the third-lowest rate after Ireland and Mexico.

◀ This reflects an important trade-off between social solidarity and individual economic freedom and independence. In the United States, you can make a lot of money and keep most of it. But all of the trade-offs inherent in competing economic systems are controversial, and there's no definitive answer about what kind of economic system is best. We make choices—from public education, to health care, to taxes, and the social safety net. Different histories, cultures, and values always lead to different choices for a country's economic system.

Are the World's Economies Converging?

Are the world's economies becoming more similar? In other words, is there convergence toward a single economic and political system? Or are the world's economies diverging?

The American political scientist Francis Fukuyama laid out an argument for the idea of convergence in his controversial 1992 book, *The End of History and the Last Man*, in which he predicted that all economies would become private enterprise, deregulated systems with little state ownership or control. But it hasn't turned out that way.

And it's not likely that economic systems will be converging anytime soon. Many different economic systems operate side by side in the world today, and there will probably be many different economic systems far into the distant future.

Readings

DRAKULIC, *Café Europa*.
FUKUYAMA, *The End of History and the Last Man*.

Questions

1 What makes Slovenia such a good example of the benefits of European economic integration and the institutions of a mixed economy? How did Slovenia's unique history prepare it to take advantage of the opportunities it was given by national independence in 1991?

2 Does the Slovenian example provide evidence for all economic systems converging to a single system of free market capitalism as exemplified by the U.S. economy? Is there another economic system that you think would be an ideal system for all the world's economies?

Both Sides Now: Experiment in Slovenia

C an a small central European country like Slovenia provide us with
some clues about the future? Slovenia was a sliver of the Hapsburg
Empire for nearly 1,000 years—right up until World War I. After the war—
torn between the forces of assimilation and independence—these south
Slavic people (along with ethnic Croats and Serbs) hitched their star to
what became the Kingdom of Yugoslavia, beginning in 1918. Later, during
World War II, much of Yugoslavia was occupied by Nazi Germany, and
temporarily broke up as the Croats formed a Nazi-allied independent state.

Under the communist partisan forces of Josip Broz Tito, the "land of the
South"—as Yugoslavia is known in translation—then reunited, and broke
away from Soviet influence in 1948. In 1961, Tito's Yugoslavia became a
founder of the non-aligned movement, which pursued a less orthodox path
to communism than in the Soviet Union and east bloc. And in June 1991,
six months before the Soviets' ultimate collapse, Slovenia declared its
independence from the disintegrating Yugoslav federation. Little more
than a decade later, in May 2004, it completed its reorientation by joining
the European Union and adopting the euro.

Today, in many ways, Slovenia is attempting to be a modern, mixed
economy with significant roles for private initiative, private property,
and market incentives. But even as some Slovene citizens embrace
participation in a European social market economy, others prefer to
look backward to what they perceive as a more secure, and less stressful,
socialist economy. In this way, the Slovenes frame a question many of us
hold about what is the best path forward? More broadly, are the world's
economies becoming more similar? Is there convergence toward a single
economic and political system? Or are the world's economies diverging?

The American political scientist Francis Fukuyama laid out an argument
for the idea of convergence in his controversial 1992 book, *The End of
History and the Last Man*. Fukuyama wrote the book as a celebration
of free-market capitalism and liberal democracy. He predicted that all
economies would become private-enterprise, deregulated systems with

little state ownership or control. Indeed, there was much triumphalism in the United States and Western Europe about how we had "won" the Cold War after the fall of the Berlin Wall in November 1989, and the demise of the Soviet Union in December 1991; and now the rest of the world would be just like us. It hasn't turned out that way.

But if the worlds' economies are not all moving in the same direction—towards one economic system—are those who believe in diverging (rather than converging) systems correct? Do national values and cultures create their own enduring economic systems? Comparative economics is the study of different systems of economic organization, notably capitalism, socialism, communism, and mixed economies. And today, debates about the nature of capitalism, socialism and communism—and whether any or all of them can be reformed to function better in the interests of the general population—are common once more.

As I stated at the outset of this Great Course on comparative economic systems 23 lectures ago, here are some questions that debates about comparative economics seek to answer: What are the goals of a good society? How should societies be organized? What is the best way to make sure that people have a decent standard of living?

Are people best motivated by self-interest and individual success? Or do we have a basic moral sense of solidarity?

Underlying these questions are arguments about: private property versus state ownership, government regulation versus free-market decisions, high taxes versus low taxes on consumption spending and other questions.

The Cold War between the United States and Russia—and between Western Europe and Eastern Europe—dominated the political atmosphere of its time, up to a generation ago. Until then, it was widely assumed that this was a life-and-death struggle between two incompatible systems. In the United States and the West, as most of us are aware, modern capitalism is based upon private property rights. The Scottish classical economist Adam Smith understood the entire system of a commercial economy in terms of the self-interest of private owners of businesses.

The reward of private gain is believed to be what motivates a business owner to produce desired products as efficiently as possible. And without a secure system of property rights, a modern capitalist economy has a very limited foundation, and will not function well.

Paradoxically, as I've also argued, this means that a free-market, private enterprise economy needs a strong government to protect the property rights of its citizens and businesses. Adam Smith was emphatic about the need for governmental roles in providing a national defense, public education, and safeguarding private property, to ensure the proper functioning of a private enterprise economy.

At the same time, the unsatisfactory—and often exploitative—conditions of industrial capitalism beginning in the late 18th century inspired many social and political movements interested in reform. Some were predominantly religious in nature—seeking spiritual inspiration and solution. Others, like the trade unions, had economic orientations with a human face. Many approaches were a mixture—combining political, social, economic and religious answers—to alleviate the miserable conditions of the increasing numbers of the poor, urban working class.

The more religious or philosophical movements got the label of "utopian socialist." And the more political and revolutionary movements referred to themselves as "scientific socialism."

The term utopian socialist probably first was used by Frederick Engels—an intellectual collaborator of Karl Marx—as a pejorative to distinguish between the religious and philosophical movements, and the more revolutionary political movement he and Marx favored. Karl Marx himself left no detailed description of what a real, functioning communist economy should look like. Marx had assumed that communism would first triumph in a modern developed capitalist economy, with sophisticated managers and literate, skilled workers. He certainly didn't envision communism starting in a poor, backward, agricultural, and largely illiterate society such as early 20th-century Russia.

Consequently, the Russian Bolsheviks led by Vladimir Lenin and his peers had to more or less make up their new economic system on their own, when they seized power in October 1917. The Bolsheviks were the prevailing power and a majority faction in the Russian Social Democratic Party, which was renamed the Communist Party after October 1917. The Bolsheviks decided on a system of direct control over the economy, with direct orders to factories and farms. The Bolsheviks' desperation and isolation was a key cause in the development of a political dictatorship at the state level, which, in turn, was to be a dominant feature of Soviet communism—almost to the end of its existence.

Vladimir Lenin and Leon Trotsky accommodated some crude, early forms of democratic socialism—and temporary compromises between communism and capitalism—but the strong man Joseph Stalin, in succeeding them, enforced a more rigid model that oversaw the rapid industrialization of Soviet society—and dramatic results—at great human costs.

Many observers and scholars studying the Soviet system believe today that dictatorship is inherent in any form of socialism or communism. Others contend that the dictatorship in the Soviet Union was created by the unique conditions of Russian and Soviet society. The controversy continues, and is one of the main contentious arguments between supporters and critics of communism.

Turning back to the Republic of Slovenia—one of whose prominent exports after independence was United States First Lady Melania Trump—Slovenia made a rapid transition in recent decades from a socialist economy to a modern, middle-income market economy. It started on this path with many advantages, including both geography and history. As part of the former Austro-Hungarian empire, Slovenia had always been linked to the important economies of central Europe. It borders Austria to the north, and Italy to the west. And as the richest of the six constituent republics of the former Yugoslavia, and the one most involved in foreign trade, this strategic location helps us to understand why.

At one time, Slovenia accounted for less than 10 percent of Yugoslavia's population yet produced more than 20 percent of the country's gross domestic product, and accounted for 40 percent of its exports. Another advantage the Slovenes enjoyed over many of their Slavic neighbors is a language that employs the Latin alphabet, unlike Serbo-Croatian, which uses the Cyrillic alphabet. This gave it a linguistic advantage over the rest of Yugoslavia in adapting to the global language of English. So, if you had to be part of a communist economic system after World War II, your best option probably would have been to be part of Yugoslavia, and, specifically, Slovenia.

The Yugoslav leader Josef Broz adopted the nickname "Tito" in the 1930s when he rose to prominence as one of the leaders of the Yugoslav Communist Party. Because the party was illegal, it had to operate underground—and anonymously. Throughout Europe at this time, communist leaders often used nicknames to conceal their identities. Vladimir Illyich Ulyanov became Lenin. Leon Davidovich Bronstein became Trotsky. And Josef Vissarionovich Djugashvili became Stalin.

During the Second World War, Tito led his army of Yugoslav partisans in the fight against Germany, Italy, as well as against domestic fascists and royalists. The partisans were victorious, and Tito would end up leading Yugoslavia from 1945 until his death in 1980. He was able to break with the Soviet Union in part because he had his own army, and had not been put in power by the Soviet Red Army. He also succeeded at creating his own version of communism, which was not as inefficient or stagnant as elsewhere in the eastern bloc. Still, Tito did adopt many components of the classic communist system. He led a one-party dictatorship that tolerated little dissent. And while communism promises equality, Tito was a bit more equal than all the rest of his fellow Yugoslavs.

One of the more beautiful parts of Slovenia is around the glacial Lake Bled, in an area known as the Julian Alps. It was a Tito favorite. He built a beautiful villa on the lake's shores. I visited this magnificent structure a few years ago. It's now a luxury hotel and conference center. One of most interesting and lavish gathering places in the villa was Tito's movie room. It's a large ballroom painted with garish frescos. Hidden in the eye of one of the painted sea maidens on the back wall is a small hole through which Tito could spy on his fellow movie watchers. Tito had other villas—and a yacht. The Croatian writer Slavenka Drakulic gives an ironic glimpse of one of Tito's villas in her book *A Guided Tour Through the Museum of Communism*. It's narrated by a profanity-laden parrot.

Tito also owned a DC-6 airplane for his personal use. You can visit the plane in Salzburg, Austria, at what is known as Red Bull Hangar-7. Dieter Mateschitz, the creator of Red Bull energy drinks, has built a magnificent museum, restaurant, and bar complex at the Salzburg airport. Along with all his Formula 1 racers, he displays quite a few aircraft in the combination art gallery/hanger.

In contrast to Tito's strict dictatorial political control, he allowed some economic freedom, including a unique system of worker self-management. Each enterprise had some discretion about where to buy its inputs, and where to sell its products. These decisions were made based on price and profit. This created—in workers and managers alike—some familiarity with market-oriented decision-making that was almost completely absent elsewhere in Eastern Europe (where virtually all important economic decisions were governed by central planners).

In the 1990s, I did some consulting for General Motors, as it was buying an automobile factory in Eisenach, Germany, that had been part of East Germany's planned economy. Despite GM's best efforts at obtaining relevant information and prospects, the company eventually had to admit that it made a mistake in buying the factory. They tore the old plant down, and built a completely new one. This was extremely costly, and probably had something to do with GM finally selling its Opel subsidiary and reducing its European operations. I wasn't giving GM advice on its business operations, but was briefing them with some history—and a description of the East German communist economic system. But I probably should have emphasized more the point that whatever information they were getting about the factory was likely just guesswork, based on no market information at all.

In contrast to the East Germans, Yugoslav enterprise managers had some knowledge of how markets determine prices and profits. And the Slovenes, in particular, had more of this knowledge than other Yugoslavs because they had constant exposure to the prices of the goods, services, and resources in their trade with Austria, Italy, and West Germany. That said, Yugoslavia's system of worker self-management was not without its idiosyncrasies. It shouldn't come as a surprise that when workers have a say in how wages should be set, and profit goals are determined, wages are pretty high—and profits rather low.

On the other hand, one of the real drawbacks of Soviet-style central planning was its emphasis on production, without equal consideration of input costs and markets. Soviet enterprises were evaluated on output. If the products actually sold, or were useful, was a secondary question. In the Soviet system, there was almost no incentive to limit resource use. In fact, the incentive was to accumulate—and use—as many resources as possible. More labor resources and stockpiled supplies, for instance, meant greater ability to meet production targets.

In the Yugoslav system, by comparison, enterprises could keep a large part of the profits they generated. This incentivized managers and workers to economize on their resources. Resource conservation, in terms of power and raw materials, meant lower costs and higher earnings; whereas hiring more workers meant a smaller slice of the profit share. Another lasting value of worker self-management is the shared sense of equality and solidarity. Modern production processes tend to turn on team efforts. You need many skills and individuals to produce most goods and services. Workers know this. Everybody working with the team is valuable. They are also human beings, with individual dignity.

Tito emphasized his independence by leading the Non-Aligned Movement of countries, along with Egypt under Gamar Abdel Nassar, and Indonesia under Sukarno. By playing both sides in the Cold War against each other, the non-aligned countries gained benefits from both sides. Tito visited Richard Nixon at the White House in 1971, and Jimmy Carter in 1978. He also toured my hometown of Houston, Texas. I remember seeing new footage of him in his blazing white military uniform riding in a Cadillac convertible down Main Street.

The Slovenian economy's many differences uniquely advantaged it to take advantage of the eventual fall of the Yugoslav Federation. At the time of independence, Slovenia had three times the per capita GDP of fellow ex-communist states Poland, Hungary, and Czechoslovakia, and was at a level of income and development not far behind Portugal. But do all the factors contributing to Slovenia's economic and social success have to do with adopting a free-market, capitalist system? Or have the Slovenes continued some of their own unique values?

The answers to these questions—to the extent I have them—are complicated. Yes, Slovenia adopted a market economy with private property and monetary incentives. It also became even more oriented to international trade. But it also retained some of the solidarity and cohesion of a more socially oriented system. Let me explain.

To be admitted to the European Union, a country must meet the three basic criteria known as the "Copenhagen Criteria," adopted by EU before the accession of some of the former communist countries of Eastern Europe in 2004. The three Copenhagen Criteria were: parliamentary democracy, human rights, and a market-based economy.

Parliamentary democracy means freedom for political parties, and voting based on non-discriminatory eligibility of citizens. Russia would fail to meet these criteria today. Human rights mean equality for women and religious, ethnic, and national minorities. It also means the abolition of capital punishment. The United States fails to meet these criteria. A market-based economy means support for private enterprise and private property. It does not mean the abolition of all state property, or the elimination of government regulation. It means the majority of production and consumption decisions are made on the basis of enterprise profit, and consumer choice. Slovenia met these criteria.

But even after joining the EU, Slovenia and the other former east bloc states had to meet a second set of requirements to adopt the euro in 2007. This was an additional step for Slovenia in its progress to becoming a full member of the European economic integration process. These additional criteria were established by the 1992 Maastricht Treaty to integrate the European economies. They include guidelines on domestic inflation, interest rates, fiscal deficits, and public debt levels. Slovenia was the first of its eastern peers to meet all these criteria.

I took some of my American students to Ljubljana a few years ago. There's a nice overnight train from Munich. We didn't have to change money or show passports.

Slovenia has benefited nicely from foreign tourism and external investment. Some of the big firms that set up shop in Slovenia include France's Renault, in automobile production; Italy's Saffa and Austria's

Bergmeister in paper products; Siemens from Germany in electrical machinery; and Henkel from Austria in chemical products. In the years since, Slovenia has been a fast globalizer and international trader. Consistent with its history in trade, Slovenia exports a sizeable portion of its gross domestic product: about three-quarters of GDP, according to the Paris-based Organization for Economic Co-Operation and Development. The OECD average is 28.9 percent.

At the same time, as an export engine, Slovenia is heavily dependent on the rest of the world's economies. And that means it gets hit hard when there is a global recession. Some other leading export countries—Korea, for example, exports the equivalent of about half of its GDP. In contrast, the United States exports 13.5 percent of its GDP and imports 16.6 percent of GDP. Stated another way, most of the U.S. economy is domestic, while most of the Slovenian economy is globalized.

Slovenia has also maintained a strong social safety net—and a high level of economic security—while achieving impressive growth and exports. The Slovenian constitution states that it is a "social state." This means that the government takes significant responsibility for the health, welfare, and economic security of the population. One of its prime ministers, Miro Cerar, has stated that, "The government has a duty to provide high-quality health care, education, and other forms of social security to the population." Cerar is a former professor of law at the University of Ljubljana, and, before that, was a Fulbright Scholar at the University of California's Berkeley School of Law. He's the author of a best-selling children's book, *How I Explained Democracy to Children*. There might be a broader market for that book, too: adults!

The results of Slovenia's social-welfare approach to caring for its population have been impressive, in my view. Not only has the life expectancy of Slovenians increased substantially, but measures of social solidarity have also been impressive. The last time I looked, the poverty rate in Slovenia was 9 percent, compared to the average poverty rate of about 11 percent among all 35 high-income OECD countries. The poverty rate in the United States was double Slovenia's, at 18 percent. And for American children up to age 17, the U.S. poverty rate was even higher: 21 percent.

Across the world incomes have been becoming more and more unequal in recent decades. In the Peoples Republic of China, there are almost as many billionaires as in the United States. In the Russian Federation, the rise of oligarchs and "new Russians" is well-known. Here's an interesting insight into the Russian example. The German automaker BMW, based in Munich, tracks the sales of all its models on a country-by-country basis. In almost every country, BMW's 3 series—its least expensive—is the largest seller, followed by the 5 series (the mid-level), and then the 7 series (the most expensive). In Russia, the order is completely reversed, with the most-expensive BMW models outselling mid- and less-expensive models.

An economist's most commonly used measure of inequality is something known as the Gini coefficient. It can range in value from 0—meaning complete equality—to 100 (meaning one guy has all the dough). For the OECD countries, as a whole, the Gini coefficient is 32, and for the European Union more narrowly, it is 29. By comparison, in the Russian Federation it's 40, and for the Peoples Republic of China it's 47. In the United States, by comparison, the Gini co-efficient is 39—almost on the level of Vladimir Putin's Russian Federation—and has been increasing since the early 1980s. In Slovenia, the Gini coefficient is 25—the lowest of all OECD countries. But, as my Texas daddy always said, "Ya git what ya pay for." And the Slovenes pay a lot.

As a percentage of total income, the Slovenes pay 44.9 percent of their incomes in taxes. The OECD average is about 40 percent. And of all the OECD countries, the Norwegians pay the most, at 54.8 percent. The United States—despite what you might have heard—is one of the lowest-tax countries in the OECD, with the third-lowest rate after Ireland and Mexico. This reflects an important tradeoff between social solidarity and individual economic freedom and independence. In the United States, you can make a lot of money and keep most of it.

But all of the tradeoffs inherent in competing economic systems are controversial, and there's no definitive answer about what kind of economic system is best. We make decisions, from public education, to healthcare, to taxes and the social safety net. Different histories, different cultures, and different values always lead to different choices for a country's economic system. So, I don't think that economic systems will be converging anytime soon.

In my humble opinion—and taking exception with Francis Fukuyama's statement that free-market liberal democracy conclusively triumphed, and would become the world's "final form of human government"—I do not believe that we are at the end of history. Not yet. Many different economic systems operate side-by-side in the world today. And I think there will be many different economic systems far into the distant future.

Bibliography

AUTOR, DAVID H., DAVID DORN, AND GORDON H. HANSON. "The China Syndrome: Local Labor Market Effects of Import Competition in the United States." *American Economic Review* 103, no. 6 (2013): 2121–2168.

BARZINI, LUIGI. *The Europeans.* New York: Penguin Books, 1983.

BERGHOFF, HARTMUT, JURGEN KOCKA, AND DIETER ZIEGLER, EDS. *Business in the Age of Extremes: Modern German and Austrian Economic History.* New York: Cambridge University Press, 2013.

BEVERIDGE, WILLIAM. *Full Employment in a Free Society: A Report.* New York: Routledge, 2015.

BUCHAN, JAMES. *Capital of the Mind: How Edinburgh Changed the World.* London: John Murray Publishers, 2004.

BUREAU OF ECONOMIC ANALYSIS. "Survey of Current Business." Various issues. Washington, DC: U.S. Department of Commerce.

BUREAU OF LABOR STATISTICS. "Beyond the Numbers." Various Issues. Washington, DC: U.S. Department of Labor.

CHANG, HA-JOON. *Bad Samaritans: The Myth of Free Trade and the Secret History of Capitalism.* New York: Bloomsbury Press, 2008.

CHANG, HA-JOON, AND ILENE GRABEL. *Reclaiming Development: An Alternative Economic Policy Manual.* London: Zed Books, 2014.

CHERNOW, RON. *Alexander Hamilton.* New York: Penguin Books, 2004.

CHOW, GREGORY C. *China's Economic Transformation.* Oxford: Basil Blackwell, 2002.

COHEN, STEPHEN, AND BRADFORD DELONG. *Concrete Economics: The Hamilton Approach to Economic Growth and Policy.* Boston: Harvard Business Review Press, 2016.

CRAIG, GORDON A. *The Germans.* New York: Penguin Books, 1983.

DE GRAUWE, PAUL. *Economics of Monetary Union.* 11th ed. Oxford: Oxford University Press, 2016.

DICKENS, CHARLES. *Hard Times.* London: The Folio Society, 1983.

DRAKULIC, SLAVENKA. *A Guided Tour through the Museum of Communism.* New York: Penguin Books, 2011.

———. *Café Europa: Life after Communism.* New York: Penguin Books, 1996.

———. *How We Survived Communism & Even Laughed.* New York: W. W. Norton & Company, 1992.

DUCHENE, FRANCOIS. *Jean Monnet: The First Statesman of Interdependence.* New York: W. W. Norton & Company, 1994.

ENGELS, FREDERICK. *Socialism: Utopian and Scientific.* New York: International Publishers, 1935.

——. *The Condition of the Working Class in England.* New York: Oxford University Press, 1993.

FRIEDMAN, MILTON, AND ROSE FRIEDMAN. *Free to Choose: A Personal Statement.* New York: Mariner Books, 1990.

FUKUYAMA, FRANCIS. *The End of History and the Last Man.* New York: Avon Books, 1992.

GALBRAITH, JOHN KENNETH. *The Great Crash: 1929.* Boston: Houghton Mifflin Company, 1988.

GEDMIN, JEFFREY. *The Hidden Hand: Gorbachev and the Collapse of East Germany.* Washington, DC: The AEI Press, 1992.

GORBACHEV, MIKHAIL. *Memoirs.* New York: Doubleday, 1995.

JUDT, TONY. *Postwar: A History of Europe since 1945.* New York: The Penguin Press, 2005.

KEYNES, JOHN MAYNARD. *The Economic Consequences of the Peace.* New York: Penguin Books, 1995.

KINDLEBERGER, CHARLES P. *Manias, Panics, and Crashes: A History of Financial Crises.* New York: Basic Books, 1989.

KOTKIN, STEPHEN. *Uncivil Society: 1989 and the Implosion of the Communist Establishment.* New York: The Modern Library, 2009.

LINDERT, PETER H., AND JEFFREY G. WILLIAMSON. *Unequal Gains: American Growth and Prosperity since 1700.* Princeton: Princeton University Press, 2016.

MALIA, MARTIN. *Russia under Western Eyes: From the Bronze Horseman to the Lenin Mausoleum*. Cambridge, MA: The Belknap Press, 1999.

——. *The Soviet Tragedy: A History of Socialism in Russia, 1917–1991*. New York: The Free Press, 1994.

MARX, KARL, AND FREDERICK ENGELS. *Selected Works in One Volume*. New York: International Publishers, 1968.

MASSIE, ROBERT K. *The Romanovs: The Final Chapter*. New York: Random House, 1995.

NOVE, ALEC. *An Economic History of the USSR: 1917–1991*. New York: Penguin Books, 1992.

ORGANIZATION FOR ECONOMIC COOPERATION AND DEVELOPMENT. *OECD Factbook 2015–2016: Economic, Environmental and Social Statistics*. Paris: OECD, 2016.

OXFAM AND DEVELOPMENT FINANCE INTERNATIONAL. *The Commitment to Reducing Inequality Index*. Oxford: Oxfam GB for Oxfam International, 2017.

PLOKHY, S. M. *Yalta: The Price of Peace*. New York: Penguin Books, 2010.

RAUCHWAY, ERIC. *The Money Makers: How Roosevelt and Keynes Ended the Depression, Defeated Fascism, and Secured a Prosperous Future*. New York: Basic Books, 2015.

REID, T. R. *The Healing of America: A Global Quest for Better, Cheaper, and Fairer Health Care*. New York: Penguin Books, 2009.

——. *The United States of Europe: The New Superpower and the End of American Supremacy.* New York: Penguin Books, 2004.

REMNICK, DAVID. *Lenin's Tomb: The Last Days of the Soviet Empire.* New York: Vintage Books, 1994.

RIASANOVSKY, NICHOLAS V. *A History of Russia.* 4th ed. New York: Oxford University Press, 1984.

RYNER, J. MAGNUS. *Capitalist Restructuring, Globalization, and the Third Way: Lessons from the Swedish Model.* New York: Routledge, 2002.

SCHNEIDER, PETER. *The German Comedy: Scenes of Life after the Wall.* New York: The Noonday Press, 1991.

——. *The Wall Jumper.* New York: Random House, 1983.

SKIDELSKY, ROBERT. *John Maynard Keynes: Hopes Betrayed, 1917–1920.* New York: Penguin Books, 1994.

——. *Keynes: The Return of the Master—Why, Sixty Years after His Death, John Maynard Keynes Is the Most Important Economic Thinker for America.* New York: Public Affairs Books, 2009.

SNOW, EDGAR. *Red Star over China.* New York: Grove Press, 1968.

SPUFFORD, FRANCIS. *Red Plenty.* Minneapolis: Graywolf Press, 2010.

STIGLITZ, JOSEPH. *Whither Socialism?* New York: MIT Press, 1996.

TAYLOR, KEITH. *Political Ideas of Utopian Socialists.* New York: Routledge, 1982.

WALDER, ANDREW G. *China under Mao: A Revolution Derailed.* Cambridge, MA: Harvard University Press, 2015.

WEBSTER, CHARLES. *The National Health Service: A Political History.* New York: Oxford University Press, 1998.

WHITE, WILLIAM FOOTE, AND KATHLEEN KING WHITE. *Making Mondragon: The Growth and Dynamics of the Worker Cooperative Complex.* Ithaca, NY: ILR Press, 1991.

WOLF, MARKUS. *Man without a Face: The Autobiography of Communism's Greatest Spymaster.* New York: Times Books, 1997.

Image Credits

206 · · · · · · · · Library of Congress, Prints and Photographs Division, LC-USZ62-117121.

208 · · · · · · · · © Justin Sullivan/Getty Images/Thinkstock.

209 · · · · · · · · © alfexe/iStock/Thinkstock.

223 · · · · · · · · © lensmen/iStock/Thinkstock.

227 · · · · · · · · © Photos.com/Thinkstock.

228 · · · · · · · · © SerrNovik/iStock/Thinkstock.

232 · · · · · · · · © wutwhanfoto/iStock/Thinkstock.

247 · · · · · · · · The Teaching Company Collection.

248 · · · · · · · · © Scharvik/iStock/Thinkstock.

252 · · · · · · · · © OperationShooting/iStock/Thinkstock.

268 · · · · · · · · © neko92vl/iStock/Thinkstock.

270 · · · · · · · · © seb_ra/iStock/Thinkstock.

273 · · · · · · · · Library of Congress, Prints and Photographs Division, LC-USZ62-117122.

277 · · · · · · · · © Monkey Business Images/Thinkstock.

294 · · · · · · · · © Pradit_Ph/iStock/Thinkstock.

295 · · · · · · · · © Ingram Publishing/Thinkstock.

301 · · · · · · · · The Teaching Company Collection.

318 · · · · · · · · © wrangel/iStock/Thinkstock.

320 · · · · · · · · © Cineberg/iStock/Thinkstock.

322 · · · · · · · · Bundesarchiv, B 145 Bild-F045625-0010/Engelbert Reineke/CC-BY-SA 3.0.

337 · · · · · · · · © Teka77/iStock/Thinkstock.

343 · · · · · · · · © kisgorcs/iStock/Thinkstock.

345 · · · · · · · · © paylessimages/iStock/Thinkstock.

365 · · · · · · · · The Teaching Company Collection.

367 · · · · · · · · © Jupiterimages/Photos.com/Thinkstock.

381 · · · · · · · · Bundesarchiv, Bild 183-B0628-0015-035/Heinz Junge/Wikimedia Commons/ CC-BY-SA 3.0.

382 · · · · · · · · © horkins/iStock/Thinkstock.

384 · · · · · · · · © fizkes/iStock/Thinkstock.

388 · · · · · · · · RIA Novosti archive, image #662287/Yuriy Somov/Wikimedia Commons/ CC-BY-SA 3.0.

404 · · · · · · · · © PhonlamaiPhoto/iStock/Thinkstock.

426 · · · · · · · · Library of Congress, Prints and Photographs Division, LC-USZ62-5972.

430 · · · · · · · · © ajafoto/iStock/Thinkstock.

432 · · · · · · · · © View Stock/Thinkstock.

433 · · · · · · · · Richard Fisher/flickr/CC BY 2.0.

447 · · · · · · · · National Archives and Records Administration.

450 · · · · · · · · © shunjian123/iStock/Thinkstock.

454 · · · · · · · · © vlana/iStock/Thinkstock.

470 · · · · · · · · © imtmphoto/iStock/Thinkstock.

476 · · · · · · · · National Archives and Records Administration.

477 · · · · · · · · National Archives and Records Administration.

478 · · · · · · · · © NattapoomV/iStock/Thinkstock.

493 · · · · · · · · © AdrianHancu/iStock/Thinkstock.

496 · · · · · · · · The Teaching Company Collection.

498 · · · · · · · · © AlxeyPnferov/iStock/Thinkstock.

514 · · · · · · · · © sewer11/iStock/Thinkstock.

522 · · · · · · · · © Azbuka/iStock/Thinkstock.